BIOMETRICS in a DATA DRIVEN WORLD

Trends, Technologies, and Challenges

BIOMETRICS
in a DATA
DRIVEN WORLD
Trends, Technologies, and Challenges

EDITED BY
Sinjini Mitra
Mikhail Gofman

CRC Press
Taylor & Francis Group
Boca Raton London New York

CRC Press is an imprint of the
Taylor & Francis Group, an **informa** business

CRC Press
Taylor & Francis Group
6000 Broken Sound Parkway NW, Suite 300
Boca Raton, FL 33487-2742

First issued in paperback 2020

© 2017 by Taylor & Francis Group, LLC
CRC Press is an imprint of Taylor & Francis Group, an Informa business

No claim to original U.S. Government works

ISBN 13: 978-0-367-57407-9 (pbk)
ISBN 13: 978-1-4987-3764-7 (hbk)

Visit the Taylor & Francis Web site at
http://www.taylorandfrancis.com

and the CRC Press Web site at
http://www.crcpress.com

Contents

List of Figures

List of Tables

Preface

When studying 31,000-year-old cave wall paintings of prehistoric humans, archeologists occasionally stumble upon a remarkable find—a human handprint. It is believed that these prints were left on the walls of caves to serve as the signatures of the artists. This concept of using human traits for purposes of identification eventually evolved into the intricate and subtle field that is known today as "biometrics."

The word *biometrics* originates from the Greek words *bio* (life) and *metric* (to measure). In traditional statistical literature, the terms "biometrics" and "biometry" have been used since the early twentieth century to refer to the field of development of mathematical methods applicable to data analysis problems in the biological sciences. Some examples include agricultural field experiments to compare the yields of different varieties of a crop and human clinical trials evaluating the relative effectiveness of competing drugs. However, recently the term "biometrics" has also been used to denote the unique physical traits, such as face, fingerprints, and iris, and behavioral characteristics, which include gait, voiceprint, and signature. *Biometric authentication* refers to the science and technology of identifying people based on their physical and behavioral traits. Technological advances as well as new discoveries about the human body and behavioral patterns continue to expand the list of human traits that are useful for identification. For example, recent research has demonstrated the viability of using ear prints, brainwaves, heartbeats, and DNA as basis for verifying identity. It is quite surprising, yet fascinating, to see how this field has evolved following the September 11 attacks in New York City in 2001, particularly over the last 10–15 years.

In today's highly connected and data-driven world, biometrics play critical roles in ensuring national security and are becoming increasingly important in securing mobile and cloud computing applications, as well as improving the quality of health care and transforming the way people experience computer gaming and entertainment.

The aim of this book is to inform readers about the modern applications of biometrics in the context of a data-driven society, to familiarize them with the rich history of biometrics, and to provide them with a glimpse into the future of biometrics.

Section I discusses the fundamentals of biometrics; provides an overview of common biometric modalities, namely face, fingerprints, iris, and voice; discusses the history of the field; and provides an overview of the emerging trends and opportunities.

Section II introduces the reader to a wide range of biometric applications as noted above.

Section III is dedicated to the discussion of case studies of biometric modalities (introduced in Section I) currently used on mobile applications. As smartphones and tablet computers are rapidly becoming the dominant consumer computer platforms, biometrics-based authentication is emerging as an integral part of protecting mobile devices against unauthorized access, while enabling new and highly popular applications such as secure online payment authorization.

Finally, Section IV concludes with a discussion of the future trends and opportunities in the field of biometrics, which pave the way for advancing research in the area of biometrics and for deployment of biometric technologies in real-world applications.

A recurring theme throughout this book is the challenge of implementing automated biometric authentication. This is because making biometrics-based authentication robust requires complex sensor technologies for capturing high biometric quality images (e.g., face photographs or voiceprints) and complex algorithms, which can accurately determine the identity of a person based on the biometric images. Addressing these challenges is an important area of biometrics research which this book discusses.

The book's intended audience includes individuals interested in exploring the contemporary applications of biometrics, from students to researchers and practitioners working in this field. Both undergraduate and graduate students enrolled in college-level security courses will find this book to be an especially useful companion.

Security is of utmost importance today to ensure the safety of the world. From the London bombings of 2005 to the more recent attacks in the airports at Brussels and Istanbul in 2016, there is imminent need to enhance security in different areas. As people will learn from reading this book, biometrics provides a way to accomplish that in many practical security applications.

Acknowledgments

Dr. Sinjini Mitra would first like to acknowledge her PhD advisor and mentor Dr. Stephen Fienberg, Maurice Falk University Professor of Statistics and Social Science at Carnegie Mellon University, who introduced her to this interesting field of biometrics that offer such huge opportunities for cutting-edge research. During her PhD, she received invaluable guidance from Dr. Fienberg and her co-advisor Dr. Anthony Brockwell, currently an adjunct associate professor of statistics at Carnegie Mellon. She also learnt much about the area of biometrics from faculty members in the Robotics Institute and CyLab at Carnegie Mellon, particularly Drs. B.V.K. Vijaya Kumar, Marios Savvides and Yanxi Liu (currently a professor of computer science at Penn State University). Dr. Mitra is grateful to Dr. Tami "Sunnie" Foy at California State University, Fullerton (CSUF) for introducing her to Dr. Mikhail Gofman, which led to the development of a successful long-term research collaboration. Finally, she is also grateful to Dr. Bhushan Kapoor, chair of the Information Systems and Decision Sciences (ISDS) Department, for supporting her biometrics research work throughout her career at CSUF.

Dr. Mikhail Gofman would like to express his sincere gratitude to his PhD advisor Dr. Ping Yang at the State University of New York at Binghamton who had made it possible for him to pursue a rewarding career in academics and research in the field of cybersecurity. In addition, he also would like to thank Drs. Kartik Gopalan and Dmitry Ponomarev at the State University of New York at Binghamton for their support and valuable advice during his student years at the State University of New York at Binghamton. He would also like to extend immense thanks to Drs. Susama Barua and Raman Unnikrishnan for encouraging him to establish and direct the Center for Cybersecurity at CSUF, where he is currently employed. The center's ability to bring together students and faculty to work on biometrics research is simply astounding.

Both authors would like to acknowledge the work done by their undergraduate and graduate student research assistants at CSUF, both at the departments of Computer Science and Information Systems and Decision Sciences (ISDS), whose valuable contributions helped move their biometrics research forward, while at the same time often providing opportunities for stimulating conversations that generated new research ideas. Most notable amongst them are Kevin Cheng, Nicholas Smith, Oyun Togtokhjav, Bo Wen, Yu Liu, and Karthik Karunanithi.

Finally, the authors are grateful to the staff at Taylor & Francis, including Randi Cohen, senior acquisitions editor, and Cynthia Klivecka, for patiently working with us through the process of writing and publishing this book.

Editors

Dr. Sinjini Mitra is currently an assistant professor at the Department of Information Systems and Decision Sciences in the Steven G. Mihaylo College of Business and Economics (MCBE) at California State University, Fullerton (CSUF). At CSUF, she is also the associate director of the Center for Information Technology and Business Analytics (CITBA), a faculty fellow of the Catalyst Center (an interdisciplinary center on teaching and research for STEM [Science, Technology, Engineering and Mathematics] courses) and a faculty associate of the ECS Center for Cybersecurity. Prior to joining CSUF, she was a postdoctoral research associate at the University of Southern California's Information Sciences Institute (USC-ISI), and a postdoctoral research associate at the Department of Statistics and *CyLab* at Carnegie Mellon University.

Dr. Mitra earned her BSc in statistics from Presidency College, Kolkata, MStat from the Indian Statistical Institute, Kolkata, and PhD in statistics from Carnegie Mellon University, USA. Dr. Mitra's research is interdisciplinary, and primary interests include data mining and business analytics, security and biometric authentication, and statistical modeling applications in education, healthcare and information systems. She started working on biometrics research for her PhD dissertation, where she developed various novel statistical models for face recognition and developed an inference-based model framework for performance evaluation of biometric systems. Currently, she is working on developing multimodal biometric systems for consumer mobile devices, and investigating other newer biometric technologies. She has established several collaborations for her research and has mentored many students at CSUF on biometrics research.

Her teaching interests include business statistics, data mining, data science and analytics. She is a member of the American Statistical Association (ASA), the Institute of Mathematical Statistics (IMS), and the Institute for Operations Research and Management Science (INFORMS). She has around 40 research publications, including 15 peer-reviewed journal articles and 8 book chapters, and presents regularly at national and international conferences. She is the recipient of several intramural awards at CSUF, the MCBE Faculty Excellence Fellowship in 2013 and 2016, and the University award for teamwork and collaboration in 2015. She has also received external grants to support her research work from the National Science Foundation (NSF) and National Institutes of Health (NIH).

Mikhail Gofman is an associate professor of computer science at California State University, Fullerton, where he also directs the Center for Cybersecurity. He earned his PhD in computer science at the State University of New York at Binghamton in 2012. His research interests include access controls, biometrics, and virtualization and cloud security, and his work has been published at top computer science venues.

Contributors

Yoonsuk Choi
Department of Computer
  Engineering
California State University
Fullerton, California

Christina Dudaklian
Department of Computer Science
California State University
Fullerton, California

Andrey Gubenko
Department of Computer Science
California State University
Fullerton, California

Mahdi Hosseini
Department of Computer Science
California State University
Fullerton, California

Kenneth Kung
Department of Computer Science
California State University
Fullerton, California

Yukhe Lavinia
Department of Computer Science
California State University
Fullerton, California

Charles Li
General Dynamics Information
  Technology
California State University
Fullerton, California

Jason Ligon
Department of Computer
  Science
California State University
Fullerton, California

Yu Liu
Department of Computer
  Science
California State University
Fullerton, California

Regan L. Mandryk
Department of Computer
  Science
University of Saskatchewan,
  Saskatchewan, Canada

Rodrigo Martinez
Department of Computer
  Science
California State University
Fullerton, California

Lennart E. Nacke
Department of Drama and Speech
    Communication
University of Waterloo
Waterloo, Ontario, Canada

Laurie O'Connor
Department of Systems
    Engineering
University of California
Los Angeles, California

Christopher Rodney
Department of Computer Science
California State University
Fullerton, California

Yun Tian
Department of Computer Science
California State University
Fullerton, California

Abhishek Verma
Department of Computer Science
California State University
Fullerton, California

Maria Villa
Department of Computer Science
California State University
Fullerton, California

Bo Wen
Center for Information Systems
    and Technology (CISAT)
Claremont Graduate University
Claremont, California

Alec Yenter
Department of Computer Science
California State University
Fullerton, California

I

Introduction to Biometrics

I

Introduction to Biometrics

CHAPTER 1

Overview of Biometric Authentication

Sinjini Mitra, Bo Wen, and Mikhail Gofman

CONTENTS

1.1 INTRODUCTION

Biometrics refer to the unique physiological (face, fingerprints, and ear) and behavioral (keystroke dynamics, voiceprint, and gait) traits of individuals that can be used for identification or verification purposes. *Biometric authentication* refers to the technology of identifying a person or verifying a person's identity based on these unique biometric traits. Such technology is widely deployed in several applications today, from immigration and border control to access control in online banking, ATM, laptops, and mobile phones [1,2]. Passwords and PINs are susceptible to loss, theft, and guessing attacks. Similarly, magnetic cards are subject to loss, theft, forgery, and duplication. Biometric-based techniques, on the other hand, are resilient to such threats: people's biological traits cannot be misplaced or forgotten, and are difficult to steal or forge [1]. Biometric techniques are categorized as either *static* or *dynamic*. Static biometrics examine physiological traits of the individual such as face, fingerprints, iris, and hand geometry. Dynamic biometrics examine behavioral characteristics such as keystroke dynamics and voiceprints. Some sample images are shown in Figure 1.1.

The rest of this chapter is organized as follows. Section 1.2 introduces the common biometrics including multimodal biometrics that combines information from multiple biometrics to perform authentication. Section 1.3 presents a history of these different types of biometrics. We discuss various challenges and issues underlying the technique of biometric authentication in Section 1.4 and conclude in Section 1.5.

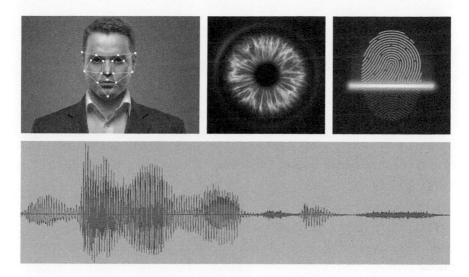

FIGURE 1.1 Commonly used biometrics—face, iris, fingerprints, and voice-print. (From Shutterstock with permission.)

1.2 OVERVIEW OF BIOMETRICS

In this section, we start with a brief description of how the authentication process works, followed by the limitations of traditional approaches like passwords and magnetic cards, and introductions to the four commonly used biometric modalities, namely, face, fingerprints, iris, and voiceprint along with an outline of multimodal biometrics.

1.2.1 Process of Biometric Authentication

There are two types of authentication problems: (1) *identification:* Who am I? and (2) *verification:* Am I whom I claim to be? A typical biometric system has the following three components:

1. *Enrollment.* A biometric image is captured by some device (known as the "sensor"), preprocessed for feature extraction where features denote the identifying characteristics that are used in the identification process, and enrolled in the system.

2. *Matching.* The enrolled image is matched against the database of features extracted earlier from existing images, typically referred to as *reference feature vectors.*

3. *Decision.* A decision is made about whether the person is genuine or an impostor.

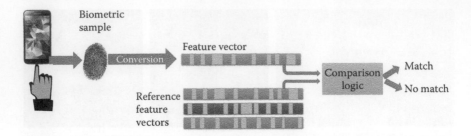

FIGURE 1.2 **(See color insert.)** The process of biometric authentication (this example is for a mobile phone).

Figure 1.2 shows a schematic of how the biometric authentication process works in practice, using the sensor (fingerprint reader) in a mobile phone.

Because of the decision-theoretic framework involved, there is scope for error in any biometric authentication scheme. In particular, there are two types of errors in the context of a verification task, namely (1) *false acceptance rate* (FAR for short) and (2) *false rejection rate* (FRR for short). The first one arises when an impostor is declared genuine by the system (i.e., the system finds a match when it should not have) and the second one arises when a genuine person is declared an impostor (when the system does not find a match when it should). These are typically determined with respect to thresholds that are set on the match scores, so that a set of FARs and FRRs are generated for a system with varying thresholds. The most commonly used metric for performance evaluation of a biometric system is called the *equal error rate* (or ERR for short) which is that value where the FAR and FRR approximately coincide.

1.2.2 Limitations of Traditional Authentication Mechanisms

First, we summarize the limitations of traditional authentication mechanisms. In particular, we will focus on the limitations of the two most pervasive methods: passwords and magnetic cards.

1.2.2.1 Passwords

Most modern systems authenticate users based on *username* and *password*. If the user-supplied password matches the password associated with the user's username, then the user is permitted to use the system [3]. A good password is easy to remember and hard to guess. Unfortunately, these can be conflicting requirements. In practice, most easy-to-remember passwords are dictionary words, names, dates, short sequences of letters and numbers, and other easily guessable pieces of information. On the other hand, difficult-to-guess passwords usually comprise of long sequences of random characters, numbers, and symbols difficult for humans to remember. The difficulty of remembering passwords is often compounded by system administrators requiring users to periodically change their passwords. Easily guessable passwords are vulnerable to *dictionary attacks*, where the attacker compiles a dictionary of commonly used passwords and then tries all words in his dictionary until the correct password is found. Because such dictionaries are usually relatively small, for example, can contain less than 100,000 terms, modern computers can try all passwords in the dictionary in a matter of minutes, or less. Mobile devices, including iPhones, iPads, and Windows Phones, are also vulnerable to similar password guessing attacks. For example, iPhones and iPads use a four-digit number password. According to Gellman [4] and Gayomali [5]:

> A large study revealed that the top 10 iPad passcodes which accounted for 15% of the whole sample were: "1234, 0000, 2580, 1111, 5555, 5683, 0852, 2222, 1212, and 1998." People also prefer using their birth years and graduation years: every number from 1990 to 2000 makes the top 50, and every one from 1980 to 1989 the top 100. Although iPads can be configured to erase themselves after 10 wrong login attempts, many passcodes can be guessed in less than 10 attempts.

1.2.2.2 Magnetic Stripe Cards

Initially developed in the 1960s, magnetic cards are one of the most pervasive methods of electronic access control. A magnetic card consists of multiple magnetic stripes storing encoded information. Magnetic stripe cards have many vulnerabilities, including (1) card duplication; (2) lack of standards for protecting information on the card; and (3) susceptibility to loss and theft. The introduction of smart card technology has greatly alleviated concerns associated with vulnerabilities (1) and (2). Because smart cards contain a processor chip capable of altering card data and require passwords to read/write data to/from the card, they are more resistant to duplication than simple magnetic cards. However, even these security features can be circumvented. For example, secret codes can be extracted by eavesdropping on the communications between the card and the card reader, by using social engineering, and by using differential power analysis techniques [3]. Moreover, smart cards are not immune to loss and theft.

1.2.3 Types of Biometrics

Next, we briefly summarize different types of biometrics and authentication algorithms based on those that are used in current applications.

1.2.3.1 Face

As one of the most successful applications of image analysis and understanding, face recognition has recently received significant attention, especially during the past few years. Face recognition can occur from both still and video images, and from both two-dimensional (2D) and three-dimensional (3D) images.

The problem of automatic face recognition involves three key steps/subtasks: (1) detection and normalization of faces, (2) feature extraction, and (3) identification and/or verification. These tasks may, however, overlap. For example, face detection and feature extraction can be achieved simultaneously using facial features like eyes, nose, etc. Depending on the nature of the application, the sizes of the training and test databases, clutter and variability of the background, noise, occlusion, and speed requirements, some of the subtasks can be very challenging. Though fully automatic face recognition systems must perform all three subtasks, research on each subtask is critical. Hjelmas and Low [6] provide a highlighted summary of research on face detection and feature extraction methods.

Existing face recognition based on intensity images can be broadly classified into three categories:

1. *Holistic methods.* Methods that use the whole face region as the raw input to a recognition system; examples include Eigenfaces that are based on principal component analysis or PCA [7], Fisherfaces that use a combination of PCA and Fisher's linear discriminant analysis or LDA [8], support vector machines or SVM [9], independent component analysis or ICA [10], etc.

2. *Feature-based methods.* Methods where local features such as the eyes, nose, and mouth are first extracted and their locations and local statistics (geometric and/or appearance) are fed into a structural classifier, some examples being the hidden Markov model (HMM) [11], pure geometry methods [12], graph matching methods [13], etc.

3. *Hybrid methods.* Methods that use both local features and the whole face. Available techniques include modular Eigenfaces [14], local feature analysis [15], and component based [16].

Zhao et al. [17] present an in-depth discussion of the practical implementations of the above methods. Apart from intensity-based methods, there are face recognition methods based on the frequency domain as well. The importance of phase in face recognition [18] was exploited to improve performance over standard algorithms where it was shown that the resulting subspace by performing PCA on the phase spectrum alone is more robust to illumination variations [19]. These principal components are termed Eigenphases (in analogy to Eigenfaces). It was shown that Eigenphases outperform Eigenfaces and Fisherfaces when trying to recognize not only full faces but also partial or occluded faces. Another family of algorithms, called advanced correlation filters (ACFs for short [20]) are also widely used for performing face recognition using the frequency domain representation of images. Of these, the most important is the minimum average correlation energy filter [21]. A detailed survey of these frequency domain and filter-based face identification methods appears in Reference 22. An illustration of the face recognition technique is included in Figure 1.3.

1.2.3.2 Fingerprints

Fingerprinting is the oldest biometric identification method. It dates back to 1891 when police official Juan Vucetich first cataloged fingerprints of criminals in Argentina [23]. Fingerprint identification is based upon unique and invariant features of fingerprints. According to the Federal Bureau of Investigation (FBI), the odds of two people sharing the same fingerprints are one in 64,000,000,000. Fingerprints differ even for 10 fingers of the same person [24]. The uniqueness of a fingerprint is determined by global features like valleys and ridges, and by local features like ridge endings and ridge bifurcations, which are called *minutiae.* The earliest work in the field was done by Moayer [25]. He considered the fingerprint as a one-dimensional character string, and another method considering the fingerprint as a 2D tree, and verified two fingerprints by grammar matching. These methods work for a rough classification but fail on low quality images and thus, are not suitable for an identification system. Among the various current fingerprint matching algorithms, minutiae-based fingerprint

FIGURE 1.3 Illustration of face detection and recognition. (From Shutterstock with permission.)

matching is dominant. Some other methods include graph-based matching, genetic algorithms, etc. Extraction of minutiae features before matching needs a series of processes, including orientation computation, image segmentation, image enhancement, ridge extraction, minutiae extraction and filtering, etc. An earlier popular minutiae-based technique was introduced in Reference 26, using the delay triangulation method. Jain et al. [27] used ridge patterns in fingerprint matching. A detailed review of the various techniques can be found in Reference 28. Another approach is the application of correlation filters to fingerprint identification. These have added features like built in shift invariance, closed-form expressions, and tradeoff discrimination for distortion tolerance, and demonstrate good performance without requiring any preprocessing [29]. The one-to-one correlation of fingerprints on a large set of data yields poor results for fingerprint matching because of the elastic distortions between two fingerprints of the same finger. Wilson et al. [30] proposed a distortion-tolerant filter for elastic distorted fingerprint matching.

Some of the common challenges related to fingerprint technology are low quality or degraded input images, noise, and problems with the fingerprint readers. The degradation can be due to natural effects like cuts,

FIGURE 1.4 Image of a fingerprint captured and digitized. (From Shutterstock with permission.)

bruises, etc. or it may be due to appearance of gaps on ridges or parallel ridge intercepts. The fingerprint enhancement techniques not only have to enhance the quality of the image but also at the same time, have to reduce noise. Much work has been done in this field and the most commonly used method for this involves application filters [31]. Figure 1.4 shows the image of a fingerprint image captured by a sensor and digitized for the purpose of recognition.

1.2.3.3 Iris

With the growing demand of high security level and contactless biometrics, iris recognition is fast gaining in popularity today. Iris recognition analyzes the random pattern of the iris in order to establish individual identity. The iris is a muscle within the eye that regulates the size of the pupil, controlling the amount of light that enters the eye. It is the colored portion of the eye; the coloring is based on the amount of melatonin pigment within the muscle. Interestingly, the spatial patterns that are apparent in the human iris are highly specific to an individual [32,33] as is a person's fingerprint, hence it is now widely employed as a biometric for identification purposes. Furthermore, it has been observed in repeated measurements that the patterns in the iris vary very little, at least past childhood [34], unlike a person's face, which shows significant changes over time. It is rarely impeded by glasses or contact lenses, and it remains stable over time as long as there are no injuries or diseases that affect the eye. Some medical and surgical procedures can affect the overall shape and color of an iris but the fine texture remains stable over many decades. Even blind people can use this scan technology since iris recognition technology is iris pattern-dependent and not sight dependent. Figure 1.5 shows some sample iris images.

Iris recognition methods use a noninvasive method for acquiring images, and have some advantages over other biometric traits. There is no need for the person being identified to touch any equipment that has recently been touched by a stranger, thereby eliminating an objection that has been raised in some cultures regarding this issue. This is definitely an advantage over other biometric-based methods where the operator is required to make physical contact with a sensing device (like fingerprint scanners) or otherwise take some special action (recite a specific phonemic sequence for voice recognition). In 1936, ophthalmologist Frank Burch proposed the concept of using iris patterns as a method to recognize an individual [35]. In 1985, ophthalmologists Leonard Flom and Aran Safir proposed the concept that no two irises are alike. In 1994, John Daugman developed the first ever algorithm to automate the identification of the human iris, and this method was used to build the first commercial iris identification system that is now owned by Iridian Technologies [36].

Conceptually, issues in the design and implementation of a system for automated iris recognition can be subdivided into three parts: (i) image acquisition, (ii) localization of the iris from a captured image, and (iii) matching an extracted iris pattern with candidate images stored in a

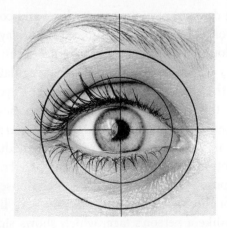

FIGURE 1.5   Image of an iris. (From Shutterstock with permission.)

database. One of the major challenges of automated iris recognition is to capture a high-quality image of the iris while remaining noninvasive to the human operator. It is desirable to acquire images of the iris with sufficient resolution and sharpness to support recognition. Initially, the cost of acquiring iris images was prohibitively high but now with the advent of several technologies and sophisticated image enhancing tools, the cost of iris image capture has gone down considerably. Most iris recognition systems now only require that the image be taken with a digital camera (preferably of high quality). Today's commercial iris cameras typically use infrared light to illuminate the iris without causing harm or discomfort to the subject. However, capturing the iris image may require some practice and thus can be more time consuming than capturing the image of a face or a fingerprint [37]. Following the image capture, a combination of image processing tools is applied prior to performing authentication. Before recognition of the iris takes place, the iris is located using landmark features [38]. These landmark features and the distinct shape of the iris allow for imaging, feature isolation, and extraction. Localization of the iris is an important step in iris recognition because, if done improperly, the resulting noise in the form of eyelashes, reflections, pupils, eyelids, etc., in the image may lead to poor performance.

1.2.3.4 Voiceprint

Speaker verification (based on the voiceprint biometric) consists of making a decision whether a given voice sample belongs to the individual in question or not. Applications of speaker verification include additional identity check during credit card payments over the Internet, automatic segmentation of teleconferences, and in the transcription of courtroom discussions [39]. A large number of methods have been proposed for speaker recognition. Specifically, Gaussian mixture model (GMM)-based systems have received much attention [40]. Since then, some hierarchical extensions of the GMM method have also been proposed [41]. Another well-known method for speech recognition is based on HMMs. One reason why HMMs are popular is because they can be trained automatically and are simple and computationally feasible to use [42]. Modern speech recognition systems use various combinations of a number of standard techniques in order to improve results over the basic approaches based on GMMs and HMMs. Neural networks have also been utilized for speech recognition [43]. Speaker recognition also suffers from several

FIGURE 1.6 Voiceprint sample

challenges, the primary one being background noise and other external factors that potentially affect the quality of the captured voiceprint. There is, therefore, a considerable amount of ongoing research in this area for improving the robustness of speech recognition systems that are used in practice. Figure 1.6 shows sample voiceprint.

1.2.4 Multimodal Biometrics

Most biometric systems deployed in real-world applications are unimodal, that is, they rely on the evidence of a single source of information for authentication (e.g., single fingerprint or face). These systems have to contend with a variety of problems such as

- *Noise in the sensed data.* A fingerprint image with a scar or a voice sample altered by cold is an example of noisy data. Noisy data could also result from defective or improperly maintained sensors (e.g., accumulation of dirt on a fingerprint sensor) or unfavorable ambient conditions (e.g., poor illumination of a user's face for face recognition).

- *Intraclass variations.* Such variations are typically caused by a user who is incorrectly interacting with the sensor (e.g., incorrect facial pose).

- *Interclass similarities.* In biometric systems comprised of a large number of users (say, at airports), there may be interclass similarities (overlap) in the feature space of multiple users.

- *Nonuniversality.* The biometric system may not be able to acquire meaningful biometric data from a subset of users. A fingerprint biometric system, for instance, may extract incorrect minutiae features from the fingerprints of certain individuals due to the poor quality of ridges (as may be caused by aging, illness, etc.).

- *Spoof attacks.* This type of attack is especially relevant when behavioral traits such as signature or voice are used. However, some physical traits such as fingerprints are also susceptible to spoof attacks occasionally.

Some of the limitations imposed by unimodal biometric systems can be overcome by including multiple sources of information for establishing identity [44]. Such systems, known as multimodal biometric systems, are expected to be more reliable due to the presence of multiple, (fairly) independent pieces of evidence [45]. Figure 1.1 gives a high-level schematic of the multimodal biometric system. These systems are able to meet the stringent performance requirements imposed by various applications. They address the problem of nonuniversality, since multiple traits ensure sufficient population coverage. They also deter spoofing since it would be difficult for an impostor to spoof multiple traits of a genuine user simultaneously. More importantly, using more than one trait ensures greater reliability of the results that is expected to maximize performance accuracy (minimize false alarm rates).

1.2.4.1 Fusion Methods
In a multimodal biometric system, information reconciliation can occur in the following ways [45]:

1. *Fusion at the data or feature level,* where either the data or the feature sets originating from multiple sensors/sources are fused

2. *Fusion at the match score level,* where the match scores generated from multiple classifiers pertaining to the different biometric modalities are combined

3. *Fusion at the decision level*, where the final output (decision: genuine or impostor) of multiple classifiers are consolidated into a single decision via techniques such as majority voting

Biometric systems that integrate information at an early stage of processing are believed to be more effective than those systems, which perform integration at a later stage. Since the feature set contains richer information about the input biometric data than the matching score or the output decision of a matcher, fusion at the feature level is expected to provide better recognition results. However, fusion at this level is difficult to achieve in practice because (i) the feature sets of the various modalities may not be compatible and (ii) most commercial biometric systems do not provide access to the feature sets (nor the raw data) which they use in their products. Fusion at the decision level is considered to be rigid due to the availability of limited information. Thus, fusion at the match score level is usually preferred, as it is relatively easy to access and combine the scores presented by the different modalities.

1.3 HISTORY OF BIOMETRICS

The word *"biometrics"* is originally from the Greek words *bio* (life) and *metric* (to measure). In traditional statistical literature, the terms "biometrics" and "biometry" have been used since the early twentieth century to refer to the field of development of mathematical methods applicable to data analysis problems in the biological sciences. Some examples include agricultural field experiments to compare the yields of different varieties of a crop and human clinical trials evaluating the relative effectiveness of competing drugs. However, recently the term biometrics has also been used in the context of security to denote an individual's unique biological traits (like face and fingerprints) that can be used for identification.

1.3.1 Ancient Times (BC to Mid-1800s)

The origin of biometrics can be traced back to 31,000 years ago. "In a cave estimated to be at least 31,000 years old, the walls are adorned with paintings believed to be created by prehistoric men who lived there. Surrounding these paintings are numerous handprints that are felt to *have acted as an unforgettable signature* of its originator" [46]. An example of an old cave painting appears in Figure 1.7. Joao de Barros, a Spanish explorer and writer, wrote that early Chinese merchants used fingerprints to settle business transactions and Chinese parents also used fingerprints

FIGURE 1.7 (**See color insert.**) Handprints used as signatures for cave paintings. (From Renaghan, J., *Smithsonian Zoogoer*, August 1997.)

and footprints to distinguish their kids from each other. Interestingly, in some places of the world today, this practice is still in use [47]. In early Egyptian history, businessmen were recognized by their physical descriptors in order to distinguish between businessmen who had known reputations from previous successful transactions and those who were new to the market [47].

1.3.2 Industrial Revolution (Mid-1800s to Mid-1900s)

By the mid-1800s, with the fast development of urbanization because of the industrial revolution and more productive farming, a formally recognized demand for individual identification was created. Merchants and authorities were confronted with progressively larger and more mobile populations and started realizing that their own experiences and local knowledge were no longer reliable for the purpose of identification [48]. As a result, in 1858, the first systematic capture of hand images for identification purposes was recorded by William Herschel who was working for the Civil Service of India. The handprint was recorded on the back of a contract for each worker in order to verify the identity of employees when getting paid. An illustration of such a handprint is shown in Figure 1.8.

In 1870, Alphonse Bertillon, an anthropologist and police desk clerk in Paris, developed a system called "Bertillonage" that used physical characteristics (body dimensions) as a means of identifying criminals. These

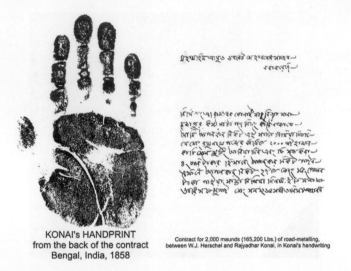

KONAI's HANDPRINT
from the back of the contract
Bengal, India, 1858

Contract for 2,000 maunds (165,200 Lbs.) of road-metalling, between W.J. Herschel and Rajyadhar Konai, in Konai's handwriting

FIGURE 1.8 Handprint at the back of the contract. (From Ed German. n.d. The history of fingerprints. With permission.)

measurements were written on cards that could be sorted by height, or arm length. This field, called *anthropometries,* however, proved to have some flaws because these body dimensions were not unique to a person. According to Ed German [49], "two men, determined later to be identical twins, were sentenced to the US Penitentiary at Leavenworth, KS, and were found to have nearly the same measurements using the Bertillon system."

In 1896, Edward Henry built up a technique that offered the ability to quickly retrieve fingerprint records as Bertillon's system did, but used a more personalized metric—fingerprint patterns and ridges. The Henry technique and its variations are still being used today [50]. A couple of years after, the NY state facilities system started utilizing fingerprints for the identification of criminals. Also, with developing interest by national police authorities, the identification division of the FBI was established by an act of Congress on July 1, 1921 [51].

1.3.3 Emergence of Computer Systems (Mid-1900s to Present Day)

The emergence of computers in the latter half of the twentieth century coincided with the emergence of modern-day biometric systems [48]. In 1969, the FBI began its push to develop a system to computerize its fingerprint identification process. They contracted the National Institute of Standards and Technology (NIST) to develop the process of automating fingerprint identification. Unlike the method introduced earlier by Edward Henry where fingerprints were simply compared by using a magnifying glass or microscope, the computer system conducted the enrollment and identification/verification fully in an automated fashion.

Since the cost of digital storage was relatively high in the late 1900s, only the minutiae were stored. Therefore, early readers were using capacitive techniques to collect the fingerprints [52]. A *capacitive scanner* measures the fingerprints electrically. At the point when a finger lays on a surface, the ridges in the fingerprint touch the surface while the hollows between the ridges stand slightly clear of it. In other words, there are differing distances between every piece of a person's finger and the surface beneath. A capacitive scanner develops a photo of a fingerprint by measuring these distances. Scanners like this are somewhat like the touchscreens on devices like iPhones and iPads.

With FBI funds, NIST centered around and drove advancements in automatic methods for digitizing inked fingerprints and the impacts of image compression on image quality, classification, extraction of minutiae, and matching [53]. The work at NIST prompted the improvement of the M40 algorithm, the first operational matching algorithm utilized at the FBI for narrowing human identification. The available fingerprint technology continued to improve and by 1981, five automated fingerprint identification systems had been deployed [54].

As the cost of digital storage dropped significantly, the *optical scanner* gained in popularity. An optical scanner works by shining a bright light over a fingerprint and taking what is effectively a digital photograph. Instead of producing a dirty black photocopy, the image feeds into a computer scanner. The scanner uses a light-sensitive chip called a charge-coupled device to produce a digital image. The computer analyzes the image automatically, selects the fingerprint from it, and uses sophisticated software to turn it into a code that could be used to perform matching [52].

1.3.4 Other Biometrics

With its long history and numerous studies in forensic science, according to Norzaliza Binti Bidin [55], "fingerprint-based authentication is by far the most often selected biometric security measure, dominating the majority of the market today." However, with huge advances in technology and increased threats of global terrorism and other dangers, new forms of biometrics gradually emerged to upgrade and improve security and identification methods.

By 1974, the first commercial hand geometry recognition system became available, which was arguably the first commercially available biometric device after the early deployments of fingerprinting in the late 1960s [48]. Like fingerprints, an individual's hand geometry must be enrolled first in the system database and then can be verified by the system. The hand geometry readers measure and record the length, width, thickness, and surface area of an individual's hand while an individual's hand is placed on a plate. The readers must capture both the top surface of the hand, and a side image using an angled mirror.

Another contactless biometrics is face recognition. Although human faces have been utilized to distinguish individuals for quite a while, automated face recognition is a moderately new idea. The first semiautomatic face recognition system was designed by Woodrow W. Bledsoe under contract to the US Government in the 1960s. This system required the administrator to locate features, for example, eyes, ears, nose, and mouth on the images. This system depended singularly on the ability to extract usable feature points, and calculated distances and ratio to a common reference point that was compared to the reference data [56]. In the 1970s, Goldstein, Harmon, and Lesk used 21 specific subjective markers such as hair color and lip thickness to automate recognition [57]. However, in both of these early solutions, measurements and locations of face features were manually computed. In 1988, Kirby and Sirovich developed the Eigenface technique described earlier [58] that solved the face recognition problem. This is considered to be a milestone in the area of face recognition because it demonstrated that a suitably aligned and normalized face image can be approximated with considerably fewer values.

1.4 CHALLENGES AND ISSUES IN BIOMETRIC AUTHENTICATION

Despite the promising role of biometrics in ensuring security in different walks of the society today, there are several issues and challenges associated with the process of biometric authentication. The most important factor is undoubtedly the *quality* of the biometric samples. It is well known that the quality of the image used for authentication purposes plays a vital role in the identification process for all biometrics.

Considerable research has been focused on investigating how the quality of an image affects identification accuracy. Hence image quality assessment plays an important role in automated biometric systems for two reasons: (1) system performance (recognition and segmentation) and (2) interoperability [59]. Biometric systems that are typically used in public places suffer from the drawback of low-quality images.

Needless to say, the role of quality in an authentication protocol varies from biometric to biometric. Hence, we first discuss the specific quality challenges for the most popularly used biometric modalities, and then present other issues and challenges that are common across all biometric authentication applications, such as false positives, privacy intrusion and user cooperation, spoofing, and so on.

1.4.1 Quality of Fingerprint Images

The absence of robustness against image quality degradation has a great impact on the performance of a fingerprint recognition system [60,61]. Low-quality fingerprint captures result in spurious and missed templates, therefore, decreasing the performance of the overall system. Hence, it is critical for a fingerprint identification system to assess the quality and validity of a fingerprint image after having captured it. A well-designed recognition system should have the ability to either reject or adjust a degraded image based on estimated quality. According to Alonso-Fernandez et al. [61], several algorithms for automatic fingerprint image quality estimation have been discussed. Also, the advantages of incorporating automatic quality measures in fingerprint identification have been shown in recent studies [62–65]. A successful solution to improve the performance of a fingerprint recognition system is to join the results of different recognition algorithms. As the key to the solution, several simple fusion rules and complex trained fusion rules have been discussed in studies [66–68]. Examples for combining minutia- and texture-based approaches can be found in References 62, 69, and 70. Also, a full study of combining different fingerprint recognition systems is done in Reference 71. Nevertheless, there is no scientific evidence to prove that complex fusion approaches outperform simple fusion approaches, thus the question on which fusion approaches are to be used requires further research.

When assessing the quality of fingerprint images, there is a number of factors to be considered, such as skin conditions (e.g., dryness, wetness, dirtiness, temporary or permanent cuts and bruises, etc.), sensor conditions (e.g., dirtiness, noise, and size), etc. [72]. These are enumerated below.

1.4.1.1 Skin Conditions

Some of the intrinsic and extrinsic factors that are linked to skin conditions of the finger are as follows:

- *Dirt.* Fingerprints may be indistinguishable or unidentifiable if one's fingertip has dirt on it or if the finger is twisted during the process of fingerprinting. For example, if one's fingertip has ink on it, twisting the fingertip can cause the ink to blur, damaging the image of the fingerprint and possibly making it unidentifiable. If there is dirt on a person's fingertip, this can mar an ink fingerprint or the image captured by a digital fingerprint scanner [73].

- *Age and occupation.* As we know, a man's finger changes size or form/pattern after a certain time period. Also, in the manual labor industry, a worker's fingers may get rough or scratched since they usually work with their hands. Therefore, an individual's age and occupation might bring about some sensor trouble in catching a complete and precise fingerprint image [74].

- *Other conditions.* Some other conditions affecting the quality of the fingerprint image include wetness, excessive coldness, temporary or permanent cuts and bruises on the fingertips caused by injuries, and so on. People with special conditions, such as no or few minutia points or medical personnel who always wash hands with strong detergents, hardly can enroll or use a fingerprinting system [75]. The small number of minutia points can be a limiting factor for security of the algorithm as well as produce inaccurate results.

1.4.1.2 Sensor Conditions

Sensor conditions are also significant in order to ensure accurate acquisition of the fingerprint image samples. Often imperfect acquisitions cause the captured fingerprint image to be far from ideal. Some factors affecting poor sensor performance are as follows:

- *Dirt.* Fingerprint sensors may occasionally pick up dust, dirt, and other unwanted particles that affect their ability to capture a clean fingerprint image.

- *Contact type.* Non-uniform and inconsistent contact resulting from physical damages to the sensor plates can lead to poor samples and feature extraction artifacts during image processing.

- *Smaller sensor size.* As the cost and size of fingerprinting decreased, many sensors have been already embedded into today's mobile devices, such as smart phones, PC tablets, personal digital assistants (PDAs), etc. Nevertheless, less information can be extracted from a fingerprint while using these small-area sensors since there is a little overlap between different acquisitions of the same finger. As a result, the overall performance of identification system could be harmed [76]. A possible solution to reduce such impact is to equip mechanical guides along with sensors in order to constrain the finger position or to capture partial images of a fingerprint several times during the enrollment and then reconstruct them into a full fingerprint image [73].

1.4.2 Quality of Facial Images

Just like in a fingerprint system, the quality of facial images is very crucial for accurate feature extraction and hence reliable authentication. For facial recognition systems, the most common attributing factors to deteriorating image quality include motion blur and occlusion, illumination conditions, poses, camera resolution, etc. which are common in uncontrolled conditions (say, when face images are captured in public places). Some of these are briefly discussed below:

- *Distance and occlusion.* Often facial images are captured by surveillance cameras (say, at airports, stores) that are placed far away and at certain angles, thus often leading to low quality images that are blurry, of low resolution, and often occluded in parts. Moreover, for video imagery, motion blur is a common occurrence that severely hampers image quality.

- *Illumination.* Nonuniform lighting can create shadows and hence affect face image quality to a great extent. Illumination can change the appearance of an object drastically and the same face appears differently due to change in lighting. Hence, it is important to overcome irregular lighting, and some available techniques for this include (i) normalization, (ii) histogram equalization, and (iii) order-statistic filtering. The study [77] contains an overview of these methods that are popularly used in many face recognition and verification routines. Some sample face images with illumination variations are shown in Figure 1.9.

FIGURE 1.9   Images of a person under various illumination conditions.

- *Pose variation.* Often cameras capture facial images that are at a certain angle, say, turned sideways. Most face recognition algorithms work best when dealing with full frontal images; however, their performance deteriorates quickly as the face is rotated more and more away from this. Figure 1.10 shows some sample images where the faces display varied poses.

- *Expression variations.* Often people's faces display different expressions and emotions, such as screaming (open mouth), angry (eyebrows scrunched), laughing, etc. that also affect the performance of face recognition systems. Figure 1.11 shows some sample images where the faces display varied expressions.

- *Facial variations.* It is not very hard to change the appearance of a face very drastically with the application of makeup (eye makeup has specially been known to significantly alter facial features [78]) and disguise (beards, glasses, etc.). Another important factor is the time delay because a face changes over time, in a nonlinear way, over long periods. In general, this problem is harder to solve with respect to the others and not much has been done especially for age variations.

- *Image size.* When a face detection algorithm finds a face in an image or in a video frame, the relative size of that face compared with the enrolled image size affects how well the face will be recognized [79]. This is often the case when the distance between the camera and the target face is large.

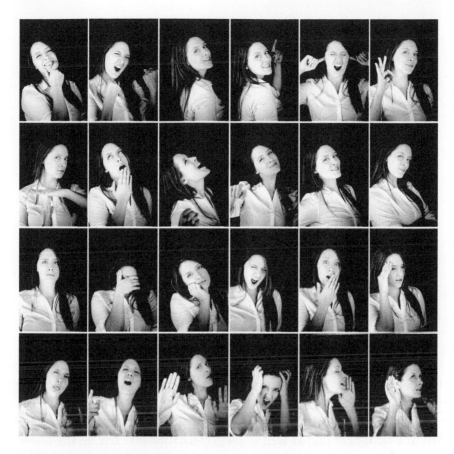

FIGURE 1.10 Images of a person under various pose variations. (From Shutterstock with permission.)

1.4.3 Quality of Iris Images

For the iris, identification performance is affected by factors such as defocus blur, motion blur, occlusion, specular reflection, lighting, off-angle, and pixel counts [80]. Among these seven factors, defocus blur, motion blur and off-angle, and occlusion (due to eyelashes and hair) are the most dominant ones, and the authors demonstrate that performance of the system improves significantly as the image quality due to these three factors gets better.

Iris recognition is known to be extremely hard to conduct at a distance more than several meters. It is also impossible if the person to be recognized is not cooperating by holding his/her head still and looking into the sensor [81]. Nevertheless, a few products, which claim to have the capability of identifying individual at distance of up to 10 m ("Standoff Iris" or

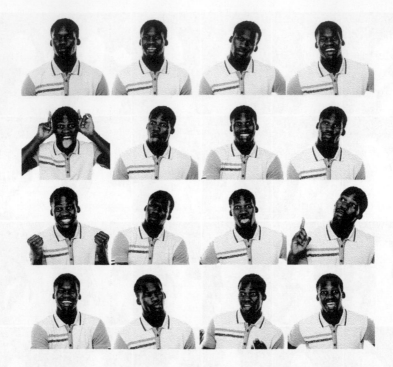

FIGURE 1.11   Images of a person with various expressions. (From Shutterstock with permission.)

"Iris at a Distance" [82] as well as SRI International's "Iris on the Move" [83] for persons walking at speeds up to 1 m/s), have been already developed by several biometric research institutions and vendors.

Whether or not the camera used in the process has the correct amount of illumination is also a key factor to the quality of iris images. In association with illumination, other problems may also greatly impact the ability of the camera to capture a quality image, such as the existence of reflective surfaces under the range of the camera and any unusual lighting that may exist. The format of images that are captured by a camera is another factor. Images in a monochrome format can result in problems with the limitation of grayscale that makes it impossible to differentiate the darker iris colorations from the pupil [84].

1.4.4 Quality of Voiceprints

An individual's speech is likely to be heavily affected by background noise due to traffic, music, people chatter, and other factors that are common in the real world. Moreover, speakers have their special voices, due to their unique physical body, style, and personality. The voice is not only different between speakers; but there are also wide variations within one specific speaker.

Men and women have different voices, and the main reason for this is that women have in general shorter vocal tracts than men. Due to this, the fundamental tone of women's voices is roughly two times higher than men's. Different people also speak in different modes of speed, and this varies over time as well. If one is stressed, he or she tends to speak faster, and if he or she is not tired, the speed tends to decrease. People also speak at varying speeds if they talk about something known or something unknown. Finally, regional dialects involve widely different types of pronunciation, vocabulary, and grammar, which vary with the geographical area where the speaker comes from. Social dialects are distinguished by characteristics of pronunciation, vocabulary, and grammar according to the social group of the speaker.

1.4.5 Other Challenges and Issues

Here, we summarize some of the other important challenges and issues with biometrics-based authentication.

1.4.5.1 Security

How to maintain the integrity of a biometric system is a critical topic. This topic not only manages how the biometric data input to the system is indeed provided by its authenticated owner, but also assures that the input data are matched with a bona fide template in the system. There are various ways an individual can endeavor to bypass a biometric system and eventually attack the weakness spot of such a system. One of the main weaknesses in a biometric system is the fact that a person's biometric data are often not hidden as a secret. Another big weakness is the reality that people cannot change their biometrics whenever they want to. As a result, there may be a chance that an attacker can use such stolen biometric information to design a fraudulent dataset in order to gain access to the system. Unlike a password or PIN number, an individual will not be able to alter their biometric data after it is compromised. A possible solution is to check whether the data originates from an inanimate object rather than the real user [85].

1.4.5.2 Spoofing

Spoofing attacks generally refer to the process of fabricating biometric traits in order to bypass the biometric authentication process. If a spoofing attack is successful, the fundamental tenet of biometrics—"something you are"—is undermined. Therefore, such attacks continue to be a concern for many biometric systems especially those based on physiological biometrics such as fingerprint, hand geometry, and iris.

Several studies dating from around 1998 have demonstrated the potential for successfully launching a spoofing attack under carefully controlled conditions. A more recent study in 2016 [86] revealed that images of the person's fingerprints printed using conductive AgIC silver printer ink, can be used to fool fingerprint readers in the modern Samsung Galaxy S6 and in Huawei Honor 7 mobile phones.

Spoofing involves two stages: (a) the capture of a biometric "image" belonging to an enrolled user and (b) transferring the biometric image onto an artifact containing the biometric features required as proof of identity. Some features generally are more difficult to capture than others, and the skill needed to create a successful artifact depends on both the biometric feature and how resistant the system is to artifacts. Faces are easily captured by photography and photos are available from multiple open and public sources. Fingerprint patterns may be captured through the lifting of latent or residual images left on smooth surfaces. Voices may be captured on tape or using any other audio recorder. The difficulty of carrying out a successful spoofing attack depends on the difficulty of acquiring the necessary biometric and defeating the counter-spoofing measures (if any) used by the system. Some biometrics, such as retinal patterns, can be difficult to capture without the use of sophisticated equipment and from an uncooperative victim. In addition, the liveness testing techniques often used for determining whether the biometric data detected by the sensors belongs to a real, living person and is not a spoof, can also further complicate the attack. For example, some fingerprint–based systems verify the presence of the pulse in the finger placed on the reader in order to help prevent attacks involving the use of fake fingers with spoofed print patterns. Similarly, some face recognition systems require people to blink and perform other gestures and facial motions in order to defeat spoofing attacks where the attacker holds the photo of the legitimate user's face in front of the camera.

Some noteworthy historical cases of spoofing attacks include the Japanese cryptographer Tsutomu Matsumoto using gelatin and plastic mold in 2002 to collect latent fingerprints left on, for example, glass, and mold fake fingers. The fabricated fingers were able to bypass 11 commercial fingerprint sensors (both capacitive and optical) available at the time [87]. The vulnerability was a result of the lack of liveness testing: determining whether the finger placed on the sensor belongs to a real, living person.

In 2014, Marasco and Ross published a survey on anti-spoofing measures for fingerprints. Some of the documented approaches included verifying the finger's vitality signs such as electrical conductivity, temperature, and pulse of the finger [88]. Though these and similar approaches can help frustrate spoofing attacks, not all systems incorporate them. For example, although Apple iPhone's TouchID fingerprint recognition system is used by millions of people around the world, it includes very limited liveness testing capabilities. As a result, German hackers bypassed the system using spoofed fingerprints after 2 days of iPhone's arrival on the market.

A similar incident happened with the face recognition feature in the Android 4.0 operating system released in 2011. The system included a novelty feature which allowed users to unlock Android-based phones and tablets by taking an image of their face. The system was demonstrated to be vulnerable to spoofing attacks where an attacker held a photo of the authorized user (perhaps procured from a social networking site) in front of the device camera. Samsung researchers attempted to counter such attacks by requiring the authenticating person to blink [89]. However, the technique was of limited effectiveness, as blinking proved easy to fake using doctored photographs of the user. Google is currently investigating means of defeating spoofing attacks, which include requiring users to use a specific facial expression when authenticating.

1.4.5.3 User Cooperation Issues
The capturing of viable biometric samples and images is dependent to a large extent on the cooperation of the user. People may choose not to cooperate while giving their biometrics because of issues related to privacy, hygiene, cultural beliefs, or other circumstantial reasons (for instance, in a rush to leave the airport). In a well-known case, Italian philosopher Giorgio Agamben refused to enter the United States by protesting against the United States Visitor and Immigrant Status Indicator (US-VISIT) program's requirement for visitors to be fingerprinted and photographed [90]. Agamben claimed that collecting of biometric information is a type of biopolitical tattooing, likened to the tattooing of Jews during the Holocaust. According to him, biometrics transform the human persona into an uncovered body. For him, this new biopolitical relationship between the general public and the state transforms people into unadulterated biological life denying them their humanity; and biometrics would define this new world.

Diseases and germs are normally spread through hands and fingertips. It is crucial to utilize clean and hygiene techniques on public machines in order to stop germs and viruses from spreading from each other. Nevertheless, in a busy location like the airport border control, use of the same glass surface by many people every day without applying hygiene techniques frequently may cause a serious hygiene hazard [74]. This might be a reason that passengers at airports may be unwilling to use fingerprint scanners due to hygiene-related health concerns.

1.4.5.4 Template Theft

If biometric data are stolen, the privacy and security of the data owner are forever compromised. This is because, any biometric trait, such as iris, retina, or palm vein, generally remain the same throughout an individual's entire life, and cannot be easily changed as in the case of a compromised password. Compounding the problem is the fact that a person has a limited number of biometrics to fall back upon if one biometric is compromised.

Hackers and other malicious actors understand the value of biometric data, as evidenced by the cyberattacks against the United States Office of Personnel Management (OPM) in 2015. After breaching OPM's systems, hackers are believed to have stolen fingerprint data of an estimated 5.6 million federal employees [91].

Therefore, it is critical that all systems which store templates of people's biometric data in order to enable matching, store them in a way that a compromise of the template does not constitute a compromise of the biometric data. The concept is often referred to as revocable or cancellable biometrics [92].

Even if feature vectors stored in a template contain condensed information about the biometric uniqueness of the user, it is still important for such a system to use cancellable biometrics. For instance, in case of fingerprints, the system often stores only the discriminatory set of minutiae points. However, given such points, an attacker can construct a fake fingerprint that has the same discriminatory information.

Approaches for implementing revocable biometrics include *feature transformation and biometric cryptosystems*. In feature transformation, the template is transformed using a piece of secret information called the key that is assigned to each user of the system. During authentication, the key is used to perform a similar transformation on the biometric data entered as an input, which is then matched against the template. In the biometric cryptosystem approach, an external key is associated with each template, such that neither the key nor the biometric template can be derived unless the genuine biometric data is presented [92].

Revocable biometrics continues to be an active area of research with a continuous emergence of new techniques.

For additional security, all databases and systems storing and processing biometric data should implement strong system, database, and network security techniques aimed at preventing the leakage of sensitive data.

1.4.5.5 Privacy Issues

Another essential issue in the biometrics field is focused on protecting privacy. A person loses some anonymity that cannot be recuperated no matter whether or not a person has a biometric identifier recorded. Most critics of biometrics argue that the government utilized biometrics data in order to monitor the behavior of its citizens. While this thought might no longer be credible in the future, the chance of inappropriate use may cause many people to be more conservative in using biometric identifiers. In addition, biometrics data often can capture more information than an individual's identity. Additional information may be extracted, such as one's health and medical conditions, age, and so on. Even though this idea currently has no proof of its viability, its possibility is also increasing public concerns on the use of biometrics [93].

Despite the negative problems connected with their deployment, biometrics still can be utilized as an exceptionally efficient technique to protect one's privacy. Assuming an individual's biometrics data can only be obtained through a biometric matching procedure, the biometric data will be much more secure if the access was preceded by a regular password. Similarly, the likelihood of a thief using a stolen card would be largely decreased if the use of the credit card must be verified with the authenticated fingerprint. Hence, these benefits have a tendency to overcome the worries over losing a level of one's privacy by providing biometric information. In fact, today's biometric systems do not store the user's template in its original copy. In the same way as with storing passwords, the user's biometric data are encrypted prior to storage in order to prevent theft [2].

Another privacy-related concern today lies in the emergence of *mass-market biometrics*. Some argue that biometrics have the ability to transform existing surveillance systems into something more powerful and much more invasive. Domain Awareness System is a network of 3000 surveillance cameras in New York City. The purpose of building such a system is to help law enforcement since the police can then monitor any suspicious activities by the video recordings. However, the user of such a system can actively track someone throughout their daily life if a facial-recognition software has been equipped with such a system. "*A person who lives and works in lower Manhattan would be under constant surveillance,*" says Jennifer Lynch, an attorney at the Electronic Frontier Foundation, a nonprofit group. Although such face recognition is known to be a powerful technique and may require public hearings, there have been many ongoing projects, including the Department of Homeland Security's Biometric Optical Surveillance System [94].

Moreover, there is concern that biometrics can be abused or misused, and infringe on our first amendment rights, such as protesters at a political rally. People could be identified from video recordings of these events and put into a government database without their knowledge. For example, many people argue that "whole body scanners," implemented by The Transportation Security Administration (TSA) at most of the busy airports in the United States is a civil liberties violation, since the TSA has affirmed that naked digital photos of a person could be stored or transmitted to other places [95].

1.5 CONCLUSIONS

After the 9/11 events, security has become a big issue in the United States and around the world. Biometrics provide a reliable and robust way of ensuring security in today's society. The growth of biometrics is happening at an exponential rate in the current world, as more and more people are becoming aware of the vast potential of the technology of biometrics-based authentication. Apart from the traditional applications in criminal identification in law enforcement and immigration and border control, biometrics is increasingly finding use in relatively newer domains such as health care, education, social networks and gaming, and mobile devices. Thus, the field of biometrics is burgeoning with endless opportunities. Nonetheless, there are concerns, and challenges as well, that need to be addressed to the extent that is practically feasible. This is important in increasing the acceptance of biometrics-based technology among the public and to mitigate many of the underlying concerns and challenges.

REFERENCES

1. Jain, A.K., Ross, A., Nandakumar, K. 2011. *Introduction to Biometrics*, Springer, USA.
2. Jain, A.K., Ross, A., Prabhakar, S. 2004. An introduction to biometric recognition, *IEEE Transactions on Circuits and Systems for Video Technology*, 14, 4–20.

3. Goodrich, M., Tamassia, R. 2010. *Introduction to Computer Security*, Addison-Wesley Publishing Company.
4. Gellman, B. 2011. Why I can guess your iPad password, June. http://techland.time.com/2011/06/15/why-i-can-guess-youripad-password (retrieved April 24, 2013).
5. Gayomali, C. 2011. The 10 most popular iPhone passwords, starring 1234, June. http://techland.time.com/2011/06/13/the10-most-popular-iphone-passwords-starring-1234 (retrieved April 23, 2013).
6. Hjelmas, E., Low, B.K. 2001. Face detection: A survey, *Computer Vision and Image Understanding*, 83, 236–274.
7. Turk, M., Pentland, A. 1991. Eigenfaces for recognition, *Journal of Cognitive Neuroscience*, 3, 72–86.
8. Belhumeur, P.N., Hespanha, J.P., Kriegman, D.J. 1997. Eigenfaces vs. Fisherfaces: Recognition using class specific linear projection, *IEEE Transactions on Pattern Analysis and Machine Intelligence*, 19, 711–720.
9. Phillips, P.J. 1998. Support vector machines applied to face recognition, *Advances in Neural Information Processing Systems*, 11, 803–809.
10. Bartlett, M.S., Lades, H.M., Sejnowski, T. 1998. Independent component representation for face recognition. In *Proceedings of SPIE Symposium on Electronic Imaging: Science and Technology*, San Jose, California, pp. 528–539.
11. Nefian, A.V., Hayes, M.H. III. 1998. Hidden Markov models for face recognition. In *Proceedings of International Conference on Acoustics, Speech and Signal Processing*, Seattle, Washington, pp. 2721–2724.
12. Cox, I.J., Ghosn, J., Yianilos, P.N. 1996. Feature-based face recognition using mixture distance. In *Proceedings of IEEE Conference on Computer Vision and Pattern Recognition*, San Francisco, California, pp. 209–216.
13. Wiskott, L., Fellous, J.M., von der Malsburg, C. 1997. Face recognition by clastic bunch graph matching, *IEEE Transactions on Pattern Analysis and Machine Intelligence*, 19, 775–779.
14. Pentland, A., Moghaddam, B., Starner, T. 1994. View-based and modular Eigenspaces for face recognition, In *Proceedings of IEEE Conference on Computer Vision and Pattern Recognition*, Vols. 21–23, Seattle, Washington, pp. 84–91.
15. Penev, P., Atick, J. 1996. Local feature analysis: A general statistical theory for object representation, *Computational Neural Processing Systems*, 7, 477–500.
16. Huang, J., Heisele, B., Blanz, V. 2003. Component-based face recognition with 3D morphable models, In *Proceedings of International Conference on Audio and Video-Based Person Authentication*, Guildford, UK, pp. 27–34.
17. Zhao, W., Chellappa, R., Phillips, P.J., Rosenfeld, A. 2003. Face recognition: A literature survey, *ACM Computing Surveys*, 35(4), 399–458.
18. Oppenheim, A.V., Lim, J.S. 1980. The importance of phase in signals, *Proceedings of the IEEE*, 69(5), 529–541.
19. Savvides, M., Vijaya Kumar, B.V.K., Khosla, P.K. 2004. Eigenphases vs. Eigenfaces. In *Proceedings of IEEE International Conference on Pattern Recognition*, Cambridge, UK, pp. 810–813.

20. Vijaya Kumar, B.V.K. 1992. Tutorial survey of composite filter designs for optical correlators, *Applied Optics*, 31(23), 4773–4801.
21. Mahalanobis, A., Vijaya Kumar, B.V.K., Casasent, D. 1987. Minimum average correlation energy filters, *Applied Optics*, 26(17), 3633–3640.
22. Savvides, M., Bhagavatula, R., Li, Y., Abiantun, R. 2007. Frequency domain face recognition, In *Face Recognition*, Delac, K., Grgic, M. (Eds), InTech. DOI: 10.5772/4853. Available from: http://www.intechopen.com/books/face_recognition/frequency_domain_face_recognition
23. National Library of Medicine. n.d. Visible proofs. https://www.nlm.nih.gov/visibleproofs/galleries/biographies/vucetich.html.
24. Federal Bureau of Investigation (FBI). 1984. *The Science of Fingerprints: Classification and Uses*, US Government Printing Office, Washington, DC.
25. Moayer, B., Fu, K.S. 1976. A tree system approach for fingerprint pattern recognition, *IEEE Transactions on Computers*, 25(3), 262–274.
26. Bebis, G., Deaconu, T., Georgiopaulos, M. 1999. Fingerprint identification using Delaunay triangulation, *IEEE Transactions on Information Intelligence and Systems*, 4, 452–459.
27. Jain, A.K., Hong, L., Bolle, R. 1997. Online fingerprint verification, *IEEE Transactions on Pattern Analysis and Machine Intelligence*, 19, 302–314.
28. Maltoni, D., Cappelli, R. 2008. Fingerprint recognition. In *Handbook of Biometrics*, Jain, A., Flynn, P., Ross, A., (Eds), Springer, USA, pp. 23–42.
29. Venkataramani, K., Vijaya Kumar, B.V.K. 2003. Fingerprint verification using correlation filters, *Lecture Notes in Computer Science, Proceedings of Audio and Video Based Person Authentication*, 2688, 886–894.
30. Wilson, C.L., Watson, C.I., Paek, E.G. 1997. Combined optical and neural network fingerprint matching, *Optical Pattern Recognition VIII, SPIE Proceedings*, 3073, 373–382.
31. OGonnan, L., Nickerson, J.V. 1988. Matched filter design for fingerprint image enhancement. In *Proceedings of International Conference on Acoustics, Speech, and Signal Processing*, New York, NY, pp. 916–919.
32. Adler, F.H. 1965. *Physiology of the Eye*, Mosby, St. Louis, Missouri.
33. Kroeber, A.L. 1948. *Anthropology*, Harcourt Brace Jovanovich, New York.
34. Kronfeld, P.C. 1968. The gross anatomy and embryology of the eye. In *The Eye*, Davson, H. (Ed.), Vol. 1, Academic, London, pp. 1–66.
35. Burch, F. 2005. Individual biometrics: Iris scan, National Center for State Courts. http://ctl.ncsc.dni.us/biomet%20web/BMIris.html (retrieved September 20, 2015).
36. Iridian Technologies. 2003. Historical timeline. http://www.iridiantech.com/about.php?page=4 (retrieved September 20, 2015).
37. Daugman, J.G. 1992. High confidence personal identification by rapid video analysis of iris texture. In *Proceedings of IEEE International Carnahan Conference on Security Technology*, pp. 1–11.
38. Wildes, R. 1997. Iris recognition: An emerging biometric technology, *Proceedings of the IEEE*, 85(9), 1348–1363.

39. Martin, A., Przybocki, M. 2001. Speaker recognition in a multi-speaker environment. In *Proceedings of 7th European Conference on Speech Communication and Technology* (Eurospeech 2001), Aalborg, Denmark, pp. 787–790.
40. Reynolds, D.A., Rose, R.C. 1995. Robust text-independent speaker identification using Gaussian mixture speaker models, *IEEE Transactions on Speech and Audio Processing*, 3, 72–83.
41. Beigi, H.S.M., Maes, S.H., Sorensen, J.S., Chaudhari, U.V. 1992. A hierarchical approach to large-scale speaker recognition. In *Proceedings of the 6th European Conference on Speech Communication and Technology* (Eurospeech 1999), Budapest, Hungary, pp. 2203–2206.
42. Hu, H., Zahorian, S.A. 2010. Dimensionality reduction methods for HMM phonetic recognition. In *Proceedings of ICASSP*, Dallas, Texas.
43. Waibel, A., Hanazawa, T., Hinton, G., Shikano, K., Lang, K.J. 1989. Phoneme recognition using time-delay neural networks, *IEEE Transactions on Acoustics, Speech and Signal Processing*, 37, 328–339.
44. Ross, A., Jain, A.K. 2003. Information fusion in biometrics, *Pattern Recognition Letters*, 24, 2115–2125.
45. Ross, A., Jain, A.K. 2004. Multimodal biometrics: An overview. *Proceedings of 12th European Signal Processing Conference (EUSIPCO)*, Vienna, Austria, pp. 1221–1224.
46. Renaghan, J. 1997. Etched in stone, *Smithsonian Zoogoer*, August.
47. McMahon, Z. 2005. *Biometrics: History*. Indiana University, Indiana University of Computer Science Department, Bloomington, Indiana.
48. The National Science and Technology Council. 2006. Biometrics history, August. http://www.biometrics.gov/documents/biohistory.pdf (retrieved September 15, 2015).
49. Ed German. n.d. The history of fingerprints. onin.com/fp/fphistory.html. (retrieved September 15, 2015).
50. Wayman, J.L. 2004. Biometrics now and then: The development of biometrics over the last 40 years. In *Proceedings of Second BSI Symposium on Biometrics*.
51. Global Security Organization. n.d. Fingerprint identification systems. http://www.globalsecurity.org/security/systems/biometrics-fingerprint.htm (retrieved September 16, 2015).
52. Woodford, C. 2014. Biometric fingerprint scanners, June. http://www.explainthatstuff.com/fingerprintscanners.html (retrieved September 16, 2015).
53. Wayman, J.L., Jain, A., Maltoni, D., Maio, D. 2005. *Biometric Systems Technology, Design and Performance Evaluation*, Springer-Verlag, London.
54. Woodward, J.D. Jr., Orlans, N.M., Higgins, P.T. 2003. *Biometrics*, McGraw Hill Osborne.
55. Norzaliza Binti Bidin. 2005. Fingerprint recognition system (reprocessing), March. http://umpir.ump.edu.my/3695/1/NORZALIZA_BINTI_BIDIN.PDF (retrieved September 16, 2015).

56. Department of Computer Science at the University of Texas at Austin. n.d. In Memoriam Woodrow Wilson Bledsoe. http://www.cs.utexas.edu/users/boyer/bledsoe-memorial-resolution.pdf (retrieved September 17, 2015).
57. Goldstein, A.J., Harmon, L.D., Lesk, A.B. 1971. Identification of human faces, *Proceedings of the IEEE*, 59(5), 748–760.
58. Sirovich, L., Kirby, M. 1987. A low-dimensional procedure for the characterization of human faces, *Journal of the Optical Society of America A*, 4(3), 519–524.
59. Kalka, N.D., Zuo, J., Schmid, N.A., Cukic, B. 2006. Image quality assessment for iris biometric. In *Defense and Security Symposium*, International Society for Optics and Photonics, Orlando, Florida, pp. 62020D–62020D-11, April.
60. Simon-Zorita, D., Ortega-Garcia, J., Fierrez-Aguilar, J., Gonzalez-Rodriguez, J. 2003. Image quality and position variability assessment in minutiae-based fingerprint verification, *IEE Proceedings Vision, Image and Signal Process*, 150(6), 402–408.
61. Alonso-Fernandez, F., Fierrez, J., Ortega-Garcia, J., Gonzalez-Rodriguez, J., Fronthaler, H., Kollreider, K., Bigun, J. 2007. A comparative study of fingerprint image quality estimation methods, *IEEE Transactions on Information Forensics and Security*, 2(4), 734–743.
62. Fierrez-Aguilar, J., Chen, Y., Ortega-Garcia, J., Jain, A. 2006. Incorporating image quality in multi-algorithm fingerprint verification. In *Proceedings of IAPR International Conference on Biometrics, ICB*, Hong Kong, China, Vol. LNCS 3832, pp. 213–220.
63. Alonso-Fernandez, F., Veldhuis, R., Bazen, A., Fierrez-Aguilar, J., Ortega-Garcia, J. 2006. On the relation between biometric quality and user-dependent score distributions in fingerprint verification. In *Proceedings of Workshop on Multimodal User Authentication—MMUA*, Toulouse, France.
64. Fronthaler, H., Kollreider, K., Bigun, J., Fierrez, J., Alonso-Fernandez, F., Ortega-Garcia, J., Gonzalez-Rodriguez, J. 2008. Fingerprint image quality estimation and its application to multialgorithm verification, *IEEE Transaction on Information Forensics and Security*, 3(2), 331–338.
65. Alonso-Fernandez, F., Roli, F., Marcialis, G., Fierrez, J., Ortega-Garcia, J. 2008. Performance of fingerprint quality measures depending on sensor technology, *Journal of Electronic Imaging, Special Section on Biometrics: Advances in Security, Usability and Interoperability*.
66. Bigun, E., Bigun, J., Duc, B., Fischer, S. 1997. Expert conciliation for multi modal person authentication systems by Bayesian statistics. In *Proceedings of International Conference on Audio- and Video-Based Biometric Person Authentication (AVBPA)*, Crans-Montana, Switzerland, pp. 291–300, March 12–14.
67. Kittler, J., Hatef, M., Duin, R., Matas, J. 1998. On combining classifiers, *IEEE Transaction on Pattern Analysis and Machine Intelligence*, 20(3), 226–239.
68. Snelick, R., Uludag, U., Mink, A., Indovina, M., Jain, A. 2005. Large-scale evaluation of multimodal biometric authentication using state-of-the-art systems, *IEEE Transaction on Pattern Analysis and Machine Intelligence*, 27(3), 450–455.

69. Ross, A., Jain, A., Reisman, J. 2003. A hybrid fingerprint matcher, *Pattern Recognition*, 36(7), 1661–1673.
70. Marcialis, G., Roli, F. 2005. Fusion of multiple fingerprint matchers by single-layer perceptron with class-separation loss function, *Pattern Recognition Letters*, 26(12), 1830–1839.
71. Fierrez-Aguilar, J., Nanni, L., Ortega-Garcia, J., Capelli, R., Maltoni, D. 2005. Combining multiple matchers for fingerprint verification: A case study in FVC2004. *Proceedings of International Conference on Image Analysis and Processing*, ICIAP LNCS-3617, Cagliari, Italy, pp. 1035–1042.
72. Alonso-Fernandez, F., Bigun, J., Fierrez, J., Fronthaler, H., Kollreider, K., Ortega-Garcia, J. 2009. Fingerprint recognition. In *Guide to Biometric Reference Systems and Performance Evaluation*, Petrovska-Delacrétaz, D., Chollet, G., Dorizzi, B., (Eds), Springer-Verlag, London.
73. Allen, J. n.d. The disadvantages of fingerprinting. http://www.ehow.com/list_7640391_disadvantages-fingerprinting.html. (retrieved September 20, 2015).
74. Vzendran. 2010. Disadvantages of the fingerprint scanner, March 29. http://vzendran.blogspot.com/2010/03/disadvantages-of-fingerprint-scanner.html (retrieved September 20, 2015).
75. Biometric News Portal. n.d. Fingerprint biometrics. http://www.biometricnewsportal.com/fingerprint_biometrics.asp. (retrieved September 22, 2015).
76. Maltoni, D., Maio, D., Jain, A., Prabhakar, S. 2003. *Handbook of Fingerprint Recognition*, Springer-Verlag, London.
77. Ramchandra, A., Kumar, R. 2013. Overview of face recognition system challenges, *International Journal of Scientific & Technology Research*, 2(8), August. http://www.ijstr.org/final-print/aug2013/Overview-Of—Face-Recognition-System—Challenges.pdf. (retrieved September 27, 2015).
78. Dantcheva, A., Ross, A., Chen, C. 2013. Makeup challenges automated face recognition systems, April. http://spie.org/newsroom/technical-articles/4795-makeup-challenges-automated-face-recognition-systems (retrieved September 30, 2015).
79. Trimpe, A., Edgell, J. 2013. 4 limitations of facial recognition technology, November 22. http://www.fedtechmagazine.com/article/2013/11/4-limitations-facial-recognition-technology (retrieved October 12, 2015).
80. Kalka, N.D., Zuo, J., Schmid, N.A., Cukic, B. 2010. Estimating and fusing quality factors for Iris biometric images, *IEEE Transactions on Systems, Man, and Cybernetics: Systems*, 40(3), 509–524.
81. Olatinwo, S.O., Shoewu, O., Omitola, O.O. 2013. Iris recognition technology: Implementation, application, and security consideration, *The Pacific Journal of Science and Technology*, 14(2), 228–233.
82. Martin, Z. 2011. Biometric trends: Will emerging modalities and mobile applications bring mass adoption? March. http://www.secureidnews.com/news-item/biometric-trends-will-emerging-modalities-and-mobile-applications-bring-mass-adoption/?tag=biometrics&tag=Law_Enforcement (retrieved October 2, 2015).

83. Terdiman, D. 2011. SRI shows the benefits of shrinking tech, May. http://www.cnet.com/news/sri-shows-the-benefits-of-shrinking-tech/ (retrieved October 6, 2015).

84. Khaw, P. 2002. *Iris Recognition Technology for Improved Authentication*. As part of the Information Security Reading Room, SANS Institute. https://www.sans.org/reading-room/whitepapers/authentication/iris-recognition-technology-improved-authentication-132. (retrieved October 7, 2015).

85. Diefenderfer, G.T. 2006. Fingerprint recognition, June. www.dtic.mil/cgi-bin/GetTRDoc?AD=ada451278 (retrieved October 8, 2015).

86. Cao, K., Jain, A.K. 2016. Hacking Mobile Phones Using 2D Printed Fingerprints. Michigan State University (MSU) Technical Report, MSU-CSE-16-2, East Lansing, Michigan.

87. Matsumoto, T., Matsumoto, H., Yamada, K., Hoshino, S. 2002. Impact of artificial gummy fingers on fingerprint systems. In *Electronic Imaging 2002*, International Society for Optics and Photonics, Orlando, Florida, pp. 275–289, April.

88. Marasco, E., Ross, A. 2014. A survey on antispoofing schemes for fingerprint recognition systems, *ACM Computing Surveys (CSUR)*, 47(2), 28.

89. Davies, C. 2012. Blink if you're human: Samsung boosts Android Face Unlock security, March 29. http://www.slashgear.com/blink-if-youre-human-samsung-boosts-android-face-unlock-security-29220515/ (retrieved January 12, 2016).

90. Agamben, G. 2008. No to bio-political tattooing, *Communication and Critical/Cultural Studies*, 5(2), 201–202.

91. US Government Hack Stole Fingerprints of 5.6 Million Federal Employees. The Guardian. Guardian News and Media, September 23, 2015. Web. August 11, 2016. https://www.theguardian.com/technology/2015/sep/23/us-government-hack-stole-fingerprints. Retrieved on August 10, 2016.

92. Nagar, A., Jain, A.K. 2009. On the security of non-invertible fingerprint template transforms. *2009 First IEEE International Workshop on Information Forensics and Security (WIFS)*. IEEE, London, UK.

93. Woodward, J.D. 1997. Biometrics: Privacy's foe or privacy's friend? *Proceedings of the IEEE*, 85(9), 1480–1492.

94. Munday, O. 2014. Biometric security poses huge privacy risks, January 1. http://www.scientificamerican.com/article/biometric-security-poses-huge-privacy-risks/ (retrieved October 10, 2015).

95. Robinson, S. 2011. Privacy issues and the use of biometrics, November. http://www.brighthub.com/computing/smb-security/articles/69433.aspx (retrieved October 12, 2015).

CHAPTER 2

Emerging Trends and New Opportunities in Biometrics

An Overview

Yoonsuk Choi

CONTENTS

BIOMETRICS ARE WHAT WE ARE and how we behave. Based on one's biometric information, authentication can be achieved to guarantee the identity of a user or a service given a set of confidence. Conventional biometric authentication has been studied and deployed in our daily lives using morphological analysis based on face, fingerprint, iris, and voice. In addition, it is possible to adopt additional biological modalities that have emerged recently, such as body odor and deoxyribonucleic acid (DNA), and behavioral modalities such as gait and signature dynamics. In this chapter, emerging trends and new opportunities in biometrics are briefly introduced and further details are discussed in the following chapters in detail. In Section 2.1, emerging unimodal biometrics are introduced in terms of dynamic signature analysis, hand geometry, retina, keystroke dynamics, gait, skin spectroscopy, vein pattern, DNA, body salinity, facial thermography, ear pattern, lip print, and body odor. In Section 2.2, emerging multimodal biometrics are introduced by discussing the fusion of various biometrics at different levels, such as sensor level, feature-extraction level, matching-score level, and decision level, and elaborating on applicable fusion scenarios for multimodal biometrics. In Section 2.3, new opportunities in biometrics are briefly discussed as an introduction to the following chapters which will discuss more in detail about biometrics in mobile systems, healthcare systems, social networks, gaming technologies, and homeland security. This chapter is concluded in Section 2.4.

2.1 EMERGING UNIMODAL BIOMETRICS

2.1.1 Dynamic Signature Analysis

Dynamic signature analysis is also called signature recognition since this method is used to authenticate a user's identity by measuring and analyzing handwritten signatures. Every person has a different pattern or habit of writing using their hands; therefore, every handwritten signature is unique. While this technology does not rely on the physical appearance of the written signature, the manner in which the signature is written is taken into consideration. During the enrollment process, users sign their names more than one time on a pressure-sensitive writing tablet that is electronically connected to a computer. Writing names multiple times ensures the accuracy of the written signature of each user, and changes in pressure, position, and velocity of the electronic pen are measured during the signing process. Moreover, the overall size of the signature as well as the quantity and various directions of the strokes within the signatures are measured and stored for authentication. Some people may think that it would be possible to duplicate the visual appearance or look of the signature; however, this signature-based method is focused on the behavioral characteristics of the person who signs which are difficult to be duplicated.

2.1.2 Hand Geometry

Besides the face, fingerprint, and palmprint, hand geometry is also one of the most widely studied and used biometric modalities for user authentication. Hand geometry is employed by the biometric recognition system to measure and analyze the overall structure, shape, and proportions of each user's hand, especially the length, width, and thickness of each user's hand, fingers, and their joints. In addition, each person has unique characteristics of the skin surface area, such as ridges, wrinkles, and creases. One interesting fact about this technology is that hand geometry is not the only trait used but finger geometry is also analyzed to increase the accuracy and reduce authentication failure. Therefore, one advantage of this method is that the users can verify their identities even when their hands are dirty, and this significantly facilitates the measuring process. However, the only limitation of this method is when users have serious arthritis and are not able to spread their hands evenly on the reader. A hand geometry-based system measures the palm of the user's hand which is properly placed on the surface of the reader, and aligns the hand with the guided pegs on the reader which indicate proper location of the fingers. The process is quite easy to use since it is very intuitive for the users to see the reader and understand where to put their hands and fingers. It only takes a few seconds for the system to check its database for user identification and verification. The image acquisition system within the reader is composed of a light source, a camera, a simple mirror, and a flat surface with five pegs. The five pegs serve as guide points for the proper positioning of the user's right hand. The system also has control knobs to change the intensity of the light and the focal length of the camera. The mirror projects the side view of the user's hand onto the camera.

Although an individual's hand features are not descriptive enough for identification, a hand geometry recognition system is fairly accurate for user verification when additional finger features are used. It is important to understand that the hand biometric is relatively nonintrusive and only a small amount of data are required to verify each user. Therefore, a large number of templates can be stored in the device for comparison with user inputs. Hand geometry systems are already deployed in some restricted areas and buildings to give access to authorized personnel and are also used in companies where attendance of each employee is checked and reported.

2.1.3 Retina

The retina is the layer of blood vessels that resides at the back of the eye from where a unique pattern can be captured. The retina is known as one of the most secure biometric modalities because of its uniqueness. When a user's eyes are scanned through the reader, the blood vessels in the eye are identified and measured. Since glasses adversely affect retina scanning, it is required that users take off their glasses prior to scanning. A low light source within the system compares unique patterns of the retina with the stored data. Each retina scan produces about the same volume of data as a fingerprint image. The retina-based method is not widely used in our daily lives due to the fact that it is intrusive and not user friendly. More importantly, the biometric system for retina scan is relatively expensive; therefore, it is suitable for applications where absolute security is required and user acceptance is not a major concern.

2.1.4 Keystroke Dynamics

Keystroke dynamics focus on a user's habit of typing where each user's keyboard inputs at thousands of times per second are evaluated. Since each individual possesses a unique typing habit, different typing rhythm patterns are created. Dynamics such as speed, pressure, time it takes a user to type particular words, the amount of time a user holds down a particular key, and the amount of time for which a user pauses between particular keys are all measured by the system. Keystroke-based methods can be classified into two categories: static and continuous. The static method analyzes keystrokes only at specifically fixed times; for example, only when the user types a username and password. On the other hand, the continuous method continuously monitors the user's typing behavior whenever the user is engaged in typing. The keystroke-based verification system is relatively easy to implement compared to other biometric systems because it is completely based on software implementation. The only necessary hardware is a set of working computer and keyboard, and no extra hardware components are needed. Therefore, the overall cost for this system is lower than any other system using different biometric modalities. Keystroke dynamics capture and monitor the username and password, but it does not replace or reset any username and password. In other words, the systems using keystroke dynamics still need to remember multiple sets of usernames and passwords, increase administrative costs of resetting passwords, and provide less convenience to the users.

Keystroke dynamics-based systems can run in two different modes: identification and verification. Identification is one-to-many mode which is the process of finding out an individual's identity by examining biometric patterns. A large amount of keystroke dynamics data are collected and the user is identified based on the previously collected profiles of all users. A pattern is matched against every known template to yield either a score or a distance describing the similarity between the pattern and the template. On the other hand, verification is in one-to-one mode where the pattern that is verified is only compared with the user's individual template. One potential application lies in computer access where keystroke dynamics could be used to verify a user's identity. For example, military control towers or air traffic control towers can adopt this method to ensure high security in monitoring users while they access confidential documents or execute restricted tasks.

2.1.5 Gait

It has been studied that each individual's way of walking, or gait, is unique, and it has been observed that an individual performs his or her walking pattern in a fairly repeatable and characteristic way. As a result, it is sufficiently possible to recognize an individual from a distance by their gait. This uniqueness can makes gait a useful biometric modality. Many conventional biometric modalities like face and fingerprints must be scanned by the reader at designated surfaces; however, gait can be used from a distance even at relatively low resolution. Identification can be achieved based on the human shape and posture as well as the body movement. Gait-based systems have the potential to be used in criminal identification when the suspects disguise or hide their faces with masks. Although their faces may not be recognized, gait-based systems can identify and verify their unique gait since it is relatively more difficult to hide body motion.

2.1.6 Skin Spectroscopy

A skin spectroscopy-based system can recognize the user's skin using an optical sensor. The sensor is able to illuminate a small part of skin with multiple wavelengths of visible and near-infrared light. The exposed skin patch reflects the light back toward the sensor and the reflected light is collected at the sensor for particular wavelengths. The collected light with the measured wavelengths are used to analyze the reflectance variability of the light frequencies after passing through the user's skin. Optical signals that travel across the skin reflect the different chemical and physical characteristics of the skin; therefore, skin spectroscopy can provide a way to verify that a sample is from a particular person. This system is suitable for multimodal biometrics where additional biometric traits can be used in addition to skin spectroscopy. Since it is required to have direct skin contact to the reader, fingerprint or hand geometry methods can be used together to ensure high security and accuracy. Actual sensors can operate on nearly any part of the skin; hence, this method is suitable for places where convenient processing is required. The sensor also consumes low power with small size and fast processing speed, which makes it promising for mobile platforms like smart phones and tablets.

2.1.7 Vein Pattern

Vein pattern-based biometric systems are also called vascular pattern recognition systems. They record vein patterns that can be found under the user's skin using infrared absorption. Subcutaneous features like veins absorb infrared and produce distinctive patterns that are suitable for user identification. The subcutaneous features show large, robust, and stable patterns which can be easily imaged from the wrist and palm surfaces of the user's hand. An image sensor in the system takes an image of the back of the user's hand. The operation mechanism behind the system is based on the temperatures; the main blood vessels have higher temperatures compared to the surrounding tissues and they look brighter in the resultant image. During this process, the selected regions of the user hand are carefully scanned and the resultant vein patterns are extracted. Additional processing called noise reduction is required where the unwanted background is removed and necessary vein patterns are obtained clearly. Veins remain the same whereas blood vessels change as people get old; therefore, only vein patterns are considered for user identification. Since the image sensor is used in the system, hands that are covered with dirt or gloves cannot be identified, and the imaging sensor device that is currently used in the system is not portable. Therefore, it is required to reduce the size of the imaging device for portable or mobile platforms. Although the imaging device is not portable, this vein pattern biometric system can be used in various applications, such as intelligent door locks and handles, safe deposit box access, membership management, and e-commerce.

2.1.8 Deoxyribonucleic Acid

DNA is one of the biometric modalities which is used in high security applications. It is impossible to counterfeit one's DNA due to its uniqueness that originates from one's parents. DNA samples are used to produce either a DNA fingerprint or DNA profile which is then used for user identification. The current processes for obtaining DNA samples are quite intrusive because DNA is collected from a physical sample of each user, such as blood, hair, saliva, and tissues. The DNA-based system has very high degree of accuracy because the chance of two individuals having the same DNA profile is impossible. However, this system is not widely used in daily applications due to its high cost and long processing time. Moreover, the users may find this biometric system to be very intrusive; however, due to the fact that is the most distinct and unique biometric trait available from human beings, it is already used in forensics and paternity testing.

2.1.9 Body Salinity

The natural level of salt in an individual's body is utilized in the body salinity biometric system. The system makes an electric field produce a small amount of electrical current that flows through the body and reacts with salt's conductivity. The induced electrical current is approximately one-billionth of an amp; hence, it does not adversely affect the human body since the amount of current is less than that of the currents that already reside in the body. The body salinity method is still in the developmental stage; however, it is a promising biometric system which can be used in the authentication of data transfer devices attached to the human body, such as watches, phones, and mobile biomedical sensors. Based on the level of salt, the user can enter a house or room and appliances can be turned on.

2.1.10 Facial Thermography

Facial thermography utilizes the pattern of heat that is present in the face which is caused by the blood flow under the user's skin. The heat is captured by infrared sensor in order to obtain unique thermal patterns. These thermal patterns obtained from each individual are distinctive; however, the dynamic nature of blood flow may cause fluctuations and secondary patterns. Although the underlying vein and tissue structures are stable, facial thermography is not yet suitable to be used in the user identification due to the possible fluctuations and secondary patterns. Moreover, environmental conditions and the use of drugs and alcohol can also change the thermal patterns of the face. At this point, facial thermography has potential in determining whether or not an individual is alive because no thermal signatures mean no liveness. Facial thermography is still in the developmental stage but may be integrated with other biometric modalities to identify and verify an individual. One important fact is that facial thermography does not need an infrared illuminator to obtain thermal patterns because the infrared emissions generated by human faces are good enough for generating distinctive thermal signatures. Surveillance and security applications may employ this special modality, especially when the surrounding light is low.

2.1.11 Ear Pattern

Every individual has their unique ear pattern because the outer ear, bone structure, earlobe, and size are all different. Unlike many other biometric systems where direct physical contact is required, the ear pattern-based system does not need direct contact of the ears. This is possible due to the detector which is called an optophone. The optophone is used in the system in order to identify the unique pattern of each individual's ear and verify the pattern to match the individual. The optophone was first introduced by a French company, ART Techniques. It looks similar to a telephone handset which is composed of two different parts: light source and camera. Since there are many detailed features that are already present in individual's ear, detected ear patterns can be collected and compared to biometric templates. The overall process is similar to that of fingerprint and palmprint systems in a way that multiple feature points are measured. This ear pattern-based biometric system is very promising in various applications, especially in a situation where an individual has a serious degree of burns on face and hands. In this situation, the ear pattern can be useful to identify the right person. In addition, ear patterns can be used together with other biometric modalities to ensure the accuracy of verification.

2.1.12 Lip Print

The human lip has its own prints that are composed of normal lines and fissures. Normal lines give outer line information of the lip whereas fissures are formed by wrinkles and grooves that provide more detailed features of each individual. Fissures reside between the inner mucosa and outer skin of the lip. Lip prints are very much like fingerprints and they are unique to every individual. Additional features that can be collected from lip print are furrows on the red part of the lip, labial wrinkles, and lip grooves. This biometric system is still in the developmental stage; however, if the record is accumulated by collecting the individual's detailed descriptive lip patterns of both upper lip and lower lip, the record can serve as a template for identifying a person. Although this modality is less likely to be used in our daily lives, well set up templates can be used to compare with postmortem lips of any unknown dead person.

2.1.13 Body Odor

The body odor biometric system is contactless unlike fingerprint and palmprint where each individual must place their hands on a detecting device. An individual is identified and verified based on the natural properties of human body scent. The biometric system based on body odor may look very intrusive; however, the scent detectors collect the scent data from nonintrusive body parts like the hand. Once the scent is collected, it is extracted and converted into a unique data string. This system is still in the developmental stage but has the potential to be used in the multimodal biometric system where more than one modality is integrated.

2.2 EMERGING MULTIMODAL BIOMETRICS

As discussed in the previous section, unimodal biometric systems are widely used in various real-world applications in order to identify and verify an individual, especially when secure access is required. However, there are technical drawbacks in unimodal biometric systems that cause some performance-related issues, such as noisy data, interclass similarities, nonuniversality, and spoofing. These technical shortcomings lead to a high false acceptance rate, false rejection rate (FRR), limited identification capability, and lack of permanence. As a result, it is necessary to overcome these technical issues in order to achieve higher accuracy, and the multimodal biometric system is a promising solution. The advantages of multiple biometric modalities can be used to enhance performance in many aspects, such as accuracy, noise resistance, universality, and spoofing prevention. The performance degradation in applications with large databases can be reduced as well. Many novel algorithms and methods of multimodal biometrics are emerging these days. Multimodal biometric systems employ multiple sensors for data acquisition, as a result, multiple samples of multiple biometric traits can be captured and analyzed for the maximum level of accuracy. Moreover, each biometric modality has its own advantages and unique characteristics which provide the system with more reliable results in identifying and verifying an individual. Multimodal biometrics can satisfy some of the stringent performance requirements of various applications by addressing the issues of nonuniversality where multiple traits are used to ensure sufficient population coverage. Spoofing attacks can be prevented because it would be hard for adversaries to spoof multiple biometric modalities of an individual at the same time. Another important advantage is that the multimodal biometric system can ask the user to provide random subsets of biometric traits that ensure a real live person is present for proper data acquisition. This will definitely add one additional layer of security at the time of collecting biometric data from an individual.

The term, multimodal is used when more than one biometric trait is combined together to achieve more reliable analysis. This technique is actually based on a study called "data fusion" where different sources of data are collected and fused to produce a high-quality resultant data which presents characteristics of each data source. For example, two different sources of medical imagery data, such as magnetic resonance imaging (MRI) and computed tomography (CT) images, can be combined to produce one high-quality image that can be provided to a doctor for better diagnosis of a medical symptom. Furthermore, different sources of satellite images, such as multispectral and panchromatic images can be fused to produce one high-quality resultant image that contains both spectral and spatial information. Therefore, the multimodal process is a very promising technology which also can be applied to the development of biometric systems.

2.2.1 Fusion of Multimodal Biometrics

In multimodal biometric systems, the fusion of different biometric traits can be performed at four different levels: *sensor level, feature-extraction level, matching-score level,* and *decision level.*

2.2.1.1 Sensor-Level Fusion

Sensor-level fusion integrates characteristics of different modalities using more than one type of sensor. Sensor-level fusion can be achieved only if the multiple sensors generate samples of the same biometric modality. Multiple sensors detect necessary biometric traits before the feature-extraction is performed. One example of the sensor-level fusion is collecting data from an infrared imaging sensor to obtain facial thermography characteristics and from a camera to collect face patterns. Both sensors collect useful traits of the human face and interpret either independently or collaboratively in order to achieve the maximum level of accuracy for user identification. Another good example is a three-dimensional (3D) imaging sensor where 3D shapes can be collected and used together with a standard imaging camera which collects regular two-dimensional (2D) patterns.

2.2.1.2 Feature-Extraction Level Fusion

Feature-extraction is widely used in the area of signal processing, especially image fusion, and it may also be applied to the multimodal biometric systems. Feature-extraction level fusion generally refers to combining different feature sets extracted from multiple biometric sensors. Each sensor acquires and collects various feature sets, and the feature sets are represented as a vector. The vectors are then concatenated to generate a new feature vector with higher dimensionality; however, concatenation is not feasible when the collected feature sets are incompatible, such as eigenface coefficients and fingerprint minutiae.

2.2.1.3 Matching-Score Level Fusion

Each biometric system produces matching-scores that indicate the proximity or similarity of the input data to the template, and the integration or fusion of the matching-scores can be achieved at the matching-score level. The matching-scores next to the feature vectors that are produced by biometric matchers contain the richest information of the input patterns. Moreover, the scores produced by different matchers can also be accessed and fused together to obtain even richer information. Matching-score level fusion is adopted to mainly reduce the FRR. Fusion at this level is very much employed by multimodal biometric systems due to the ease in accessing and consolidating the matching-scores.

2.2.1.4 Decision-Level Fusion

Biometric information can be fused or integrated at the decision level. In order to achieve fusion at the decision level, each different biometric system should make a decision about an individual's identity and determine if the claimed identity is true. Therefore, each of the biometric systems used in making a final decision must have both the identification system and the verification system. Decisions that are rendered by each system can be fused based on techniques such as majority voting (Lam and Suen 1997) and weighted voting (Xu et al. 1992). Decision-level fusion is very important, since all of the individual systems that are used in multimodal biometric system generate decisions, and the final decision is made based on the combined decisions. Commercial biometric systems may use the final resultant decision for user identification and verification.

2.2.2 Applicable Fusion Scenarios for Multimodal Biometrics

In multimodal biometric systems, multiple biometric traits of a person are obtained from multiple sensors. Each sensor can collect raw biometric data of each trait; therefore, various characteristics can be obtained with regard to each of the biometric traits. Fusion of the characteristics of each biometric modality is achieved at different levels as mentioned in the previous section. The final analysis to establish one's identity can significantly enhance the accuracy compared to the analysis based on unimodality. Different fusion scenarios are possible based on the number of biometric modalities, sensors, and feature sets that are employed in the multimodal biometric system (Ross and Jain 2004).

2.2.2.1 Single Biometric Modality and Multiple Sensors

Each sensor detects and collects the data of the same biometric modality. However, since each sensor can provide different aspects of the same biometric modality, their fusion can enhance the performance of the system. An example of this fusion scenario is combining both 2D and 3D images of the face at the matching-score level to improve the overall performance of the face recognition system (Chang et al. 2003).

2.2.2.2 Single Biometric Modality and Multiple Classifiers

In this fusion scenario, only one sensor is used to collect biometric data; however, multiple classifiers are applied to the data. The classifiers can operate on the same extracted feature set or they can generate their own feature sets. The logistic function was used to combine the matching-scores of three different fingerprint matchers operating on the same minutiae sets (Jain et al. 1999). Another example of this fusion scenario is based on face images. Three different types of feature sets from the face image are extracted and the output of the corresponding classifiers are fused at the matching-score level (Lu et al. 2003).

2.2.2.3 Single Biometric Modality and Multiple Units

With only one biometric modality, we can obtain multiple sets of biometric data. In other words, it is possible to use the fingerprints from two or more fingers, the palmprints from both hands or the iris data from both eyes. This fusion scenario is relatively simple and less expensive since additional sensors and extra modules for feature-extraction and score-matching are not necessary.

2.2.2.4 Multiple Biometric Modalities

In this fusion scenario, more than one biometric modality is employed in the system to identify and verify an individual. The system needs extra sensors and hardware components to acquire biometric data of different modalities. Since each biometric modality provides unique characteristics, the system can have enhanced performance in identifying an individual. Face and voice were fused together using HyperBF network to combine the normalized scores of five different classifiers operating on the voice and face feature sets (Brunelli and Falavigna 1995). Different confidence measures with the individual matchers were used to integrate the face and fingerprint characteristics of an individual (Hong and Jain 1998). In 2000, a commercial multimodal system was proposed and named as BioID (Frischholz and Dieckmann 2000). In this system, lip motion and face images were extracted from a video and fused at the feature-extraction level.

2.2.3 Recent Developments in Multimodal Biometric Fusion

- Fusion of face and finger veins at the matching-score level (Razzak et al. 2010)

- Fusion of face and speech information at the matching-score level (Soltane and Doghmane 2010)

- Fusion of palmprint and palm vein at the feature-extraction level (Vaidhya and Pawar 2014)

- Fusion of face and fingerprints at the feature-extraction level (Rattani et al. 2007)

- Fusion of palm vein and face at the feature-extraction level (Bahgat et al. 2013)

- Fusion of fingerprint and finger vein at the matching-score level (Cui and Yang 2011)

- Fusion of fingerprint and palmprint at the feature-extraction level (Krishneswari and Arumugam 2012)

- Fusion of face and ear patterns at the decision level (Boodoo and Subramanian 2009)

- Fusion of palm print and face pattern at the matching-score level (Nageshkumar et al. 2009)

- Fusion of face and speech information at the decision level (Krzyszof et al. 2007)

- Fusion of fingerprint and iris at the decision level (Abdolahi et al. 2013)

- Fusion of palmprint and face pattern at the decision level (Hong and Jain 2008)

- Fusion of face and palmprint at the feature-extraction level (Bokade and Ashok 2012)

- Fusion of fingerprint and iris at the feature-extraction level (Jagadessan and Duraisamy 2010)

2.3 NEW OPPORTUNITIES IN BIOMETRICS

In this section, a brief introduction to the following chapters is presented in the areas of mobile, health care, social networks, gaming technologies, and homeland security.

2.3.1 Biometrics in Mobile Systems

As the usage of mobile systems grows, the needs for security rise significantly. Modern mobile devices such as smartphones and tablets have a high memory capacity that stores large amount of personal data. Moreover, it is not only constrained to the users' personal data since all the mobile devices can be connected to the Internet to access even larger amount of sensitive on-line data that are stored in banking, e-mail, cloud, and social networking sites. Biometrics can be a promising solution to secure the personal data that is stored on mobile devices, and by doing so, the more sensitive data that can be accessed via mobile Internet is also secured. Most of the mobile devices have already implemented some protection using passwords and patterns; however, password-based methods are susceptible and pattern-based methods are vulnerable to smudge attacks. Therefore, it is necessary to employ another layer of security based on biometrics that is unique to each user and less vulnerable to attacks. The integration of mobile devices and biometric technologies will definitely leverage biometric authentication into a wide range of services that include online banking, online payment, and e-commerce. Mobile biometric technologies can be implemented using a built-in camera, microphone, and touch screen which enable the collection of multimodal biometric data of a user. These built-in sensors can offer a strong alternative to conventional password or pattern schemes for user authentication. Biometrics will become more relevant due to the rapid growth in mobile devices and social media. It is expected that the industry will move into a direction of employing multimodal biometrics for user authentication on mobile platforms.

2.3.2 Biometrics in Healthcare Systems

Biometrics are now considered in the healthcare field due to the rising demands for data security. The healthcare industry is adopting various biometric technologies because accuracy has improved, public acceptance has increased, and overall cost has reduced. Some hospitals have begun to move away from traditional password-based system since the passwords can always be used in unauthorized situations where they are shared or stolen. Most of the computer systems in the hospital are designed to automatically time out and force the users (doctors and nurses) to log on repeatedly between shifts. Once biometrics are widely deployed, the total amount of time for logging back into the systems will be significantly reduced with a simple touch of biometric modalities like a finger. In the near future, healthcare industries will employ biometric technologies to identify a patient. Blood banks in the United States are starting to use fingerprints of a donor to follow the federal regulations that require accurate verification of each donation. By using the biometric information of a donor, no personal data like social security numbers will be used anymore, which in turn, will reduce personal data breach. Biometrics will also replace patient wristbands or barcodes that are currently used to identify each patient for their medication or treatment. Using biometrics like fingerprints and palmprints will also improve the ability to deal with medical emergencies where patients are unconscious by quickly checking their identities along with their medical histories. Furthermore, biometrics will also help reduce medical insurance fraud and billing fraud by replacing patients' insurance or credit cards to prevent situations where a patient poses as another to take advantage of insurance benefits and where unauthorized providers file an illegal medical claim.

2.3.3 Biometrics in Social Networks

Social networks like Facebook have attracted a large number of people around the world for its ease in creating an online human network. With the number of users significantly increased, social network companies started adopting biometric technologies to attract even more users and also to deal with security issues that have arisen recently. One example of biometric technology that is used in social networks to provide the users with a better experience is facial recognition for identifying people in online social networks and photo storage services. For example, Facebook has employed a tool, "tag suggestion" based on facial recognition that scans uploaded pictures and identifies network friends by suggesting who should be tagged. This is done by calculating an individual's facial features such as distance between eyes, nose, and ears. The template is based on the user's profile pictures and photos. Facebook has recently introduced a new tool, namely "Moments," which syncs photos stored on a user's phone based on which friends are depicted in the photos. All these biometric tools provide the users with a better experience in connecting with their friends across online social networks; however, despite the advantages, there are security issues that we need to think about. Users are concerned about using social network services because the lack of security may put them at the risk of identity theft and potential cyber-crimes like sexual violence or stalking. A major security concern nowadays is the exposure of a user's personal account since social network services like Facebook are used by many websites that allow a single sign-in. For example, online shopping websites let users sign in via their Facebook account information including ID and password. If the Facebook account is exposed, all the other websites that have gained access via Facebook will be compromised as well. As a result, the personal bank account, credit card, and other payment information may be exposed to potential attacks. Therefore, it is necessary to add another layer of security to the current password-based authentication using biometric technologies. However, social network providers will have to find a way to receive consent from the users for collecting and storing their biometric data because many users feel uncomfortable with providing their personal biometric data. Recently, a less intrusive method has been proposed by AuthenWare (www.authenware.com), which uses a keystroke-based system, namely "Cool ID." The Cool ID is based on behavioral biometrics, especially in the form of keystroke authentication. A user's keystroke habit is measured and used for authentication since every user has their own unique keystroke rhythm that does not have regularity.

2.3.4 Biometrics in Gaming Technologies

Over the past few years, many people have been playing computer or video games using new technologies such as virtual reality and motion sensors. Due to the development in gaming technologies, people have been enjoying games with their bodies; hence, it is not motionless play in a couch anymore. Moreover, we are very close to a situation where we will be employing real-time biometrics such as heart rate and respiration rate that will definitely provide users with a new experience. New games based on the heart rate can help users manage their stress by lowering the heart rate not only during the gameplay but also in the real world. This can be achieved by collecting a player's biometric emotional states based on heart rate variability, and as a result, players can learn how to manage their stress without even noticing it. The heart rate also can control the difficulty level of game; for example, player's shooting accuracy may improve by maintaining a lower heart rate or sports games can adopt the player's heart and respiration rates to create a very realistic virtual environment. Game designers and companies will be able to produce a game which can sense the player's biometric information and learn about the player on a real-time basis, which in turn, will make the game more interesting and realistic. Physically fit people can play well in the virtual game as if they were playing in the real world. On the other hand, people with less fit bodies can improve their physique by playing the game that tracks the player's biometric data. In other words, games will be interacting with real players by sharing biometric data that change dynamically during gameplay. Furthermore, educational games can also be developed for young children to learn proper behavior in a dangerous situation; for example, when they are in a building that is on fire. Children will be able to learn how to react in a certain situation by playing the virtual game with their biometric data continuously monitored.

2.3.5 Biometrics in Homeland Security

National security and public safety have always been the top priority of the government to protect people from any potential threats. The United States, especially after experiencing the tragedy of 9/11, has adopted various methods to secure the homeland including biometric technologies. The United States Department of Homeland Security released a biometric strategic framework which outlines plans for its use of biometric technologies until 2025 (https://www.dhs.gov). This framework is introduced here because it projects the right direction for government agencies or countries to follow in deploying their biometric systems. The framework has three major goals to achieve: (i) enhance effectiveness of subject identification; (ii) transform identity operation to optimize performance; and (iii) refine processes and policies to promote innovation. The first goal is to replace outdated biometric systems, centralize the access to the federal database, improve real-time access in the field, and expand the use of multimodal biometrics. Fingerprints have dominated biometric systems so far; however, both the law enforcement and the other government agencies will employ additional biometric traits like the face and iris to better identify individuals based on the multimodal approach. The second goal is to improve the overall process speed using biometric data rather than documents and credentials of individuals. This biometric verification will speed up the processing time and reduce possible vulnerabilities and fraud. The third goal is to refine processes by implementing standardized biometric solutions among the government agencies. If every government agency employs their own biometric systems without organized standards, collaboration among the agencies will be destroyed; hence, the homeland will be vulnerable to potential threats.

2.4 CONCLUSIONS

As discussed in this chapter, various biometrics can be added to conventional password-based security systems as an additional layer of protection. Using either unimodal or multimodal biometrics as another authentication mechanism provides a much higher level of security to verify users' identities. However, there are still some issues that need to addressed due to people's concerns over a number of biometrics-related technologies. Many people are skeptical about using their biometric information for authentication because both the collecting and the storing of data and records are perceived as intrusive and very personal. Moreover, now that the technology has been implemented on mobile devices like iPhones, users are concerned with the safety of their unique biometric data since there is possibility of misuse and forgery that may significantly affect one's privacy. However, although biometrics may have some security concerns, if the rules and policies to protect the collected data are well set up, biometrics is still a promising solution to securely identify and verify users prior to accessing sensitive data. Moreover, multimodal biometrics which use multiple biometric traits and sensors for data acquisition can be a good alternative to increase matching accuracy for identification and verification. Various multimodal biometrics were introduced in this chapter in addition to unimodal biometrics, and new opportunities for biometrics were also briefly discussed which are explained more in detail in the following chapters. As biometrics technologies become more secure, accurate, and affordable, the extra security that they provide will surpass the shortcomings of the technologies as well as the concerns and issues on privacy.

REFERENCES

Abdolahi, M., M. Mohamadi, and M. Jafari, Multimodal biometric system fusion using fingerprint and iris with fuzzy logic, *International Journal of Soft Computing and Engineering*, 2(6), 504–510, 2013.

AuthenWare, Cool ID, 2013. http://www.authenware.com

Bahgat, S. F., S. Ghonieny, and M. Alotabi, Proposed multimodal palm veins-face biometric authentication, *International Journal of Advanced Computer Science and Applications*, 4(6), 92–96, 2013.

Bokade, G. U. and M. Ashok, Feature level fusion of palm and face for secure recognition, *International Journal of Computer and Electrical Engineering*, 4(2), 157–160, 2012.

Boodoo, N. B. and R. K. Subramanian, Robust multi-biometric recognition using face and ear images, *IJCSIS—International Journal of Computer Science and Information Security*, 6(2), 164–169, 2009.

Brunelli, R. and D. Falavigna, Person identification using multiple cues, *IEEE Transactions on PAMI*, 12, 955–966, October 1995.

Chang, K. I., K. W. Bowyer, and P. J. Flynn, Face recognition using 2D and 3D facial data, in *Proceedings of Workshop on Multimodal User Authentication*, (Santa Barbara, California), pp. 25–32, December 2003.

Cui, F. and G. Yang, Score level fusion of fingerprint and finger vein recognition, *Journal of Computer Information's Systems*, 16, 5723–5731, 2011.

Frischholz, R. W. and U. Dieckmann, Bioid: A multimodal biometric identification system, *IEEE Computer*, 33(2), 64–68, 2000.

Hong L. and A. K. Jain, Integrating faces and fingerprints for personal identification, *IEEE Transactions on PAMI*, 20, 1295–1307, December 1998.

Hong, L. and A. K. Jain, Integrating faces and fingerprints for personal identification, *IEEE Transactions on Pattern Analysis and Machine Intelligence*, 20(12), 1295–1307, 2008.

Jagadessan, A. and K. Duraisamy, Secured cryptographic key generation from multimodal biometrics: Feature level fusion of fingerprint and iris, *International Journal of Computer Science and Information Security*, 7(2), 28–37, 2010.

Jain, A. K., S. Prabhakar, and S. Chen, Combining multiple matchers for a high security fingerprint verification system, *Pattern Recognition Letters*, 20, 1371–1379, 1999.

Krishneswari, K. and S. Arumugam, Multimodal biometrics using feature fusion, *Journal of Computer Science* 8(3), 431–435, 2012.

Krzyszof, J. R., P. Prodanov, and A. Drygajlo, Reliability-based decision fusion in multimodal biometric verification systems, *EURASIP Journal on Advances in Signal Processing*, Article ID 86572, 2007, 9pp, 2007.

Lam, L. and C. Y. Suen, Application of majority voting to pattern recognition: An analysis of its behavior and performance, *IEEE Transactions on Systems, Man and Cybernetics, Part A: Systems and Humans*, 27(5), 553–568, 1997.

Lu, X., Y. Wang, and A. K. Jain, Combining classifiers for face recognition, in *Proceedings of IEEE International Conference on Multimedia and Expo (ICME)*, vol. 3, (Baltimore, Maryland), pp. 13–16, July 2003.

Nageshkumar, M., P. K. Mahesh, and M. N. S. Swami, A efficient multimodal biometric fusion using palmprint and a face image, *International Journal of Computer Science*, 2(3), 49–53, 2009.

Rattani, A., D. R. Kishu, and M. Bicego, Feature level fusion of face and fingerprint Biometrics, in *First IEEE International Conference on Biometrics: Theory, Applications and Systems*, Crystal City, Virginia, 2007.

Razzak, M. I., R. Yusof, and M. Khalid, Multimodal face and finger veins biometric authentication, *Scientific Research and Essays*, 5(17), 2529–2534, 2010.

Ross, A. and A. K. Jain, Multimodal biometrics: An overview, in *The 12th European Signal Processing Conference (EUSIPCO)*, Vienna, Austria, pp. 1221–1224, 2004.

Soltane, M. and N. Doghmane, Face and speech based multimodal biometric authentication, *International Journal of Advance Science and Technology*, 21(8), 41–46, 2010.

The United States Department of Homeland Security. https://www.dhs.gov

Vaidhya, D. and S. Pawar, Feature level fusion of palmprint and palm vein for personal authentication based on entropy technique, *International Journal on Electronics and Communication Technology*, 5(Issue spl-1), 53–57, 2014.

Xu, L., A. Krzyzak, and C. Y. Suen, Methods of combining multiple classifiers and their applications to handwriting recognition, *IEEE Transactions on Systems, Man and Cybernetics*, 22(3), 418–435, 1992.

II

Applications of Biometrics in a Data-Driven World

CHAPTER 3

Mobile Device Biometrics

Maria Villa, Mikhail Gofman, Sinjini Mitra, Christopher Rodney, and Mahdi Hosseini

CONTENTS

3.1 INTRODUCTION

"In Less Than Two Years, a Smartphone Could Be Your Only Computer," wrote Christina Bonnington on wired.com in 2015 [1], referring to the rapid takeover of the consumer computing market by smartphones and tablet computers.

Modern phones and tablet computers provide unparalleled convenience to users, allowing them to browse social networks, check emails, take photographs, and bank and shop online on the go. Many modern mobile devices are equipped with high-resolution cameras, GPS, radios, accelerometers, and other sensors that enable novel applications, such as instant video calls, navigation, fitness, and support for many other applications not practical with traditional laptop and desktop computers.

The number of mobile phone users worldwide is expected to pass the five billion mark by 2019 [2], and by 2018, the number of tablet computer users is projected to reach 1.43 billion [3].

This proliferation of smartphones and tablets raises concerns about the security and privacy of data stored on mobile devices if they are lost, stolen, or hacked. An attacker with physical access to a mobile device can potentially steal a user's banking information, read his/her emails, look at his/her private photos, and perform other criminal actions. The scale of the problem is vast; according to ConsumerReports.org, 2.1 million mobile phones were stolen and 3.1 million phones were lost in 2013 in the United States alone [4].

The initial countermeasures for restricting unauthorized access to mobile devices were passwords (e.g., Google Android-based devices) and four-digit PIN codes (e.g., Apple iPhone smartphones and iPad tablets). However, this approach has proven ineffective; for the sake of convenience, many users chose easily guessable passwords and PINs. For example, according to *TIME* magazine, the most widely used iPhone PIN numbers in 2011 were as follows:

1. "1234"

2. "0000"

3. "2580"

4. "1111"

5. "5555"

6. "2683"

7. "0852"

8. "2222"

9. "1212"

10. "1998"

Similar problems still exist in 2016 [5,6].

Recognition of the above problems prompted mobile device manufacturers to consider what they believed would be a more robust approach to authentication in mobile devices—*biometrics*. With biometrics, users do not have to design and remember strong passwords or PIN numbers. At the same time, biometric traits are fairly difficult to fabricate when attempting to bypass the authentication process.

With the integration of biometric sensors, such as fingerprint readers, into modern mobile devices, mobile biometrics have found applications beyond simply protecting mobile devices against unauthorized access. One such popular application is secure payment authorization. For example, the ApplePay feature of the iPhone deployed by Apple in 2014 allows users to authorize online payments by scanning their finger.

The trend of integrating fingerprint readers into mobile devices is expected to continue. By 2021, more than one-third of all mobile devices are expected to have fingerprint readers, bringing the total number of such devices to one billion [7].

This chapter discusses the past and present research on, and practice of, using keystroke dynamics, and fingerprint, face, voice, and iris biometrics in mobile devices. This chapter concludes with a discussion on multimodal biometric systems as a promising future solution for strengthening biometrics-based authentication in mobile devices. Moreover, this chapter makes generous use of the State of the Art of Mobile Biometrics, Liveness, and Noncoercion Detection report published by the Personalized Centralized Authentication System Project group [8].

3.1.1 History

Mobile biometrics have come a long way since their early days and have become more portable and affordable for the average consumer. The first documented use of fingerprint sensors, or biometric authentication, on a mobile device dates back to 1998. Siemens PSE and Triodata developed a GSM phone prototype called SL10 with a Siemens/Infineon fingerprint sensor on the back of the phone. Figure 3.1 shows an image of the SL10. The fingerprint module was integrated into the battery pack and could capture and recognize the user's fingerprint. The feature granted access only if the user's fingerprints had been recognized.

Two years later in 2000, Sagem released MC 959 ID, which was the first commercially available mobile device to comprise a dual-band GSM phone with a built-in fingerprint reader. However, the use of consumer mobile biometric technology did not quite catch on at the time, and sensitive data was generally not stored on the mobile devices of the late 1990s and early 2000s—colloquially referred to as *dumb phones.*

A brief timeline of mobile fingerprint sensors is presented below:

- Siemens (1998): Siemens PSE and Triodata developed a phone prototype with a Siemens/Infineon fingerprint sensor on the back.

© Bromba Biometrics

FIGURE 3.1 (**See color insert.**) Siemens mobile phone presented in 1999 at Centrum für Büroautomation, Informationstechnologie und Telekommunikation (CeBIT), which the user could unlock using their fingerprint. The fingerprint module was integrated into the phone's battery pack and integrated the functionality for capturing and recognizing the fingerprint. (From Bromba Biometrics.)

- Sagem (January, 2000): Sagem MC 959 ID with a ST/Upek fingerprint sensor on the back.

- HP (November, 2002): The HP iPAQ h545 was the first personal digital assistant (or PDA) with a built-in fingerprint sensor: the FingerChip AT77C101, from Atmel.

- Casio (February, 2003): Casio & Alps Electric unveiled a new fingerprint optical sweep sensor designed for the cell phone, such as the Casio cell phone prototype.

- Fujitsu (February, 2003): The Fujitsu F505i cell phone contained an AuthenTec sensor was demoed in Japan.

- Hitachi (July, 2004): A Hitachi G1000 PDA phone prototype containing the Atrua swipe sensor was shown in Japan.

- LG TeleCom (August, 2004): The LG-LP3800 camera phone containing the AuthenTec AES2500 was released.

- Yulong (February, 2005): Yulong announced the Coolpad 858F GSM with the Atrua swipe fingerprint sensor.

- Samsung (October, 2005): Samsung unveiled the SCH S370 Anycall cell phone using the AuthenTec swipe fingerprint sensor.

- Lenovo (October, 2005): Lenovo unveiled the ET980 phone using the AuthenTec swipe fingerprint sensor.

- HTC (March, 2006): Release of the HPC Sirius P6500 phone with an AuthenTec sensor.

- Toshiba (February, 2007): At 3GSM, Toshiba unveiled the G900 phone with an Atrua ATW310 sweep fingerprint sensor.

- Asus (March, 2008): Asus unveiled the M536 PDA phone.

- Motorola (July, 2008): Motorola unveiled the Q9 Napoleon phone with an Atrua swipe fingerprint sensor.

- Sharp (August, 2008): Sharp unveiled the SH907i (aka SH-01A) phone with an optical swipe fingerprint sensor.

- Lexun/Leson (September, 2008): Lexun/Leson unveiled the G2 phone featuring the Atrua fingerprint sensor.

- Acer (February, 2009): Acer unveiled the Tempo M900 phone with a fingerprint sensor.

- Philips (July, 2010): Philips unveiled the Xenium X712 phone with an AuthenTec AES2260 sensor.

- Samsung (January, 2013): Validity Sensors Company demonstrated a modified Galaxy S2 phone with a swipe fingerprint sensor.

- Apple (September, 2013): Apple unveiled the iPhone 5S with a fingerprint sensor (a year after buying the Authentec authentication/biometric company).

- Bull (October, 2013): Bull unveiled the Hoox m2 phone with a Upek TCS5 fingerprint sensor (released in 2008).

- Fujitsu (October, 2013): The Fujitsu Arrows Z FJL22 was announced with a round swipe fingerprint sensor.

- HTC (November, 2013): HTC announces One Max phone with a swipe sensor [9].

- Samsung (July, 2014): Samsung announces the Galaxy S5 Mini phone with a swipe fingerprint sensor.

- Fujitsu (September, 2015): Fujitsu unveils Arrows Fit F-01H phone with a fingerprint sensor on the back [10].

- Vivo (November, 2015): The Vivo X6 is unveiled with a FPC1035 fingerprint sensor [10].

- LG (February, 2016): The LG G5 phone is unveiled at the Mobile World Congress. It features a Cards FPC1035 fingerprint sensor [10].

As can be seen, many companies have tried integrating fingerprint sensors with mobile phones, with most attempts failing to gain popularity. These failures can be attributed to their lack of user-friendliness, the limited applications of the fingerprint reader (i.e., the reader was only used for unlocking the device), and, overall, poor user experience. They can be seen in sharp contrast to the success enjoyed by more recent devices, beginning with Apple's iPhone (5S released in 2013 and later models), which also feature a fingerprint reader. The iPhone's success has been attributed to Apple improving the user-friendliness of the technology and finding novel and highly popular applications for their fingerprint reader, such as the ApplePay payment authorization system.

In 2012, Apple acquired AuthenTec, which specialized in biometric authentication. This union with AuthenTec resulted in a new design for the iPhone's fingerprint reader [11]. The fingerprint reader was placed on the home button and a capacitive contact sensor was added which captures a high-resolution image of the finger from the subepidermal layer of the skin. The fingerprint data are processed by the Secure Enclave coprocessor integrated into the Apple A7, or later A-series processors. Although there are no official reports on the accuracy of Apple's fingerprint recognition system, some researchers estimate a 0.05% false acceptance rate (FAR) and a 2%–10% false rejection rate (FRR) [11].

According to Tomorrow's Transactions press release on September 11, 2013, two days after the iPhone 5s was released, a hacker group based in Germany, called Chaos Computer Club, released a tutorial documenting a technique for bypassing the device's fingerprint recognition system using a fabricated finger [12,13]. Notwithstanding these concerns, the system remains popular, owing to its convenience and powerful applications [14].

Although fingerprints remain the most popular biometric modality on consumer mobile devices, other modalities such as face, iris, voice, ear, and teeth have been, and continue to be, experimented with as well.

An early prototype of a facial recognition system for a mobile device was developed in 2005 by the OMRON Corporation. The prototype was demonstrated at the "Security Show Japan 2005" held at Tokyo Big Sight from March 2 to 4, 2005 [15].

As of the time of writing, all mobile devices powered by Google's Android operating system allow users to unlock their phones using their face. However, the system is considered vulnerable, as it can be bypassed by an attacker holding a photograph of the legitimate user's face in front of the camera (which he/she can easily obtain from, e.g., a social networking website). Although liveness detection techniques have been developed to help thwart such attacks, many have been successfully bypassed [16,17].

One of the first mobile voice recognition applications was developed by Google in 2008 for Apple's iPhone. The application allowed users to use their voice to input search queries into Google's search engine. It digitized the voice and sent it to Google's cloud servers, which would analyze the speech and return search results back to the phone.

Modern, mobile devices (e.g., iPhones and Android-based phones) feature digital assistant applications, which enable users to use their voice to manage their device, search the web, and perform other tasks by simply speaking to their phone. Some well-known digital assistant applications include Apple's Siri, Microsoft's Cortana, and Google Now. The voice recognition capabilities of these programs are highly robust and continue to improve.

Kim et al. (2010), McCool et al. (2012), and other researchers have experimented with using photos of a user's teeth as a means of authentication. In 2014, Descartes Biometrics Company demonstrated a prototype system that allowed the user to unlock the device by holding his/her ear to the screen. In 2015, Amazon Corporation patented the mobile device ear recognition technology, which recognizes the user's ear from an image taken by the smartphone's front-facing camera. The same year, Fujitsu Corporation released the Arrows NX F-04G Android-based smartphone, which is the first smartphone equipped with an iris scanner.

3.2 MODALITIES

3.2.1 Fingerprints

Fingerprint recognition refers to identifying people based on their fingerprints and is the most widely used biometric method for authenticating users of computer systems [9]. It is implemented in commercial, government, immigration, and border control applications [18]. Its popularity is attributed to the ease with which fingerprint images can be captured and to the method's long history of use and general acceptance.

Technological progress in the last few decades has resulted in a fingerprint scanner that is sufficiently small to be integrated into a mobile device. This innovation has marked the entry of fingerprint recognition into the consumer mobile market and its eventual popularity there.

3.2.1.1 Modern Devices with an Embedded Fingerprint Scanner

Modern mobile phones (as of 2016) with an embedded fingerprint scanner include the Apple iPhone 6, Samsung Galaxy S7, Google Nexus, Samsung Galaxy Note 5, Huawei Mate S, OnePlus 2, and LG V10. It is interesting to note that iPhones and Galaxy devices integrate their fingerprint scanners into the home button, which is typically used by users to navigate to a device's main menu. In contrast, Google Nexus, OnePlus 2, LG V10, and Huawei Mate S integrate their fingerprint readers into the back panel of the phone. Some argue that the placement of the fingerprint reader on the back panel is the more user-friendly design because it makes it easier for the user to place his/her finger on the scanner while holding the device in his/her hand [19].

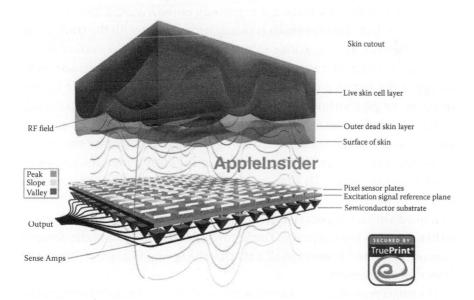

FIGURE 3.2 **(See color insert.)** Cross-section of AuthenTec's fingerprint sensor. (From AppleInsider, http://www.appleinsider.com)

Similar to smartphones, the Apple iPad Pro, Google Nexus, and Samsung Galaxy tablet computers also feature a fingerprint scanner.

3.2.1.2 Fingerprint Acquisition Methods on Mobile Devices

There are two general methods of acquiring fingerprints on a mobile device. The first is by using the device's integrated generic photo camera to capture a fingerprint image. The second is by using a semiconductor-based fingerprint reader. We discuss both methods in Sections 3.2.1.2.1 and 3.2.1.2.2.

3.2.1.2.1 Camera Fingerprint Capture

This method has the advantage of not requiring contact between the camera and the finger and is used in the ICE Unlock Fingerprint Secure application (designed for the Android system) [9]. The other approach is using a capacitive or a thermal sensor in the mobile phone to acquire the fingerprint.

3.2.1.2.2 Semiconductor-Based Reader

iPhone's approach to fingerprint acquisition contrasts with the above approach. Instead, it uses a semiconductor-based fingerprint reader based on the design by AuthenTec (see Figure 3.2), which works by using small radio frequency signals to detect the fingerprint's peak and valley patterns. As a result, it is able to obtain a sharp image of the live skin layer beneath the skin's surface. This approach is in marked contrast with the traditional optical, thermal, and capacitive solutions that only read the surface of the skin [20]. Another interesting feature of Touch ID fingerprint sensor technology is the fact that each enrolled fingerprint stays within the device and does not get transmitted to a remote system for analysis (e.g., a cloud).

The Secure Enclave is a component of the iPhone's main A7 processor chip and is responsible for handling the data acquired by the Touch ID sensor. Each Secure Enclave is provisioned during manufacture with its own unique ID (UID) that cannot be accessed by other parts of the system. In fact, the UID is not even known to Apple. The device UID is combined with a temporary randomly generated key. The resulting value is then used as a key to encrypt the Secure Enclave's portion of the device's memory space and to encrypt all data that the Secure Enclave writes to the device's flash memory.

The fingerprint sensor communicates with Secure Enclave through the main A7 processor across a serial peripheral interface bus. Although the processor can relay data received from the sensor to the Secure Enclave, it cannot read the data it relays because the data are encrypted with a secret session key known only to the sensor and the Secure Enclave. The session key is collaboratively generated by the two sides using the device's shared key built into the Touch ID sensor and the Secure Enclave. All messages passed during the key exchange phase are encrypted using the Advanced Encryption Standard (AES) algorithm with key wrapping. The session key is derived from the two random keys generated by both sides and is then used to encrypt all sensor-Secure Enclave communications with the AESCCM transport encryption algorithm [21].

Starting in September 2014, Apple introduced Apple Pay technology with the unveiling of the Apple iPhone 6. This technology allows mobile users to authenticate payments by moving the iPhone device near the payment terminal. Near field communication (NFC) technology allows the terminal to receive the payment information from the phone and initiate a transaction. To authorize the transaction, the users can verify their identity via the Touch ID system.

Other mobile devices with fingerprint readers also have techniques for securely acquiring and storing biometric data (some of which are similar to those of iPhones). For example, consider the Google Android operating system 6.0, which is designed to run on many different types of mobile devices. To be compatible with Android 6.0, Google mandates that

> Device implementations with a secure lock screen SHOULD include a fingerprint sensor. If a device implementation includes a fingerprint sensor and has a corresponding application program interface (API) for third-party developers, it

- MUST have a false acceptance rate not higher than 0.002%.
- Is STRONGLY RECOMMENDED to have a false rejection rate not higher than 10%, and a latency from when the fingerprint sensor is touched until the screen is unlocked below 1 s, for 1 enrolled finger.
- MUST rate limit attempts for at least 30 s after 5 false trials for fingerprint verification.
- MUST have a hardware-backed keystore implementation, and perform the fingerprint matching in a trusted execution environment (TEE) or on a chip with a secure channel to the TEE.
- MUST have all identifiable fingerprint data encrypted and cryptographically authenticated such that they cannot be acquired, read or altered outside of the TEE as documented in

the implementation guidelines on the Android Open Source Project site [Resources, 96].

- MUST prevent adding a fingerprint without first establishing a chain of trust by having the user confirm existing or add a new device credential (PIN/pattern/password) using the TEE as implemented in the Android Open Source project.
- MUST NOT enable third-party applications to distinguish between individual fingerprints.
- MUST, when upgraded from a version earlier than Android 6.0, have the fingerprint data securely migrated to meet the above requirements or removed.
- SHOULD use the Android fingerprint icon provided in the Android Open Source Project [22].

The cases of iPhone and Samsung Galaxy are particularly interesting, as the fingerprint readers used therein were among the first to successfully penetrate the mobile market.

Considering the current market trends, we can expect to see more and more mobile devices with fingerprint readers in the future. With the evolution of mobile sensing technology, these fingerprint reading systems will be more secure, robust, and user-friendly.

3.2.2 Keystroke Dynamics

3.2.2.1 Introduction

Keystroke dynamics, or typing dynamics, is a behavioral biometric used to identify people based on the manner and the rhythm of their typing on a keyboard or a touch screen [9,23]. The interaction between a person and a keyboard or touch screen creates a type of signature that is generally unique to each individual [24] (e.g., Figure 3.3).

Although traditional keystroke pattern recognition techniques in computer keyboards can also be used in smartphones, computer keyboards are limited to their keys. This limited hardware only allows for the measurement of typing speed. This is measured based on the time between pressing and releasing keys. For a traditional keyboard, the typing speed is the only characteristic that can be used to differentiate between users [25].

Smartphone touch screens allow for the measurement of much more than simply the user's typing speed. The force of keypresses, phone orientation, and finger size can be measured [9]. These features can be used to design a more robust biometric system based on keystroke dynamics.

FIGURE 3.3   Woman using keystrokes on a mobile device. (From bigstockphoto. com)

3.2.2.1.1   Advantages of Keystroke Dynamics

The keystroke dynamics biometrics scheme is inexpensive to implement, is noninvasive to the user, does not require extra hardware, allows for continuous authentication, and can be easily integrated into a computer system with minor modifications (assuming the system has a means of collecting keystroke data) [9,23].

3.2.2.1.2   Disadvantages

A disadvantage of keystroke dynamics is that it is less robust than many other biometric techniques. Injury, or even exhaustion, may alter a user's keystroke patterns. Keystroke patterns can also change with time, thus requiring keystroke classification systems to keep up with such variations [9]. Liveness detection is particularly challenging in keystroke dynamics because it is difficult to differentiate between a keypress generated by a real person and a keystroke generated by a machine (e.g., a robot) [9].

3.2.2.2   Integration of Keystroke Dynamics with a Mobile Device

The verification of a user's keystroke dynamics on a mobile device can be done either statically at login, periodically dynamically, continuously dynamically, keyword specifically, or application specifically [26]. We describe each of these methods below.

> *Static at login.* As soon as the smartphone is turned on, the user keystroke data are acquired as the user enters the PIN number to unlock the device [27].

Periodic dynamic. In this method, the data are obtained on a periodic basis after the user turns the device on to either unlock the screen or make a call [27].

Continuous dynamic. The measurements are taken nonstop, typically with an application running in the background, which detects the keypresses of the user [27].

Keyword specific. This method measures the user's keystroke data when the user types a word or draws a shape [27].

Application specific. Mobile applications are created specifically to identify and authenticate users with images or graphical patterns, in which keystroke dynamics is used [27].

3.2.2.3 Keystroke Recognition Background
3.2.2.3.1 Timing Strokes
The measurements of the user's keystroke dynamics features are divided into two categories: dwell time and flight time. Dwell time is the amount of time it takes to press and release a single key, or the duration of the keypress [9,28]. Flight time, or latency, on the other hand, is the amount of time between releasing a key and pressing the next key.

The term Di-Graph refers to the amount of time that elapses between pressing two consecutive keys. The same concept extended to three or more keypress sequences is referred to as an N-Graph [9]. These measurements can then be used as features.

3.2.2.4 Keystroke Dynamics Technology and Research
As mobile phones support more and more secure applications (e.g., email, bank accounts, calendars, and more), it is essential to integrate more security measures into these applications and into the devices as a whole. Keystroke dynamics can help here.

This section introduces some of the state-of-the-art mobile keystroke dynamics applications, services, and ongoing research.

3.2.2.4.1 BehavioSec
BehavioSec is a Swedish company that uses keystroke dynamics, mouse movements, and other behavioral biometrics to deliver user authentication services [29]. Its system consists of the application that runs on the mobile device itself and collects the keystroke data, and a server

application that runs on a remote system and studies and records the user's keystroke dynamics behavior (usually when entering a PIN or password) and matches the pattern against the database of known keystroke dynamics patterns of authorized users. It then computes confidence scores indicating the likelihood of the behavior matching that of the authorized user [29].

What makes BehavioSec interesting is that the system learns continuously. It looks at behaviors, such as keystroke and touch dynamics, and then compares them to earlier interactions of the same person. This generates a score comparing current activity to prior activity. An implementation-defined response is then generated. For example, the security level can be adjusted if needed, depending on the score received [29].

3.2.2.4.2 Keystroke Dynamics on the Battlefield

"The whole concept of authentication is a necessary evil from the soldier's standpoint... If I could walk up to the computer and have the computer automatically recognize me, confirm my identity and provide me access without me even touching the keyboard, that's kind of the ideal situation," said Bob Fedorchak, tactical public key infrastructure technical lead at the Army Communications-Electronics Research, Development and Engineering Center in an interview with NextGov (information/newsource resource for federal decision makers) on April 11, 2016. He was referring to the lengthy authentication processes that soldiers often have to go through on the battlefield in order to gain access to their battle systems. For example, the time it takes the soldier to enter his/her password or insert an ID card into the mobile computer of his/her Humvee in order to obtain a map of field mines could be the difference between life and death.

To reduce authentication times, the US Army has been testing keystroke dynamics-based authentication methods to improve their efficiency on the battlefield [30]. One proposal was to use biometric keystroke-equipped touchpads that would allow soldiers to quickly and easily sign in by swiping their finger across the screen, by using the relative uniqueness of the finger swiping motion as a biometric [30]. According to NextGov.com, the army may deploy this approach as early as 2018.

3.2.2.4.3 Sensor-Enhanced Keystroke Dynamics

Cristiano Giuffrida and Kamil Majdanik, the creators of the sensor-enhanced keystroke application, used accelerometers and the gyroscope hardware available on many Android phones to enhance the robustness of keystroke dynamics-based authentication [31]. Their sensor-enhanced keystroke dynamics mechanism was demonstrated with an Android-based device prototype named Unagi. Unagi used sensor data from the accelerometer, gyroscope, and keystroke timing data when measuring the user's keystroke dynamics. Their authentication scheme, which involves the user entering a predefined string of characters, results in an equal error rate (EER) of 0.08%.

Even though Giuffrida and Majdanik obtained relatively low error report rates, they hope to further reduce these rates by using more sophisticated sensors and algorithms. Their goal is an FRR of less than 1% and an FAR of no more than 0.001%. They also plan to explore free-text with noise suppression methods for further robustness, as well as further testing of the scheme [31].

3.2.2.5 Conclusion

Although keystroke dynamics was traditionally applied only to computer keyboards, in the age of smartphones and tablets it can be successfully applied to mobile devices. Commercial applications, such as BehavioSec, have more than four million users, which is evidence of user acceptance of the biometric. However, keystroke dynamics in general is still in its early stages in the mobile world. It can be expected that the integration of new sensors into mobile devices will enhance the accuracy of keystroke measurements, thus making the keystroke dynamics biometric more secure and robust.

3.2.3 Facial Recognition

Facial recognition, or face recognition, refers to identifying an individual based on his/her face [32]. Since the pioneering work of Woody Bledsoe in the 1960s, focusing on matching photographs of people to mugshots, facial recognition systems have forayed into homeland security, surveillance, and other applications, and in the last decade have begun penetrating the consumer mobile device market. The goal of face recognition on mobile devices is to provide a more convenient alternative to passwords and PIN numbers, which are the most commonly used authentication schemes in mobile devices.

3.2.3.1 Advantages of Face Recognition

Using face recognition on mobile devices has several advantages. First, capturing an image of the face does not require making physical contact with a sensor and can be performed from a distance [33]. The same is not true of, for example, fingerprint recognition, which requires users to physically place their finger on the sensor.

Second, an image of person's face can be easily captured using the built-in camera of a smartphone or a tablet and does not require special equipment, as is the case with fingerprint recognition and recognition based on irises.

3.2.3.2 Challenges of Face Recognition

The challenges of face recognition on mobile devices include constrained computational resources, uncontrolled conditions, and liveness detection.

A significant challenge of implementing face recognition on a consumer-grade mobile device is limited computational resources. Constrained memory and processing resources preclude the use of the best available face recognition algorithms that tend to be resource intensive. Another challenge is uncontrolled conditions, which include poor facial illumination and varying camera angles. Such conditions are very common in mobile applications and are known to degrade the accuracy of face recognition.

Finally, implementing robust liveness detection techniques to prevent spoofing attacks continues to be a major challenge. For example, Google Android's Face Unlock face recognition feature, which allows the user to unlock his/her device with a photo of his/her face, can be bypassed by an attacker simply by holding a high quality photograph of the authorized user's face in front of the camera [34]. Attempts to protect the system against such attacks have included requiring the user to blink. However, this measure can also be bypassed, since blinking can be easily faked using photo editing techniques or by simply playing a video of the user's face (where he/she naturally blinks) in front of the camera [35].

For example, consider the following account given by David Moren from *Popular Science* magazine [35]: "I shot a quick video of myself—blinking included. I held my phone up to the screen, and sure enough, the bank app let me right in. So much for high security."

Other techniques for face spoofing attacks include the use of three-dimensional (3D) face models [36] and physical face masks. Other techniques include tracking the mouth movements as well as the use of 3D features [9].

In summary, many types of face spoofing attacks can be frustrated using liveness detection techniques and many face spoofing attacks are generally challenged by systems based on a 3D image of the face. However, most consumer mobile devices currently do not have the camera hardware (e.g., 3D cameras) necessary for supporting highly robust liveness detection.

FIGURE 3.4 Face recognition concept image. (From Face Recognition. Bigstockphoto.com)

3.2.3.2.1 Mobile Face Recognition Applications

Many face recognition methods and commercial products have been developed in the last 20 years. Figure 3.4 illustrates the underlying concept of a typical face recognition application. We discuss some of these products and recent research below.

3.2.3.2.2 Visidon

Visidon Ltd. builds imaging technologies and provides camera solutions for face recognition in mobile devices and embedded platforms. Its commercial method for face recognition offers face identification, face detection and tracking, gender and age detection, blink and smile detection, and face beautification [37]. For face identification, it uses one-to-one verification to validate each user while performing instant searches to recognize the persons in the pictures. Among the features, it includes (1:N) matching to identify individuals according to their facial characteristics. Visidon also includes a spoofing detection application, which helps to prevent spoofing attacks [37].

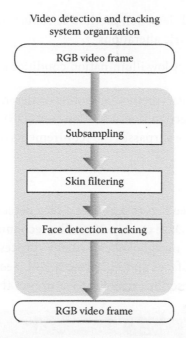

Video detection and tracking
system organization

FIGURE 3.5   Organization of the projected face recognition and tracking technique. (From S. Pachalakis and M. Bober. 2004. Real-time face detection and tracking for mobile videoconferencing. *Real-Time Imaging*, 10(2):81–94.)

3.2.3.2.3 Pachalakis and Bober

Pachalakis and Bober [15] introduced a face detection and tracking system for use in mobile videoconferencing applications [39]. Figure 3.5 illustrates the high-level logic used in the face detection/tracking algorithm they developed. The algorithm employed in their application detects user faces and samples skin color. It achieves over 400 frames per second (fps) on the 33 MHz ALTERA APEX 20 K CPU with a narrow computational complexity using less than 700 bytes of memory. Figure 3.5 is a diagram showing the organization of the projected face recognition and tracking techniques.

Pachalakis and Bober cite the following advantages of their approach [39]:

- Improved visual effect through face stabilization

- Reduction in the bandwidth requirements through the encoding and transmission of only the established face

- Provision of high-quality video on practical display sizes

- Skin color-based detection method is robust to illumination variations and geometric alterations

- Robust under very low illumination conditions [39].

Pachalakis and Bober's method of mobile conferencing face recognition provides a 99% face recognition detection rate (DR) at a speed of 400 fps [39]. Such performance surpasses the requirements of a typical videoconferencing application.

3.2.3.2.4 Droid

The DROID phone (see Figure 3.6) uses a face detection and recognition process developed by Dave et al. in 2010. The recognition process includes color segmentation, morphological image processing, and template matching using Eigenfaces and Fisherfaces [40]. See Figure 3.7 for some sample images. We describe each of the features of their approach below.

FIGURE 3.6 (**See color insert.**) Photo of Motorola Droid Turbo 2 64 GB Black taken by Motorola Droid Maxx. (Data from https://en.wikipedia.org/wiki/File:Motorola_Droid_Turbo_2.png)

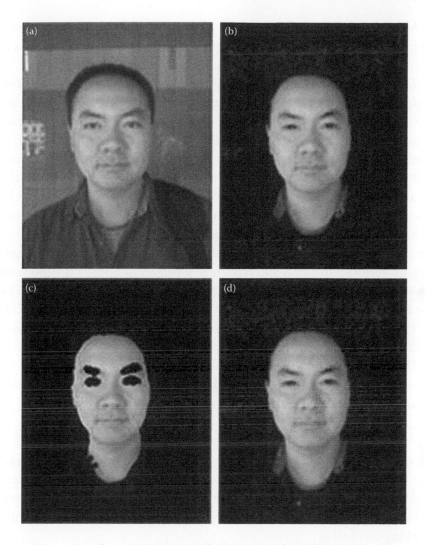

FIGURE 3.7 Face detection process. (a) Down sampling, (b) color segmentation with Cr classifier, (c) erosion, and (d) dilation. (From G. Dave, X. Chao, and K. Sriadibhatla. 2010. *Face Recognition in Mobile Phones*. Department of Electrical Engineering Stanford University, Stanford, California.)

Color segmentation. Using color section values, the color segmentation procedure categorizes each pixel as skin or nonskin. Dave et al. first reduce the sample by a factor of eight to avoid extra computation. Then, a scale-by-max color-balancing technique, which applies predistorted gamma values, is used to diminish the illumination effects [40]. A correct rejection (Cr) classifier is then used to categorize a pixel as either skin or non-skin.

Morphological image processing. Once the color separation is performed, a nonskin pixel's mask is acquired. The purpose of this process is to reject the nonskin visible pixels and to reorganize the skin pixels.

Template matching. This is the final step in face detection. The template matching system finds the entity represented by the template $T(x,y)$ in an input image $I(x,y)$ and associates the template with the input [440]. Fast Fourier transform (FFT) and inverse fast Fourier transform (IFFT) frequency domains are employed. About 400 faces, including male and female and diverse background subjects, were used in the testing. However, the results were not favorable, as this method only works well if the faces in the images taken by the DROID are lined up looking straight at the camera. [40].

Eigenfaces and Fisherfaces. Another approach using Motorola DROID for face recognition was to use Eigenfaces and Fisherfaces [40]. The algorithms were able to detect and recognize a person in under 1.6 s and with a total correct rate of 24.3% (with an EER of 35%) using the Eigenface. For the Fisherface, by contrast, the rate of detection increased to 94% (an EER of 25%). The Fisherfaces' system operated better, recognizing faces under fluctuating lighting settings, as predicted by the authors [40].

The Eigenfaces and Fisherfaces algorithms employed by Dave et al. incorporated a nonintrusive method using low-cost sensors, thus there was no need for significant investment in hardware.

3.2.3.3 Conclusion

Face recognition systems have been integrated into mobile commercial products and research prototypes. Constrained computational resources and liveness detection continue to be ongoing problems that researchers, device manufacturers, and mobile application developers are currently working to address.

The increasing computational power of mobile devices and constant liveness detection innovations will continue to drive the creation of more and more robust face recognition systems.

3.2.4 Voice Recognition

Voice is a behavioral biometric with a long history of use in health care, military, and traffic control applications [41]. Today, voice recognition technologies are widely used in mobile platforms for implementing user authentication, allowing users to control their device with their voice, and to interact with the popular digital assistant applications whose capabilities are expanding rapidly.

In the subsections that follow, we give a brief overview of voice recognition and then discuss modern applications of voice recognition in consumer mobile devices.

3.2.4.1 How It Is Performed

Voice recognition uses a microphone or a sensor that detects a voice and then sends the data for analysis by a computer. Figure 3.8 demonstrates a user waveform. Most mobile devices (even some smart watches) have means of capturing voices. Figure 3.9 shows an individual using a mobile device with voice detection.

Voice recognition techniques can be divided into two categories: text-dependent and text-independent. In text-dependent speech recognition, the speaker recognition system (SRS) knows beforehand the exact words, sentences, or phrases the user will say in order to be recognized. This means that the same text must be used for both enrollment and recognition [42]. Therefore, text-dependent methods are mostly used in applications where users are expected to cooperate with the speech recognition system.

The text-independent speech recognition method recognizes the user based on the sound of his/her voice, regardless of the words or phrases he/she utters. This makes the method flexible and particularly well suited for noncooperative speech recognition applications, as well as liveness detection. A disadvantage of text-independent voice recognition is that it takes longer to identify the vocal features and requires more training data than text-independent speech recognition [42].

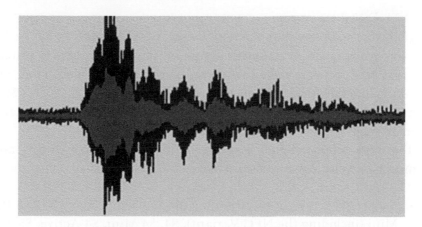

FIGURE 3.8 Waveform representation of the user saying "mobile device."

FIGURE 3.9   Using voice biometrics on a mobile device. (From bigstockphoto.com)

3.2.4.2 Voice Recognition on Mobile Devices

Recent advancements in both text-dependent and text-independent voice recognition have resulted in mobile applications that help make mobile devices more convenient and secure. We discuss a few of these applications, which we believe illustrate the power of implementing voice recognition on mobile devices, below.

3.2.4.2.1 Digital Assistants

Digital voice assistants allow users to interact with their devices by speaking voice commands [43]. Modern digital assistants allow users to search the web, get directions, make and receive phone calls, and much more, by speaking into their device. Some digital voice assistants (e.g., Apple's Siri and Microsoft's Cortana) even include learning capabilities to entertain users through singing, humor, and other functions.

The most popular digital assistants at the time of this writing are Samsung's S-Voice, Microsoft's Cortana, and Apple's Siri.

- *S Voice.* This is an application for the Samsung Galaxy S III, S III Mini (including the NFC Variant), S4, S4 Mini, S4 Active, S5, S5 Mini, S II Plus, Note II, Note 3, Note 4, Note 10.1, Note 8.0, Stellar,

Mega, Grand, Avant, Core, Ace 3, Tab 3 7.0, Tab 3 8.0, Tab 3 10.1, Galaxy Camera, and other Samsung Android devices dating from 2013 or later [44].

- *Cortana.* This is an application for Microsoft Windows Phones and PCs that has the ability to manage a calendar, track packages, find files, chat, and tell jokes [43]. These devices have Cortana: Windows Phone 8.1 (where it now supersedes Bing Mobile), Microsoft Band, Xbox One, iOS, and Android [43].

- *Siri.* Speech Interpretation and Recognition Interface (Siri) is a built-in feature on the iPhone, which was first implemented in the model 4S in October 2011 [45].

3.2.4.2.2 VoiceVault

A current commercial application for voice-based biometric authentication on mobile devices is made by VoiceVault (Figure 3.10) [46]. The application relies on a cloud based service and is currently (at the time of this writing) available for Android- and iOS-based devices. It delivers multiple voice biometric-based services, including VOICESIGN, which allows users to generate legally binding voice signatures, and ViGO, which allows users to unlock mobile devices with their voices.

The VOICESIGN service allows users to sign legal contracts by speaking a sequence of numbers (as instructed by the VoiceVault software). The service allows people to conveniently sign contracts over the phone and is approved for use by the American Bar Association, US E-Sign Act, US Health Insurance Portability and Accountability Act (HIPPA) of 1996/ CMS, US Food and Drug Administration (FDA) 21 CFR 11, and EU Directive 1993/93/EC.

Another service offered via VoiceVault is ViGo, a voice-based authentication service which allows users to unlock their device using their voice. First, the user trains the system to recognize their voice by speaking a phrase displayed on the screen. From that point on, the user can unlock the device by simply uttering that same phrase. Since the application recognizes the user based on the sound of their voice, the user does not need to remember the specific phrase; they can be prompted to read the phrase at the time of authentication.

VoiceVault also delivers a similar service called ViGo Wear For Wearables, which allows wearable devices (e.g., smartwatches) to take advantage of the ViGo features.

FIGURE 3.10 Mobile device with a VoiceVault application. (Mobile voice biometrics for iOS and Android—VoiceVault. n.d.)

In the benchmark tests conducted by VoiceVault, ViGO had "99.99% success at rejecting impostors, and 97% success for accepting genuine users (at their first login attempt)" [46].

3.2.4.2.3 Sesame

Sesame is a proposed application for voice biometrics in mobile devices developed by Aliasgary et al. [49]. At the time of writing, Sesame's application is available at no cost in the Google Play online store under the name Open Sesame—Password Vault. The application allows users to securely manage their passwords and generate strong passwords using their voices.

Open Sesame encrypts each password with a new random key, then stores the passwords locally on a mobile device and backs them up in a cloud selected by the user. Open Sesame servers encrypt and store the encrypted keys. To retrieve the keys, users are required to authenticate using their voices. Speech recognition and the words spoken are used to confirm the user's identity.

3.2.4.2.4 Liveness Detection

It is relatively easy to record the voice of an individual and to use the recording to gain access to resources that are protected by a voice-based biometric authentication system [15]. This is called a voice spoofing attack.

Voice spoofing attacks can be categorized according to how they are performed: via impersonation, replay, speech synthesis, and voice conversion [48,49].

Impersonation. The impersonation voice approach encompasses the imitation of the prosodic (intonation, tone, stress, and rhythm [50]) or stylistic signs, rather than features associated with the vocal region. People can be misled with this technique, but automatic speaker verification (ASV) systems are able to recognize this type of spoof [15].

Replay. Replay uses speech fragments taken from a real person. These recordings are used to fool voice recognition systems in order to gain access to resources [48]. Villalba and Lleida's case study [48] indicates that replay attacks are able to transform the "spectrum and modulation indexes" in a way that makes it possible to use them as discriminating classifiers to sense spoofs [48].

Speech synthesis. Speech synthesis is the reproduction of a human voice by a computer [51]. The attacker can attempt to use computer-synthesized speech in order to spoof the voice of the legitimate user and hence obtain access to the system. Multiple approaches have been developed in order to help overcome such attacks.

For example, in a 2013 study, De Leon and Stewart et al. used a Gaussian mixture model—universal background model (GMM-UBM), a support vector machine using GMM super vectors, and selected word discriminators in order to differentiate between real and synthetic voice samples. Overall, they were able to achieve a discrimination accuracy of 98%.

Their results are applicable to text-dependent voice speaker verification systems where the speaker is required to utter a specific phrase.

Voice conversion. Voice conversion takes speech synthesis a step further. The purpose of voice conversion is to transform an individual's voice into that of another [9] by mining automated speaker verification (ASV) features to match the selected speaker. Text-to-speech and speech-to-speech facilitate speech spoof attacks.

3.2.4.3 Conclusion

The approaches to voice biometrics for mobile devices presented in this section indicate that voice biometrics has some advantages over other modalities. For instance, all mobile phones are already equipped with a microphone to capture voices. Voices are easy to capture, but at the same time, they are also easy to duplicate. Voice duplication can be combatted through effective liveness detection techniques, but this is challenging.

Services such as VoiceVault are quite promising options for companies and individuals wishing to protect their devices and sign contracts using their voices.

Nevertheless, voice biometrics in mobile devices still faces many challenges. In addition to spoofing attacks, voice recognition systems must cope with background noises and changes in people's voices due to emotions or sickness, all of which can frustrate recognition.

3.2.5 Iris Recognition

3.2.5.1 Introduction

Iris recognition is a method of identifying people based on their iris patterns. "The iris is a muscle (the colored portion of the eye) that controls the size of the pupil regulating how much light comes into the eye" [53]. The anatomy and color of the iris are genetically related, but the complex random patterns are unique and unchanging. Figure 3.11 shows the complex patterns of the iris.

Iris recognition is a growing research area, especially in the mobile realm, as the iris is considered a robust biometric [24,54]. In addition, unlike fingerprint recognition and some other biometrics, iris recognition does not require physical contact with the biometric sensor. For these reasons, researchers and companies are exploring the potential of implementing iris recognition in smartphones. Some of these devices are already available to consumers. We discuss some of these models in the sections that follow.

3.2.5.2 Iris Recognition versus Retinal Recognition

Iris recognition is often mistaken for retinal scanning. The difference between the two is that iris recognition analyzes the iris muscle for

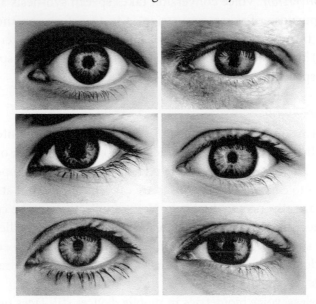

FIGURE 3.11   Unique pattern of the human iris. (Stock Photo by Phakimata. n.d.)

verification, while retinal scanning uses the distinctive shape of blood vessels in the retina, located in the back of the eye [53]. Figure 3.11 shows a close-up of the human eye. Note the locations of the iris and the retina in Figure 3.12, which displays the anatomy of the eye. Researchers are constantly testing ways in which spoofing attacks may compromise the security of iris-based recognition systems.

3.2.5.3 Advantages of Iris Recognition in Mobile Devices

As with any biometric technique, there is a trade-off when integrating iris recognition into a mobile device.

Advantages of iris recognition in mobile devices include the following [9]:

- In controlled circumstances, it provides competitive performance.

- People are familiar with the idea of having their eyes scanned for authentication purposes.

- The iris template can be updated constantly.

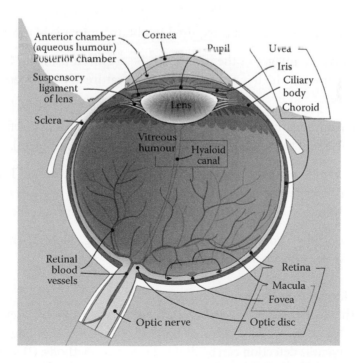

FIGURE 3.12 **(See color insert.)** Eye anatomy. (Stock Vector by Microvector. n.d.)

FIGURE 3.13 **(See color insert.)** Example of an iris occluded by a corneal SR.

Disadvantages of iris recognition in mobile devices include the following [9]:

- A high-quality camera is required to obtain an image of the iris.

- Ideally, the images of the iris should be acquired using an infrared (IR) camera, which is not yet a common feature of consumer mobile devices.

- Environmental conditions, such as lighting and specular reflections (SRs), affect the ability to capture an iris image (Figure 3.13).

- Reflections in the image of the iris can obscure features. This scenario is expected to be common in many mobile use cases, as the conditions in which the images are acquired are uncontrolled.

- Uncontrolled conditions, such as dim lighting, motion, and angle can distort the quality of the iris image.

3.2.5.3.1 Liveness Detection in Iris Images

One of the challenges of iris recognition, especially in mobile devices, is liveness detection, which is critical for preventing iris spoofing attacks [24]. Iris liveness detection can be divided into two methods: (1) software-based and (2) hardware-based. In the software-based method, the iris image is acquired, then the features of the iris's image, not the eye itself, are examined to distinguish between real and fake eyes [24]. Conversely, the hardware-based technique requires hardware in order to detect the liveness properties of an iris, such as eye hippus (pupil fluctuation) or the pupil's reaction to light variations [24].

3.2.5.4 Iris Recognition Research

Next, we provide an overview of several important studies exploring iris recognition in mobile devices. Most of the research focuses on the methods used for acquiring images of the iris. Such methods can be grouped into two areas based on how the iris information is collected: first, using the IR wavelength, and second, using the visual wavelength [9].

3.2.5.4.1 Binarization and Modified Edge Detector by Cho et al.

In this study, the authors proposed a pupil and iris localization algorithm optimized for cellular phones [57]. At the heart of their approach is the detection of the dark pupil and corneal SR by changing brightness and contrast values (Figure 3.14). In addition, the authors used a technique to shorten the processing time by avoiding floating point computations in their algorithm.

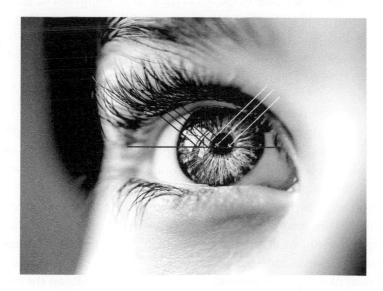

FIGURE 3.14 **(See color insert.)** Corneal SR. Yellow represents the incident light and red represents the reflected light.

They used a halogen lamp and an IR pass filter to capture the image of the iris [9,57]. To locate the corneal reflections and the pupil, they employed binarization. Binarization is a technique used to differentiate the pupil and other regions, such as the iris, sclera, and facial skin [57]. They then located 10 points around the pupil and 10 points around the iris. The radii of both were calculated. Finally, a modified circular edge detector was used to calculate the difference between the smaller and larger radii. They made enhancements to the modified edge detector to work better indoors and outdoors [9].

Among the experiments presented in the paper, the authors measured the accuracy of their algorithm using 1000 iris images from 20 people and captured the iris images by using a Samsung SPH-S2300 cellular phone. The accuracy measurements were obtained by calculating the root mean square (RMS) error between the detected iris center and the manually chosen center.

Their results showed that the RMS error of the calculated iris center position was about 1.2 pixels and that of the pupil center position was 0.6 pixels. Results also showed that the error in determining the iris radius was 2.2 pixels and that of the pupil radius was 0.55 pixels. The authors argue that their approach yields similar accuracy to the approaches used by other earlier researchers in the field, such as Daugman et al. [58,59], but has better processing time (<180 ms compared to Daugman et al.'s algorithm, which yields a total of 340 ms as a result of doing floating point computations). The authors also argue that these and other results presented in the paper "make their scheme well suited for real-time iris localization for iris recognition in cellular phones."

3.2.5.4.2 IR-Illuminator and IR Pass Filter by Jeong et al.

Jeong et al.'s study proposes an iris recognition method for mobile phones based on corneal SRs [60]. Corneal SRs are a mirror-like reflection on the surface of the cornea of the eye (see Figure 3.13) where light from one incoming direction is reflected into a single outgoing direction.

This project addresses three main challenges. First, if the user is wearing glasses, then many SRs may appear on the surface of glasses, thus making it difficult to detect the genuine SR on the cornea. The authors propose to address this issue (of noncorneal SRs) by using a successive on/off dual illuminator scheme to help detect genuine SRs on the corneas of users wearing glasses. Second, the authors correct for noncorneal SRs by estimating the size, shape, and brightness of the SRs based on eye, camera, and illuminator models. Finally, they verify their results using the AdaBoost detector algorithm [61].

The approach was evaluated using 400 facial images from 100 people captured with a Samsung SPH-S2300. The resulting rate of correct iris detection was 99.5% (for images without glasses) and 98.9% (for images with glasses or contact lenses). The resulting accuracy of iris authentication using this approach was 0.05% of the EER based on detected iris images.

In the process, the authors added an IR illuminator and an IR pass filter to the SPH-S2300's 2048x1536 pixel charge-coupled 3X optical linear zoom image sensor to obtain an image of the iris. Figure 3.4 shows the image of the device with the two components added (taken from Reference [62]). They then used the algorithm presented by Cho et al. [9,57] to detect the boundaries. Finally, they ran an image segmentation process by detecting eyelid and eyelash regions. The extracted iris image was then matched against the template using the hamming distance method [62–64].

3.2.5.4.3 FotoNation Iris Recognition Biometric Algorithm

The FotoNation algorithm for the iris has been popular among defense, law enforcement, and border control institutions [65]. The company has also released a version of the algorithm for mobile device platforms [65]. The iris identification method uses denoising and image stability techniques to ensure the iris image is of good quality. It also includes liveness and spoof detection techniques.

The company holds a patent for iris and pupil matching and segmentation. In addition, the company offers MIRLIN SDK which is "FotoNation's starting point for customers developing iris recognition solutions. This fully featured toolkit enables [FotoNation] to support [their] partners to build iris recognition engines, enrollment, and ID management applications that use iris image or template databases" [65].

3.2.5.4.4 Iris Database

The MoBIOfake database is a set of 800 iris images with corresponding counterfeit copies. The fake copies were derived from images of the original and taken with the same mobile camera under the same circumstances (Figure 3.15). The MoBIOfake dataset is provided by Mobile Iris Liveness Detection Competition (MobILive) [24]. MobILive organized the first Mobile Iris Liveness Detection Competition in 2014 held during the International Joint Conference on Biometrics in 2014.

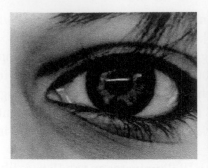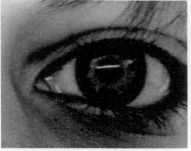

FIGURE 3.15 MobioFAKE dataset sample corresponding to real and fake images. (From A. F. Sequeira et al. 2014. MobILive 2014—Mobile Iris Liveness Detection Competition. In *2014 IEEE International Joint Conference on Biometrics [IJCB]*. IEEE, pp. 1–6, September.)

3.2.5.5 Iris Biometrics in Mobile Applications

Next, we discuss a few commercially available smartphones that support iris recognition.

3.2.5.5.1 Fujitsu NX F-04G

In May 2015, Fujitsu launched the ARROWS NX F-04G [66] phone, which featured an iris scanner. Figure 3.16 shows the different models.

NX F-04G had the following features:

- 5.2-inch display

- WQHD (1440 × 2560)

- Octa-core Qualcomm® Snapdragon™ 810 CPU clocked at (2 GHz × 4 + 1.5 GHz × 4)

- Qualcomm® Adreno™ 430 GPU clocked at 600MHz

- LPDDR43 dual channel 3 GB RAM

The iris scanner is located in the front panel and is designed using two components, an IR LED and an IR camera. The LED illuminates the iris while the camera takes an image. Unlocking the system takes less than 1 s at a maximum of 910 in. or 2225 cm distance from the face. This is 6 inches more than a traditional iris scanner and according to Fujitsu, it works under any lighting conditions [66].

Iris green White Black

ARROWS NX F-04G

FIGURE 3.16 (**See color insert.**) ARROWS NX F-04G. (From プレスリリースバ
ックナンバー 2015年5月 [Fujitsu Press Release May 5, 2015].)

3.2.5.5.2 Vivo X5Pro

In May 2015, Vivo Communication Technology Co. Ltd., a Chinese manufacturer, launched a mobile phone with an integrated iris scanner with a
powerful front camera able to take photos at 32 MP [66].

The device had the following specifications:

- 4G dual SIM phone

- 5.2-inch Super AMOLED display

- Snapdragon 615 octacore CPU (divided into two clusters [Quad-core
  1.5 GHz Cortex-A53 & Quad-core 1.0 GHz Cortex-A53])

- Funtouch OS 2.1 on top of Android 5.0

- 16 GB internal memory

- 128 GB expandable

- No separate SD card slot

- MicroSD can fit in the SIM2 slot

The iris scanner examines the white area of the eye and scans the blood
vessel patterns by capturing 32 megapixel images. No IR LED light is needed.

3.2.5.5.3 ZTE Grand S3

ZTE Grand S3 partnered with biometric developer EyeVerify and launched
EyeSpring ID in December 2015. Through a front camera, the sensor reads
the vein patterns located in the white area of the eye [66].

- The device had the following features:
  - 5.5-inch IPS LCD FHD display
  - Quadcore Snapdragon 801 processor clocked at 2.5 GHz
  - 3 GB RAM
  - 16 MP primary camera
  - 8 MP front-facing camera
  - 16 GB internal storage
  - 64 GB microSD card slot
  - 3100 mAh battery

3.2.5.6 Conclusion

The iris modality is gradually gaining popularity in the mobile world [68]. Researchers and manufacturers are rapidly developing new mobile iris recognition technologies which will contribute to the wider availability of this modality on the mobile consumer market. For example, recently, according to webcusp.com, mobile device giants Samsung and LG have been actively working with partners on efforts to develop iris scanning-enabled devices. LG in particular has partnered with Irience (a Korean enterprise) to equip the LG G5 with iris scanner technology [66].

Such advances in iris-scanning hardware and iris-matching algorithms may well make iris recognition a common feature of consumer mobile devices in the near future.

3.3 MULTIMODAL BIOMETRICS

Multimodal biometrics refers to using different biometric traits to identify people, such as face, voice, and fingerprints. Since each type of biometric has its own limitations, identifying people based on multiple biometrics can help increase the overall security and robustness of the biometric system. First, we discuss the limitations of each type of biometric and then follow this with a discussion of the benefits of using multimodal biometrics on mobile devices. We then provide an overview of the recent research on multimodal biometrics for consumer mobile devices. Finally, we discuss a few commercially available consumer mobile devices that make use of multimodal biometrics.

3.3.1 Limitations of Biometric Modalities

- *Fingerprints.* Although many mobile devices today feature fingerprint readers, not all people have fingerprints (for example, people without limbs or missing appendages). In addition, young children, the elderly, and some ethnic groups, such as Asian women, have difficulty in having their fingerprints captured. These groups will find it difficult or impossible to benefit from mobile biometrics.

- *Face.* Faces can change due to aging, the use of accessories, such as glasses, jewelry, and makeup, and the presence or absence of facial hair. In addition, the face may appear quite different based on the camera angle, lighting, and other environmental conditions common in mobile use cases, which can affect the ability of the biometric system to recognize the user.

- *Voice.* Voice recognition is highly sensitive to noise from the environment, changes in the person's voice due to varying emotions or illness, and other environmental conditions common in mobile use cases that are known to distort voice features and degrade recognition accuracy.

- *Iris.* Eye trauma or disease can render iris recognition impossible.

3.3.2 Benefits of Multimodal Biometrics on Mobile Devices

Multimodal biometrics in mobile devices deliver multiple advantages. According to Gofman et al. [70], some benefits are

- *Increased mobile security.* It is more challenging for an attacker to spoof two or more biometric modalities than merely one [1].

- *More robust mobile authentication.* In the multimodal system, one biometric modality can compensate for the deficiencies of another modality to create an overall stronger authentication for mobile devices [1].

- *A market ripe with opportunities.* Mobile devices already include biometric sensors such as cameras, microphones, and fingerprint scanners. Hence, multimodal biometric schemes can be implemented on the existing mobile devices without investing in additional hardware. The greater security afforded by a multimodal system will help make mobile devices more marketable.

3.3.3 Challenges of Multimodal Biometrics on Mobile Devices

Multimodal biometrics requires users to provide samples from multiple modalities to prove their identity. Although this helps to increase security and has the benefits discussed in the previous section, such schemes are less convenient than those based on a single biometric. These challenges can be addressed through a user interface that allows the user to simultaneously and seamlessly capture multiple biometric modalities.

3.3.4 Multimodal Biometrics Research

3.3.4.1 Aronowitz et al. (2014)

Aronowitz et al. [69] proposed a scheme for securely signing into a remote server based on face, voice, and chirography (i.e., signature recognition) biometrics. In their scheme, the user employs his/her mobile device to capture an image of a face, a voice recording, and a signature. These are then sent to the remote server for analysis and matching [69].

This scheme integrated the modalities at the score level. That is, the match scores output by the face, voice, and signature recognition algorithms were combined into a single score, which was then compared against a threshold to make a decision to grant or deny access. Match scores from modalities whose images were of greater quality were allowed to have significant weight in determining whether to grant or deny access. For example, if the voice sample was noisy (thus a less reliable identifier), its match score contributed less to the final decision.

Aronowitz et al. tested their scheme on a homegrown database of faces, voices, and signatures obtained in a quiet office environment and in more challenging, noisy environments. Their system achieved an EER of 0.1% and an EER of 0.5% in the former and latter cases, respectively.

3.3.4.2 Gofman et al. (2015–2016)

Gofman et al. [70–72] developed a multimodal biometric scheme for unlocking a consumer mobile device [70–72]. Unlike the scheme of Aronowitz et al., where matching was performed on the remote server, the scheme in this study was implemented completely on the mobile device (Samsung Galaxy S5 smartphone) itself. In addition, unlike the scheme of Aronwitz et al., which targeted an enterprise user, their scheme was designed for the average consumer.

In addition to developing their own quality-based score-level fusion scheme, they also implemented a feature-level fusion scheme based on Linear Discriminant Analysis (LDA). Their results on both good-quality

TABLE 3.1   EER Results Form Score-Level Fusion

Modality	ERR (%)	Testing Time (s)
Face	27.17	0.065
Voice	41.44	0.045
Score-level fusion	25.70	0.108

TABLE 3.2   EER Results Form Score-Level Fusion

Modality	ERR (%)	Testing Time (s)
Face	4.29	0.13
Voice	34.72	1.42
Score-level fusion	2.14	1.57

and degraded-quality face photographs and voice samples confirmed that both schemes result in a lower EER than individual modalities by around ~2% (as shown in Tables 3.1 and 3.2).

Finally, the authors tried to make multimodal biometrics user-friendly by developing a graphical interface that allowed users to easily capture both face and voice modalities by recording a short video of their face while speaking a phrase.

3.3.5 Consumer Mobile Devices That Use Multimodal Biometrics

Some cutting-edge mobile devices that use multimodal biometrics are presented in this section.

3.3.5.1 MorphoTablet™

The Morpho Tablet manufactured by Morpho Safran Group uses multimodal biometrics, fingerprint, and facial recognition, combined with cryptographic functions [5]. Morpho provides biometric solutions, including identity management, for individuals, businesses, and the government. The MorphoTablet is an innovative mobile multibiometric solution. It has the following features:

- Uses face recognition, smart cards, and a password
- Has encryption functions
- Uses SAM card readers, which integrate digital certificates and cryptographic keys
- Is compatible with Android antivirus and Fleet Management solutions
- Has live online verification capability [5]

3.3.5.2 MorphoIDent™

MorphoIDent was developed by Morpho (Safran Group) and was designed for public safety agents and officers. MorphoIDent has the following features [45]:

- Multimodal biometric system based on face and fingerprint recognition.
- Small size (it is the size of the palm) and lightweight
- Designed for public safety agents and officers
- Has the accuracy of an FBI PIV IQS optical fingerprint scanner
- Vibration alerts
- Fully certified and very robust
- Provides alerts and a color screen that is visible outdoors
- Remote matching from the device [45]

3.3.6 Conclusions

Multimodal biometrics promises to be the future of mobile authentication and to make mobile devices more secure. Even though all mobile devices are equipped with various biometric sensors, such as cameras, microphones, and fingerprint sensors, more research is needed in order to robustly consolidate the different biometric modalities on a single mobile device. In addition, multimodal mobile biometric systems must continue to be improved to make multimodal biometrics available to all users [1].

3.4 CONCLUSION AND FUTURE DIRECTIONS

The explosion of smartphones and tablets has created a market for mobile devices with biometric capabilities. Many mobile users prefer fingerprint scanning to remembering and entering a strong password or a personal identification number (PIN) when unlocking their device or authorizing an online payment. Although modern mobile biometric systems must contend with limited computational resources, the limited capabilities of biometric sensors, uncontrolled conditions, and liveness detection challenges, their popularity is growing quickly. Research undertaken in both the academic and the commercial sectors is making progress in addressing the challenges and developing new mobile biometric applications.

According to the Acuity Market Intelligence report, the mobile market is expected to grow to $34.6 billion by the year 2020 [75]. Moreover, with advancements in sensor technologies and matching algorithms, we expect that biometrics-based authentication will become a standard feature in all consumer mobile devices. Using a mobile device to securely authorize an online payment, sign into a website, or to simply unlock the device will become a standard practice that will either supplement or completely replace passwords and PINs.

REFERENCES

1. C. Bonnington. In less than two years, a smartphone could be your only computer. Wired.com. Conde Nast Digital, February 10, 2015. Web. April 27, 2016. http://www.wired.com/2015/02/smartphone-only-computer/
2. http://www.statista.com/statistics/274774/forecast-of-mobile-phone-users-worldwide/
3. Tablet users to surpass 1 billion worldwide in 2015—eMarketer. n.d. http://www.emarketer.com/Article/Tablet-Users-Surpass-1-Billion-Worldwide-2015/1011806 (retrieved April 23, 2016).
4. D. Tapellini. Smart phone thefts rose to 3.1 million in 2013—Consumer Reports. ConsumerReports, May 28, 2014. Web. May 3, 2016. http://www.consumerreports.org/cro/news/2014/04/smart-phone-thefts-rose-to-3-1-million-last-year/index.htm
5. "QWERTY" and "123456" Top List of 2015's (Worst) Passwords. n.d. http://blogs.wsj.com/digits/2016/01/19/qwerty-and-123456-top-list-of-2015s-worst-passwords/ (retrieved April 27, 2016).
6. The most popular passwords of 2015 are the worst, again. n.d. http://www.smh.com.au/digital-life/consumer-security/the-most-popular-passwords-of-2015-are-the-worst-again-20160119-gm9n6c.html (retrieved April 27, 2016).
7. A billion fingerprint readers in mobile devices by 2021|Payment week. Payment Week. 2015. Web. April 23, 2016. http://paymentweek.com/2015-6-17-a-billion-fingerprint-readers-in-mobile-devices-by-2021-7494/
8. http://www.apple.com/ios/siri/ (accessed August 15, 2016).
9. Project No: FP7-610713 Project Acronym: PCAS Project Title: Personalized Centralized Authentication System—Scheme: Collaborative project—Deliverable D3.1.
10. Biometrics: Cellphones & PDA with fingerprint sensors. n.d. http://biometrics.mainguet.org/appli/appli_smartphones.htm (retrieved May 3, 2016).
11. Patent application: Differential measurements. August, 2013. http://biometrics.mainguet.org/types/fingerprint/fingerprint_apple.htm (accessed August 15, 2016).
12. Chaos computer club breaks Apple touch ID. https://www.ccc.de/en/updates/2013/ccc-breaks-apple-touchid (accessed August 15, 2016).

13. How to fake fingerprints? http://dasalte.ccc.de/biometrie/fingerabdruck kopieren?language=en
14. D. Birch. The focus on biometrics in the mass market. Tomorrow's Transactions. N.p., September 11, 2013. Web. August 16, 2016. http://www.chyp.com/the-focus-on-biometrics-in-the-mass-market/
15. World's first face recognition biometric for mobile phones. World's First Face Recognition Biometric for Mobile Phones. Web. April 23, 2016.
16. Face Recognition Security, Even With A "Blink Test", Is Easy to Trick. n.d. http://www.popsci.com/its-not-hard-trick-facial-recognition-security (retrieved May 3, 2016).
17. Android Jelly Bean Face Unlock "Liveness Check" Bypassed with Photo Editing [VIDEO]. 2012. http://www.ibtimes.co.uk/android-jellybean-face-unlock-hacked-photo-editing-370426 (retrieved May 3, 2016).
18. S. Memon, N. Manivannan, and W. Balachandran. 2011. Active pore detection for liveness in fingerprint identification system. In *19th Telecommunications Forum (TELFOR)*, Belgrade, Serbia. IEEE, pp. 619–622, November.
19. A. Martonik. 2015. Android fingerprint sensors, ranked. http://www.android-central.com/android-fingerprint-sensors-ranked (retrieved May 3, 2016).
20. P., & A. n.d. Silver ring around "iPhone 5S" home button may be integral to fingerprint reader, not just for looks. http://appleinsider.com/articles/13/09/06/silver-ring-around-iphone-5s-home-button-may-be-integral-to-fingerprint-reader-not-just-for-looks (retrieved May 3, 2016).
21. Apple details touch ID and the A7's Secure Enclave in updated iOS security document. http://techcrunch.com/2015/12/15/vayyar-a-startup-that-looks-to-produce-3d-image-sensors-raises-22m/ (accessed August 15, 2016).
22. "Google." Google. Web. April 23, 2016. https://static.googleusercontent.com/media/source.android.com/en//compatibility/android-cdd.pdf
23. P. S. Teh, A. B. J. Teoh, and S. Yue. 2013. A survey of keystroke dynamics biometrics, *The Scientific World Journal*, 2013, 24 pages. Article ID 408280, doi:10.1155/2013/408280.
24. A. F. Sequeira, H. P. Oliveira, J. C. Monteiro, J. P. Monteiro, and J. S. Cardoso. 2014. MobILive 2014—Mobile Iris Liveness Detection Competition. In *2014 IEEE International Joint Conference on Biometrics (IJCB)*, Clearwater, Florida. IEEE, pp. 1–6, September.
25. H. Saevanee and P. Bhattarakosol. 2009. Authenticating user using keystroke dynamics and finger pressure. In *2009 6th IEEE Consumer Communications and Networking Conference*, Las Vegas, Nevada. pp. 1–2, January.
26. Griaule Biometrics. n.d. http://www.griaulebiometrics.com/new/ (retrieved April 24, 2016).
27. D. Shanmugapriya. 2009. A survey of biometric keystroke dynamics. *Approaches, Security and Challenges*, 5(1):115–119.
28. N. Zheng, K. Bai, H. Huang, and H. Wang. 2012. You are How You Touch: User Verification on Smartphones via Tapping Behaviors, College of William & Mary Department of Computer Science.

29. BehavioSec accuracy report for native mobile application: White paper. https://www.behaviosec.com/resources?resourceid=4369 (retrieved August 15, 2016).

30. "Hey Siri, call in an Airstrike": Army seeks to outfit soldiers with voice-controlled gear. n.d. http://www.nextgov.com/cybersecurity/2016/04/army-testing-talk-start-computers-war-zones/127359/ (retrieved April 26, 2016).

31. C. Giuffrida, K. Majdanik, M. Conti, and H. Bos. 2014. I sensed it was you: Authenticating mobile users with sensor-enhanced keystroke dynamics. In *Detection of Intrusions and Malware, and Vulnerability Assessment*, Egham, UK. Springer International Publishing, pp. 92–111.

32. What is facial recognition?—Definition from WhatIs.com. April. http://whatis.techtarget.com/definition/facial-recognition (retrieved April 22, 2016).

33. D. Moren. Face recognition security, even with a 'Blink Test,' is easy to trick. Popular Science, March 18, 2015. Web. August 8, 2016. http://www.popsci.com/its-not-hard-trick-facial-recognition-security

34. A. Serban. Face unlock can still be hacked in Android 4.1—Here's how. Technology Personalized (TechPP) August 6, 2012, n. p. Web. April 26, 2016. http://techpp.com/2012/08/06/face-unlock-can-be-hacked-in-android-4-1/

35. Face recognition security, even with a "blink test," is easy to trick. n.d. http://www.popsci.com/its-not-hard-trick-facial-recognition-security (retrieved April 26, 2016).

36. Y. Kim, J.-H. Yoo, and K. Choi. 2011. A motion and similarity-based fake detection method for biometric face recognition systems. *IEEE International Conference on Consumer Electronics*, 57(2):756–762.

37. Visidon, http://www.visidon.fi/en/Home. Web. Last access December, 2013.

38. Face Recognition. Bigstockphoto.com (retrieved April 21, 2016).

39. S. Paschalakis and M. Bober. 2004. Real-time face detection and tracking for mobile videoconferencing. *Real-Time Imaging*, 10(2):81–94.

40. G. Dave, X. Chao, and K. Sriadibhatla. 2010. *Face Recognition in Mobile Phones*. Department of Electrical Engineering Stanford University, Stanford, California.

41. Voice Recognition. 2013. https://www.fbi.gov/about-us/cjis/fingerprints_biometrics/biometric-center-of-excellence/modalities/voice-recognition (retrieved April 22, 2016).

42. A. Alarifi, I. Alkurtass, and A.-M. S. Al-Salman. 2011. Arabic text-dependent speaker verification for mobile devices using artificial neural networks. In *10th International Conference on Machine Learning and Applications and Workshops (ICMLA)*, Honolulu, Hawaii. Vol. 2, pp. 350–353.

43. Siri v Google Now v S-Voice v Cortana. 2014. http://www.ukmobilereview.com/2014/09/siri-v-google-now-v-svoice-v-cortana/#!prettyPhoto (retrieved April 28, 2016).

44. https://en.wikipedia.org/wiki/S_Voice

45. Siri vs. Windows speech recognition. n.d. http://translationjournal.net/journal/61dictating.htm (retrieved April 28, 2016).

46. Mobile voice biometrics for iOS and Android—VoiceVault. n.d. http://voicevault.com/ (retrieved April 22, 2016).
47. M. Aliasgari, N. Sabol, and A. Sharma. 2015. Sesame: A secure and convenient mobile solution for passwords. In *2015 First Conference on Mobile and Secure Services (MOBISECSERV)*, Gainesville, Florida. IEEE, pp. 1–5, February.
48. J. Villalba and E. Lleida. 2011. Detecting replay attacks from far-field recordings on speaker verification systems. In C. Vielhauer, J. Dittmann, A. Drygajlo, N. C. Juul, and M. C. Fairhurst (eds), *Biometrics and ID Management*, volume 6583 of Lecture Notes in Computer Science, Springer Berlin, Heidelberg, pp. 274–285.
49. P. Perrot, G. Aversano, and G. Chollet. 2007. Voice disguise and automatic detection: Review and perspectives. *Lecture Notes in Computer Science*, 101–117. http://portal.acm.org/citation.cfm?id=1768226.1768233
50. Prosody (linguistics). Wikipedia. Wikimedia Foundation. Web. April 23, 2016.
51. Speech synthesis. Wikipedia. Wikimedia Foundation. Web. April 23, 2016.
52. P. L. De Leon and B. Stewart. 2013. Synthetic speech detection based on selected word discriminators. In *2013 IEEE International Conference on Acoustics, Speech and Signal Processing (ICASSP)*, Vancouver, BC, Canada, pp. 3004–3008.
53. FBI. Iris scan 2013. https://www.fbi.gov/about-us/cjis/fingerprints_biometrics/biometric-center-of-excellence/modalities/iris-scan (retrieved April 23, 2016).
54. Iris Recognition Technology. n.d. http://www.irisid.com/productssolutions/technology-2/irisrecognitiontechnology/ (retrieved April 24, 2016).
55. Stock Photo by Phakimata. n.d. http://www.bigstockphoto.com/image-57204995/stock-photo-biometric-iris-scan-security-screening (retrieved April 23, 2016).
56. Stock Vector by Microvector. n.d. http://www.bigstockphoto.com/image-97699442/stock-vector-eye-anatomy (retrieved April 23, 2016).
57. D. H. Cho, K. R. Park, D. W. Rhee, Y. Kim, and J. Yang. 2006. Pupil and iris localization for iris recognition in mobile phones. In *Seventh ACIS International Conference on Software Engineering, Artificial Intelligence, Networking, and Parallel/Distributed Computing (SNPD 2006)*, Las Vegas, Nevada, pp. 197–201.
58. J. G. Daugman. 2003. The importance of being random: Statistical principles of iris recognition. *Pattern Recognition*, 36(2):279–291.
59. J. G. Daugman. 2004. How iris recognition works. *IEEE Trans. on Circuits and Systems for Video Technology*, 14(1):21–29.
60. D. S. Jeong, H.-A. Park, K. R. Park, and J. Kim. 2006. Iris recognition in mobile phone based on adaptive Gabor filter. In D. Zhang and A. K. Jain (eds), *International Conference on Biometrics*. Springer, Berlin Heidelberg, pp. 457–463.
61. P. Viola and M. J. Jones. 2004. Robust real-time face detection. *International Journal of Computer Vision*, 57(2):137–154.

62. J. G. Daugman. 1993. High confidence visual recognition of persons by a test of statistical independence. *IEEE Transactions on Pattern Analysis and Machine Intelligence*, 15(11): 1148–1161.

63. J. Daugman. 2004. How iris recognition works. *IEEE Transactions on Circuits and Systems for Video Technology*, 14(1):21–30.

64. J. G. Daugman. 2003. Demodulation by complex-valued wavelets for stochastic pattern recognition. *International Journal of Wavelets, Multi-Resolution and Information Processing*, 1(1):1–17.

65. http://www.fotonation.com/products/biometrics/iris-recognition/

66. List of all eye scanner (iris, retina recognition) smartphones. 2015. http://webcusp.com/list-of-all-eye-scanner-iris-retina-recognition-smartphones/ (retrieved April 24, 2016).

67. プレスリリースバックナンバー 2015年5月 [Fujitsu Press Release May 5, 2015]. http://pr.fujitsu.com/jp/news/2015/05/25al.jpg (retrieved April 24, 2016).

68. Solutions—FindBiometrics. n.d. http://findbiometrics.com/solutions/iris-scanners-recognition/(retrieved April 24, 2016).

69. H. Aronowitz, M. Li, O. Toledo-Ronen, S. Harary, A. Geva, S. Ben-David, and D. Nahamoo. 2014. Multi-modal biometrics for mobile authentication. In *2014 IEEE International Joint Conference on Biometrics (IJCB)*, Clearwater, Florida. IEEE, pp. 1–8, September.

70. M. I. Gofman and S. Mitra. 2016. Multimodal biometrics for enhanced mobile device security. *Communications of the ACM*, 59(4):58–65.

71. M. Gofman, S. Mitra, K. Cheng, and N. Smith. 2015. Feature-level multimodal biometric authentication in consumer mobile devices. In *IEEE 7th International Workshop on Information Forensics and Security*, Rome, Italy. Poster/Demo.

72. M. Gofman, S. Mitra, K. Cheng, and N. Smith. 2015. Quality-based score-level fusion for secure and robust multimodal biometrics-based authentication on consumer mobile devices. In *ICSEA 2015, The Tenth International Conference on Software Engineering Advances (ICSEA)*, Barcelona, Spain. International Academy, Research and Industry Association (IARIA).

73. MorphoTablet. 2015. http://www.morpho.com/en/biometric-terminals/mobile-terminals/morphotablet (retrieved May 4, 2016).

74. MorphoIDent. 2015. http://www.morpho.com/en/biometric-terminals/mobile-terminals/morphoident (retrieved May 4, 2016).

75. The global biometrics and mobility report: The convergence of commerce and privacy. n.d. http://www.acuity-mi.com/GBMR_Report.php (retrieved May 1, 2016).

76. R. P. Wildes, J. C. Asmuth, K. J. Hanna, S. C. Hsu, R. J. Kolczynski, J. R. Matey, and S. E. McBride. 1996. Automated, non-invasive iris recognition system and method. US Patent, 5572596.

77. R. Raguram, A. M. White, J. Frahm, P. Georgel, and F. Monrose. 2013. On the privacy risks of virtual keyboards: Automatic reconstruction of typed input from compromising reflections. *IEEE Transactions on Dependable and Secure Computing*, 10(3):154–167.

78. J. R. M. Filho and E. O. Freire. 2006. Multimodal biometric fusion, a joint typist (keystroke) and speaker verification. In *2006 International Telecommunications Symposium*, Fortaleza, Ceara, Brazil, pp. 609–614, September.
79. Montalvao Filho and Freire. 2006. Biochaves Project database. http://www.biochaves.com/en/download.htm
80. K. S. Killourhy and R. A. Maxion. 2009. Comparing anomaly-detection algorithms for keystroke dynamics. In *2009 IEEE/IFIP International Conference on Dependable Systems & Networks*, pp. 25–44, June.
81. K. Killourhy and R. Maxion. 2009. Anomaly-detection algorithms database. http://www.cs.cmu.edu/~keystroke/
82. Trusted biometrics under spoofing attacks (tabula rasa). http://www.tabularasa-euproject.org/
83. F. Ahmad, A. Najam, and Z. Ahmed. 2013. Image-based face detection and recognition: "State of the art." *International Journal of Computer Science Issues*, 9(6):3–6.
84. A. Al-Ajlan. 2013. Survey on fingerprint liveness detection. In *2013 International Workshop on Biometrics and Forensics (IWBF)*, Lisbon, Portugal. IEEE, pp. 1–5.
85. P. Coli, G. L. Marcialis, and F. Roli. 2007. Vitality detection from fingerprint images: A critical survey. *International Conference on Biometrics*. Springer, Berlin Heidelberg.
86. T. Matsumoto, H. Matsumoto, K. Yamada, and S. Hoshino. 2002. Impact of artificial gummy fingers on fingerprint systems. In *Electronic Imaging 2002*. International Society for Optics and Photonics, pp. 275–289.
87. H. Kang, B. Lee, H. Kim, D. Shin, and J. Kim. 2003. A study on performance evaluation of the liveness detection for various fingerprint sensor modules. In *Knowledge-Based Intelligent Information and Engineering Systems*. Springer, Oxford, UK, pp. 1245–1253.
88. S. T. V. Parthasaradhi, R. Derakhshani, L. A. Hornak, and S. A. C. Schuckers. 2005. Time-series detection of perspiration as a liveness test in fingerprint devices. *IEEE Transactions on Systems, Man, and Cybernetics, Part C: Applications and Reviews*, 35(3):335–362.
89. J. Jia, L. Cai, K. Zhang, and D. Chen. 2007. A new approach to fake finger detection based on skin elasticity analysis. In *International Conference on Biometrics*. Springer, Berlin Heidelberg, pp. 309–318.
90. Y. Zhang, J. Tian, X. Chen, X. Yang, and P. Shi. 2007. Fake finger detection based on thin-plate spline distortion model. In *International Conference on Biometrics*. Springer, Berlin Heidelberg, pp. 742–749.
91. S. B. Nikam and S. Agarwal. 2010. Curvelet-based fingerprint anti-spoofing. *Signal, Image and Video Processing*, 4(1): 75–87.
92. Y. S. Moon, J. S. Chen, K. C. Chan, K. So, and K. C. Woo. 2005. Wavelet based fingerprint liveness detection. *Electronics Letters*, 41(20): 1112–1113.
93. M. Espinoza and C. Champod. 2011. Using the number of pores on fingerprint images to detect spoofing attacks. In *2011 International Conference on Hand-Based Biometrics (ICHB)*, Hong Kong, China. pp. 1–5.

94. G. L. Marcialis, F. Roli, and A. Tidu. 2010. Analysis of fingerprint pores for vitality detection. In *2010 20th International Conference on Pattern Recognition (ICPR)*, Istanbul, Turkey, pp. 1289–1292.

95. J. Jia and L. Cai. 2007. Fake finger detection based on time-series fingerprint image analysis. In *Advanced Intelligent Computing Theories and Applications with Aspects of Theoretical and Methodological Issues*. Springer, Qingdao, China, pp. 1140–1150.

96. P. Z. Patrick, G. Aversano, R. Blouet, M. Charbit, and G. Chollet. 2005. Voice forgery using ALISP: Indexation in a client memory. In *Proceedings of IEEE International Conference on Acoustics, Speech, and Signal Processing (ICASSP '05)*, Philadelphia, US, Vol. 1, pp. 17–20.

97. J. Mariéthoz and S. Bengio. 2005. Can a professional imitator fool a GMM-based speaker verification system? No. EPFL-REPORT-83202. IDIAP.

98. M. Faundez-Zanuy. 2005. Data fusion in biometrics. *IEEE Aerospace and Electronic Systems Magazine*, 20(January):34–38, 2005.

99. N. Poh and S. Bengio. 2006. Database, protocols and tools for evaluating score-level fusion algorithms in biometric authentication. *Pattern Recognition*, 39(2):223–233.

100. C. McCool, S. Marcel, A. Hadid, M. Pietikdinen, P. Matejka, J. Cernocky, N. Poh et al. 2012. Bi-modal person recognition on a mobile phone: Using mobile phone data. In *IEEE International Conference on Multimedia and Expo Workshops (ICMEW)*, Melbourne, Australia, pp. 635–640.

101. H. Bredin and G. Chollet. 2007. Audio-visual speech synchrony measure for talking-face identity verification. In *IEEE International Conference on Acoustics, Speech and Signal Processing, 2007*, Honolulu, Hawaii. *ICASSP 2007*. Vol. 2, pp. II–233–II–236.

102. B. Fauve, H. Bredin, W. Karam, F. Verdet, A. Mayoue, G. Chollet, J. Hennebert et al. 2008. Some results from the biosecure talking face evaluation campaign. In *IEEE International Conference on Acoustics, Speech and Signal Processing, 2008*, Las Vegas, Nevada. *ICASSP 2008*. pp. 4137–4140.

103. MOBIO face and speaker verification evaluation. n.d. http://www.mobio-project.org/icpr-2010 (retrieved April 22, 2016).

104. A. F. Machado and M. Queiroz. 2010. Voice conversion: A critical survey. In *Proceedings of Sound and Music Computing (SMC)*, Barcelona, Spain. pp. 1–8.

105. RHU keystroke dynamics benchmark dataset. Coolest Tech RHU KeyStroke Dynamics Benchmark Dataset Comments. Web. April 24, 2016. http://www.coolestech.com/rhu-keystroke/

106. Coolest tech. n.d. http://www.coolestech.com/download/14441/ (retrieved April 26, 2016).

107. B. Saini, N. Kaur, and K. Bhatia. 2016. Keystroke dynamics for mobile phones: A survey. *Indian Journal of Science and Technology*, 9(6), DOI: 10.17485/ijst/2016/v9i6/82084.

108. https://www.behaviosec.com/

109. US Army evaluating biometrics for mobile devices on the battlefield. 2016. http://www.biometricupdate.com/201604/u-s-army-evaluating-biometrics-for-mobile-devices-on-the-battlefield (retrieved April 26, 2016).

110. Keystroke dynamics. n.d. http://www.biometric-solutions.com//solutions/index.php?story=keystroke_dynamics (retrieved April 26, 2016).

111. C. Gottschlich, E. Marasco, A. Y. Yang, and B. Cukic. 2014. Fingerprint liveness detection based on histograms of invariant gradients. In *2014 IEEE International Joint Conference on Biometrics (IJCB)*, Clearwater, Florida. IEEE, pp. 1–7, September.

112. What are cognitive abilities and skills, and how to boost them? 2006. http://sharpbrains.com/blog/2006/12/18/what-are-cognitive-abilities/ (retrieved April 27, 2016).

CHAPTER 4

Biometrics in Health Care

Kenneth Kung and Laurie O'Connor

CONTENTS

4.1 INTRODUCTION

Social and technological advances have increased the availability, accessibility, and quality of health care. However, recent transformations in health care—such as remote health monitoring, personalized medicine, privacy laws, and electronic health records—have also created new challenges. The introduction of remote health monitoring and treatment is creating a growing need for automatic authentication, based upon patient characteristics, where physicians or other caregivers are not present to identify the patient. The compartmentalization and specialization of the medical field, paired with new emphasis on Provider Accountability, has increased the need for authentication of healthcare providers. The pervasiveness of electronic information and processes in health care is increasing the number and diversity of opportunities for healthcare identity theft and fraud. Additionally, the use of data collected for healthcare processes has recently been constrained by laws and policies protecting privacy. As a result, the field of health care offers significant opportunities and challenges for the application of biometrics.

The application of biometrics in health care has many similarities with other applications, where automatic authentication is based upon physical characteristics. Secure storage and management of biometric data are essential. Cost, quality, and speed of delivery are all factors. Trusted processes, as in other fields, may require authentication at multiple points in the process by individuals and information systems, in a variety of roles, for specified actions.

On the other hand, the healthcare field is unique in several ways. Access to additional types of physical and physiological parameters may be available in a healthcare setting, measured and stored as an integral part of the healthcare process, not available anywhere else. Privacy laws require that access to patient information is limited to those who have a legitimate need to know, based upon their role in the healthcare process. Healthcare laws and policies may limit the application of biometric authentication, when it affects an individual's right to basic healthcare services. Finally, there are many unknowns regarding the application of biometrics to health care. For example, does the healthcare setting require a higher or different standard of accuracy for identification? How will biometric data be securely stored and managed in healthcare processes, so as to protect privacy? What happens to a person's healthcare access when their biometric identity is invalidated or stolen? These and other questions must be addressed.

This chapter identifies and discusses opportunities, challenges, and open questions in the application of biometrics to health care. We begin by creating a case for biometrics in health care by first identifying potential stakeholders, and then examining current and future trends, gaps, and needs that are driving the increased importance of biometrics. Addressing this evolving social and business environment, we create a conceptual framework for biometrics in health care by: (1) identifying basic elements, (2) examining important processes with special attention to the digital signature process, (3) reviewing relevant biometrics technologies, and (4) presenting a set of criteria and tradeoffs for evaluating the applicability of biometrics elements. With this framework as a foundation, we present several diverse healthcare scenarios featuring the current or proposed use of biometrics, discussing issues specific to these scenarios. We conclude by reviewing open challenges and questions in technology, law, and policy for biometrics in health care.

4.2 CASE FOR BIOMETRICS IN HEALTH CARE

Even though biometrics in the digital world is a relatively new field, the use of some types of biometrics has a long history. For example, the fingerprint has been used since the late 1800s for law enforcement applications. But the addition of new biometrics, and the ability to digitize, characterize, and share almost all data at reasonable cost and tremendous speed, has led to many new biometrics methods and processes that, in the past, were either not discovered or not practical. Intelligent and productive use of biometrics requires that we evaluate the need before implementing solutions. In this section, we first look at the healthcare environment and potential stakeholders. With this as a foundation, we then look at the important gaps and needs—to create a case for biometrics in health care.

4.2.1 Multidimensional Environment of Health Care

One of the most interesting and challenging aspects of biometrics in health care is the immense diversity of settings that must be accommodated due to its multidimensional nature. Example dimensions include terrain (urban to rural to wilderness), affiliation (military vs. civilian), care setting (home vs. doctor office vs. hospital), treatment aim (preventative vs. diagnostic vs. treatment vs. urgent care), specialization (primary care vs. various specialties), severity of need (minor vs. life-threatening vs. postdeath vs. prenatal care), and type of application (direct medical care vs. supply chain or chain of custody for medical materials, such as devices, pharmaceuticals, or biospecimens). Adding to this complexity is the universality of the need for health care that spans age, gender, race, occupation, citizenship, location, and socioeconomic status, among others.

4.2.2 Diversity and Number of Stakeholders

Another challenging aspect is the diversity and number of stakeholders in the healthcare process. Generally, stakeholders are those who are affected by or who affect a system operation. In the context of health care, we define stakeholders to be individuals, organizations, and information systems, that receive services, provide care, or participate in the healthcare process, and who, consequently, will be affected by the use of biometrics in health care. Figure 4.1 shows key stakeholder groups interacting with each other and with a generic biometrics in healthcare process in the context of common healthcare scenarios. We describe each stakeholder group, and their role in interacting with the healthcare system.

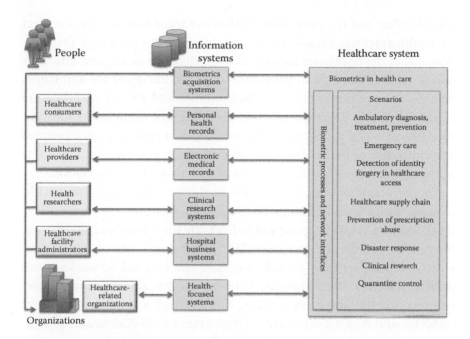

FIGURE 4.1 Stakeholders include individuals, organizations, and information systems. Individual and organization stakeholders work through systems to use the biometrics in healthcare process in many different scenarios.

Individual stakeholders, or people, may include healthcare consumers, healthcare providers, health researchers, and healthcare administrators. Healthcare consumers utilize a variety of health services in order to obtain assessment, diagnosis, prevention, treatment, and maintenance of health conditions. Healthcare consumers can be patients, or those who actively participate in managing the health of family, friends, or others. Examples of health services utilized by healthcare consumers include primary care, immunizations, emergency care, and specializations such as pediatric, oncology, pain, dental, vision, and a variety of others.

Healthcare providers offer health services directly or indirectly to the health consumer. Providers include physicians, nurses, technicians, pharmacists, emergency personnel—including paramedics, military health providers (on and off the battlefield), and medical volunteers. *Health researchers*, who design and conduct clinical research, include investigators, subinvestigators, coordinators, biostatisticians, and operations personnel for patient enrollment and site monitoring. Biometrics feature identification and the association with other traits may also be a subject for health research. *Healthcare facility administrators* manage the business side of the healthcare facility for cycle time, efficiency, and effectiveness, as well as quality and adherence to policy. Examples are admission, records management, administration, billing, and service coordination (O'Connor 2013). A person can have many stakeholder roles in a healthcare system—as a patient or legal guardian, as a physician, as a hospital administrator, or as an insurance submitter, for example. Each of these roles requires access to different services and associated information.

Organization stakeholders include healthcare organizations, health-focused institutions, and some financial organizations (O'Connor 2013). Organizations comprise groups of individuals who create and share goals, policies, standards, and processes. Healthcare organizations, which provide healthcare services, include hospitals and hospital networks, small private practices and networks, Veterans Health Administration, correctional institution health services, Health Maintenance Organizations (HMOs), and Non-Governmental Organizations (NGOs) health providers, such as the American Red Cross. They may also include organizations that are assembled to address a new or ongoing health risk, such as response to a natural disaster, or an epidemic, such as Ebola. Health-focused organizations do not directly render healthcare services, but participate in information sharing and healthcare improvement. Examples of these are payers, such as government or organizations that offer health insurance, regulatory and government agencies, such as the Centers for Disease Control and Prevention (CDC), Federal Drug Administration (FDA), National Cancer Institute (NCI), National Institute of Health (NIH), the World Health Organization (WHO), and accreditation organizations for hospitals and other healthcare organizations, as well as Internet-provided sources of medical information, information sharing, and suppliers. Some financial institutions, such as banks, which fund health and biometric investments, may also be stakeholders.

Information systems stakeholders include a wide variety of health care and other information systems that will be affected by the use of biometrics, since many systems participate in the healthcare process by storing, retrieving, utilizing, and managing the health information of healthcare consumers and healthcare providers. Many systems will need to interact with a biometrics repository—a database of the biometric characteristics of individual stakeholders supporting multiple modalities to authenticate healthcare workers, organizations, and patients. Electronic health record systems, managed either by a health organization or by a healthcare consumer, as their personal health record, maintain individual histories of health conditions, procedures, lab measurement, diagnoses, prescriptions, and doctors' narratives. Hospital business systems manage information related to operations, cost, quality, and efficiency. Many systems support the practice of clinical research, including clinical data management systems, adverse event reporting systems, and clinical research management systems. Overall, the number and scope of information systems in the healthcare process is rapidly increasing.

4.2.3 Need for Confidentiality, Authorization, and Accountability in Health Care

As we continue to digitize and use computer and communication networks within the healthcare system, the ability to identify and authenticate individual stakeholders becomes crucial to maintaining the *confidentiality*, *authorization*, and *accountability* of vast number participants in the healthcare process, for a wide range of needs. There are many laws, rules, and regulations that these healthcare industry participants must comply with, with financial penalties for violating them. The Health Insurance Portability and Accountability Act (HIPAA) and Health Information Technology for Economic and Clinical Health Act (HITECH) define the laws for medical record privacy. Individual states may have additional laws to protect individual privacy. HIPAA does not preempt state privacy laws that are more stringent or more protective (ASTHO 2005, White 2009).

Ultimately, we want to protect the well-being of individuals in the healthcare system. Furthermore, corporate or medical practice brand names can be damaged as the consequence of unauthorized release of medical information, financial information, or competitive research information. To accomplish this wide range of needs, we must start with the fundamental assumption that *we know who is in the system, doing what to the information, and acting on whose behalf.* The underlying access control system will either permit or deny the access request.

Until recently, the social security number has been the de facto number to identify an individual in the United States healthcare system. This is not a best practice, for several reasons, as the social security number was created originally for collecting tax and distributing benefits. There was no protection mechanism built into this number to prevent misidentification. There is little checking to make sure that the person using the social security number is actually the person the number was assigned to. Not everyone using the healthcare system possesses this number. For example, a temporary visitor to this country, such as a foreign scholar on an exchange program, may not have a social security number, yet will need access to the healthcare system while staying here. There are not adequate controls. An undocumented visitor who does not have a tax identification number (equivalent to the social security number) may create an arbitrary number when registering for medical service. This arbitrary number may collide with a legitimate number used by another (rightful) person.

The healthcare record created from a misuse of the social security number or tax identification number, and the associated financial responsibility, can take a long time to sort out by the legitimate holder of the identification number. Increasingly, large quantities of identity information have been stolen from major organizations (government, retail industry, insurance company, financial industry, etc.) (IDT911 2015), and have been fraudulently used to steal valuable resources, including tax refunds (McKinnon and Saunders 2015, Warren 2015), bank account funds (PresidentRemark 2015), and credit line access (FBI 2015) as well as access to or reimbursement for medical services rendered (FTC 2011). Due to these weaknesses, the U.S. Medicare Program will remove the social security number from its benefit card and switch to another identification number for the participants in this program (SSA OIG 2015). But as cybercrime and healthcare fraud evolves, other precautions will need to be taken.

Even if there is a different unique identification number used for healthcare services, there is still the problem of verifying identity, associating that number with the patient. The Healthcare IT Policy Committee (Health IT Policy Committee 2012) recognized the need to have individuals authenticated at a higher level than identification and password. The Health IT Standards Committee (White et al. 2015) formalized a multifactor authentication where biometrics can be applied as one of the factors within the healthcare industry as of 2015. The standard states:

> For one or more configurable functions, enable a system administrator to configure the technology to require that at least two distinct forms of authentication (which may include knowledge of a secret, possession of a physical object, or *possession of a biometric*) be presented as verification that a person seeking access to those functions is the individual associated with the unique identifier, as claimed.

4.2.4 Promise of Biometrics in Health Care

Currently, biometrics offers the most promising approach to show "who you are" in the system. Your biometric characteristics remain the same (e.g., deoxyribonucleic acid [DNA]) or changes very slowly, if at all. For example, the fingerprints of a mason change over his or her working career and can be accurately captured in the biometrics database (Harmon 2009). They are not easily available to be falsified. Some (such as voice signatures) can be modified to fit new situations. There is a variety of biometrics, each as unique as the individual person. Using multiple, coordinated biometrics techniques, we can increase the certainty of individual authentication to a high degree of accuracy, pending consideration of the usability of the system. With the use of appropriate biometrics, it should not be possible to masquerade as another person when accessing a healthcare system, either as a provider or a receiver of services.

Biometrics offers significant advantages in some situations, relative to other methods. If a patient neither carries identification nor contact information, and is unconscious, then biometrics offers the most effective and efficient way to identify the patient. See the *Patient in Emergency* scenario described later in this chapter. Another advantage is that the healthcare system can identify a user without the cooperation of the user. This is important when a person is either unable or unwilling to cooperate, for example, a young child, a mentally unstable individual, or a person connected with a crime.

Biometrics identification can also enhance the accuracy of the medical treatment for the individual. Accidents, such as allergic responses, and inappropriate treatments can be avoided if the appropriate identity is available as needed to access existing medical records. Biometrics can also ensure that the right person is being treated. If a person in an emergency situation has already been sedated and cannot provide the identification information to the medical team, a biometrics identity can prevent misidentification during surgical and other procedures. For example, when a healthcare worker is providing a flu shot, the patient is positively identified via biometrics to verify any potential adverse reaction (e.g., Guillain Barre Syndrome). This can prevent the problem where a patient inadvertently forgets to let the flu shot administer to know about this potentially deadly reaction.

Associated with the positive identification and authorization of the user is the accountability of any actions taken by healthcare providers while in the healthcare system. With strong authentication offered by biometrics, identifying who is doing what in the system, and when, it becomes harder to deny the actions taken by either the provider or the receiver of a healthcare visit or session, when accessing the healthcare system.

Furthermore, biometrics can help the healthcare industry to comply with various laws. In the United States, this includes the Healthcare Insurance Portability and Affordability Act (HIPAA), the Privacy Act of 1974, and others (US General Services Administration). Other countries, especially in Europe, have stronger privacy laws that exist to protect the patient information. These laws and regulations stipulate the access privileges of individuals to view, use, or modify the data. In the healthcare process, it is not easy to anticipate the access rights of specific individuals. Who is authorized to what information depends on the individual's identity and their role when accessing the information. Biometrics can give us the confidence that we know who the person is, and that the individual requesting information has the proper role before information is released.

For example, a doctor accessing medical records as an attending physician should be able to see the complete medical history of a patient. When a doctor sees a patient as a referred patient, the access privilege should be limited to the part of medical records relevant to the illness being treated. If the same doctor logs into a system as the owner of a medical practice, he should be able to view the state of his company or corporation, but not specific health records. Finally, a doctor who seeks medical care as a patient should not be able to see any medical records except his or her own. As another example, a patient enrolled in a clinical trial who is traveling from one city to another may need to visit a physician who is participating in the same trial. As a clinical investigator for that clinical trial, the physician needs to know who the patient is to ascertain the accuracy of the medical records. With biometrics, the remote physician does not need any other information to guarantee the identification of the patient.

The diversity of healthcare settings, the large number of stakeholders, and the need for confidentiality, authentication, and authorization create a need for biometrics in health care that is great, and is evolving quickly. The rapid digitization of our health information and the increasingly online, collaborative healthcare process requires new ways to ensure that we know who is using the healthcare system, how, and in what role. Biometrics is a promising technology to address those needs. As can be seen from the number and variety of stakeholders, the use of biometrics in health care can have a wide, deep, and profound impact on how health care is delivered, consumed, administered, and paid for, in the not-so-distant future.

Because of the diversity of healthcare settings and stakeholders, there is no one right approach for biometrics in health care. Instead, the use of biometrics processes and technologies will be dependent on each situation to which it is applied. Later in this chapter, we will look at several different scenarios that illustrate the variety of healthcare settings, needs, and application of biometrics.

4.3 FRAMEWORK FOR BIOMETRICS IN HEALTH CARE

Biometrics is a new and rapidly evolving field, with many unknowns. If we focus only on biometric technologies and what *can* be done with them, we will not have the perspective that we need in order to decide what *should* be done with them. Hence, we will broaden our perspective to look at health care as a system, where biometrics processes provide important functions in the context of healthcare processes. From that perspective, we develop a framework for biometrics in health care. This framework will identify and discuss important elements, the biometrics process, and important considerations for selecting and applying biometrics methods.

4.3.1 Elements of Biometrics in Health Care

There are many different elements involved in the application of biometrics to the healthcare system. In most cases, individual stakeholders will not directly interact with a biometrics system. Instead, they will interact through healthcare processes that utilize biometrics processes to identify the individual. In turn, biometrics processes will rely on a wide range of biometrics technologies and data. Figure 4.2 illustrates how stakeholders may participate in healthcare processes, drawing upon appropriate biometrics processes and technology, to ensure confidentiality, authorization, and accountability. We will further discuss these basic elements: first the healthcare processes, then the biometrics technologies, then the biometrics processes that provide the connection between health care and biometrics.

4.3.2 Healthcare Processes

Healthcare processes, which provide care to individuals, are many and varied. We will define and examine the following, which will be especially impacted by the use of biometrics in health care: Healthcare Access, Provider Accountability, HIPAA Privacy, Health Data Acquisition, Health Record Management, Emergency Services, and Digital Signature. Healthcare Access is the process of granting access to specific healthcare

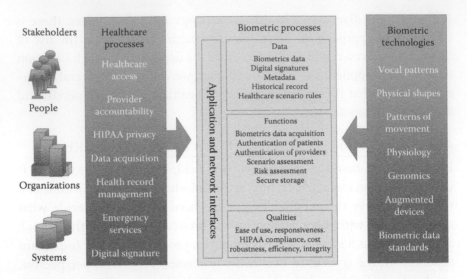

FIGURE 4.2 Basic elements for biometrics in health care include the stakeholders, processes, biometrics systems, and biometric technologies.

services. Provider Accountability is the process of ensuring that the appropriate people perform healthcare actions. HIPAA Privacy is the process of ensuring that people have access only to the information that is required to perform their assigned healthcare roles. Health Data Acquisition is the process of collecting and consolidating health information from various sources and formats into a logical data repository with metadata permitting the search and retrieval of the medical information. Health Record Management is the process of enabling the collection, maintenance, backup, replication, sharing, and consistency of medical data in various databases and repositories so that medical data are accessible whenever needed. Emergency Services is the process of responding to urgent and unforeseen situations, which may require granting access or providing treatment without 100% knowledge of identity. The reader can refer to Benefield et al. (2006) and Bradley (2004) to study the specifics of these processes.

Digital signature is the process of signing documents to ensure the veracity of the information. This process can be supported by biometrics and is elaborated further. In the healthcare context, documents are often health records, which may be in electronic form. With electronic patient record systems implemented across the medical field, a digital signature is needed to ensure the integrity and authorship of electronic documents.

For example, a doctor can electronically issue a prescription to a pharmacy, or specify a test to a laboratory for a specific patient. If there is any question later, on the accuracy of the order, digital signatures can be used to verify and ascertain the order. Digital signature may be a subprocess of any of the other healthcare processes, and may be performed with or without the use of biometrics.

4.3.3 Digital Signature Considerations

Digital signature is an important part of the healthcare process that, currently, does not rely on biometrics. But the strong case for biometrics in health care encourages us to envision a digital signature process that is powered by biometric data. The electronic signature process consists of two operations: the signing of a document and the verification of the signature. Both of these operations have associated considerations and characteristics, but a biometrics-based process for digital signature is augmented by biometrics technologies. Figure 4.3 illustrates the use of biometrics in the digital signature process. In this section, we discuss the use of biometrics for authenticating a healthcare system stakeholder.

The signing of a "document" has three components. First we need to define the "document" to be signed. In the healthcare industry, the

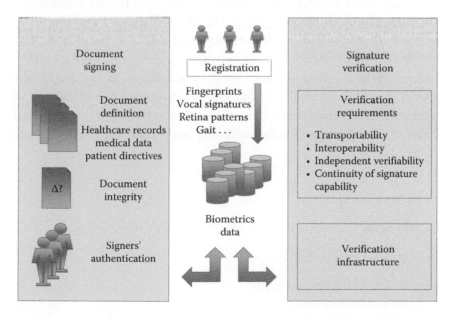

FIGURE 4.3   Digital signature process in health care using biometrics data.

document could be, for example, a laboratory test result, a prescription, a patient's Advance Directive, a family's agreement to organ donation, a doctor's note after patient examination, or the healthcare record for a hospital patient. Let us expand upon the last one, the hospital healthcare record. It is typically not a single file. Rather, it could be a composite of word files, Excel spreadsheets, Adobe pdf files, a record or several records in a large database, physicians' dictated notes, laboratory raw data, analysis results, or some other combination of digital healthcare records. For an accurate and complete healthcare record, each of those records should be verified for authenticity of source. For example, after a nurse records the vital signs, then the record of vital signs, as a document, can be signed by the nurse. The head nurse may review records signed by individual nurses and sign each of them, or multiple ones. A digital signature should allow the hospital process to be carried out as best meets the healthcare needs, instead of forcing the staff to change how they do their daily business to meet the needs of an information system.

Looking further into the details of these individual items, we must determine what metadata (e.g., date and time of the document creation) must be or should be included in the "document" to be signed. In addition, should the head nurse-signed document include the digital signature of the individual nurses? The head nurse may wish to add annotations to individual records before signing. The order of signing also should be preserved in case this is needed for any legal issues involved in patient treatment.

Some of these issues are addressed by standards in the healthcare industry. Specifically, Health IT Standards Committee recommended in Perlin et al. (2011) and Department of Health and Human Services (2011) including the following metadata with any healthcare records:

- Tagged data element (TDE) identifier

- A time stamp

- The actor

- The actor's affiliation

- The actor's digital certificate

According to the standard, the TDE is needed "to preserve clinical context by allowing other TDEs to link to this particular instance and allow users to keep a log of the set of TDEs used for a particular task." The other metadata information is recommended to assure the user of the information on the integrity and authentication of the data. The last metadata is related to the digital signature verification. Please refer to Sedona Principles (Redgrave et al. 2007) for further discussion on the best practices recommendation and principles for creating electronic documents.

The second component of document signing deals with the integrity of the signed documents. The content of a document may have different values at different times. This is the case if a document incorporates a data value from another source, such as a database, or if there is macro-like code inside a document that modifies the content of a document. This issue is not specific to the healthcare industry. It is highlighted here so that the reader is aware of this issue when applying digital signatures in the healthcare industry.

The third component of document signing deals with the authentication of the digital signers. In the healthcare industry, we need positive identification of the author of the digital health records. Biometrics technologies promise to meet this need because the biometric data is personalized, can be very accurate, changes slowly or not at all, and can be used for nearly all people. There are many different biometric technologies, as will be discussed in the next section.

Next, we need to look at the verification of the digital signatures in the healthcare industry. The verification requirements for the healthcare industry are not different from others. There are four requirements for signature verification: transportability, interoperability, independent verifiability, and the continuity of signature capability (Kung 1995). Transportability refers to the ability for a healthcare document and digital signature to be transported (possibly over an insecure network) to another system while maintaining the integrity of the document and signature. Interoperability requires that the healthcare document and signature can be processed by a recipient on a variety of platforms (e.g., tablet, laptop, desktop, etc.) while still maintaining the integrity of the document. In other words, we can verify the signature as many times as needed. Independent verifiability requires that a signature can be verified without the cooperation of the signer. Finally, the continuity of signature capability requires that the public verification of a signature does not compromise the ability of the signer to apply future secure signatures.

To complete the verification, we must verify the integrity of the healthcare document and associated document metadata included in the digital signature as described above. In the case where multiple signatures have been attached to the document, we need to be able to verify the order of the signature. We should not be able to change or replace signatures, without discovery by anyone verifying the document. A backup system should be able to recover the signature if someone purposely deletes a digital signature. With the use of biometrics, we should be able to identify a digital signer with high confidence.

In order for the biometrics to function properly as the authentication mechanism for digital signature, we must have the participant stakeholders register their biometrics and store them in a biometrics database. This registration process must be verified in order to establish the fact that accurate biometrics have been captured for a specific person. Once the biometrics is captured and stored, the integrity of parameters must be guaranteed and protected against unauthorized tampering.

Additional supporting systems associated with digital signature are similar to other industries. Please refer to Ponnapalli and Saxena (2103), Hyla et al. (2012), and Alrehily et al. (2015) for discussion on digital signature generation, verification, storage, integrity protection, nonrepudiation service, algorithms selection, performance comparison, and architecture considerations.

Specifically, long-term storage and verification of a digital signature may be needed in the healthcare industry. A typical healthcare record needs to be kept for a period defined by various Federal and State requirements (AHIMA 2011, Tavakoli and Jahanbakhsh 2013, Tavakoli et al. 2013). It could be as long as 75 years from the last date of activity (AHIMA 2015). However, AHIMA recommends a retention period of 10 years after the most recent encounter (AHIMA 2011). Hence, a digitally signed document needs to be stored and potentially verified for the nonrepudiation able proof of the original document to cover the required period of time. The digital signature infrastructure, therefore, must support the keys, algorithms, and all other needed information.

4.3.4 Application of Biometric Methods

There are a variety of biometrics technologies or methods that may be used in health care. Many of these may be used to support the digital signal process, and other healthcare processes such as Healthcare Access, HIPAA privacy, and Emergency Response. Commonly used biometrics include vocal patterns, physical shapes, patterns of movement, physiology and biochemistry, and DNA matching of genetic markers. Physical shapes include fingerprints, patterns of veins in hands, neck, or other easily accessible areas, eye retina or iris patterns, the shapes of appendages such as hands, feet, and ears, dental patterns. Patterns of movement may include gait, facial expressions, and pen movement dynamics (Ashbourn 2015). Physiology and biochemistry although not unique, may be used as part of a multimodal biometric profile.

The use of biometrics in health care has unique challenges. Some applications, such as banking and mobile environments can make valid and useful assumptions about the stability of the user and environment. However, those same assumptions may not be valid for health care. Biometrics, by definition, uses identifiable characteristics of the human body. In contrast, health care, by definition, often treats anomalies or modifies characteristics of the human body, some of which may be biometric in nature. In a healthcare situation, the biometric that identifies the individual may not act as it normally does, may not be accessible (for instance if the individual is unconscious), or may not be in place where it should be. For example, biometrics, such as voice, are very convenient, but may change with illness, age, training, or extreme stress, or may be modified by surgery. Pen movement dynamics—probably the most acceptable method for the patients and other users—may be highly variable, and may not be sufficient to uniquely identify a person. Registration of a user's biometric pen movement requires the user to copy or write a long sentence. However, the signature characteristics may not be available if the patient is unconscious, or may change as the user ages, experiences injuries (broken finger, carpal tunnel syndrome), or experiences time pressures, resulting in a deteriorating handwriting. They may even change when the signature purpose changes, as some people may use a more careful, complete signature for important documents, such as mortgages, than they do for quick transactions, such as signing into a doctor's office or a credit card purchase.

The healthcare environment presents many other unique challenges for biometrics as a result of healthcare law and policies, insurance practices, medical ethics, and privacy. For example, even in the United States, there are many variations in state law with regard to healthcare access and who is able to make what decisions; internationally, the variation is even greater. Both state and federal laws affect what documentation is considered to be legal identification for those who are noncitizens. Insurance practices are evolving to adapt to changes in medicine, changes in laws, and financial incentives. Privacy practices are rapidly evolving with the rapidly expanding Internet ecology. Finally, as identified in the introduction to this chapter, the diversity of the healthcare recipients, providers, and scenarios is unmatched in any other field.

Since biometrics in health care are so deeply dependent upon the state of the human body, which may not be functioning correctly, it may be useful to consider the application of biometrics in combination with other technologies. This is becoming feasible, as more and more implantable devices are connected wirelessly to information platforms for remote monitoring and care. Implantable devices, such as pacemakers, defibrillators, insulin pumps, and others might provide signals uniquely identifying the user, when combined with other biological signatures. Wearable devices, such as watches, may monitor heart rate and motion patterns, and provide information regarding the health condition of the individual. Biometrics information might also be supplemented with input from accessible medical devices such as hearing aids, contacts, dental work, which may be marked with an identifying marker.

Microchips are currently used for animals, and have been used in several human applications (Smith 2008) for personal identification. These may be used in combination with other biometrics to uniquely identify the individual. However, the use of these is voluntary, and is not required by law.

When multimodal biometrics are available, it may be possible to have the identification system select one or a combination of biometrics that are most likely to be functional, given the medical situation. In some cases, decisions have to be made to tradeoff the risk of misidentification with the risk of nontreatment. Probabilistic methods and risk-assessment algorithms might be applied to inform and advise this decision-making process (Bazin 2006).

Other technologies that impact the effectiveness of biometrics in health care include the Electronic Health Records, and standards applicable to biometric data. Example standards include: Health Level-7 (HL7), continuity of care (CCD) document, digital imaging and communications in medicine (DICOM), Extensible Markup Language (XML), and Electronic Data Interchange (EDI).

4.3.5 Biometrics Processes

Biometrics processes interact with healthcare processes and biometric methods to ensure that we can know *who is in the healthcare system, doing what to the information, and acting on whose behalf.* Biometric processes, comprising one or more biometric systems, include both information and functions, which are needed to apply biometric technologies to healthcare processes. Information used in biometric processes may include biometrics data, metadata, digital signatures, historical record, and healthcare scenario rules. Healthcare scenario rules are interpretable policies and instructions that are needed to guide the situation-dependent application of biometrics. For example, in an emergency situation, some identification rules may be bypassed in order to provide rapid response and treatment.

Functions required by biometric processes may include biometrics data acquisition, including registration, authentication algorithms, biometric digital signature data, scenario assessment, risk assessment, and secure storage of biometric data. Biometric processes should be easy to use, have responsiveness consistent with the needs of the application, be compliant with HIPAA requirements, and be of reasonable cost and efficient. They should also be robust to system failure, disaster, and changing conditions, and preserve the integrity of information.

A representative biometrics process, supporting the healthcare access process, depicted in Figure 4.4, includes the following elements:

- Biometrics data acquisition process

- Algorithms and functions for interpreting and representing biometrics data

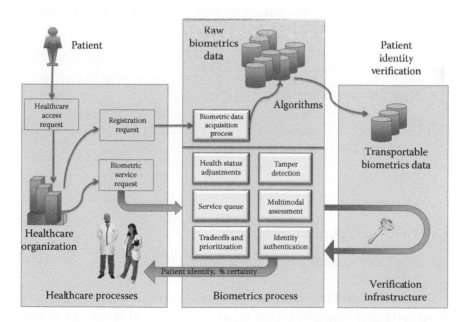

FIGURE 4.4 Biometrics processes for registration and healthcare access.

- One or more data stores for biometric data
- Request for service interface to healthcare systems
- A managed queue for service requests
- Rules addressing tradeoffs and prioritization (e.g., time vs. accuracy)
- Biometric digital signature process
- A data store for recording system operations and history
- Algorithms and processes to detect tampering
- Functions to enable the aggregation of multiple biometrics for a multimodal identity assessment
- Physical tamper detection
- Ability to adjust authentication strategy depending upon health status
- Interface to a public verification infrastructure

4.3.6 Criteria and Tradeoffs

The applicability of a specific biometric or biometric process can be evaluated using performance and quality criteria that are developed for assessment. Examples of criteria include

- Accuracy for unique identification of user
- Need for user cooperation
- Speed
- Accessibility
- Cost
- Mutability
- Vulnerability to theft or hacking
- Possibility to cause harm

Depending upon the situation, tradeoffs may need to be made among the criteria. For example, highly accurate identification may be slower. Nonmutable biometrics, if stolen, may be rendered useless. Biometrics requiring consent and cooperation by the individual may not be useful when the patient is in an unconscious state. For a healthcare system, there are four characteristics of biometrics usage that should be assessed for the target environment, which may range from the relatively tranquil office environment to the hectic emergency center. These are universality, distinctiveness, permanence, and collectability (Goodrich et al. 2011). Universality addresses whether each person has this specific biometrics. Using hand geometry and fingerprints may not work if a person lost his or her hand. Distinctiveness addresses the uniqueness of individual's biometrics such that we can identify a specific person. Using the movement of gait may not identify a specific individual. However, a combination of the gait movement and partial facial features might be specific enough to identify an individual. Permanence addresses whether the biometrics is stable enough for patients. As long as the characteristics are not changing on a daily or monthly basis, we will not need to reregister patients to use biometrics identification purpose. Collectability addresses the collection and registration of the biometrics into a database. In the healthcare system, we assume the healthcare service providers and consumers are willing participants of the biometrics use so that they are willing to provide the needed biometrics data.

We have presented a conceptual framework for biometrics in health care that identifies the important elements, and shows how biometrics technologies and processes can work within the healthcare system. It is clear from this framework that any application of biometrics has to work within existing infrastructure and healthcare processes in order to be successful. In addition, applications of biometrics must meet the needs of a variety of stakeholders, in real healthcare environments.

4.4 SCENARIOS SHOWING APPLICATION OF BIOMETRICS IN HEALTHCARE INDUSTRY

To illustrate how biometrics can be used in realistic healthcare environments, several scenarios are described in this section and evaluated within our framework. These scenarios can demonstrate how biometrics can be applied and integrated with other healthcare applications to authenticate the healthcare stakeholders, and facilitate the healthcare services with or without the cooperation of patients. The scenarios that we will address are (1) ambulatory patient, (2) patient in emergency, (3) detection of healthcare identity forgery, (4) healthcare supply chain, (5) prevention of prescription abuse, (6) disaster response, and (7) quarantine control.

4.4.1 Ambulatory Patient

4.4.1.1 Background

Ambulatory care is provided on an outpatient basis, not in a hospital. Technically, an ambulatory patient is defined as the one who can walk, although a person in a wheelchair would be considered an ambulatory patient. We assume that biometrics is used widely in the healthcare industry. Hence, the individual's biometrics data are registered in a secure biometrics database, for example, a public key database, where we can retrieve the appropriate individual's biometrics for verification. For the operational environment, we assume we have a communication network (be it voice network or data network) that connects the patient to the doctor's office.

4.4.1.2 Scenario

A patient with back pain makes an appointment to visit a physician. The appointment is made via phone or doctor's office web portal. Since the patient initiates the contact, we assume the patient can reasonably be assured of the identity of the doctor's office, and that a biometrics process to authenticate the doctor's office staff to the patient is not needed. See Figure 4.5 on the interactions between the patient and the doctor's office and the usage of the biometrics information. Authenticating a network remote node is not within the scope of this book. The reader can refer to a network authentication

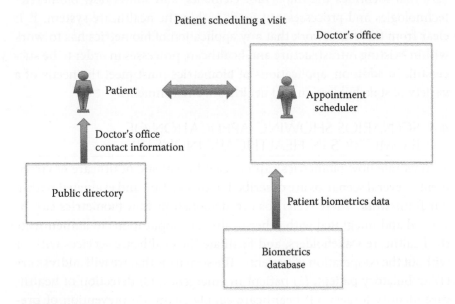

FIGURE 4.5   Patient initiates contact with doctor.

book to learn more about this topic, for example, Stallings (2014). After the appointment is made, the doctor's office knows the identity of the patient, by name, or possibly healthcare ID. This identity is not authenticated as anyone can make a phone call or use the web to make this appointment.

On the appointment date, the patient walks into the doctor's office as shown in Figure 4.6. Since the patient made the reservation in advance, the doctor's office can retrieve the patient's biometrics in advance. As the patient approaches the doctor's office door, a camera system can collect, measure, and analyze gait movement, facial features, and potentially the iris data (pending the camera resolution and patient's iris is visible, biometric data can be gathered for identification purpose). Figure 4.6 shows the patient walking toward the office with the camera capturing the biometrics to identify him or her to the office staff. Thus, as soon as the patient enters the door, the office staff is aware of the identity of the patient, and can immediately notify the medical team that the patient is available. In some cases the patient may not have to sign in or fill in any forms before being called in to see the doctor.

As the patient enters the office, additional biometrics can be applied to increase the certainty of the patient's identity. The patient can greet the

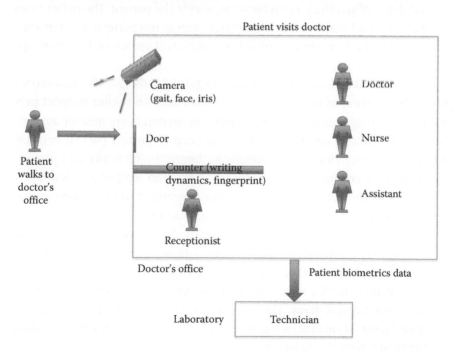

FIGURE 4.6 Patient walks into doctor's office with the biometrics data already retrieved from the database.

receptionist and be recognized by the office via voice biometrics. The patient can sign in using a pen where writing dynamics can be applied for authentication. A digital pad can collect and verify fingerprints. Furthermore, continuous authentication of the patient can be ascertained, if this is a requirement, using various biometrics while the patient is in the doctor's office, for example, for laboratory test sample collection or for minor surgical procedures.

While the doctor is examining the patient, the doctor dictates notes to the medical assistant, which are then recorded in the medical record of the patient. The doctor's voice pattern can be used to authenticate his or her identity. The existing medical record is also consulted to determine if there are any preexisting conditions, such as spinal stenosis, or a previous injury, that might be contributing to the back pain and current condition of the patient. At the end of the consultation, the doctor electronically signs the medical record of the consultation, where the doctor's registered biometrics is used to sign the medical record.

Suppose the doctor, after examining the patient, prescribes various tests such as MRI and x-ray to establish the cause of the back pain. The prescription can be forwarded to the laboratory along with patient biometric data. When the x-ray technician meets the patient, the patient can be authenticated with various biometrics such as iris pattern, facial geometry, footprints, fingerprints, or others. Incorrect match of the prescription and the patient can easily be avoided.

The associated healthcare provider organizations can use biometrics for authentication of doctors, nurses, technicians, and other support personnel, ensuring that the security policy requirements are met for authentication and access control. To meet the need to protect patient privacy, we can use biometrics to continuously authenticate the healthcare providers who are accessing medical records. Users who temporarily leave any workstation can have their authorization suspended until the authorized user is recognized to be present at the workstation.

Biometrics can be used as follow-up to doctor office visits as well. Voice authentication can be used for the follow-up phone calls from the patient to the doctor's office, and from the office to the patient, to ensure that any private health information is conveyed only to patients or their authorized representatives. The patient interface with the insurance company or financial institutions can also use biometrics, possibly replacing or supplementing the existing process used by many service providers, which require birthdate, mother's maiden name, or social security number, which are currently too readily available, to the public, online.

4.4.1.3 Observations

Much of this usage is similar to other office settings, where information must be handled in a secure manner. Note the variety of healthcare processes that are involved in a simple visit to the doctor: Healthcare Access, Provider Accountability, HIPAA Privacy, Health Data Acquisition, Health Record Management, and Digital Signature.

One question that comes to mind is, with the variety of biometrics available, how will healthcare facilities decide which biometrics to use? Is the need for accuracy high enough to justify the cost of a multimodal approach? Although standards may be desirable, they may not be practical. For example, if this doctor's office was that of an ophthalmologist, the iris biometric might not be very reliable due to the number of swollen eyes, eye patches, and other conditions related to the eye, that present to the office. With several biometrics available, lack of any one biometric will not invalidate this approach to authenticate either patient or other players in the healthcare system. See Section 4.3.6 for the criteria tradeoff discussion.

4.4.2 Patient in Emergency

4.4.2.1 Background

The above scenario is a nominal use case for a patient. The next scenario is for a case where the patient is the one who may not be ambulatory. In fact, he or she could be unconscious. We investigate how the biometrics can be applied in this case.

4.4.2.2 Scenario

A person travels alone from Los Angeles to Lake Placid, New York for vacation. This person is in a ski accident, and is found unconscious by emergency personnel. He or she did not carry an identification card, or any health insurance information.

The patient is taken to the local emergency hospital via ambulance. During transportation, as shown in Figure 4.7, multiple types of biometrics data such as finger prints and facial image from the patient can be collected and transmitted to a national biometrics repository for identification purpose. If the patient has registered biometric data, he or she is identified uniquely.

If the patient is not registered with the biometrics central repository, then additional searches can be performed. For example, the fingerprint can be transmitted to the FBI, Department of Homeland Security, and potentially other state Department of Motor Vehicles. The FBI keeps a

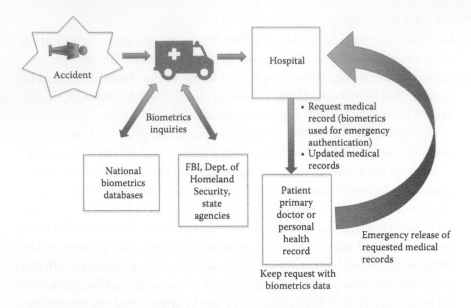

FIGURE 4.7 Identity of various players and the record transmission among them for the case where patient is unconscious.

record of fingerprints for anyone who has an interface with law enforcement. For example, anyone who has security clearance or anyone with an arrest record has their fingerprints stored in the FBI Integrated Automated Fingerprint Identification System database (FBI IAFIS; Tilstone et al. 2006). The Department of Homeland Security US-VISIT captures fingerprints for all foreign nationals in its IDENT system (legal immigrants and visitors) when they pass through the border checkpoints (Gantt 2012). Each state's driver license department may have the fingerprint(s) for those with a driver license or state-issued identification card. If the unconscious individual has a fingerprint for any of the above cases, he or she is identified. Medical information can be obtained via the contact information associated with the identification. It takes time to do these searches, which may be longer than needed in order to provide rapid medical response.

Figure 4.7 shows the relationship of various players when the patient is unconscious. The biometrics collected during the transportation to the hospital can gain precious time to identify the patient, and request patient health records when patient reaches the hospital.

With the identification information, the first responder can request further medical information about this patient. Fingerprint, iris pattern, or facial features could be captured and sent to the patient's home doctor's office to authenticate and to authorize the release of medical records. This release must meet the security policy for emergency release conditions. The patient may also have a universal Personal Health Record that contains relevant information. Biometrics can be used for authentication and authorization for releasing information per security policy.

Biometrics enables emergency or approved access to information in the patient's Personal Health Record.

Without identification, the emergency personnel proceed without taking into account the patient's medical history, such as drug allergy, current medical treatment, and any special circumstance that the healthcare workers need to know. There are many important things that first responders and medical personnel need to know quickly without extensive testing: existing conditions, for example, diabetes, recent medical treatments or surgeries, pregnancy, embedded devices, mental history that might account for unusual behaviors, vaccination history, whether and where there is an Advance Directive/living will, prescription history, and drug response or resistance. If the patient has the human immunodeficiency virus, then special precaution might be needed while the patient is being treated.

Let us assume after intense treatment, this patient recovers. After discharge, the patient's health record in the remote city is submitted, using health records information standards, to the primary doctor's office back in Los Angeles or to the patient-owned Personal Health Record. Network authentication should be used to authenticate where the new patient records are coming from. Network authentication and public key certificates are used to prevent information from getting into a wrong medical record. Digital signature can be used to authenticate the origin of the records and the integrity of the medical data while being transmitted to the primary doctor or to the patient-owned health record. To uniquely identify the remote hospital medical staff, the biometrics steps described in the first scenario, a medical office environment, can be applied here as well.

4.4.2.3 Observations

Some additional issues the reader should consider, but beyond the scope of this book are listed below.

- How can we detect if someone at the point of care center has altered medical records?

- In the scenario, we assume all systems are within the United States. If any part of the biometrics is located in another country, we need to revisit various steps in the process to ascertain the interoperability of the authentication steps.

- Do we need to keep the patient biometrics in the remote facility to prove the authorization for obtaining the patient information? This is relevant where wrong information, which should be rare, was obtained for the patient. The emergency medical personnel may need to show that they have done due diligence in using biometrics to obtain the identity of the patient.

- Should the transfer of information include the history of the information, as well, to ensure it is authentic?

- We may need not only authentication of identity but also authentication of information that is used to create or build an identity. Do we authenticate all of the sources of information too?

4.4.3 Detection of Identity Forgery

4.4.3.1 Background

The United States is moving toward healthcare insurance coverage for all residents. However, it will be a few years before all eligible persons obtain health insurance, while visitors and foreign nationals continue to lack insurance. In an environment without biometrics-verified identification, a patient can use a false identification number (e.g., social security number) when seeking medical services. There is no method for the healthcare provider to verify the authenticity of the patient's identity claim. It is different when we can use biometrics.

As in other scenarios, one assumption that we will make is that there is a repository of the biometrics data associated with individuals. This database could be limited to the healthcare industry application. It can also be extended and used by other industries such as financial, retail, critical infrastructure protection, national security, law enforcements, etc. Relevant references include Luhby (1997), Heun (2014), Smith (2015), and Swanson (2015).

4.4.3.2 Scenario

When a patient or healthcare worker, requests a service, the associated treatment is billed to the person, and with an identification number. The associated insurance company then processes the bill to determine the negotiated price for each service, the deductible, and percent covered by the insured. If the person has no insurance, then he or she is responsible for the billed amount.

Now, suppose the identity is stolen, who is responsible to pay the service? The person with the stolen identity may need to spend time to prove to the healthcare provider that the patient does not match the description of the claimed person (e.g., age, sex, race, other identifiable characteristics, etc.). If any negative credit history has been entered into the credit database, then the victim must have way to submit a statement as to why the record should not be considered when determining the credit worthiness.

These problems can be avoided if we use biometrics when the original medical service is requested. The identity of the patient can be ascertained, assuming the proper procedure was applied when a person registers the biometric data into the repository. The biometric identification methods described in the ambulatory patient scenario can be applied here to authenticate a patient.

The repository can also provide the current insurance information for the provider to submit bills. In countries such as Canada where the government is the single payer of healthcare service, the identity also provides the associated insurance information.

4.4.3.3 Observations
One shortcoming of the biometrics repository method is for the case where the patient has not registered any biometric data prior to the service request. In this case, the healthcare provider can record the biometrics in a local medical record. For example, the fingerprint pad for authenticating patients can also be a collection tool. If there are any discrepancies with the identity, the healthcare provider can submit the biometric data to the law enforcement agencies. Another potential problem that should be considered is the potential for criminal elements to cause harm to individuals in order to gain access to biometric aspects of an individual's identity. In dealing with these legal issues, we should also consider the fact that healthcare workers are not law enforcement agents. Hence, the system should not prevent those who need healthcare worker attention from seeking these services.

4.4.4 Healthcare Supply Chain
4.4.4.1 Background
In the cyberspace, supply chain risk management is a major concern to the integrity of the silicon components to major infrastructure systems. Similar concern occurs in the biological space. When medical supplies

and therapeutics are manufactured and transported, we need to prevent counterfeited supplies being mixed in with legitimate supplies. To achieve this integrity, we need to positively identify all people in the chain of custody. To this end, we can leverage the biometrics to identify each person who has contact with the supplies. The challenge is how to collect, store, and track the large volume of the biometrics associates with each medical supply. Solutions have to be created and integrated into each individual supply chain system. Since the medical supply chain is global, the positive control may need to start at another country.

4.4.4.2 Scenario

A pharmaceutical company manufactures and markets a biological therapeutic, which can cost thousands of dollars per gram. To positively control each step of the manufacturing and distribution, we can incorporate biometrics to authenticate and to control individuals who have contact with the raw material, intermediate products, and final products. Due to automation of the manufacturing process, the number of persons who may have contact with the products should be manageable. During packaging, storing, and transporting of the products, similar positive control on who has contact with the products can incorporate biometrics. This control information must be stored in a secure database where tampering is not possible or could be detected. This will protect patients and will be needed if chain-of-custody records are used in any legal proceedings.

4.4.4.3 Observations

The design and engineering of chain-of-custody systems should consider the following input when developing a conceptual system model that incorporates biometrics techniques.

- What are the medical supply entities that must be positively protected? Will it be at the level of a container storing medical devices, crates, or pallets of pharmaceuticals being moved, individual boxes of biological material, or individual tubes of blood specimen?

- How can the biometrics authentication method be incorporated cost-effectively? If we are tracking a container or pallets, we can identify workers (using biometrics) who are handling the container and tracking the records associated with the container. If we are tracking a box, we can use a device similar to that which Fedex or UPS drivers carry. For this application, continuous authentication can be accomplished by using fingerprint and voice print biometrics of the drivers or handlers who carry this device.

- The supply must be tracked from the time that it is stored into a container, through various transportation and storage stages, and until delivered to the destination custodial person.

- In order to positively identify a person using biometrics method, we need to create a biometrics database that stores the individual biometrics data. This could be a large database since potentially thousands of individuals could touch any medical supply in the medical supply chain. The systems engineer needs to consider the storage, distribution, and integrity of this biometrics database; design the verification system to meet the performance response time requirement; and develop the strategy to ensure the biometrics database can scale to the desired level after deployment.

- The pharmaceutical industry is worldwide. Hence, potentially, we need to track all the biological components throughout the world. This scale of implementation can face many challenges. For example, political or trade agreements and treaties might be needed to exchange the biometrics data.

- Larger number of adversaries—we may need to face threats from multinational criminal organizations. They have the means to craft work-around method for the biometrics. The potential profits for crime are high.

- Long period of transportation—if the container is traveling on the international sea lanes of communication, additional methods must be used to ensure the container cannot be tampered while on the ship.

For additional considerations, please refer to Bartol (2014), the NIST Special Publication 800-161, Supply Chain Risk Management Practices for Federal Information Systems and Organizations (Boyens et al. 2015, Hammond 2015), and ISO/IEC 27036 (ISO/IEC 27036-1 2014), Information security for supplier relationships. The ISO/IEC standard has three parts: Part 1: Overview and concepts, Part 2: Requirements, and Part 3: Guidelines for information and communication technology supply chain security (ISO/IEC 27036-3 2013, ISO/IEC 27036-2 2014).

4.4.5 Prevention of Prescription Abuse

4.4.5.1 Background

There exists an epidemic of drug addiction where patients become habitual users of pain killer medication (Daum et al. 2015, Kolodny et al. 2015).

4.4.5.2 Scenario

A physician may have prescribed strong prescription to reduce the pain level for a patient. Through long-term use or other causes, patients may begin to abuse the prescription by taking higher dosage or more frequent intake of the medication. This leads to the need for more prescriptions to obtain this controlled substance. The patient can visit multiple doctors to obtain these prescriptions, and then go to different pharmacies to feed on the habit. Using biometrics associated with doctor visits, patient's true identity can be confirmed while the controlled substance prescription can be submitted to a central database. Applying this method, we can verify that the patients are not abusing the system to have access to the drug.

4.4.5.3 Observations

We need to consider several issues when applying this method of controlling prescription distribution. First, who is to construct, manage, and monitor this centralized database? Access to this database may reveal competitive intelligence where competing pharmaceutical distributors or manufacturers can determine the sales information. Employers may discover which workers to let go, due to the physical nature of a job. Government agencies may use this information beyond regulating the controlled substances.

Second, this method does not prevent multiple persons going to doctors for treatment while obtaining prescriptions for others. If an addicted person has family members or friends who pretend to have the pain symptoms, doctors' prescriptions to multiple persons may not raise the alarm of the drug abuse of a specific person.

Third, we do not want this method to prevent individuals from shopping for a physician that can give them a true, unbiased second opinion (without influence from prior doctor opinion) or for finding a physician that meets their needs—better expertise, consistent with personal beliefs.

4.4.6 Usage during a Disaster

4.4.6.1 Background

When a disaster hits a region, there needs to be a backup mechanism to the biometrics.

4.4.6.2 Scenario

There is an earthquake or a massive fire where the local communication channels are down. During this period, doctor's office, laboratories, pharmacies, hospitals, and other related facilities are disconnected from the biometrics database. Will biometrics for health care still be effective? Should we rely entirely on electronic data? Should some biometrics be encoded and carried with the individual? If the biometrics authentication prevents the continued healthcare operation just as we need them the most, it can jeopardize the welfare of citizens.

4.4.6.3 Observations

The designer of the system can consider the three authentication parameters (what you are, what you know, and what you have) to determine the operational rules during a declared emergency. For example, during the emergency, what are the minimum authentication processes that still need to be done? Even during an emergency, we need to be reasonably assured who are the various stakeholders carrying out the various actions. After the emergency, we can consolidate various actions that have taken place during the emergency.

Another potential disaster and emergent threat to the biometrics system could be a cyberattack against the critical infrastructure of the nation. When that occurs, additional work-arounds must be considered. Different disasters may need different sets of operational procedures, which should be in place as part of the biometrics system design.

4.4.7 Quarantine Control

4.4.7.1 Background

When there is an epidemic, the health department may institute a quarantine to prevent the spread of the contagion.

4.4.7.2 Scenario

Individuals may be declared to be quarantined and travel is limited. To enforce this quarantine, we can apply the biometrics to check individuals who wish to pass any quarantine line. No need to carry any paperwork for authorization to pass any checkpoint. We can use the biometrics information and a central database to determine the clearance of any individual who may pass through any quarantine line. The quarantine database can be updated by authorized healthcare officials, for control of travel from one location to another.

4.4.7.3 Observations

Healthcare researchers can have the added benefit of keeping treatment and other genetic information associated with an epidemic to determine the most effective treatment.

During the Ebola outbreak that started in 2014, no effective quarantine was put into effect. It is possible that a potentially large percentage of a population must be placed into a quarantine area or put under observation. If biometrics is to be used for quarantine purpose, designers must consider scalability, performance, and update control.

Some healthcare workers may be in a protective suit. If that is the case, then many biometrics may not work well. Voice can be muffled, fingerprint and other physical characteristics cannot be visible, and gait movement can be restricted. But other characteristics such as iris scan and other facial metrics may still be used as the facial mask is still transparent.

4.4.8 Scenario Common Themes and General Observations

Although each of these scenarios is quite different, there are some common themes and lessons learned, which we can apply.

- In order to use biometrics, an infrastructure for biometrics database, registration, communication, and verification must be established.

- Not all biometrics can be used in all cases. Specific biometrics should be selected as applicable to each specific situation.

- Multimodal biometrics can be useful to increase the certainty of an individual's identity match, and to ensure identification even when certain biometrics are missing or not accessible.

- Biometrics should not be the only authentication mechanism. It should be used to assist in identifying a stakeholder in the healthcare industry.

- Standards are needed to facilitate interoperability among systems and between geographic regions.

- During emergency, work-arounds must be applied such that biometrics can still contribute to the accurate authentication of players in the healthcare system.

4.5 BIOMETRICS IN HEALTH CARE: SUMMARY AND CONCLUSIONS

In this chapter, we have made the case for using biometrics in healthcare applications. The diversity of stakeholder distributed across a large geographic area provides a basis for the justification of using biometrics for authentication. There are many characteristics of this field that permit and can benefit by the use of various biometrics. There are also many challenges that need to be considered before adopting this authentication method in the healthcare industry.

We developed and described a framework for biometrics in the healthcare system. Basic elements of this framework were identified. Healthcare processes that incorporate biometric processes and biometrics technologies were elaborated. Factors for consideration were presented. Due to its essential and central role, we highlighted the application of digital signatures using the biometrics authentication. When adopting the biometrics, the stakeholders should consider the aspects included in this framework so that they are incorporated into the healthcare system architecture.

Finally, we provided several possible scenarios where biometrics can be applied to the healthcare industry. In each scenario, we augmented the application with observations on the effective use of biometrics.

In the future, biometrics identification in health care is likely to play an increasingly important role. As can be seen from a variety of scenarios, there are a wide range of considerations and challenges that must be addressed in order to ensure that the use of biometrics technologies and processes are wisely deployed in health care. Although no attempt to be exhaustive, the scenarios show how the biometrics could be incorporated into various medical settings. Readers can extend these scenarios when applying biometrics in their systems.

REFERENCES

AHIMA 2011. Retention and destruction of health information. Appendix C: AHIMA's Recommended Retention Standards. (Updated August 2011). Retrieved August 15, 2015, http://library.ahima.org/xpedio/groups/public/documents/ahima/bok1_049250.hcsp?dDocName=bok1_049250

Alrehily, A.D., A.F. Alotaibi, S.B. Almutairy, M.S. Alqhtani, and J. Kar 2015. Conventional and improved digital signature scheme: A comparative study. *Journal of Information Security*, 6(1), 59–67.

American Health Information Management Association (AHIMA) 2011. Retention and destruction of health information. Retrieved August 21, 2015, http://library.ahima.org/xpedio/groups/public/documents/ahima/bok1_049252.hcsp?dDocName=bok1_049252

American Health Information Management Association (AHIMA) 2015. Practice brief—Retention of health information. Retrieved August 15, 2015, http://library.ahima.org/xpedio/groups/public/documents/ahima/bok1_012546.pdf

Ashbourn, J. 2015. *Practical Biometrics: From Aspiration to Implementation*, 2nd ed. Springer-Verlag, London.

Association of State and Territorial Health Officials (ASTHO) 2005. Information management for state health officials—HIPAA privacy rule implementation in state public health agencies—Successes, challenges, and future needs. Retrieved November 2015, http://www.astho.org/Programs/e-Health/Privacy/Materials/HIPAA-Privacy-Rule-Implementation-in-State-Public-Health-Agencies

Bartol, N. 2014. Cyber supply chain security practices DNA—Filling in the puzzle using a diverse set of disciplines, *Technovation*, 34(7), 354–361.

Bazin, A. 2006. *On Probabilistic Models for Object Description and Classification*. University of Southamptom, United Kingdom.

Benefield, H., G. Ashkanazi, and R.H. Rozensky 2006. Communication and records: HIPPA issues when working in health care settings. *Professional Psychology: Research and Practice*, 37(3), 273–277.

Boyens, J. et al. 2015. Supply Chain Risk Management Practices for Federal Information Systems and Organizations. NIST Special Publication 800-161, April.

Bradley, D. 2004. HIPAA compliance efforts. *Pediatric Emergency Care*, 20(1), 68–70.

Daum, A.M., O. Berkowitz, and J.A. Renner, Jr. 2015. The evolution of chronic opioid therapy and recognizing addiction. *JAAPA: Official Journal of the American Academy of Physician Assistants*, 28(5), 23–27.

Department of Health and Human Services 2011. Metadata standards to support nationwide electronic health information exchange. *Federal Register*, 76(153), August 9.

FBI IAFIS. The Integrated Automated Fingerprint Identification System (IAFIS). Press release. Retrieved August 17, 2015, http://www.fbi.gov/hq/cjisd/iafis.htm

Federal Bureau of Investigation (FBI) 2015. *Houston Man Sentenced for Conspiring to Steal from Home Equity Lines of Credit of Unsuspecting Victims*. U.S. Attorney's Office, Southern District of Texas. Retrieved August 17, 2015, https://www.fbi.gov/houston/press-releases/2015/houston-man-sentenced-for-conspiring-to-steal-from-home-equity-lines-of-credit-of-unsuspecting-victims

Federal Trade Commission (FTC) 2011. *Medical Identity Theft, FAQs for Health Care Providers and Health Plans*. Federal Trade Commission, BCP Business Center. January 2011, business.ftc.gov, https://www.ftc.gov/system/files/documents/plain-language/bus75-medical-identity-theft-faq-health-care-health-plan.pdf

Gantt, K. 2012 Privacy Impact Assessment for the Automated Biometric Identification System (IDENT). Department of Homeland Security. Retrieved August 17, 2015, http://www.dhs.gov/sites/default/files/publications/privacy/PIAs/privacy_pia_usvisit_ident_appendixj_jan2013.pdf

Goodrich, M.T. et al. 2011. *Introduction to Computer Security.* Addison-Wesley, Boston.

Hammond, B. 2015. NIST Offers Guidance for Minimizing Security Risks to ICT Supply Chains. Cybersecurity Policy Report.

Harmon, K. 2009. Can you lose your fingerprints? *Scientific American,* May 29.

Health IT Policy Committee 2012. Tang, P., Vice Chair, Letter to Department of Health and Human Services on Broad Charge for the Privacy & Security Tiger Team. Retrieved August 15, 2015, http://www.healthit.gov/sites/default/files/transmittal092512psttrecommendationsprovider-authentication.pdf.

Heun, D. 2014, Sep 10. Apple makes its move in mobile payments. *American Banker.* Retrieved August 17, 2015, http://search.proquest.com/docview/1561034057?accountid=9840.

Hyla, T., I. El Fray, W. Mackow, and J. Pejas 2012. Long-term preservation of digital signatures for multiple groups of related documents. *IET Information Security,* 6(3), 219–227.

IDT911. 2015. Data Breach Reports. Retrieved August 11, 2015, http://idt911.com/

ISO/IEC 27036-1. 2014. Information technology—Security techniques—Information security for supplier relationships—Part 1: Overview and concepts.

ISO/IEC 27036-2. 2014. Information technology—Security techniques—Information security for supplier relationships—Part 2: Requirements.

ISO/IEC 27036-3. 2013. Information technology—Security techniques—Information security for supplier relationships—Part 3: Guidelines for information and communication technology supply chain security.

Kolodny, A., et al. 2015. The prescription opioid and heroin crisis: A public health approach to an epidemic of addiction. *Annual Review of Public Health,* 36(1), 559–574.

Kung, K. 1995. RFC on Digital Signature Issues. Open Software Foundation Security Working Group, June 26.

Luhby, T. 1997, Nov 05. Biometric scanners to identify clients, employees shrink to mouse size series: 10. *American Banker.* Retrieved August 17, 2015, http://search.proquest.com/docview/249817920?accountid=9840

McKinnon, J.D., and L. Saunders 2015. Breach at IRS Exposes Returns. *Wall Street Journal* (Eastern edition), May 27. ProQuest. Web. Retrieved November 10, 2015 http://search.proquest.com/docview/1683306104?accountid=9840

O'Connor, L.J. 2013. The Health Research Exchange: A collaborative model for improving participation in health research. PhD thesis Computer Science 0201, UCLA.

Office of the Inspector General, Social Security Administration (SSA OIG) 2015. New Medicare Cards Will Not Display Social Security Numbers. April 29.

Perlin, J. et al. 2011. Health IT Standards Committee Metadata Power Team Recommendations. Retrieved August 15, 2015, http://www.ahier.net/2011/06/metadata-power-team-recommendations.html

Ponnapalli, H.K.B. and A. Saxena 2013. A Digital Signature Architecture for Web Apps. *IT Professional*, 15(2), 42–49.

President Remark 2015. United States: Remarks by the President at the Federal Trade Commission-Federal Trade Commission-Constitution Center-Washington, DC. *Asia News Monitor*, Nov 10. ProQuest. Web. Retrieved November 10, 2015, http://search.proquest.com/docview/1731914500?accountid=9840.

Redgrave, J.M. et al. 2007. *The Sedona Principles (Second Edition) Best Practices Recommendations & Principles for Addressing Electronic Document Production.* The Sedona Conference, June 2007.

Smith, C.E. 2008. Human microchip implantation. *Journal of Technology Management & Innovation*, 3(3), 151–160.

Smith, D.F. et al. 2015. Face recognition on consumer devices: Reflections on replay attacks. *IEEE Transaction on Information Forensics and Security*, 10(4), 734–745.

Stallings, W. 2014. *Crytography and Network Security.* Prentice-Hall, New Jersey.

Swanson, E. 2015. Visa and Samsung Bring Mobile Payments to the New Samsung Galaxy S6. *Business Wire.* Retrieved from http://www.business-wire.com/news/home/20150301005067/en/Visa-Samsu.

Tavakoli, N. and M. Jahanbakhsh 2013. Investigation of retention and destruction process of medical records in the hospitals and codifying appropriate guidelines. *Journal of Education and Health Promotion*, 2, 17.

Tavakoli, N. et al. 2013. Investigation of retention and destruction of medical records in the hospitals and codifying appropriate guidelines. *J Educ Health Promot*, 2, 17. http://www.ncbi.nlm.nih.gov/pmc/articles/PMC3778649/?report=printable

Tilstone, W., Savage, K., and Clark, L. 2006. *Forensic Science: An Encyclopedia of History, Methods, and Techniques.* ABC-CLIO, Santa Barbara, California.

US General Services Administration. Privacy Laws, Regulations, and more. Retrieved August 14, 2015, http://www.gsa.gov/portal/content/104250

Warren, Z. 2015. IRS a Data Breach Victim, 104,000 Taxpayers' Records Stolen. *Inside Counsel. Breaking News.*

White, J. et al. 2015. Recommendations for Health IT Standards Committee. Retrieved August 15, 2015. https://www.healthit.gov/facas/health-it-standards-committee/health-it-standards-committee-recommendations-national-coordinator

White, P.J. and J. Daniel 2009. Privacy and Security Solutions for Interoperable Health Information Exchange—Report on State Medical Record Access Laws. RTI Project Number 0209825.000.015.100, RTI International, August 2009.

CHAPTER 5

Biometrics in Social Media Applications

Charles Li

CONTENTS

5.1 WIDESPREAD SOCIAL MEDIA ADOPTION

The use of the Internet and social media has become pervasive in all aspects of our global society. Social media is a new frontier applicable to virtually all walks of life. Its use and operation is relevant globally to individuals, technology providers, governments, criminals, terrorists, and professionals such as social scientists, scientific researchers, salespersons, publishers, and entertainers. We are embracing an exciting new era of the unknown. Personal identification and identity verification have become that much more important because we human beings have lost a fundamental element of social activity through physical interaction. Much of what we do is now virtual via remote electronic interaction. As users of the Internet and social media, we want secure and reliable identity techniques that ensure privacy, secure financial transactions, and authenticate social media users. Biometric identification technologies have their roots in law enforcement applications. However, with the increasing need to fight global terrorism and the availability of more powerful and lower cost computing platforms and new sensor technologies, biometrics have become more reliable and commoditized. Biometric identification technologies offer the ability to reliably verify or determine the identity of individuals both in person and online. This chapter will focus on the application of biometrics for the purposes of identity authentication and data mining. Specifically, this chapter will discuss that biometric technologies can facilitate data mining in various web and social media applications (e.g., business/marketing and law enforcement/intelligence); how biometric technologies incorporated into social media applications can enhance the utility of the applications (e.g., face recognition that can be used to help search for a desired photo in a photo library); and how biometric technologies can be applied to assure user identity (security).

The fingerprint has been widely studied by researchers, and is used in mobile phones and desktop computers; due to its popular application and wide discussion, we will only briefly discuss the fingerprint in this chapter. Biometric modalities such as face, iris, keystroke dynamics, mouse dynamics, and several other behavioral biometrics will be the primary focus of discussion. Since face images are the most prevalent biometric data existing in social media and potentially provide the most identity-related value, this chapter will discuss face recognition extensively to cover the basic approach, current research, challenges, and resources available.

Finally, biometric spoofing occurs when an individual tries to evade identification or masquerade as another individual. This is an inherent challenge not unique to social media; however, social media is prone to spoofing because participants are generally remote and not physically visible to one another. The topic of biometric spoofing has been omitted from this chapter because it is still emerging and would require extensive discussion that tends to be application specific [1].

5.1.1 Widespread Use of Social Media and Networking

In the past decade, the emergence and maturation of social media tools based on both website and mobile platforms have created a profound impact on people's lives whether they are an executive, a merchant, a teacher, a student, an IT developer, a reporter, or a politician. We use social media tools for sending text messages, writing blogs, sharing locations and photos, exchanging money, banking, taking classes, and making reservations. People use social media tools in the cyber society including cyber gathering, cyber parties, and cyber workshops. A whole new social phenomenon has been emerging as a result of maturing social media tools, enhancing people's participation, increasing the level of trust put in by normal users, and enriching the number of activities occurring in cyber society. To put this into perspective, the current world population is 7.2 billion, and approximately 40% of that population uses the Internet. Among the Internet users of mobile and desktop platforms, the number registered is around a billion. Table 5.1 shows a selected list of major social networking websites and their registered users, illustrating the proliferation of Internet and social media usage.

As shown in the above table, social media users generate large amounts of data.

The majority of data is multilingual unstructured text, provided in the form of blogs, microblogs, and instant messages. Most importantly, the amount of photos, videos, and user activities presented on social media make it possible to collect a large number of media behavior biometrics, of great interest to commercial companies, research institutions, and the government.

TABLE 5.1   Popular Social Media Platforms and Estimated Registered Users (Alphabetic Order)

Name	Description and Data Available	Registered Users (Estimated for 2015)
Facebook	General: photos, videos, blogs, apps	1,590,000,000
Google+	General: photos, videos, blogs, apps	500,000,000
Habbo	General for teens. Over 31 communities worldwide Chat room and user profiles	268,000,000
Instagram	Photo and video	300,000,000
LinkedIn	Business and professional networking	400,000,000
Qzone	General, mainland China users	645,000,000
Sina Weibo	General, mainland China users	503,000,000
Tumblr	Microblogging platform and social networking website	282,000,000
Twitter	General, Microblogging, RSS, updates	332,000,000
VK	General, including music upload, listening, and search. Popular in Russia and former Soviet republics	280,000,000

Note: This table doesn't represent a ranking based on any criteria; they are popular social media sites. The numbers are derived from many resources and estimated to the best of the author's knowledge at the time of publication.

To illustrate the scale of data that is relevant to biometrics applications, we estimated the data scale by comparing among a few large biometrics systems and potential biometrics data collected via mobile devices shown in Figure 5.1 by using image size of a face 200 KB, a pair of irises of 10 KB, and a set of 10 flat fingerprints of 1 MB. As a result, this has created great opportunities for biometrics adoption.

5.1.2 Social Media Landscape and Demand

To understand the role biometrics play in social media and all other involved players, we need to understand the landscape and the relationships among the players (Figure 5.2). Social media categorically serves the follow functions:

1. Sharing and publishing—such as Pinterest, Facebook, YouTube, Slideshare, and Instagram

2. Discussing through instant messaging and chat forums—such as include Reddit, Facebook, and Quora

3. Networking—including LinkedIn, renren, and WeChat

DHS IDENT over 150 million identities;
Over 250,000 transactions daily
~100–300 Terabytes

ID cards/border crossings/benefits/multiple instances
7,000,000,000x (10 Print 0.5⊠1 MB + Face 200 KB + IRIS KB)
7 Exabytes

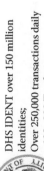

FBI NGI ~ over 100 million fingerprints and more coming plus faces/iris
~100–200 Terabytes

Prolific usage of mobile phones
7 billion mobile phones
7 Exabytes of behavior data

US DoS has in the range of 100 million faces and others
~10–50 Terabytes

1 Billion arrivals 2012 world wide
United States⊠100⊠200 million international arrivals 2012

1 Exabyte traveler data

EU VIS biometrics matching system (BMS) at 70 million individuals and 100 K daily enro lment
~100 Terabytes

Unique identification authority of India (UIDAI) plans to enroll 1.2 billion citizens. (UID Program) (enroll million/day; half billion by 2014) 3–4 Exabytes biometrics and biographic data

FIGURE 5.1   Illustrative data scale of biometrics applications.

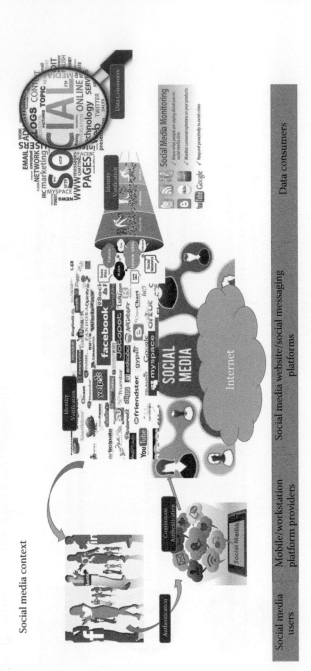

FIGURE 5.2 Different players in social media context.

From the perspective of the industrial domain, social media spreads across industries extending from media providers, commerce platforms, and service companies to technology providers. Some big players in this domain include AOL, Yahoo, Google, Tencent, and Alibaba just to name a few. In addition, some virtual meeting tools like GoToMeeting, WebEx, and Microsoft Lync can benefit from face and voice biometrics to verify participating identities.

The two distinctive groups of players in social media are data providers (individuals who communicate via social media) and data consumers (individuals who analyze data available on social media and the Internet). Social media users want friendly and reliable methods to protect them from fraudsters. On the other hand, data users such as emerging technology and software companies rely on social media data being authentic and accurate to

1. Track the actions of competitors, consumers, and adversaries

2. Engage customers in commerce

3. Market promotions of products and services

4. Perform analytics to study all aspects of social media, to include the users and data content

5. Better understand how social media can be used to influence its participants

In addition, commercial companies, citizen service entities, governments, and intelligence agencies can all benefit from identifying individuals as they perform these functions. To be useful, identification doesn't necessarily require the use of sensitive personally identifiable information; it may be sufficient to know fundamental characteristics of an individual and that various data items simply came from the same individual. In fact, current social media analytics techniques can aggregate data from different contexts and can build personality profiles, which combined with biometrics, allows drilling down into the data on a personal level. In this case, anonymity may be acceptable in certain social media exchanges and biometrics might be a way to assure that two or more identities are simply unique. Biometrics is the enabling technology to achieve all these objectives. Technologists are finding new ways to allow users to conveniently and securely gain access to secure devices and areas even though the usability remains the most challenging issue. Mobile and platform developers, such as Samsung and Apple, are continuously working on sophisticated biometrics to improve security without compromising user convenience.

5.2 SOCIAL MEDIA AND BIOMETRIC IDENTITY

Social media usage has become so widespread that it has created new opportunities, giving rise to many new technologies but also bringing about challenges at the same time. Among them are demands for easier and more secure access to users' blogs, chatrooms, and websites. As a result of the proliferation of social media, large amounts of data about users and their behavior and activities have been generated. Commercial companies, special interest groups, and the government have started data mining social media biometrics in order to identify users in the wild world of social media society. Biometric technologies, the primary identity assertion technique, can be used for both user authentication and identification.

Biometric development accelerated as a result of the tragedies of September 11, 2001. Prior to that, biometrics was primarily used in government and regulated industries including criminal justice, banking, border protection, critical infrastructure protection, and in the vetting process of critical infrastructure employees. According to many market research reports and industry projections from various market research groups,* biometrics development and application will be a primary growth sector in social media and mobile applications in the next decade.

In the last 10 years, biometric application in social media has been accelerated because of the following factors:

1. Commoditized capture sensors and matching technologies

2. Expiration of major patents

3. Development and adoption of biometric standards

The following sections will discuss some key concepts and characteristics of biometrics pertinent to social media.

---

* There are quite a few market research reports by industry groups yearly; some are based on expert opinions, economic data, oil export values, very few are based on actual planning data. So as not to provide a biased view of the market, I have intentionally not provided any specific report names.

5.2.1 Fundamental Biometric Concepts

In order to discuss biometrics applications in social media, this section describes some basic concepts that are pertinent throughout this chapter.

Biometrics is the science of identifying, or verifying the identity of, a person based on physical or behavioral characteristics. The biometric modality needs to be measurable on the basis of physical and/or behavioral characteristics and to be used to verify the identity of an individual.

Person identity and biometrics—typically, there are three traditional ways to verify the identity of a person:

1. What you have—physical tokens including keys, passports, and smartcards

2. What you know—personal knowledge including secret (passwords, pass phrases, etc.) and nonsecret knowledge (user id, mother's maiden name, favorite color, etc.)

3. Who you are—personal biometrics including physical (fingerprints, face, iris, etc.) and behavioral (walk, keystroke pattern, vocal characteristics, etc.)

Physical tokens such as smartcards can be lost, stolen, duplicated, or forgotten, and passwords can be forgotten, shared, observed, or broken (or guessed). Generally speaking, biometric identification characteristics are unique to an individual, are measurable, and remain fixed over the individual's or specific application's lifetime (a property called "permanence"). Biometrics are used to establish or verify a person's physical identity. As shown in Figure 5.3, some modalities are more popular than others due to different usage needs.

In the context of social media, application users constantly face a dilemma: demanding privacy protection and requesting easy access to social media apps and/or websites.

As you will discover throughout this chapter, users can authenticate themselves through various means to access social media accounts. Initially, solutions were influenced by mainstream biometric techniques: physical biometrics such as faces, fingerprints, and irises, which all require quality sensors on mobile devices. In fact, early desktop-type applications also required high quality, discrete sensors. As sensors have become higher

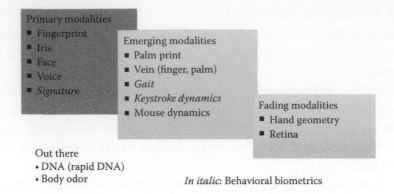

Out there
• DNA (rapid DNA)
• Body odor   *In italic:* Behavioral biometrics

FIGURE 5.3   Biometric technology types.

quality and more miniaturized, they have been integrated into mobile or handheld devices. Behavioral biometrics, including voice, mouse dynamics, and keystroke dynamics, are further investigated and found to be viable authentication modalities.

5.2.2 Social Media and Biometric Data

There are some intrinsic challenges that accompany social media data collection for both verification and identification purposes due to the unconstrained capture environment. These characteristics include

1. The data collected are frequently low quality due to unhabituated users and an unconstrained collection environment. As a result, verification is feasible; however, large-scale identification is a challenge.

2. Much behavioral data can be collected; however, technology is not yet mature enough to use the behavioral data for authentication and identification in real operations.

3. Biometric data collection requires quality sensor capabilities and extra computing resources. As a result, it creates latency and usability challenges for users.

Due to the large number of social media users and the amount of data collected, there is a fundamental accuracy challenge when identification is performed using data collected from social media. We can call this a challenge—biometric performance on a giga scale. For an individual to be enrolled into a biometric system, an $N \times N$ search is performed initially to ensure no duplicate identity is enrolled, which is called the deduplication process. If we perform a "brute force" deduplication, the challenge looks like the following:

1. If the system performs a cumulative deduplication, this is a combination problem and the total number of biometric sample comparisons is $N(N-1)/2$

2. If the system deduplicates a population of 100 million, then the enrollment results in 4,999,999,950,000,000 checks required

3. The task above needs 15 years to complete if the matching speed is 10 million matches per second—an expensive and challenging endeavor

Another challenge is the biometric accuracy.

1. If the false match rate (FMR) was one identification false match per million, there would be 500,000 false matches with one million enrollment population (deduplicate)

2. If the system needed to enroll 100 million subjects, there would be 500 million false matches

3. Many social media websites have hundreds of millions users

The question is posed as what you do with the 500 million false matches; this results in a mission impossible.

5.2.3 Biometric Processes Performance Metrics

Social media as a system, which consists of users, system components, and data collected, has some measurable performance metrics when using biometrics to verify or identify users. Social media application data collected are mainly for authentication and/or identification purposes. The three fundamental identity-related processes are enrollment, verification, and identification:

1. Enrollment is, for a known individual, when a high quality biometric sample is obtained for each modality (e.g., face or voice) of interest and stored in a database of biometric samples.

2. Verification is commonly described as a 1-to-1 matching process and is typically used for access control. An individual's newly captured

biometric sample is matched against the biometric sample on file for claimed identity. Classically, receiver operating characteristic (ROC) depicts the accuracy for verification purpose.

3. Identification is commonly described as a 1-to-N matching process and is typically applied to determining an unknown identity, determining if someone is on a security watch list, and for deduplication of identities when enrolling biometric samples in a database. An individual's newly captured biometric sample (referred to as the probe) is searched against a database of biometric samples, each of which is associated with a unique identity.

- For user-driven searches and forensic analysis, the accuracy is based on the number of top-ranked candidates' retrievals and what percentage of probe searches return the probe's gallery mate within the top rank-ordered results. The cumulative match characteristics (CMCs) depict this performance measurement because it reports the percentage of probes identified within a given rank.

- For large-scale systems, human experts examine search results that produce a matcher score exceeding a preset match threshold. There is a tradeoff between false alarms—FMR and misses—false nonmatch rate (FNMR). These measurements are generally compared using a detection error tradeoff plot.

To understand how to implement and understand biometrics with social media platforms, we need to examine the metrics and graphs specifically used for the biometrics data collected from social media and networking.

Score probability graph—the probability graph in Figure 5.4 illustrates distributions of genuine biometrics matching scores versus imposters matching score frequency distribution. The threshold line indicates false matches and false nonmatches. With low quality social media data (both verification and identification), there would be large number of false match and false nonmatch.

ROC curve—for a verification system, this graph in Figure 5.5 illustrates the verification accuracy—(1-FNMR) versus the operating point of FMR. This is a good measurement for the authentication type of application. For social media users, the false acceptance rate needs to be raised higher in order for "friendlier" access to the device or platform.

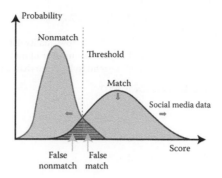

FIGURE 5.4　Probability graph: False nonmatch is also referred to as type I error and false match is also referred to as type II error in conventional statistics.

CMC curve—for an identification system, this is a measurement of accuracy to identify an individual in the top-ranked matches. The graph in Figure 5.6 shows the identification accuracy—(1-FNMR)—with predefined gallery size and number of matches returned. In case of data mining in social media collection, this measures the chance that an individual can be identified from the social media data. For examples, it answers the question of what the chances are that someone's face will be found in the sea of data collected on Facebook.

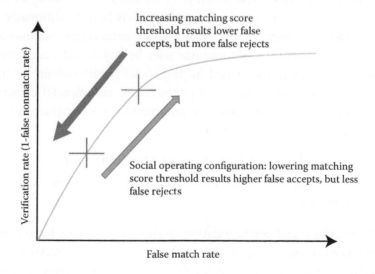

FIGURE 5.5　ROCs curve.

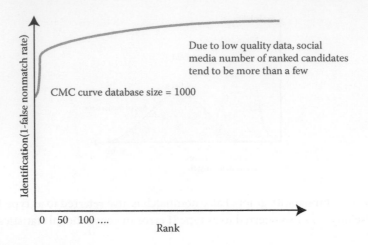

FIGURE 5.6   CMC curve.

5.3 BIOMETRIC TECHNOLOGIES APPLICABLE TO SOCIAL MEDIA

This section discusses the biometric modalities most applicable to social media based on the considerations and characteristics already discussed.

The discussion focuses on each technology's underlying basis, application in a social media context, operational challenges, and future expectations. Biometrics must support authentication on all applicable platforms including mobile, tablet, and desktop. In addition to providing authentication capabilities at times when a password has been traditionally used (such as at login), biometrics can facilitate periodic repeat or continuous authentication—continuously monitor user behavior and reauthenticate periodically—when implemented on the social media website or in the mobile application. From different perspectives, commercial companies and government can collect, analyze, and monitor user interactive behavior and data stored at social media sites.

5.3.1 Conceptual Architecture of Social Media Platform

In social media, there are two types of biometric applications as discussed in previous sections:

1. Verification and authentication authorize the user to access the social media site or apps. This includes two steps (a) initial authentication using sensors on the platform and (b) continuous authentication based on behavior biometrics.

2. Identification for forensic analysis or large-scale recognition applications by consuming the social media. Examples include videos, photos, blogs from Facebook, Google+, and Flicker.

In Figure 5.7 of a social media conceptual architecture for biometrics, users use apps on the mobile device or web browser to access social media websites; in both cases, the user can be authenticated using biometrics. All the data collected on social media activities are stored in the data store(s); companies or government can apply analytics on the data through stages "collect," "process," "analyze," and "recognize" for identity analysis.

5.3.2 Fingerprint Recognition

Many books and articles have been written on fingerprint technologies and their applications [2]; in this section, we will not cover many details due to widely available information. As shown in Figure 5.8, fingerprint technology was the first adopted biometric modality for computer authentication; since then, from separate single-finger sensors to embedded swipe sensors, fingerprint capture sensors became widely available on most computer and mobile platforms. In recent years, fingerprint technology has become further commoditized on phones, tablets, and computers. Even though fingerprint technology has been used in criminal justice applications historically, making the technology more publicly acceptable and removing the "criminal stigma" of fingerprints has helped further adoption of fingerprint for both mobile and computer platforms authentication purposes. Social media users can leverage the fingerprint technology enabled platforms for initial authentication and have access to social media apps and websites. However, fingerprint technology usage in social media has vulnerabilities similar to those of other biometrics modalities. Especially when implemented in an unsupervised fashion, measures must be taken to mitigate the risk of spoofing. Furthermore, some known challenges related to fingerprint image capture remain to be addressed, including contaminated fingertips, ghost images, oil residue left on the sensor surface, and improper finger pressure on the sensor surface. In fact, study [3] shows that the fingerprint unlock screen for the iPhone suffers from wet fingers and usability remains a challenge. Therefore, fingerprint technology for social media authentication still need improvement; and also, it would be interesting

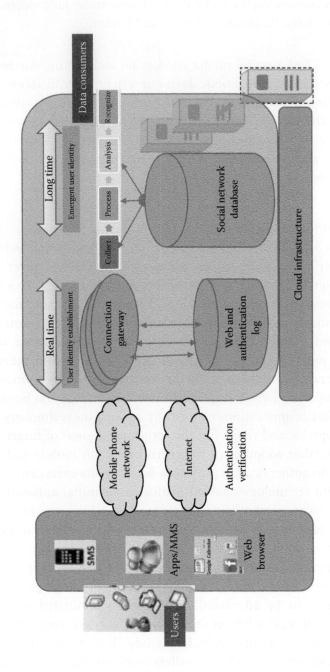

FIGURE 5.7 Social media conceptual architecture from an identity perspective.

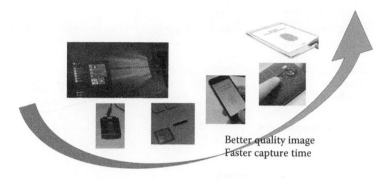

Better quality image
Faster capture time

FIGURE 5.8   Fingerprint sensors used for desktop and mobile platforms.

to see more studies on the performance of the system/sensor false reject and false accept rates.

5.3.3 Traditional Face Recognition

Face recognition has been the most researched and most useful biometric technology with regard to social media. Face recognition is noninvasive and supported by many commercial products; users can conveniently use face recognition for authentication by leveraging the on-board camera sensor on a workstation or mobile phone. In the context illustrated in Figure 5.7, cameras on either desktop or mobile platforms can capture the facial images that can be used either with on-board facial verification or with cloud-based services. From the data consumer perspective, users upload facial images or video footage into social media sites as part of their everyday sharing of information with family, friends, and colleagues; meanwhile, those data can be consumed by tools for data mining and analysis, including face recognition for various purposes, including law enforcement, marketing, and intelligence gathering.

Many commercial face recognition systems have been developed and enhanced significantly over last several decades. Typically, still images or video frames are input to the face recognition system that then process the image data through stages of face detection (also referred to as segmentation), feature extraction, and face recognition (matching) to complete the verification (1-to-1) or identification (1-to-N) cycle as shown in Figure 5.9.

1. *Face detection.* Usually a multistage algorithm is used, initially, to rapidly search for faces in low-resolution. The system switches to a high-resolution search only after a head-like shape is detected.

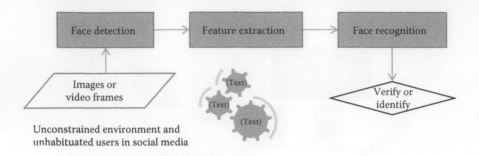

FIGURE 5.9   Stages of face recognition.

In social media, this process may be hampered by poor image quality due to unconstrained imaging environments and unhabituated users. Poor habituation also relates to users not knowing how to obtain the best image quality from their cameras in the environments they are operating (e.g., backlighting and low light).

2. *Feature extraction.* The system detects image facial features and encodes them into a features template. This coding process allows for comparison of the newly acquired facial data to previously stored facial data. In the future, this step may be dramatically accelerated with faster and more capable electronic chip technology and advanced processing algorithms, some of which may be implemented in hardware.

3. *Face recognition.* Holistic templates, feature geometry, or hybrid are typical approaches for this step.

At this present state of technology, most social media authentication requires all three stages; therefore, sufficient computing resources are needed. This poses a challenge to mobile devices and many other sensors that require processing at the point of biometrics capture. Even if the authentication is supported via a cloud identity service, the face detection stage is processed at the point of capture.

5.3.3.1 Classic Face Recognition Techniques

Social media authentication applications generate better quality face images compared with faces that are collected simply for social media sharing because users concerned with authentication are cooperative and motivated to present images that are of sufficient quality to match previously stored images. Image quality characteristics that impact the success and accuracy of face recognition include subject lighting, pose, and facial expression; facial occlusions include eyeglasses, hats, headscarves, or even background. Over the years, researchers and technology developers have developed many algorithms and techniques to support each step of the face recognition process. The next section will review some classic approaches for face recognition. The discussion focuses on face recognition for identification using images obtained from social media. Most face recognition algorithms can be categorized simply into two categories:

1. Appearance-based approaches that utilize the entire facial appearance. The methods represent a face in terms of several raw images (like eigenface or fisherface). An image is usually considered to be a high dimensional vector of features; then, statistical techniques are usually used to derive a feature space from the image distribution.

2. Model-based approach that builds a model of a human face, two-dimensional (2D) or three-dimensional (3D). These models are often morphable models—capable of being morphed—that they allow faces to be classified even when pose changes are present.

Principal component analysis (PCA) is a linear transformation algorithm in which a training set of faces is created and eigenfaces are calculated first, then the new image is projected on the eigenfaces and closeness to one of the known faces is checked. One major advantage of this approach is the dimensionality reduction in the process of removing un-useful information and precisely decomposing the face structure into orthogonal (uncorrelated) components known as eigenfaces. In Figure 5.10, feature vectors are derived from eigenfaces. Again, unknown faces are added to the training set and the eigen value is recalculated until matching is achieved. The PCA approach typically requires the full frontal face to be presented each time; otherwise, the image results in poor performance. Cooperative social media users for authentication purposes usually present frontal images.

Linear discriminant analysis (LDA) is a statistical approach for classifying samples of unknown classes based on training samples with known classes. This technique aims to maximize between-class variance (i.e., across users) and minimize within-class variance (i.e., within users). Therefore, it is better for classification than PCA techniques. LDA has its own shortcomings; PCA outperforms LDA when the training set is small

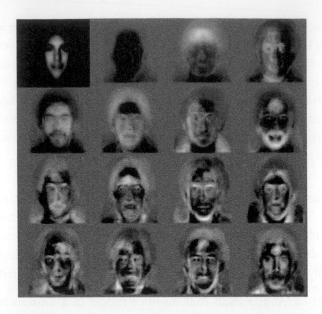

FIGURE 5.10   Standard eigenfaces: Feature vectors are derived using eigenfaces. (From Wiskott, L. et al., *IEEE PAMI*, 19(7), 1997, 775–779.)

because PCA is less sensitive to different training sets. Many LDA algorithm implementations use PCA for dimensionality reduction, that is, to solve the problem of size, and then LDA is used to maximize the discriminant power of extracting features. In Figure 5.11, where each block represents a class, there are large variances between classes, but little variance exists within classes.

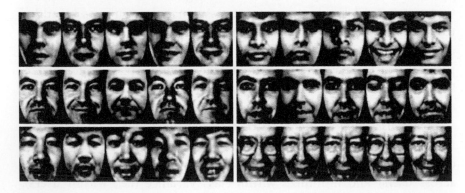

FIGURE 5.11   Examples of six classes using LDA. (From Wiskott, L. et al., *IEEE PAMI*, 19(7), 1997, 775–779.)

Elastic bunch graph matching (EBGM) is a geometry feature-based technique that analyzes local facial features and their geometric relationships. EBGM relies on the concept that real face images have many nonlinear characteristics that are not addressed by the linear analysis methods discussed earlier (PCA and LDA), such as variations in illumination (outdoor lighting vs. indoor fluorescents), pose (standing straight vs. leaning over), and expression (smile vs. frown). A Gabor wavelet transform creates a dynamic link architecture that projects the face onto an elastic grid. The Gabor jet is a node on the elastic grid, notated by circles on the image as shown in Figure 5.12, which describes the image behavior around a given pixel. A Gabor filter results in a convolution of the image; the filter is used to detect shapes and to extract features using image processing. Recognition is based on the similarity of the Gabor filter response at each Gabor node. This biologically based method using Gabor filters is a process executed in the visual cortex of higher mammals. The difficulty with this method is the requirement of accurate landmark localization, which can sometimes be achieved by combining PCA and LDA methods.

A lot of 3D approaches have gained popularity over the years due to applicability to images captured from video frames with increased accuracy; however, they are all constrained by how the images are captured and require expensive computing resources. Example techniques include facial curve-based, shape descriptor-based, holistic matching-based, and prominent regions (points)-based approaches. These algorithms can be

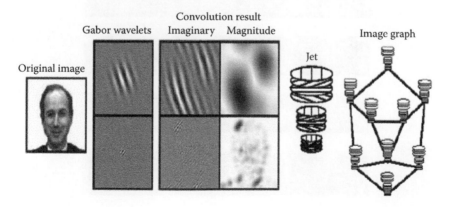

FIGURE 5.12 Face recognition using EBGM. (From Wiskott, L. et al., *IEEE PAMI*, 19(7), 1997, 775–779.)

useful for video-based face recognition because a 3D model can be constructed from multiple frames of video clips without multiple cameras or scanning sensors. With increasing processing power that brings processing to the edge (to the point of data captured), we may see 3D algorithms deployed for authentication in the future. As video capture becomes ever more pervasive, there is a realistic possibility of 3D face recognition based on multiple frames with increasing processing power and better mobile platform sensors.

5.3.3.2 Current Face Recognition Challenges

Fundamentally, face recognition is difficult due to acquisition conditions and inherent challenges including aging and weight gain or loss. Among them all, illumination and pose are the most important factors that affect accuracy. Figure 5.13 shows some face images. Regardless of authentication or identification problems, the challenges are further pronounced in social media due to the platform camera lens quality, unhabituated users, and ambient environment.

Illumination remains the biggest challenge to face recognition systems. Lighting intensity and uniformity across pixels may vary significantly, and sometimes two images of the same person may show more differences between them than compared to another person. Unfortunately, the habits of users with mobile or workstation devices that access social media regardless of lighting conditions will not change for a long time to come.

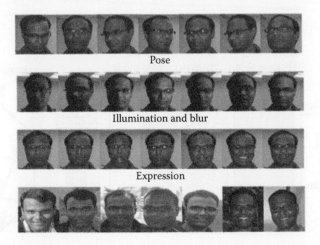

Pose

Illumination and blur

Expression

FIGURE 5.13 Examples of different poses, illumination, and expressions. (From Chellappa, R. et al., *IEEE Computer*, 2010, 46–55.)

Fortunately, researchers have developed many approaches to address this problem including

1. The heuristic approach, which leverages the natural symmetry of human faces; this approach has shown significant accuracy improvement on frontal face images under different lighting conditions.

2. The statistical approach, which produces varied results with different feature extractions. The LDA method performs better than the PCA method does. Bayesian methods and some nonlinear methods deal with illumination changes better than the linear method, like PCA and LDA.

3. The light-modeling approach, which attempts to model a lighting template in order to build illumination invariant algorithms. Some research has shown improved recognition accuracy.

4. The model-based approach, which makes intrinsic shape and texture fully independent of the light variations, examples including building 3D models.

Pose [5] is another major challenge for algorithms that work well with frontal images. Social media users pose their faces liberally (they actually seek to obtain more interesting, atypical poses) and face recognition challenges are further amplified. One approach is to make templates of all the possible pose variations taken either from multiple shots or video frames. Even though the technique improves accuracy, there is added computational cost. Another approach is to use a few images to build a model or model head rotation so that every single pose can be deducted. This is called the active appearance model. Lastly, EBGM is one geometric approach to build a sublayer pose-invariant information of a face.

In addition, there are many other challenges that are not unique to social media; these challenges include face expression, resolution of interest region (pixels in the face region, especially between the eyes), natural aging, and weight gain or loss [6]. Furthermore, additional variations can be caused by disguises or occlusions, such as glasses, hats, beards, and certain haircuts, posing even bigger challenges for identification problems in social media. Figure 5.14 is an example of facial expression variation with aging.

FIGURE 5.14 Aging with expression (Albert Einstein's face images collected from Internet).

Researchers have been improving accuracy by developing evolutionary algorithms based on known algorithms and finding the best features to extract. Approaches may apply different combinations of feature extraction methods and classifiers; some algorithms gather additional data including 3D and/or multispectral data to build better face models; some apply artificial neutral network and boosting techniques. For system developers, implementing automated image quality assessment improves the matching accuracy; however, there is a compromise on speed during the capture process.

To understand the state of art face recognition used in real operations, the NIST Face Recognition Vendor Test (FRVT) [4] is among the best resources where commercial face recognition algorithms are evaluated. Figure 5.15 shows some example images used in NIST evaluations. Most images are of the mug shot and frontal image variety.

For beginners who want to exercise face recognition, OpenCV Open source software comes with face recognition software; hence, you can start experimenting. The currently available algorithms include eigenfaces, fisherfaces, and local binary patterns histograms.

5.3.4 Face Recognition in the Wild

Some social media sites such as Facebook, Instagram, Flickr, and Google+ have collected an enormous amount of data with faces, which we want to identify. For face images captured in a controlled environment and with a frontal pose, commercial algorithms have achieved quite good results based on NIST evaluations [4]. With increasing resolution and quality of webcam and mobile phone cameras, face recognition can be a viable modality for authentication purposes. However, face images appearing in social media "wild" society can be problematic for identification since the data are frequently of very low or inconsistent quality, as shown in Figure 5.16. Such "unconstrained face images" may be described as partial face, blurred, all possible poses, all possible lighting variations, glasses, beards, and objects in front of faces. This amplifies the challenges

FIGURE 5.15 Example images used in the NIST FRVT evaluation. (a) Webcam and (b) mug shot. (From P. Grother et al., *Performance of Face Identification Algorithms*, NIST Interagency Report 8009, May 2014.)

described above as shown in Figure 5.17. While numerous research projects such as the IARPA JANUS program [9,10] have been undertaken to address "face recognition in the wild" head-on, the JANUS program is still an extremely challenging task for even the latest commercial face recognition systems. Specific details on what is meant by good quality for face images can be found in the international standard ISO/IEC 19794-5:2011 "Information technology—Biometric data interchange formats—Part 5: Face image data."

The types of faces described above are the most challenging problems for face recognition research and solution development. Fortunately, some significant progress has been made to improve the matching accuracy as a result of applying deep learning techniques [11]. Deep learning allows computational models that are composed of multiple processing layers to learn representations of data that have dramatically improved the state-of-the-art in speech recognition, visual object recognition, object detection, and many other domains such as drug discovery and genomics. Recent development of DeepFace [12] by Facebook and FaceNet [13] by Google represents state of art research; however,

FIGURE 5.16 (**See color insert.**) Faces randomly collected from the Internet.

the algorithms don't give a good indication of how they would perform under real operational conditions. At least from a research perspective, the algorithm developers have achieved significant accuracy by identifying most faces in the dataset described by Labeled Face in the Wild (LFW).

The Google team uses 128-dimensional representations from very deep networks, trained on a 260-million image data set using a *triplet loss* at the final layer. The loss separates a positive pair from a negative pair by a margin. They report results in the range of 98%, which is among the most accurate algorithms on LFW [14].

Facebook has developed two main novelties: a method for 3D face frontalization and a deep neural net trained for classification. The neural network featured 120 million parameters and was trained on 4000 identities having four million images (the nonpublic *SFC* dataset). The DeepFace networks are able to achieve an accuracy of 97% on LFW.

In addition, Tencent-BestImage [7] is a commercial system that built their solution combining an alignment system, a deep convolutional neural network with 12 convolution layers, and the joint Bayesian method for verification. The whole system was trained on their data set, "BestImage Celebrities Face" (BCF), which contains about 20,000 individuals and one million face images and is identity-disjoint with respect to LFW. The researchers divided the BCF data into two subsets for training and validation. The network was trained on the BCF training set with 20 face patches. The features from each patch were concatenated, followed by PCA

FIGURE 5.17 Example faces in the IJB-A with pose and illumination variations. (From B. Klare et al., Pushing the frontiers of unconstrained face detection and recognition: IARPA Janus Benchmark A, *CVPR*, 2015; FaCE, Face Recognition Challenges and Evaluation.)

and the joint Bayesian model learned on BCF validation set. They report an accuracy of around 99% on LFW.

In order to advance research and solution development, it is always a challenge to have representative labeled data for training purposes. Fortunately, there are some publicly available data sets that can be used for algorithm and solution development:

1. *LFW* is a database of face photographs designed for studying the problem of unconstrained face recognition. The data set contains more than 13,000 images of faces collected from the web. The only

constraint on these faces is that they were detected by the Viola–Jones face detector. More details can be found in the technical report below and at http://vis-www.cs.umass.edu/lfw/index.html

2. *PubFig* database is a large, real-world face dataset consisting of *58,797* images of *200* people collected from the Internet. The database can be accessed from http://www.cs.columbia.edu/CAVE/databases/pubfig/

3. *YouTube Faces* is a database of face videos designed for studying the problem of unconstrained face recognition in videos. The data set contains *3425* videos of *1595* different people. All the videos were downloaded from YouTube. This database can be accessed from http://www.cs.tau.ac.il/~wolf/ytfaces/

4. *Point and Shoot Face Recognition Challenge* is an inexpensive "point-and-shoot" camera technology combined with social network technology that motivates the general population to use face recognition technology. The challenge includes 9376 still images and 2802 videos of 293 people. The images are balanced with respect to distance to the camera, alternative sensors, frontal versus not-frontal views, and different locations. Verification results are presented for public baseline algorithms and a commercial algorithm for three cases: comparing still images to still images, videos to videos, and still images to videos. This dataset can be found at http://www.nist.gov/itl/iad/ig/pasc.cfm

5. *IARPA Janus Benchmark A (IJB-A)* is a publicly available media in the wild dataset containing 500 subjects with manually localized face images found at http://www.nist.gov/itl/iad/ig/facechallenges.cfm

In summary, deep learning techniques have helped advance algorithm development for identification problems on faces collected in the wild. The speed of operation might still be a challenge; in the near future, some practical applications will be available.

5.3.5 Iris Recognition for Social Media Authentication

Iris recognition is one of the most promising authentication modalities for social media applications. This section will discuss various aspects of iris technology and its challenges with respect to social media. Iris recognition technology was first patented in 1994 by Dr. John Daugman and has become one of the premier technologies for user identification and verification applications even though the use of iris patterns as biometric

FIGURE 5.18   Afghan woman verification.

identifiers was studied much earlier. In 2005, the broad patent covering the basic concept of iris recognition expired, providing marketing opportunities for other companies that have developed their own algorithms for iris recognition. Dr. Daugman's patent on the IrisCodes® implementation of iris recognition expired in 2011.

One of the success stories for iris recognition came when *National Geographic Magazine* published a cover photo of an Afghan girl in 1984, shown in Figure 5.18. The magazine tried to locate the girl for an updated photograph. The magazine used iris recognition to find the woman, 18 years later. Currently, the iris recognition system has been deployed for border management, airport access control, residential access control, refugee registration, secure worker's access, and ATM banking among its many applications.

5.3.5.1 Iris Recognition Basics
The iris is the plainly visible, colored ring that surrounds the pupil, as shown in Figure 5.19. The iris begins to form during the third month of gestation. The structures creating its distinctive pattern are completed by the eighth month of gestation, but pigmentation continues into the first years after birth. No two irises are alike; there are correlations between the iris patterns of an individual's left and right eyes or between identical twins. Iris formation is epigenetic. Furthermore, the amount of information that can be measured in a single iris is much greater than fingerprints, and the accuracy is greater than DNA [16].

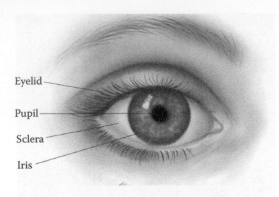

FIGURE 5.19   Iris is the colored ring that surrounds the pupil.

The process of iris recognition consists of several major steps: iris detection, segmentation, feature extraction, and recognition. Landmark features are used for localization to detect the iris, as shown in Figure 5.20. These landmark features and the distinct shape of the iris allow for imaging, feature isolation, and extraction.

Today's commercial iris cameras typically use infrared light to illuminate the iris and a high quality digital camera to capture the iris image. A 2D Gabor wavelet filters and maps the segmented iris into phasors (vectors). These phasors include information on the orientation, spatial frequency, and position of these areas. This information is used to map the IrisCodes, a sequence of 0's and 1's, depicted visually in the top left corner of Figure 5.20.

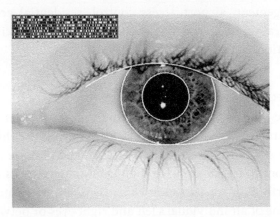

FIGURE 5.20   Iris localization and IrisCode pictorial representation. (Data from http://biometrics.gov/Documents/Glossary.pdf; J. Daugman, University of Cambridge: Computer Laboratory: From John Daugman.)

To perform iris recognition, two IrisCodes are compared. The amount of difference between two IrisCodes is called the Hamming distance (HD). HD is used as a test of statistical independence between the two IrisCodes. The key concept in iris recognition is the failure of the test of statistical independence.

Some challenges still remain in deploying iris applications because the iris is a small anatomical target of 1 cm diameter located behind a curved, wet, reflecting surface (the cornea). Humans regularly blink their eyelids for protection and lubrication, and the eyes are constantly in motion. In addition, the iris can be obscured by eyelashes, lenses, and reflections, and partially occluded by eyelids, which can droop.

In social media, the primary application of iris recognition is to authenticate users for reidentification. The challenges are how to deploy an economical sensor to the mobile phone or workstation user platform and how to capture a user's iris conveniently and with sufficient clarity. Iris recognition utilizes infrared light to illuminate the eye to maximize the visibility of iris features, particularly for dark-colored irises. The illumination poses some challenges from a usability perspective because it creates a perception of causing health effects. Recently, miniaturized commercial iris capture sensors have been installed on smart phones as an additional camera. Ultimately, the front high-resolution camera is needed in order to capture the iris; however, the approach is a challenge because most onboard cameras have an infrared filter built-in, which is detrimental to iris capture.

5.3.5.2 Outlook with Iris Scanning in Smartphones

Iris scanners stand out as the next best biometric solution for mobile devices. They promise a high reliability and can be designed in a very compact manner. The contrast of recorded images is very important for the quality of the scanner as the iris pattern can only then be securely identified. For brown eyes, the eye color most predominant worldwide, high-contrast recordings can only be achieved using infrared light. With blue and green eyes, the best results are achieved using visible light; however, infrared wavelengths also deliver good results. The typical wavelength for iris scanners is between 700 and 900 nm. Many experts currently set 810 nm as a good compromise in order to realize images with a high contrast for all eye colors. An advanced sensor can compensate various needs; in the very near future, we may have an iris scanning capability with the front camera of the mobile phone.

In the last couple of years, smart phone makers started building iris recognition technology into their smartphones either using a separate iris sensor or using the higher resolution front-facing camera. It is desirable to have one single camera to capture both iris scans and normal images for better usability. With increasing acceptance and usability improvement, users can log into social media apps by staring at their home screen: the Android or iPhone iris scanner uses infrared light to unlock the phone and accounts.

5.3.6 Speaker Recognition

Speaker recognition is a promising biometric modality for social media authentication platforms due to its nonintrusive and touchless nature. Actually, speaker recognition or voice recognition technology can apply to the identification problem when we identify people in multimedia stored at social media sites or mobile apps. Speaker recognition is one of many speech processing related applications as shown in Figure 5.21.

Speaker recognition dates back four decades and uses the acoustic features of speech to differentiate individuals. These acoustic patterns reflect both anatomy (e.g., size and shape of the throat and mouth) and learned behavioral patterns (e.g., voice pitch and speaking style). Based on speeches, the techniques can apply to recognize the language spoken, the words spoken, the gender of the speaker, and the speakers themselves. In this section, this discussion focuses on recognition of the speaker. Speaker recognition has been applied to applications such as access control, transaction authentication, speech database management, personalization, and law enforcement. Commercial products exist and extensive research has

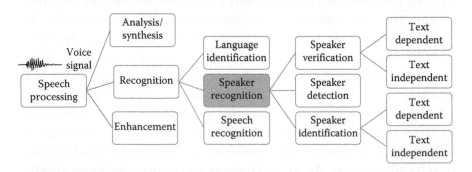

FIGURE 5.21   Taxonomy of speech processing with the speaker recognition indicated. (From LeCun, Y., Bengio, Y., Hinton, G., *Nature*, 521, 2015, 436–444.)

been performed. Most successful speaker recognition solutions combine different levels of features including semantic, dialogic, dialectal, phonetic, prosodic, and spectral features by separately modeling them and fusing them at the score level to obtain a decision.

To date, the most prevalent modeling techniques are the Gaussian mixture model and support vector machine approaches. Neural networks and other types of classifiers have also been used, although not in significant numbers. Recently, the speaker-verification community has enjoyed a significant increase in accuracy from the successful application of the factor analysis framework and some key techniques developed in recent years [18,19].

A major advantage of speaker verification is its widespread familiarity and acceptability, and ease of use. Speaker verification can be implemented with rather inexpensive basic microphones embedded in workstations and mobile phones; however, a related challenge is that there is really no standardization in terms of the quality of the capture microphones (e.g., sensitivity, noise pickup, and noise canceling) or the channels over which the voice signal is transmitted (e.g., a cell network). Nevertheless, voice biometrics allow users to verify their identity simply by speaking, making it easier and faster to gain access to secure apps by way of mobile devices and web browsers. Since usability is the number one challenge for any biometrics adopted, voice biometrics ranks among the desirable choices for users. Some market research projects that voice recognition will be widely adopted for social media apps and mobile platforms. In the context of social media applications, there are some fundamental challenges that impact performance:

1. Acoustic environment (e.g., background noise)

2. Channel (e.g., microphone, handset, or recording equipment)

3. High signal-to-noise ratio

4. Audio degradation through compression

5. Speaker's physical condition (emotion, intoxication, or illness)

6. What is said (text independent vs. text dependent)

Some inherent concerns still remain over privacy when users speak into the microphone. However, speaker recognition will be one primary modality to be adopted regardless of these challenges.

5.3.7 Behavioral Biometrics in Social Media

In social media applications, there are quite a few user behavior induced biometrics that can be used for authentication. Some modalities include keystroke dynamics, mouse dynamics, and signatures; the primary usage is for authentication and continuous identity monitoring. Because of the data quality and size of population, behavioral biometrics application in identification problems could be a challenge.

5.3.7.1 Keystroke Dynamics for Authentication

Keystroke dynamics refers to the process of measuring and assessing a human's typing rhythm on digital devices, such as a computer keyboard, mobile phone, or touch screen panel (Figure 5.22). A form of digital signature is created upon human interaction with these devices. These signatures are believed to be rich in cognitive qualities, which are fairly unique to each individual and holds huge potential as a personal identifier.

A user's identity is verified by comparing a sufficiently large set of keystroke data accumulated since the last verification to a previously established keystroke profile. A key-logger can record the press and release times for each key that a user presses. Utilizing these timings, a keystroke sensor derives five features for each letter pair. Currently, these features consist of

1. Key press latency: time from the press of the first key to the press of the second key

2. Key release latency: time from the release of the first key to the release of the second key

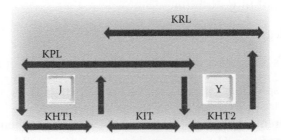

FIGURE 5.22   Keystroke features (pressing and releasing keys "J" and "Y").

3. Key interval time: time from the release of the first key to the press of the second key

4. Key hold time: the amount of time a key is held down

Like any other biometric recognition modalities, keystroke dynamics includes stages of acquisition, feature selection, matching, and decision. Keystroke dynamics biometrics is unlikely to replace existing knowledge-based authentication entirely, and is also not robust enough to be a sole biometric authenticator. However, the advantages of keystroke dynamics are indisputable, such as the ability to operate in stealth mode, low implementation cost, high user acceptance, and ease of integration into existing security systems. These create the basis of a potentially effective way of enhancing the overall security rating by playing a significant role in a larger multifactor authentication mechanism.

5.3.7.2 Mouse Dynamics for Authentication

Recent research suggests that mouse dynamics is a viable solution for identification on a small scale; Yampolskiy et al. provide a good review of the subject [11]. This modality could be a part of the multifactor authentication process. Commercial products have not yet matured as a number of challenges exist, including

1. Identification of stable features for each user application

2. Developing adaptive algorithms as the user's mouse dynamics change over time

3. Scalability of mouse dynamics to large populations

In addition, some external environmental and user emotional variables can cause subject behavior to change over time. Also, the time to authenticate a user based on mouse dynamics depends on their frequency of interaction with the mouse. Some research shows that it may require long time to reliably authenticate a user; however, some recent studies indicate authentication times as fast as less than 10 s with some closed datasets. Reducing this time period is imperative to making this approach a viable option.

Naturally, mouse dynamics features can utilize simple mouse events (down, up, wheel, and movement), mouse composite actions (clicks,

TABLE 5.2   Mouse Events

Common operation patterns	Creating new document
	Copying text
	Pasting text
Mouse actions	Single/double clicks
	Movement
	Drag/drop
	No activity
Mouse events	Mouse up, down, wheel, move

movement, and drag/drop), and operations (creating a new document, copying, and pasting a file), shown in Table 5.2. Researchers can aggregate features extracted from common operation patterns, and remove features that do not contribute discriminating information to user authentication. Table 5.3 shows some commonly investigated features.

Even though some work has achieved a low false alarm rate and a high true positive rate, most of the work has been on small population sizes. Much work remains to be done. Meanwhile, performance requirements will be attained through information fusion among keystroke analysis, mouse dynamics, and user behavior patterns. In social media applications, this technique is used for verification purposes, not for identifying an individual. Some pilot projects have been conducted but have not yet resulted in real deployment applications.

TABLE 5.3   Mouse Dynamics Features

Feature Type	Description of Feature
Movement	Lack of activity—ratio of time when there is no movement
	Distance distributions—frequency of movements within discrete distances
	Direction distributions—frequency of movements within discrete directions (e.g., north, northeast, northwest, west, east, south, southeast, and southwest)
	Speed—average speed calculated for each discrete distance
	Acceleration—average acceleration calculated for each discrete distance
Click	Overall single click elapsed time—elapsed time between mouse down/up event for left and right mouse buttons
	Overall double click elapsed time—elapsed time between mouse down/up event of left and right mouse buttons for a double click
	Intermediate double click times—intermediate elapsed time between mouse down/up events of first and second click
Location	Screen location distributions—frequency of where mouse actions occur on the user display

5.3.7.3 Signature Recognition

Most applications require a signature pad as shown in Figure 5.23, commonly used for financial transactions and document signing. Verification is usually done by visual inspection. Unlike the iris, fingerprint, and face, which use physical features, signature biometrics is behavior-based and is already widely accepted by general public. There are some obvious advantages

1. Achieving high accuracy academically (current accuracy can reach to a high 90 s percentile depending on the academic test datasets)

2. Eliminating fraud

3. Implementing economically

4. Substituting PIN or password

5. Attracting increasing interest, academic and commercial

Though signature recognition can be used for authentication on the platform; this modality has not gained much attention yet in social media applications. Potentially, users could use a stylus to sign up their signatures on the standard smart phone screen or touchable workstations.

5.3.7.4 Application of Behavioral Biometrics in Social Media

In recent years, the academic community has researched user social media behavior and their patterns on workstation and mobile platforms. Some example topics include behavioral biometrics with audit logs, command

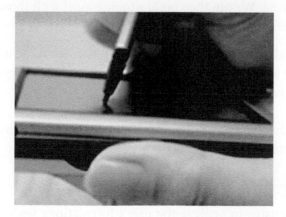

FIGURE 5.23   Signature recognition.

line lexicon, e-mail behavior, human machine user interface interaction, keystroke dynamics, mouse dynamics, network traffic, programming style, registry access, storage activity, and any other user actions that are potentially unique to the user. Though most of the research is at its relative infancy, researchers still continue to look for discriminatory features, various combinations, and classification techniques to address the continuous authentication problem, since most modalities are not suitable for identification. In previous sections, several forms of conventional biometrics have been discussed pertinent to social media, and additional areas of interest that researchers discovered include [20–22]

1. Application switches: this captures desktop behavior habits that a user possesses. For example, frequent switching versus staying with one application for a long time.

2. Temporal patterns: this captures how long the user typically spends on a specific resource or application. For example, a user might usually spend 1 h on program development and then 10 min on reading news.

3. Resource accesses: this captures the way the user accesses resources. For example, a user might usually go to a folder, open a file and start editing. If we observe that the user then goes to one specific folder, keeps opening and closing different files, this could be a different user.

4. Resource used: this captures the way the user creates and edits documents.

5. Content signatures: this captures snippets of the resources the user is accessing. We can then build a topic model with those snippets to characterize various users.

6. Temporal activity fingerprints: this captures what the user is usually doing at a specific time of day. For example, a user might usually log out at 8 p.m.

However, there are some fundamental challenges to deploy this type of operations because:

1. Searching for behavior patterns is computing expensive

2. It is intrusive to analyze the user's interactions with applications/resources

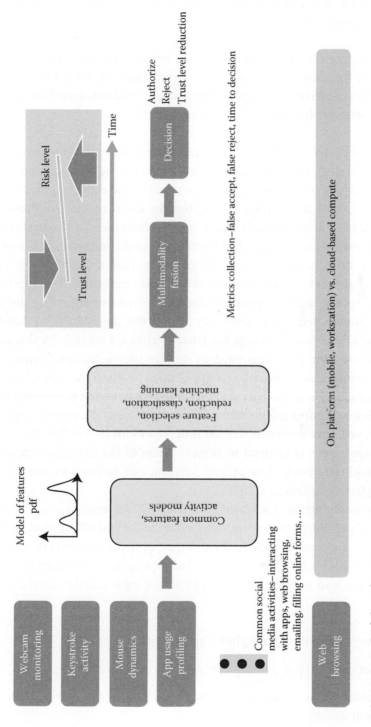

FIGURE 5.24   Risk-based continuous authentication and trust management.

3. Limited data and time are allowed to use behavioral biometrics for authentication

In the very near future, we should see revolutionary advances in chip design, sensor design, and analytics technologies; subsequently, social media users can take advantage of more secure solutions based on various kinds of behavior biometrics in a real situation.

5.3.7.5 Risk-Based Continuous Authentication and Trust Management

With increasing advanced sensors and various biometric modalities available, as discussed above, usability remains the most important and challenging issue for biometrics adoption in social media. As shown in Figure 5.24, a likely approach would be a combination of the traditional biometric modalities for initial authentication and continuous authentication based on behavior. The continuous authentication process will be a risk-based authentication approach, a dynamic authentication approach that takes into account the profile of the user or system requesting authentication. Risk-based implementation allows the application to build a trust level of users and manage the trust level based on risk. In this case, mobile or desktop platforms need to capture user activities, timing features of mouse and keyboard, and application profiles; therefore, the system can formulate a decision that incorporates trust levels continuously. As increasing computing power becomes available and analytics capability enhances, this approach will become economical and feasible. Some systems have been developed to achieve some of the discussed capabilities through government or private funding (see http://www.darpa.mil/program/active-authentication).

In the near future, a social media user will be able to use a mobile phone with a built-in fingerprint sensor and a face and iris unified camera to access social media website. In addition to the traditional biometrics data captured, built-in software can also capture users' human machine interactions and applications. A typical use case can be described as follows:

1. User brings the mobile phone in front of the face.

2. User can also present fingerprint using the touch screen.

3. Mobile phone captures face and/or iris and/or fingerprint with different quality.

4. Phone unlocks its screen based on the biometrics captured and authenticates the user:

   a. User starts using Instagram app

   b. User then switches to weather.com

   c. User starts google.com to search

   d. User starts using Facebook to chat

5. The system detects some unusual activities because the owner usually doesn't use weather.com at the initial sessions.

6. The system still allows browsing on Facebook, but locks the features of chatting, editing, and adding functions to avoid impersonation.

7. The system locks all apps accessing online banking apps.

8. The system locks all edits to user profile.

9. The system prompts and asks user to present fingerprint/face/iris to reauthenticate.

The series of events above depicts a possible future scenario in which social media users potentially experience with enhanced initial biometrics-based authentication and continuous authentication based on behavior biometrics.

5.4 SUMMARY

In the current state of social media, impersonation is rather easy to implement and difficult to detect. In order to benefit businesses, improve the quality of people's lives, and ease concerns over privacy violation, user-friendly technology is needed to authenticate users, initially and continuously. Biometric technologies offer the most promising and feasible solutions to this need. On the other hand, consumer marketing companies and government agencies can also build profiles on individuals for targeted marketing and identifying potential threats by leveraging biometrics collected via social media. With the advancement of processing to the edge, more computing resources available, and more data collected, social media users should have biometric-based solutions for authentication in the very near future. Meanwhile, efforts will continue to build identity intelligence based on social media for targeted marketing and fighting terrorism.

REFERENCES

1. A. Adler, S. Schuckers, Security and liveness: Overview. In: *Encyclopedia of Biometrics*, S. Li (ed.), Springer, 2009.
2. J. Wayman et al., *Biometric Systems: Technology, Design and Performance Evaluation*, Springer, Nottingham, 2004.
3. C. Bhagavatula et al., Biometric authentication on iPhone and Android: Usability, perceptions, and influences on adoption. *NDSS Symposium*, San Diego, 2015.
4. L. Wiskott et al., Face recognition by elastic bunch graph matching, *IEEE PAMI*, 19(7), 1997, 775–779.
5. X. Zhang et al., Face recognition across pose: A review, *Pattern Recognition*, 42(11), 2009, 2876–2896.
6. Y. Fu et al., Age synthesis and estimation via faces: A survey, *IEEE PAMI*, 32(11), 2010, 1955–1976.
7. R. Chellappa et al., Face recognition by computers and humans, *IEEE Computer*, 43(2), 2010, 46–55.
8. P. Grother et al., *Performance of Face Identification Algorithms*, NIST Interagency Report 8009, www.nist.gov, May 2014.
9. B. Klare et al., Pushing the frontiers of unconstrained face detection and recognition: IARPA Janus Benchmark A. *CVPR*, Boston, Massachusetts, 2015.
10. FaCE, Face recognition challenges and evaluation. http://www.nist.gov/itl/iad/ig/facechallenges.cfm
11. Y. LeCun, Y. Bengio, G. Hinton, Deep learning, *Nature*, 521, 2015, 436–444.
12. N. Zhang et al., Beyond frontal faces: Improving person recognition using multiple cues. In: *Computer Vision and Pattern Recognition (CVPR), 2015 IEEE Conference*, Boston, US, 2015.
13. Y. Taigman et al., DeepFace: Closing the gap to human-level performance in face verification. In: *2014 IEEE Conference on Computer Vision and Pattern Recognition*, Columbus, Ohio, 2014.
14. G. Huang et al., Labeled faces in the wild: A survey, Erik Learned-Miller.
15. A good source of biometric glossary can be found at http://biometrics.gov/Documents/Glossary.pdf
16. J. Daugman, How iris recognition works, http://www.cl.cam.ac.uk/~jgd1000/irisrecog.pdf
17. J. Daugman, University of Cambridge: Computer Laboratory: Webpage for John Daugman, http://www.cl.cam.ac.uk/~jgd1000/
18. J. Campbell, Speaker recognition. In: *Personal Identification in Networked Society*, A. Jain, R. Bolle, S. Pankanti (Eds.), Chapter 8, Springer, USA, pp. 165–189, 1996.
19. E. O'Neil King, *Speech and Voice Recognition White Paper*, Biometrics Research Group Inc., Toronto, Canada, 2014.

20. O. Brdiczka, From documents to tasks: Deriving user tasks from document usage patterns. In: *Proceedings of the 15th International Conference on Intelligent User Interfaces*, Hong Kong, China, pp. 285–288, 2010.
21. O. Brdiczka, M. Langet, J. Maisonnasse, J. L. Crowley, Detecting human behavior models from multimodal observation in a smart home, *IEEE Transactions Automation Science and Engineering*, 6(4), 2009, 588–597.
22. O. Brdiczka, N. M. Su, J. B. Begole. Temporal task footprinting: Identifying routine tasks by their temporal patterns. In: *Proceedings of the 15th International Conference on Intelligent User Interfaces*, Hong Kong, China, pp. 281–284, 2010.

CHAPTER 6

Biometrics in Gaming and Entertainment Technologies

Regan L. Mandryk and Lennart E. Nacke

CONTENTS

6.1 INTRODUCTION

Within biometric research, digital games are of particular interest as experimental stimuli and application scenarios, not just because they provide safe environments to explore the benefits and drawbacks of physiological sensor interaction without the concern of serious repercussions, but also because games have become a popular entertainment medium deserving of technological innovation in and of themselves. Recent estimates suggest that more money is spent purchasing games ($92 billion) than music ($18 billion) and movies ($62 billion) combined (Dring, 2015). Four out of five American households own a device that is used to play video games, and 115 million Americans play games, resulting in an average of 6.5 h of weekly gameplay (Entertainment Software Association, 2015). Internationally, the global game market is expected to exceed $102 billion by 2017 (Newzoo, 2015). Although games have a reputation of appealing to a stereotypical young male gamer, the appeal of digital game play is actually much broader. The latest report from the Entertainment Software Association (2015) shows that 26% of game players are younger than 18, but that 27% are over 50 (30% are 18–35, whereas 17% are 36–49). In addition, 44% of game players are female and women over 18 represent a significantly larger part of the game-playing population (33%) than boys age 18 or younger (15%).

With so much time and money being spent (by choice) on digital games, researchers have questioned what it is about games that make them so motivating to play (Ryan et al., 2006) and how we can translate these motivating features into nongame environments—a process known as gamification (Deterding, 2011). Serious games—games that leverage this ability to motivate behavior and retain attention in serious contexts—have been applied to, for example, encourage behavior change, improve the efficacy of therapy, and foster activities that lead to learning. The desire of

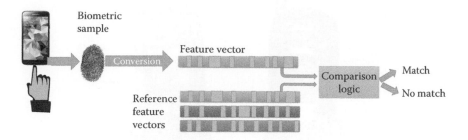

Biometric sample

Feature vector

Conversion

Reference feature vectors

Comparison logic

Match

No match

FIGURE 1.2 The process of biometric authentication (this example is for a mobile phone).

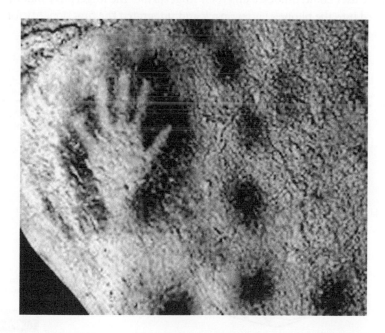

FIGURE 1.7 Handprints used as signatures for cave paintings. (From Renaghan, J., *Smithsonian Zoogoer*, August 1997.)

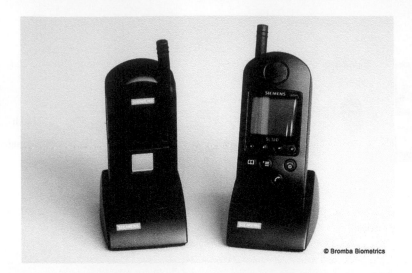

FIGURE 3.1 Siemens mobile phone presented in 1999 at Centrum für Büroautomation, Informationstechnologie und Telekommunikation (CeBIT), which the user could unlock using their fingerprint. The fingerprint module was integrated into the phone's battery pack and integrated the functionality for capturing and recognizing the fingerprint. (From Bromba Biometrics.)

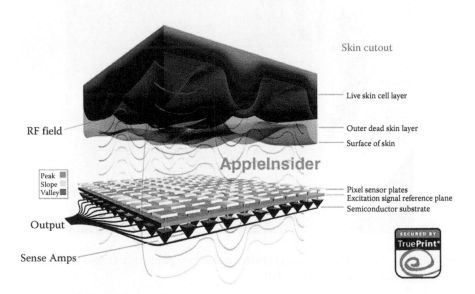

FIGURE 3.2 Cross-section of AuthenTec's fingerprint sensor. (From AppleInsider, http://www.appleinsider.com)

FIGURE 3.6   Photo of Motorola Droid Turbo 2 64 GB Black taken by Motorola Droid Maxx. (Data from https://en.wikipedia.org/wiki/File:Motorola_Droid_Turbo_2.png)

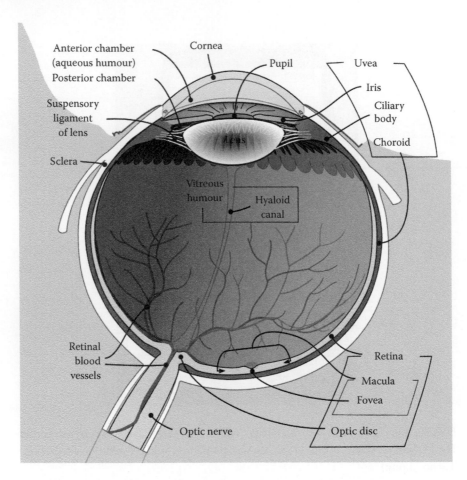

FIGURE 3.12   Eye anatomy. (Stock Vector by Microvector. n.d.)

FIGURE 3.13 Example of an iris occluded by a corneal SR.

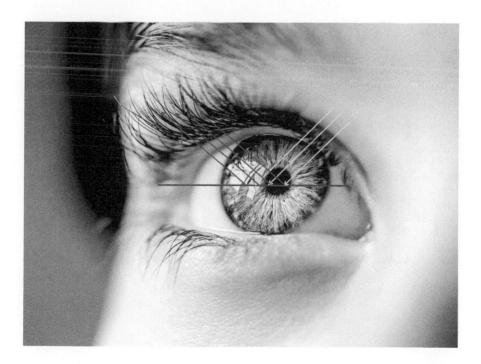

FIGURE 3.14 Corneal SR. Yellow represents the incident light and red represents the reflected light.

Iris green   White   Black

ARROWS NX F-04G

FIGURE 3.16 ARROWS NX F-04G. (From プレスリリースバックナンバー 2015年5月 [Fujitsu Press Release May 5, 2015].)

FIGURE 5.16 Faces randomly collected from the Internet.

FIGURE 7.1 A person using a US-VISIT program to provide fingerprints at Washington Dulles Airport. (Photo by Department of Homeland Security, Public Domain.)

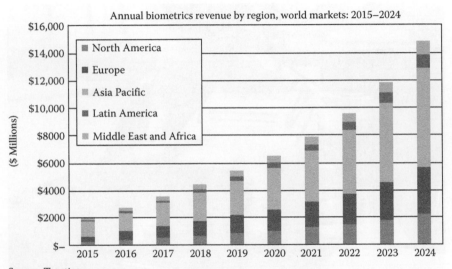

FIGURE 17.1 Biometrics market overview over the next 10 years. (From Tractica. 2015. Biometrics market revenue to total $67 billion worldwide over the next 10 years. With permission from Tractica.)

researchers and developers to innovate new forms of play, to understand how people engage with playful technologies, and to leverage the motivational pull of games in serious contexts has created an environment with the need for new forms of interaction. Understanding how people interact with technology is a challenging task—the desire of researchers to access the attitudes, feelings, and behaviors of people while they engage with technology has spawned innovation in evaluation methods in the field of human–computer interaction. Biometrics provides a means to assess thoughts and feelings in games, but in addition, biometrics contributes to positive player experiences by creating new forms of play that leverage real-time physiological signals as input. Nacke (2011) distinguishes between these two contributions of biometrics to games research—that is, (1) biometrics for innovating game interaction and (2) biometrics for evaluation (understanding players and their experiences). Players experience a dynamic range of emotions including joy, excitement, and even fear. These emotions can be used as input into digital games, and also used in iterative evaluation to improve game design (Nacke, 2013, 2015).

Within this framework of understanding biometrics for input or evaluation, we can also distinguish biometric game research into sensors that gather information from brain functions—so called brain-based sensing methods—and sensors that gather information from the surface of the skin and use body information, so called body-based sensing. This categorization of game interaction or evaluation with either brain or body sensors provides the structure that we use in this chapter to describe the current state of biometrics in games research. In Part I, we describe the use of biometrics as input into game systems. In Part II, we describe the use of biometrics for evaluating game systems. In each case, we address both brain and body-based input. To begin, we provide a very brief primer on the types of biometric signals that are used in games research, which will be discussed more in depth throughout this chapter.

6.1.1 A Primer of Biometrics Used in Games

Although the other chapters in this book also provide overviews of biometric measures, when used in games, different signals are employed. We are not aware of gaming systems that leverage fingerprints or irises in the design of their interaction. However, the following physiologically derived signals are commonly used in game interaction and evaluation. For a more in-depth description of these signals, please see Mandryk (2008), Kivikangas et al. (2011a), or Nacke (2015).

Electromyography (EMG) describes the measurement of electrical activation of muscle tissue. While game evaluation uses facial EMG, it has also been used to sense muscle activation as a more direct form of input.

Electrodermal activity (EDA, also: skin conductance level or SCL) or galvanic skin response (GSR; when referring to points in time) is a common psychophysiological measurement with easy application. Sweat production in the eccrine glands regulates EDA, in which increased activity is associated with psychological arousal.

Electrocardiography (EKG) is the sensing of heart activity through physiological sensors on the body. It is hard to control directly, but hyperventilation or increased physical activity often results in an increased heart rate (HR). The EKG signal can also be used to extract heart rate variability (HRV).

Electroencephalography (EEG) is the sensing of brain activity through sensors placed on the scalp. Brain activity is usually distinguished by the amplitude and frequency of the signal in comparison to a reference location on the head and differentiated into standard frequency spectra.

6.2 PART I: BIOMETRICS IN GAME INTERACTION

In this section, we present how gaming systems use biometrics as input. Whether controlled directly or indirectly, whether players are aware of the physiological adaptation or not, and whether the biometrics adapt the players' skills or the game environment, the examples in Part I all incorporate biometrics specifically into the game as input into the system, rather than as an evaluation of the player experience.

6.2.1 A Brief History of Physiologically Based Game Interfaces

Modern physiological sensor systems, capable of capturing signals unobtrusively from electrodes placed on the skin, have become more affordable for consumers. With each new system released, we have seen a surge of new applications, and many of these systems predominantly use games as a showcase of their main functionalities. Video games are usually considered a safe environment to explore the advantages and disadvantages of physiological sensor technologies because the consequences of failure are far less severe than those in life-critical systems or clinical applications.

There is a significant history of researchers exploring physiological input and interaction with biofeedback games. These games are often developed to make users more aware of their physiological state, conditioning them to control specific biological responses using digital game environments. In brain–computer interface (BCI) systems, users are commonly trained to control their brain activity, explicitly using brain signals as the primary input into the computing system. Similar concepts have been explored within the business community throughout the history of modern video gaming. Industry biofeedback gaming applications include early forays from Canadian biofeedback equipment manufacturer Thought Technology, who investigated physiological input with a modified GSR sensor (integrated into an Apple II mouse) and built the simple racing game CalmPrix in 1984. CalmPrix modified properties of the racing game based on the arousal values generated by the player. Around the same time, Atari developed the aforementioned Mindlink, an EMG headband based on an earlier medical plugin product called the Atari Bionics System. The Mindlink was eventually canceled as a consequence of player headaches resulting from repeated, deliberate movement of facial muscles.

Physiological game development continued for some years with varying success, including the creation of a Nintendo 64 electrocardiographic biosensor that was shipped with the Japanese version of Tetris 64. The game adapted its speed based on the user's HR. A little later, a device called the Lightstone was developed for the game The Journey to Wild Divine, which was moderately successful, but has since been turned into a web-compatible product called the Iom (see http://www.wilddivine.com). The Wild Divine biofeedback game trained people to control their physiological activation, with the goal of promoting and aiding relaxation.

In this section, we outline recent work conducted on using biometrics as input into a game system. First, we address body-based interaction, involving sensors such as GSR and HR. Second, we address brain-based interaction, sensed using EEG.

6.2.2 Body-Based Interaction

The intention of early research in games that use physiology as input was to create compelling player experiences. Sensed physiology can be indicative of a user's emotional state, and if used to manipulate a player experience, could create engaging affective games (Gilleade et al., 2005). For example, Relax-to-Win (Bersak et al., 2001) involved racing dragons whose speed was controlled by GSR; as players relaxed, their dragons raced faster, creating winning conditions. BalloonTrip (Sakurazawa et al., 2003) also used GSR as a game control; as players were excited, the game introduced more enemies and became more difficult as a result.

Body-based biometrics have also been used to enhance off-the shelf games. In AffQuake (Picard, 1997), the player's avatar jumps when startled and grows with player excitement. Dekker et al. (2007) developed a game modification using the Source software development kit (SDK) and Half-Life 2—GSR and HR were used to control game shader graphics, screen shaking, and enemy spawn points (i.e., number of locations in which enemies are put into the game world) (Dekker, 2007).

These examples all demonstrate how biometric input is not directly controlled, but is mediated by some other player interaction, such as meditation or deep breathing. In this way, the biometric sensors are indirectly controlled (Nacke et al., 2011a,b). In addition to the indirect control of biometric sensors seen in the previous examples, researchers have also investigated how to use biometric control directly. Death Trigger is a side-scrolling shooter that was played with a traditional gamepad and control scheme, but also adapted game elements (e.g., length of the flamethrower, size of the enemies, and density of snowfall) using different physiological signals (Nacke et al., 2011a). As an exploration of both how to augment—rather than replace—traditional control with physiological input, the Death Trigger project also characterized player response to whether the physiological input was controlled directly (e.g., EMG) or indirectly (e.g., electrodermal response).

In related work, Kuikkaniemi et al. (2010) studied how awareness of the biometric-based manipulation affected player experience in a first-person shooter game, where affective input modulated character walking and turning speed, aiming direction, recoil amount, and firing rate. The results show that people enjoyed the explicit biofeedback conditions more and their conscious control of the respiratory sensor led to a better game experience.

Negini et al. (2014) were interested in exploring whether adapting the player's abilities (as in Relax-to-win), the enemy's strengths (as in BalloonTrip), or the environment (as in DeathTrigger) changed the player experience. They created a custom zombie survival level for Half-Life 2 that adapted based on GSR. They varied the strength of the player's avatar (through speed and access to weapons), the strength of the zombie opponents (through their speed and number), or the surrounding environment to increase or decrease support for the player (through varying the spawning of health packs and the visibility of the environment due to fog). Results suggested that decreasing the challenge by adapting the number and strength of the zombie enemies was not as effective as giving the players the tools needed to overcome greater challenges, as done when adapting the strengths of the player or the supportiveness of the environment. These results are in line with recent work that suggests that thwarting the need for competence within the context of a game negatively affects player experience (Ryan et al., 2006).

6.2.3 Brain-Based Interaction

From its invention in 1929, EEG research has made invaluable contributions in the fields of psychology, medicine, biology, and more recently, human–computer interaction (HCI). Though the most straightforward use of EEG involves the passive measurement and analysis of brain activity to retroactively infer details of emotional or neurological state, the current state of the art allows researchers to explore more complex applications. For the evaluation of user interfaces and video games, EEG can provide valuable input, because it allows us to infer a current cognitive state in real time.

EEG collects data by measuring the electrical impulses generated when neurons fire in the brain. Technically speaking, the chemical reaction that occurs when a neuron is stimulated can be measured using a passive electrode placed on the scalp of the user. This data are collected over time. The result is a continuous reading from the user (Cacioppo et al., 2007; Wehbe and Nacke, 2013). In a brain–computer interface (BCI) application, these brain waves are translated by the software and linked to actions in the interface. As a result, the user can control the interface with their brain (Nijholt et al., 2008). The primary use of EEG to drive game interaction has been in the context of therapeutic applications. In this section, we will provide a brief primer on EEG and present some of the examples for which it has been used to drive interaction with a game.

6.2.3.1 Electroencephalography

The brain consists of billions of neurons, which communicate by electrical currents (Thompson and Thompson, 2003). These electrical currents can be measured using an electroencephalograph (EEG), which places several electrodes on the participant's head. The amount of electrical activity corresponds to the amount of brain activity. Brain activity is usually distinguished by the amplitude and frequency of the signal in comparison to a reference location on the head (Nacke, 2013, 2015). Standard EEG devices differentiate the captured signal into different frequency bands. The frequency bands are named alpha (8–13 Hz), beta (13–30 Hz)—again divided into low beta (13–20 Hz) and high beta (20–30 Hz), theta (4–8 Hz), delta (1–4 Hz), and gamma (30–50 Hz). Not all frequency bands show the same activity all the time; they are associated with certain states. Beta activity, for example, is related to alertness, attention, vigilance, and excitatory problem solving activities while delta is mostly seen during sleep. Theta activity is associated with decreased alertness, drowsiness, and lower information processing (Thompson and Thompson, 2003; Nacke, 2013).

6.2.3.2 Brain Input in Games

There are only a few examples of games that use brain input (as measured by EEG) to drive interaction—the more common use of EEG in the domain of games is in evaluation (see Part II of this chapter). Brainball (Hjelm et al., 2003) is a game in which a user's EEG signal controls a physical ball rolling on a table. The objective for a player is to keep the ball away from their end of the table while their opponent tries to move it toward them. The movement of the ball is controlled through relaxation, which creates an interesting dynamic for players—although they naturally start to feel panicked when the ball rolls toward them, they must relax in order to triumph. Although Brainball was developed as an exploration of game interaction, other researchers specifically look at integrating brain–computer interfaces with video games (Loup-Escande et al., 2015). Another game that explored BCI with different interaction paradigms was *Bacteria Hunt*, which used steady-state visually evoked potentials (SSVEP) as an indicator of concentration, and alpha activity as a measure of relaxation (Mühl et al., 2010). Controlling both of these BCI paradigms simultaneously yielded progress in the game (i.e., eating bacteria). Holz et al. (2013) discuss a BCI version of the game Connect Four for severely motor-restricted end users, where three classes of motor movements were imagined by players in order to control the game. Tangermann et al. (2008) discussed how to control the paddles of a physical pinball machine using a BCI. Common to all of these approaches is that they are using games with very simple input mechanisms, because the mapping and processing of brain signals is often not possible in the same time as direct input provided by controlling buttons or joysticks with a hand. Gürkök et al. (2013) also discuss how to use BCI as input in an entertainment game called *Mind the Sheep*, to herd sheep as quickly as possible, but they discuss three categories of BCI games: mental state, movement imagery, and evoked potential games. In mental state games, players try to trigger brain states (e.g., relaxation, concentration, or stress) (van de Laar et al.,

2013; Gürkök et al., 2014). Players of movement imagery games visualize body movements that help them navigate a virtual or physical environment (Hjelm et al., 2003; Krepki et al., 2007; Tangermann et al., 2008). In evoked potential games, the two prominent paradigms are SSVEP (Mühl et al., 2010) and P300 (Finke et al., 2009). The principle behind SSVEP is that the frequency of a visual stimulus (e.g., flickering images) is enhanced in our visual cortex when measured. Usually, a game stimulus will then trigger a directional command (i.e., movement imagery) through the BCI, often aiming and steering (Martinez et al., 2007; Müller-Putz et al., 2007; Jackson et al., 2009). As with body-based input, there are also examples of game projects that use SDKs to integrate EEG input with existing games. For example, in *Alpha WoW* (Nijholt et al., 2009; Bos et al., 2010), players trigger their shapeshifting ability through controlling their EEG (van de Laar et al., 2013). Although there are few examples of games that use EEG as input to explore new forms of interaction, there are several examples of EEG input in games for therapeutic purposes—in which the game simply exists in service of a biofeedback training system.

6.2.3.3 Neurofeedback Training Games

Biofeedback training systems encourage a specific mental or physical state in a user through a closed biofeedback loop. These systems gather a player's physiological state through sensing hardware, integrate this state into a computer-based interactive system, and present the feedback to the user so that they can work to adjust their state; biofeedback training that uses brain-based sensing is referred to as neurofeedback training. In 1976, Lubar and Bahler (1976) showed that it is possible to self-regulate one's brain activity with neurofeedback training and thereby decrease the intensity and duration of seizures. Based on their findings, neurofeedback training started to be explored to treat various conditions (e.g., attention deficit hyperactivity disorder [ADHD] [Monastra et al., 2006; Bakhshayesh et al., 2011], fetal alcohol spectrum disorder [Mandryk et al., 2013], and Asperger's syndrome [Thompson et al., 2010]). Because video games were available in combination with low-cost home computer systems, and because they are fun and motivating to interact with—especially for children who do not like to sit still and focus on training activities, researchers started to combine neurofeedback training with video games (Wilkinson et al., 2008). In this section, we present a short description of neurofeedback training and then present training games in which interaction is driven by a player's EEG activity.

6.2.3.3.1 Neurofeedback

Lubar et al. (1976) originally showed that neurofeedback training could significantly reduce seizure intensity and duration for epilepsy patients, when they focused on increasing the 12–14 Hz activity of EEG referred to as sensorimotor rhythm (SMR). Further research showed similar success in reducing symptoms for seizure patients (Sterman, 2000; Heinrich et al., 2007), and neurofeedback training began to be explored to treat other conditions. Monastra et al. (1999) showed that participants with ADHD have a distinctive difference in their brain activity compared to people without ADHD. Specifically, they showed that people diagnosed with ADHD have significantly higher levels of slow wave (i.e., theta, 4–8 Hz) in relation to fast wave (i.e., beta, 13–21 Hz) EEG activity. Research focused especially on children with ADHD used different training mechanisms, that is, suppressing or increasing activity in different frequency bands (e.g., SMR, theta, and beta) to try to help children learn to self-regulate their brain activity (e.g., Lubar and Lubar, 1984; Lubar et al., 1995; Heinrich et al., 2007; Gevensleben et al., 2009; Bakhshayesh et al., 2011; Moriyama et al., 2012; Steiner et al., 2014). The results showed that people who were able to change their brain activity through neurofeedback training also showed significant improvements along several other metrics: their performance on attention tests and intelligence tests increased, behavioral ratings improved, and feedback from parents and teachers was positive (Lubar et al., 1995; Kaiser and Othmer, 2000; Monastra et al., 2002). Neurofeedback training has proven itself effective not just in case studies, but also in large-scale studies in treating attentional dysfunction (Kaiser and Othmer, 2000). The results of neurofeedback training also seem to be sustainable, as shown by follow-up studies after years without continued neurofeedback training (Monastra et al., 2006). One study demonstrated the positive effect of neurofeedback training with school children that were taking medication to treat the symptoms of ADHD. The positive effect of the altered brain activity was sustained even when the medication was discontinued (Monastra et al., 2002).

In addition to helping people with different medical conditions modulate brain their activity, neurofeedback training also showed positive results when used for healthy people who were not diagnosed with a medical condition (Kaiser and Othmer, 2000; Vernon, 2005; Heinrich et al., 2007; Nan et al., 2012). For example, to determine whether neurofeedback training could result in improvements in areas such as memory or performance in sports or artistic activities, Vernon (2005) documented that by training healthy subjects to modulate their SMR/beta and SMR/theta ratios, they were able to observe improvements in semantic working memory. Other researchers showed that by increasing the low frequency activity in the left hemisphere, the targeting ability in pre-elite archers improved significantly (Landers et al., 1991). Finally, researchers showed that the performance of a dancer could be improved with neurofeedback training (Raymond et al., 2005). For a more detailed review of the possibilities of neurofeedback training, see Vernon (2005).

6.2.3.3.2 Neurofeedback Games

During neurofeedback training, most setups give auditory or visual feedback (Lubar and Bahler, 1976; Kaiser and Othmer, 2000), that is, a sound or/and a light signal that the desired brain frequency threshold was achieved or maintained long enough. Visual feedback could also include points or color wheels advancing around the periphery (Lubar et al., 1995). Because several participants in the early neurofeedback studies were children, the researchers tried to make the feedback more fun and the training more engaging. One good way to keep children engaged is through computer games, as they have been shown to capture the attention of children (Rigby and Ryan, 2011). Therefore, instead of staring at a lamp or waiting for an auditory signal, the children had to complete tasks such as: changing the color of a pole to enable a famous mouse from German TV to jump (Heinrich et al., 2007), make a diver sink to reach a treasure (Cmiel et al., 2011), make an emoticon smile, a monkey climb a tree for food, or a ball blink (Bakhshayesh et al., 2011), or make a dolphin dive to the ocean ground to collect coins (Steiner et al., 2014). Although these are not games by standard definitions (e.g., they do not include an uncertain and quantifiable outcome) (Salen and Zimmerman, 2004), they are rather playful applications that provide more fun and engagement than standard training approaches (Rigby and Ryan, 2011). To introduce more engaging games, researchers at NASA decided to try a different approach and modulated the control of off-the-shelf games using the EEG signal (Pope and Palsson, 2001). If the player increased his or her beta activity, the game controller or joystick became more responsive and the player had greater control; whereas, if theta waves increased, the controller was more sluggish (Pope and Palsson, 2001). Mandryk et al. (2013) developed a similar approach where the view of any off-the-shelf computer game was obfuscated by graphics if the player's brain activity was not in the desired theta/low beta range. Although agnostic to the underlying game, Mandryk et al.'s system was able to display game-relevant graphics that appeared to be integrated with the underlying premise or theme of the game. They deployed their system over 12 weeks of training (three sessions per week) and observed significant differences in the theta/low beta rations between the first and final weeks of training.

Neurofeedback training games have also captured the attention of commercial EEG headset companies (Brainmaster Technologies Inc., 2015; NeuroSky, 2015). Neurosky and Brainmaster both sell equipment and games for neurofeedback training. NeuroSky's focus is more consumer oriented, whereas the equipment sold by Brainmaster takes a somewhat more clinical approach. These EEG headsets are low-cost consumer-grade headsets, often using a single electrode and a ground, and the games are compelling as they are generally developed with the latest game development engines (e.g., Unity 3D). For example, the NeuroSky headset features Focus Pocus—a 2012 biofeedback game designed specifically for children with ADHD.

6.2.4 Summary of Biometrics as Input

In Part I, we have described how biometrics have been used as input into a game system. Used for increasing engagement, adapting difficulty of a game, exploring innovative interaction, and supporting neurofeedback training, various physiological sensors have been used as input into a game. In Part II, we investigate the other major use of biometrics in games—to evaluate player experience.

6.3 PART II: BIOMETRICS IN GAMES USER RESEARCH

In Part I, we described how biometrics drives interaction with games; however, because physiological data can be indicative of a person's psychological state (both cognitive and emotional), it is also good for assessing experience. Used for evaluating experience with other interactive technologies, such as search engines, websites, or productivity software, biometric evaluation is also popular for evaluating experience with computer games. Physiological signals yield large amounts of contextually relevant data, provide an objective indicator of user experience without interrupting the gameplay experience, and can be used to infer underlying emotional states relevant to gameplay. It would be a boon to the game evaluation community if there were a plug-and-play system, in which a user is sat down in front of a computer game, physiological sensors are attached, and a few minutes later we know how much fun she is having, and which parts of the game are more fun than other parts. Unfortunately, using physiological signals are not this straightforward, and there are complexities in data collection and analysis that currently prevent us from achieving this plug-and-play level of ease. But research in this area is advancing, and the ease of a plug-and-play system is not far off.

In this section, we will describe why people would want to use biometrics for game evaluation, and outline the current state of the art on assessing player experience using biometrics, both derived from body- and brain-based sensors.

6.3.1 What Is Games User Research?

Games User Research (GUR) is a field that combines knowledge from human–computer interaction (HCI), game design, and experimental psychology, with the overall objective of improving the player experience within a variety of design contexts (Isbister and Schaffer, 2008; Bernhaupt, 2010; Bernhaupt, 2015). GUR aims to create methods, techniques, and tools to collect data and evaluate player experience, informing the game design process to improve the resulting experience.

Many aspects of GUR draw from knowledge accumulated within the field of HCI. However, many of the measures and tools used in traditional HCI are intended to assess productivity applications for the purposes of maximizing user performance. Consequently, many traditional HCI techniques do not fit well with GUR, because the entertainment value or positive experience arising from a game is not merely a matter of user efficiency or objective ease of interaction. For example, common user experience measures such as task efficiency or error rate cannot be applied to games in the same way. Moreover, gameplay introduces new aspects of user experience that are inherent to play, but are inconceivable within the context of a productivity application. For example, while an error of any sort is considered unquestionably negative in the realm of productivity, repeated failure preceding the mastery of a challenge is a commonly accepted paradigm in games, serving to foster a player's desire to attain superiority over the game system. Games are a dynamic form of interaction, which can lead to a variety of sensations in a short space of time. The goal of GUR, then, is to find ways to assess player experience both over time and with a fair amount of precision, while simultaneously avoiding the interruption of gameplay with obtrusive evaluation methods, such as eliciting subjective user opinion.

Some of the methods used to access individual player experience are (Nacke et al., 2010a,b)

- *Psychophysiological player testing.* Controlled measures of gameplay experience with the use of physical sensors to assess user reactions.

- *Eye tracking.* Measurement of eye fixation and attention focus to infer details of cognitive and attentional processes.

- *Persona modeling.* Constructed player models.

- *Game metrics behavior assessment.* Logging of every action the player takes while playing, for later analysis.

- *Player modeling.* AI-based models that react to player behavior and adapt the player experience accordingly.

- *Qualitative interviews and questionnaires.* Surveys to assess the player's perception of various gameplay experience dimensions.

The assessment of player experience by means of postplay surveys or interviews is the easiest and least expensive approach, however, it has some drawbacks. Because it relies on the player's memory, information may be lost in the delay between action (gameplay) and recall (interview or questionnaire). Besides, this approach is only able to discover the conscious sensations experienced by the player, lacking the power to recognize unconscious sensations that may be an important part of the experience. Finally, it is an explicit approach that requires direct interaction with the player. Surveys are excellent for explicitly eliciting user attitudes, but are not capable of implicitly assessing user behaviors.

The use of methods capable of detecting players' emotions and actions in real time allows the user researcher to access a richer set of information; however, these techniques require more work and expertise, and are typically more expensive. For this reason, GUR often relies on mixed methods that combine data from self-reported surveys or interviews with methods such as psychophysiological measures or game analytics. This combined approach allows the researcher to balance the advantages and drawbacks of each method to achieve a clear and robust result. Of the methods commonly used in GUR, physiological measures are the most recent innovation; surveys and interview techniques used in GUR are grounded in decades of research from psychology, human factors, and human–computer interaction, whereas game metrics build on a history of instrumentation and logging in software development. Physiological measures have only been used in evaluation in the last decade, meaning that many of the innovations have been relatively recent. In this section, we describe biometrics for game evaluation. Because of the volume of work in this area and the scope of this chapter, we present the basic fundamentals of physiological game evaluation. For a more in-depth treatment of the topic, please see Mandryk (2008) or Nacke (2015).

6.3.2 Evaluation Using Body-Based Sensors

When choosing which physiological sensors to use, the main question to ask yourself is what you want to know about the user's experience. Additional considerations include the feasibility of data collection and the impact that sensor choice might have on gaming experience. In this section, we describe a number of physiological sensors relevant to digital game play. Organized by anatomical system, each subsection presents: the measure, why it is important in the context of GUR, how it is generally measured, and any special considerations for its use in a gaming context.

6.3.2.1 Electrodermal Activity

EDA refers to the electrical properties of the skin and is one of the most common biometric signals in GUR. EDA is comprised of the general conductivity of the skin (tonic baseline—also called EDA of the skin) and the short-term response to an event (phasic response—also called the GSR) (Boucscin, 1992). There are specific sweat glands, called the eccrine sweat glands—located in the palms of the hands and soles of the feet—that are used for measuring EDA. These glands response to psychological stimulation instead of simply to temperature changes in the body (e.g., cold and clammy hands when nervous), and were thought to evolve in this manner for locomotion, manipulation, and defense (Stern, 2001). Participants do not have to be actually sweating for sensors to detect changes in EDA; as sweat rises in a gland, the resistance of that gland decreases even though the sweat may not overflow onto the surface of the skin (Stern, 2001).

EDA is correlated to arousal (Lang, 1995) and reflects both emotional responses and cognitive activity (Boucsein, 1992). EDA has been used extensively as an indicator of stress and mental workload, and is considered the most sensitive response used in the detection of deception (i.e., lie detectors) (Bouscein, 1992). EDA has also been used extensively to indicate arousal in a digital game context, for example, by differentiating between playing against a friend or a computer opponent (Mandryk and Inkpen,

2004). Many other things also affect EDA, including age, sex, race, temperature, humidity, stage of menstrual cycle, time of day, season, sweating through exercise, deep breathing, and individual traits such as extroversion (Bouscein, 1992). As such, it is difficult to compare GSR between participants or within participants over multiple repeated sessions.

EDA is easily measured in a gaming context using dry electrodes attached to the fingers, the palm of the hand, or soles of the feet (Mandryk, 2008). Although operating a mouse or game controller can affect the measurement of EDA on the hands by affecting the connection between the electrode and skin (thus affecting the measured conductivity), our experience has been that using surface electrodes sewn in Velcro straps that were placed around two fingers on the same hand was robust enough for EDA measurement. We tested numerous electrode placements to ensure that there was no interference from movements made when manipulating the game controller, and found that finger clips were as responsive as pregelled electrodes on the feet, while electrodes on the palms suffered from movement artifacts (Mandryk, 2005).

6.3.2.2 Electromyography

EMG measures the activity level in our muscles by detecting voltages on the surface of the skin that occur when a muscle is contracted (Stern, 2001). Because muscles are directly controlled, EMG is an excellent candidate for biometric input in games (see Part I of this chapter); however, EMG can also be used in an evaluative capacity—in particular, through the measurement of muscle activity on the face, where it has been used to distinguish between positive and negative emotions (Fridlund and Cacioppo, 1986). When emotions are positive as opposed to negative, EMG activity over the brow region (corrugator supercilii, the frown muscle) is lower and EMG activity over the cheek (zygomaticus major, the smile muscle) and periocular (orbicularis oculi) muscle regions are higher (Cacioppo et al., 2000). These effects are stronger when averaged over a group rather than for individual analysis, and can differentiate between positive, neutral, and negative valence when viewing image-based stimuli (Partala et al., 2005). In addition, EMG on the forehead (musculus frontalis, the eyebrow-raising muscle) has been used as an indicator of mental effort (Fridlund and Cacioppo, 1986).

To measure EMG, electrodes are placed on the skin over the muscle of interest—two electrodes are placed along the muscle and a third ground is placed off the axis (Mandryk, 2008). There are many factors that can interfere with EMG measurement, such as body hair, interference from proximal muscles, and movement of the skin. In addition, players may feel self-conscious with sensors attached to their face.

In the context of games, facial EMG has been used to differentiate positive or negative reactions to an emotional moment in a game (Hazlett, 2006), to indicate positive emotional responses in play (Mandryk et al., 2006a), and even fun and flow in a game (Nacke and Lindley, 2008). Combined with video observation and gameplay logs, Mirza-Babaei et al. (2013) used EMG to identify key positive and negative moments during gameplay that were then correlated with in-game behavioral events (e.g., button press, interaction). In addition, for longer-term evaluation (i.e., over a few minutes of gameplay), the eye muscle (orbicularis oculi) is helpful for identifying high arousal pleasant emotions (Ravaja et al., 2008).

6.3.2.3 Cardiovascular Measures

There are a variety of cardiovascular measures that relate to heart activity that are useful for assessing player interaction with games (Mandryk, 2008). HR indicates the number of contractions made by the heart each minute, and is affected by age, posture, level of physical conditioning, breathing frequency, and circadian cycle (Stern, 2001). HR can be measured using EKG (i.e., electrodes placed on the surface of the skin), but a standard exercise HR monitor would suffice for evaluating player experience. HR has been used to differentiate between positive and negative emotions, with further differentiation made possible with finger temperature, and has also been used to differentiate between anger and fear (Papillo and Shapiro, 1990). In the context of games, HR responds to competition with human as opposed to nonplayer character (NPC) opponents (Lim and Reeves, 2010). We also used HR to model emotional response to games (Mandryk and Atkins, 2007), which is discussed in the section on sensor fusion.

There are factors, other than HR, that can be extracted using the cardiovascular signal. If quality sensors are used, the oscillation between consecutive heartbeats can be used to calculate HRV, which is an interesting biometric signal for player experience evaluation. Normally, the HR of an individual is slightly irregular; however, this irregularity can be suppressed for a variety of reasons, including mental effort and cognitive workload (Kalsbeek and Ettema, 1963; Kalsbeek and Sykes, 1967). Used extensively to evaluate interaction with computing systems (see Mandryk, 2008), the great potential of HRV for player experience evaluation is still untapped.

6.3.2.4 Other Physiological Measures

Outside of the scope of this chapter, there are several other physiological measures that could be of interest for evaluating player experience with digital games. For example, gaze tracking (Duchowski, 2007) has been used alone and in combination with other measures. Pupillometry, which investigates fluctuations in the size of the pupil (Stern, 2001), is a potential signal for evaluation as the pupil responds to mental effort and interest; however, the pupil is also affected by changing screen luminance, color, and spatial patterns, meaning that further research needs to be done to extract the meaningful signal. Respiration, blood pressure, and blood volume pulse (see Mandryk, 2008) have also been explored as evaluation measures, but are not as used in the context of GUR as the ones described in this chapter.

6.3.2.5 Sensor Fusion

Each signal described in this section has its own unique advantages for characterizing player experience and accesses a different aspect of player emotional state. To get the best picture from biometric measures, it is reasonable to take a sensor fusion approach and simultaneously examine multiple signals. Taking a sensor fusion approach has multiple advantages. First, it creates a more robust picture of player experience by accessing different physiological signals; second, it helps researchers map the signals to properties that are more directly tied to player experience—concepts like valence, arousal, or emotional state. Our initial work in this area (Mandryk et al., 2006b; Mandryk and Atkins, 2007) developed mathematical models of four emotional states—based on physiological signals—that are relevant to player experience. Using a fuzzy logic approach, our first model mapped four physiological signals (GSR, HR, EMG smiling, and EMG frowning) into levels of arousal and valence, which are two orthogonal dimensions commonly used to describe human emotion. Representing both the positive–negative aspect of experience and the level of activation, the arousal–valence space is a great method of objectively and quantitatively representing player experience when engaged with computer games. Our second model took the mapping further and transformed arousal and valence into four emotional states: boredom, excitement, frustration, and fun. We compared the modeled emotions to subjective reports and found that the modeled and subjective emotions showed the same trends for fun, boredom, and excitement; however, the modeled emotions revealed statistically significant differences between play conditions, whereas the subjective reports failed to reach significance. Our modeled emotions were based on fuzzy transformation functions from physiological variables to arousal and valence, and then from arousal–valence space to emotional labels. For more information on the development of the mathematical models, see Mandryk and Atkins (2007), while a validation of the modeling approach, as well as a description of its use in player experience evaluation can be found in Mandryk et al. (2006b).

Although this initial work successfully modeled states relevant to computer game play from physiological signals, there are still many unanswered research questions that have to be addressed before these types of models can be practically employed by games user researchers. Later in this chapter, we discuss issues with analyzing physiological signals for GUR, and inferring emotional states based on physiological measures. In addition, recent theories of player experience focus on established constructs grounded in research on human psychology. For example, the self-determination theory has been used to describe the motivational pull of games (Ryan et al., 2006) and is a leading subjective measure in player experience research (e.g., Birk and Mandryk, 2013; Birk et al., 2015). Although used in numerous studies of player experience, constructs from self-determination theory that describe play experience have not yet been modeled using biometric signals.

In addition to building models based on the sensor fusion of several biometric signals, researchers have also been combining physiological signals with other methods of evaluation. For example, Nacke et al. (2008, 2011a) and Kivikangas et al. (2011b) both examined physiological responses in the context of game events logged from the computer game software. Combining game analytics and physiological measures allows games user researchers to better characterize their findings and creates a more robust and complete picture of user experience.

6.3.3 Evaluation Using Brain-Based Sensors

As discussed in Part I of this chapter, EEG provides a method by which we can use an inference of the player's cognitive state as input into a game. Primarily for the purposes of neurofeedback training, there have also been a few examples of EEG game input to enhance the enjoyment of a leisure game. Traditionally, however, EEG is used as a method by which we can evaluate a person's cognitive state, and thus it also has great promise in terms of game evaluation. A full detailed summary of analysis techniques in BCI can be found in Wehbe and Nacke (2013); in this section, we specifically address frequency analysis, hemispheric asymmetry, event-related potential (ERP), or connectivity as measurement approaches.

The high temporal resolution of EEG makes it useful as a real-time evaluation tool for aspects of player experience during gameplay (Salminen and Ravaja, 2008; Salminen et al., 2009). In recent studies, EEG has been used to evaluate parts of user experience and to interact with computing systems, most often for users with interaction constraints, but also more often to investigate antecedents of player experience (Nacke, 2010; Nacke et al., 2010b; Schild et al., 2012; Johnson et al., 2015; Wehbe and Nacke, 2015). In many of these studies, it is paramount to correlate EEG with subjective measures to establish ground truth. However, EEG is maturing as a reliable tool for providing games user researchers with an additional data gathering instrument for assessing player experience.

6.3.3.1 EEG Data Collection in GUR

EEG data in GUR are recorded using a series of electrodes. Electrodes should align to the 10–20 map of electrode placement, a reference map commonly used to align electrodes to scalp locations corresponding to brain lobe areas. The electrical activity recorded by all electrodes (corresponding to neural activity) is often referenced against one or two reference points. Reference points may include, for example, the center of the scalp, nose, or mastoids. Alternative reference methods may include calculating the average as a global reference or using driven right leg and common mode sense. The electrical activity of each electrode is subtracted from the reference point to obtain information about the brain of the participant. Once obtained, the information can be analyzed using different techniques, such as frequency analysis, hemispheric asymmetry, ERP, or connectivity. EEG recordings may be done with a dense electrode array of 132 electrodes down to as few as one electrode plus references. Introducing multiple electrodes can increase spatial resolution but also increases the cost of the system and it may also increase complexity of the analysis, depending on the technique used. In contrast, certain evaluation techniques may not be possible with the available electrode arrangements. For example, hemispheric asymmetry techniques cannot be used with a single electrode system.

6.3.3.2 EEG Analysis Techniques

EEG analyses that depend on power of a frequency band or decomposition of the EEG signal include frequency analysis, neurofeedback, hemispheric asymmetry, and synchrony techniques. ERP techniques are used to look at the brain changes after an event or stimulus presentation. Lastly, synchrony and power change are of interest during connectivity studies or studies that further explore the connections within the brain. The analysis will dictate the specifications of the equipment and setup. It will also affect the study design and statistical analysis.

6.3.3.2.1 Frequency Analysis

Questions involving the brain state of the user may employ frequency analysis. In frequency analysis, the EEG data are divided by frequency bands determined by separating the signal into its component waves. A common approach to this analysis is to use a fast Fourier transform. Information obtained by this analysis depends on the area of collection. For example, for skull collection, the alpha band consisting of 8–13 Hz frequency can be an indication of a drowsy or relaxed state. The delta band is defined from 1 to 4 Hz. The theta band is from 4 to 12 Hz and can be associated with sleepiness. The beta band is from 13 to 30 Hz and can represent concentration. Lastly, the gamma band is from 30 to 50 Hz (Nacke, 2013). Salminen and Ravaja (2008) showed that in response to violent game events, there is an increase in oscillatory theta activity.

Precalculated frequency measures for entertainment and relaxation are available from commercial retailers, such as Neurosky, Emotiv, and Interaxon. Schild et al. (2012) investigated player experience and compared these formulas to questionnaire data after playing a game. The resulting data from the EEG, however, contrasted with the results of the questionnaire. Common to these approaches is that the overall frequency of the brain waves was analyzed. However, depending on the research question, researchers may to choose to analyze signals from only a few areas of the skull by limiting the electrodes.

Another approach worth mentioning is the mu rhythm, which is collected in the alpha frequency range of 8–12 Hz over the motor cortex. To specifically look at this rhythm only, data from electrodes overlapping or near the motor cortex (i.e., horizontally between the ears) are used. The mu rhythm fires when observing an action performed using the hand or mouth, and is suppressed when the participant mirrors that action (McFarland et al., 2000). Topography can be used as part of mu rhythm analysis, which allows for visualization of the decomposition of the signal into component frequencies overlaid on a depiction of the skull. Researchers have also looked at mu rhythms to study learning in video games (Wehbe et al., 2013). They showed that learning depends on the order of playing versus watching a video of the game being played. The results also indicated that the order of play also affected player arousal.

6.3.3.2.2 Hemispheric Frontal Alpha Asymmetry

Hemispheric frontal alpha asymmetry (HFAA) involves frequency analysis. This technique processes hemispheric activity of the opposing lobes of the brain. This may include comparing the statistical power of the frequency analysis of a wave in the right hemisphere versus the left. Further statistical tests can be used to analyze the data by lobe, to look for significant differences in activation between lobes. Coan and Allen (2004) presented a protocol that can be followed for analysis.

This technique has been used to study user experience in gaming. Salminen et al. (2009) used the game Super Monkey Ball 2 and examined game events (i.e., falling off the track) to determine their effects on the player's physiology—including on EEG. The researchers proposed that games that are more arousing are more engaging. HFAA can also be used as a measure of negative emotions such as stress or aggression.

6.3.3.2.3 ERP Technique

Questions that involve cognitive understanding may be answered using the ERP technique. Researchers employing this methodology look at different components or patterns that appear poststimulus or after an event. This technique uses time markers to identify the point of the stimulus in a presentation. Researchers often record around 800 ms after an event. They then search for the expected component within the time range. For instance, the P300 component is a component that occurs 300 ms after a visual stimulus. When looking for this component pattern, one would record an overlapping time section and expect the peak to occur 300 ms after the presentation of the visual stimulus (Luck, 2014). A common approach is to examine pre- and poststimulus data by summing the EEG response curves after removing artifacts. Random fluctuations will be resolved through this process, leaving only systematic differences. Patterns of activation previously established in the literature are sought to make inferences about the cognitive state of the participant. The appearance of the component can also depend on the population being studied. As an example, the N170 component appears 170 ms after presentation of a face or face-like stimuli but in children it appears around 250 ms after a stimulus (Luck, 2014).

Stimuli or events are not always concrete. ERP analysis can be used to study more abstract concepts such as creativity and insight (Dietrich, 2004a,b; Dietrich et al., 2010). In addition, components can also include patterns that occur indirectly or as a result of cognition following a task or stimuli. For example, error-related negativity is a negatively occurring peak that occurs after an error is made.

6.3.3.2.4 Connectivity and Coherence

When two or more regions of the brain fire synchronously, they are said to be functionally connected despite the absence of a physical connection. Unlike other EEG techniques, the functional connectivity technique is not exclusive to EEG. Other techniques such as functional magnetic resonance imaging and diffusion tensor imaging also employ functional connectivity. The brain is able to change in response to stimuli. Connectivity techniques can be used to show real-time changes in the brain state in response to stimuli.

6.3.4 Considerations for Analysis and Inference

As we have shown in Part II of this chapter, there has been significant investment into evaluating player experience using both body- and brain-based measures. It would benefit everybody in the game development industry if biometric measures were plug-and-play. Unfortunately, physiological measures are sensitive and finicky and are generally collected in controlled experimental settings, which is not ideal for evaluating computer games. However, following some simple rules can support the successful use of biometrics for game evaluation.

6.3.4.1 Analyzing Biometric Data

For a detailed description on how to analyze physiological data for GUR, see Mandryk (2008), Nacke (2013, 2015), or Wehbe and Nacke (2013). Here, we address some of the basic issues of using biometrics to evaluate game experience.

First, most biometric measures have high individual variability, making comparison across participants very difficult without some form of normalization. To correct for these individual differences, you can normalize the data; the most common method is to represent the biometric value as a percentage of the total span for that individual participant (see Mandryk, 2008). One of the drawbacks with normalizing biometric data is that you must know the minimum and maximum values for an individual participant, requiring that all analyses happen after all of the data have been collected, rather than in real time while the data are being collected.

A second issue with using biometric data to evaluate play experience is that sensor readings can change for reasons not related to the participant's experience. Although some of these factors can be controlled, noisy data can occur when the sensor produces random fluctuations, and sensor error can occur when other factors systematically affect the sensor readings. Consider, for example, a participant who sneezes, which would affect the EMG gathered on the face. Variations like this cannot technically be referred to as sensor noise because the sensor is measuring what it is intended to measure; however, for a researcher hoping to measure smiling and frowning behavior, these variations obscure the useful data. One of the most prevalent examples of sensor error is with the contact electrodes used in GSR sensors. Because the GSR sensor measures the conductivity of the skin between two contact electrodes, if the contact between the electrode and the skin varies, the GSR will appear to change. For example, if you place GSR electrodes on the palm of a participant's hand using standard sticker electrodes, and she bends her hand so that the palm "scrunches," the likely result is that the electrode will not be contacting as much skin as when the palm is stretched out. As a result the GSR will appear to drop (since the conductivity drops), when the user's actual GSR did not change. In this case, the sensor is not measuring what it is supposed to and we can call this sensor error. Alternative electrode placements (e.g., toes, finger clips) can alleviate this particular problem.

There are multiple ways of dealing with sensor error. If you know when the errors occurred, you can simply remove these data from subsequent analyses. If the data are noisy, with minor random fluctuations, there are standard signal processing methods you can use to clean up your data, such as a moving-average window, or a low-pass filter (see Mandryk, 2008). While both methods achieve a smoother signal, the moving-average window can easily be achieved with simple spreadsheet programing, while the low-pass filter requires more powerful tools and approaches. On the other hand, the low-pass filter approach is more powerful, allowing you greater control over which frequencies you keep and which you discard.

6.3.4.2 Issues with Inference

The physiological signals of players vary due to multiple stimuli, and as such, it is important to ensure that the biometric responses observed are due to the game stimulus and not another factor. Whenever using physiological data, researchers must ensure that other factors that affect physiology (e.g., physical activity, changing light, moving, and talking) are controlled. Even the act of applying sensors to the body and monitoring the body's responses can be a stressful experience for a participant, and every effort must be made to allow the participant to feel at ease. Anticipation and nervousness can also be present at the beginning of a user study and cause the resting baselines to be artificially high, creating a problem for a researcher who wants to use resting rates to normalize biometric data. Vicente et al. (1987) recommend collecting a number of baselines throughout the experimental session and averaging them to create a single baseline value. In addition, using participants who are familiar with the process of being connected to physiological sensors would help lower the resting values. Beginning the experiment with a training or practice condition, before collecting the resting values, might also help the participants relax.

Aside from the methodological issues, there are also theoretical challenges associated with making inferences from biometric data. After having identified correlations between events related to the game, psychological events, and physiological data, the eventual goal of a mathematical model is to be able to index psychological events from sensor readings. Although possible, there are various issues to address. Let us take a very simple example of a neurofeedback game to train focus in which a player's EEG activity reflects a loss of concentration after each level is completed. Basic logic prevents us from assuming that every time the player loses focus, they have just completed a level. Although this example is obvious, it demonstrates the care that must be taken when making inferences.

Cacioppo and Tassinary (1990) discuss four classes of psychophysiological relationships called outcomes, markers, concomitants, and invariants. These relations are based on the specificity (one-to-one vs. many-to-one), and generality (context bound vs. context free) of the relationship between the psychological event and the physiological response. Outcomes are many-to-one, situation-specific relationships, and reflect the fact that a physiological response varies as a function of a psychological event in a specific situation. When the physiological response follows the psychological event across situations (generality), the relationship is concomitant (many-to-one, cross-situational associations). With outcomes and concomitants, it is unclear whether the physiological response only follows changes for that psychological event or whether other psychological events (specificity) can also inspire the same physiological response. Markers are one-to-one, situation-specific relationships, and reflect that a physiological response can predict the occurrence of a psychological event in a specific situation. Invariants are like markers, except that the psychophysiological relationship is maintained across situations (one-to-one, cross-situational associations). Invariants provide a strong basis for inference; the issue for a researcher is in establishing the invariant relationship instead of simply assuming that the relationship between a psychological event and a physiological response is an invariant.

6.3.5 Summary of Using Biometrics for Game Evaluation

In Part II, we have described how biometrics have been used to evaluate player experience. Used to describe differences in various play conditions, as high-resolution correlates of player experience constructs, and to model emotional experiences with games, biometrics have been increasing in popularity as a meaningful and robust method of assessing player experience.

6.4 CONCLUSIONS

Although digital games have been a form of entertainment for decades, their dominance of leisure technologies is recent. Spawned by advances in hardware and software, game interaction has also seen several recent innovations. Natural interaction, gestural control, and virtual reality are all technologies that are seeing increased presence in digital gaming. Alongside these technologies, biometric control of digital games has been explored and is increasing in popularity. In Part I of this chapter, we present the advances in using physiological signals to control digital games.

Because digital games are such a dominant form of entertainment, game studios stand to make economic gains if their games are well designed and developed. To aid in creating excellent games, games user researchers employ several traditional and advanced methods of iteratively evaluating games and players' experiences during play. Alongside methods such as subjective evaluation, observation, and log-based game analytics, biometric player assessment has increased in use as a meaningful indicator of player experience. In Part II of this chapter, we present the state of the art in using physiological signals for game evaluation.

The role of biometrics in digital gaming is young and there is room for continued innovation in the signals used, the processing algorithms, the integration into standard processes, and the analysis and visualization of the data. The next decades will surely see incredible advances in the use of biometrics in digital games.

ACKNOWLEDGMENTS

The authors wish to thank Rina Wehbe and Anke Reinschlüssel for their part in the research that was presented in this chapter. Thanks also to NSERC and SSHRC for funding.

REFERENCES

Bakhshayesh, A. R., S. Hänsch, A. Wyschkon, M. J. Rezai, and G. Esser. Neurofeedback in ADHD: A single-blind randomized controlled trial. *European Child & Adolescent Psychiatry* 20(9), 2011: 481–491.

Bernhaupt, R. *Evaluating User Experience in Games: Concepts and Methods.* Human-Computer Interaction Series. Berlin: Springer, 2010.

Bernhaupt, R., ed. *Game User Experience Evaluation.* Switzerland: Springer, 2015.

Bersak, D., G. McDarby, N. Augenblick, P. McDarby, D. McDonnell, B. McDonald, and R. Karkun. Intelligent biofeedback using an immersive competitive environment. *Paper at the Designing Ubiquitous Computing Games Workshop at UbiComp,* Atlanta, Georgia, 2001.

Birk, M. and R. L. Mandryk. Control your game-self: Effects of controller type on enjoyment, motivation, and personality in game. In *Proceedings of the SIGCHI Conference on Human Factors in Computing Systems,* Paris, France. ACM, pp. 685–694, 2013.

Birk, M. V., R. L. Mandryk, M. K. Miller, and K. M. Gerling. How self-esteem shapes our interactions with play technologies. In *Proceedings of the 2015 Annual Symposium on Computer–Human Interaction in Play,* London, England. ACM, pp. 35–45, 2015.

Bos, D. P.-O., B. Reuderink, B. van de Laar, H. Gürkök, C. Mühl, M. Poel, A. Nijholt, and D. Heylen. Brain–computer interfacing and games. In *Brain–Computer Interfaces,* D. S. Tan and A. Nijholt (Eds.). London: Springer, pp. 149–178, 2010.

Boucsein, W. 1992. *Electrodermal Activity.* New York: Plenum Press, 1992.

Brainmaster Technologies Inc. 2015. Neurofeedback Games. September 21. http://www.brainmaster.com/page/neurofeedback-games/

Cacioppo, J. T., G. G. Berntson, J. T. Larsen, K. M. Poehlmann, and T. A. Ito. The psychophysiology of emotion. In *Handbook of Emotions,* M. Lewis, J. M. Haviland-Jones, and L. F. Barrett (Eds.). Vol. 2, pp. 173–191, 2000.

Cacioppo, J. T. and L. G. Tassinary. Inferring psychological significance from physiological signals. *American Psychologist* 45(1), 1990: 16.

Cacioppo, J. T., L. G. Tassinary, and G. Berntson, eds. *Handbook of Psychophysiology.* Cambridge, UK: Cambridge University Press, 2007.

Cmiel, V., O. Janousek, and J. Kolarova. EEG biofeedback. In *Proceedings of the 4th International Symposium on Applied Sciences in Biomedical and Communication Technologies,* Barcelona, Spain. ACM, p. 54, 2011.

Coan, J. A. and J. J. B. Allen. Frontal EEG asymmetry as a moderator and mediator of emotion. *Biological Psychology* 67(1), 2004: 7–50.

Dekker, A. and E. Champion. Please biofeed the zombies: Enhancing the game-play and display of a horror game using biofeedback. In *Proceedings of DiGRA*, Tokyo, Japan. pp. 550–558, 2007.

Deterding, S., D. Dixon, R. Khaled, and L. Nacke. From game design elements to gamefulness: Defining gamification. In *Proceedings of the 15th International Academic MindTrek Conference: Envisioning Future Media Environments*, Tampere, Finland. ACM, pp. 9–15, 2011.

Dietrich, A. Neurocognitive mechanisms underlying the experience of flow. *Consciousness and Cognition* 13(4), 2004a: 746–761.

Dietrich, A. The cognitive neuroscience of creativity. *Psychonomic Bulletin & Review* 11(6), 2004b: 1011–1026.

Dietrich, A. and R. Kanso. A review of EEG, ERP, and neuroimaging studies of creativity and insight. *Psychological Bulletin* 136(5), 2010: 822.

Dring, C. 2015. More money is spent on games then on movies or music combined, says IHS (Blog post). Retrieved from: http://www.mcvuk.com/news/read/more-money-is-spent-on-games-than-movies-and-music-combined-says-ihs/0151059

Duchowski, A. *Eye Tracking Methodology: Theory and Practice*. Vol. 373, London, UK: Springer Science & Business Media, 2007.

Entertainment Software Association. 2015. Essential Facts. Retrieved from: http://www.theesa.com/wp-content/uploads/2015/04/ESA-Essential-Facts-2015.pdf

Finke, A., A. Lenhardt, and H. Ritter. The MindGame: A P300-based brain–computer interface game. *Neural Networks* 22(9), 2009: 1329–1333.

Fridlund, A. J. and J. T. Cacioppo. Guidelines for human electromyographic research. *Psychophysiology* 23(5), 1986: 567–589.

Gevensleben, H., B. Holl, B. Albrecht et al. Distinct EEG effects related to neuro-feedback training in children with ADHD: A randomized controlled trial. *International Journal of Psychophysiology* 74(2), 2009: 149–157.

Gilleade, K., A. Dix, and J. Allanson. Affective videogames and modes of affective gaming: Assist me, challenge me, emote me. In *DiGRA '05—Proceedings of the 2005 DiGRA International Conference: Changing Views: Worlds in Play*, Vancouver, Canada. 7p., 2005.

Gürkök, H., A. Nijholt, M. Poel, and M. Obbink. Evaluating a multi-player brain–computer interface game: Challenge versus co-experience. *Entertainment Computing* 4(3), 2013: 195–203.

Gürkök, H., B. van de Laar, D. Plass-Oude Bos, M. Poel, and A. Nijholt. Players' opinions on control and playability of a BCI game. In *Universal Access in Human-Computer Interaction. Universal Access to Information and Knowledge*, Held as Part of HCI International 2014, Heraklion, Crete, Greece, June 22–27, 2014, Proceedings, Part II, C. Stephanidis and M. Antona (Eds.). Springer International Publishing, pp. 549–560, 2014.

Hazlett, R. L. Measuring emotional valence during interactive experiences: Boys at video game play. In *Proceedings of the SIGCHI Conference on Human Factors in Computing Systems*, Montreal, Canada. ACM, pp. 1023–1026, 2006.

Heinrich, H., H. Gevensleben, and U. Strehl. Annotation: Neurofeedback—Train your brain to train behaviour. *Journal of Child Psychology and Psychiatry* 48(1), 2007: 3–16.

Hjelm, S. I. Research+design: The making of brainball. *Interactions* 10(1), 2003: 26–34.

Holz, E. M., J. Höhne, P. Staiger-Sälzer, M. Tangermann, and A. Kübler. Brain–computer interface controlled gaming: Evaluation of usability by severely motor restricted end-users. *Artificial Intelligence in Medicine* 59(2), 2013: 111–120.

Isbister, K. and N. Schaffer. *Game Usability: Advancing the Player Experience.* Burlington, MA: CRC Press, 2008.

Jackson, M. M., R. Mappus, E. Barba, S. Hussein, G. Venkatesh, C. Shastry, and A. Israeli. Continuous control paradigms for direct brain interfaces. In *Human-Computer Interaction. Novel Interaction Methods and Techniques.* Heidelberg: Springer Berlin, pp. 588–595, 2009.

Johnson, D., P. Wyeth, M. Clark, and C. Watling. Cooperative game play with avatars and agents: Differences in brain activity and the experience of play. In *Proceedings of the 33rd Annual ACM Conference on Human Factors in Computing Systems*, Seoul, Korea. ACM, pp. 3721–3730, 2015.

Kaiser, D. A. and S. Othmer. Effect of neurofeedback on variables of attention in a large multi-center trial. *Journal of Neurotherapy* 4(1), 2000: 5–15.

Kalsbeek, J. W. H. and J. H. Ettema. Scored regularity of the heart rate pattern and the measurement of perceptual or mental load. *Ergonomics* 6(3), 1963: 306–307.

Kalsbeek, J. W. H. and R. N. Sykes. Objective measurement of mental load. *Acta Psychologica* 27, 1967: 253 261.

Kivikangas, J. M., G. Chanel, B. Cowley et al. A review of the use of psychophysiological methods in game research. *Journal of Gaming & Virtual Worlds* 3(3), 2011a: 181–199.

Kivikangas, J. M., L. Nacke, and N. Ravaja. Developing a triangulation system for digital game events, observational video, and psychophysiological data to study emotional responses to a virtual character. *Entertainment Computing* 2(1), 2011b: 11–16.

Krepki, R., B. Blankertz, G. Curio, and K.-R. Müller. The Berlin brain–computer interface (BBCI)—Towards a new communication channel for online control in gaming applications. *Multimedia Tools and Applications* 33(1), 2007: 73–90.

Kuikkaniemi, K., T. Laitinen, M. Turpeinen, T. Saari, I. Kosunen, and N. Ravaja. The influence of implicit and explicit biofeedback in first-person shooter games. In *Proceedings of the SIGCHI Conference on Human Factors in Computing Systems*, Atlanta, Georgia. ACM, pp. 859–868, 2010.

Landers, D. M., S. J. Petruzzello, W. Salazar, D. J. Crews, K. A. Kubitz, T. L. Gannon, and M. Han. The influence of electrocortical biofeedback on performance in pre-elite archers. *Medicine & Science in Sports & Exercise* 23(1), 1991:123–129.

Lang, P. J. The emotion probe: Studies of motivation and attention. *American Psychologist* 50(5), 1995: 372.

Lim, S. and B. Reeves. Computer agents versus avatars: Responses to interactive game characters controlled by a computer or other player. *International Journal of Human–Computer Studies* 68(1), 2010: 57–68.

Loup-Escande, E., F. Lotte, G. Loup, and A. Lécuyer. User-centred BCI videogame design. In *Handbook of Digital Games and Entertainment Technologies*, R. Nakatsu, M. Rauterberg, and P. Ciancarini (Eds.). Springer, pp. 1–26, 2015.

Lubar, J. F. and W. W. Bahler. Behavioral management of epileptic seizures following EEG biofeedback training of the sensorimotor rhythm. *Biofeedback and Self-Regulation* 1(1), 1976: 77–104.

Lubar, J. F., M. O. Swartwood, J. N. Swartwood, and P. H. O'Donnell. Evaluation of the effectiveness of EEG neurofeedback training for ADHD in a clinical setting as measured by changes in TOVA scores, behavioral ratings, and WISC-R performance. *Biofeedback and Self-Regulation* 20(1), 1995: 83–99.

Lubar, J. O. and J. F. Lubar. Electroencephalographic biofeedback of SMR and beta for treatment of attention deficit disorders in a clinical setting. *Biofeedback and Self-Regulation* 9(1), 1984: 1–23.

Luck, S. J. *An Introduction to the Event-Related Potential Technique.* Cambridge, MA: MIT press, 2014.

Mandryk, R. L. Modeling user emotion in interactive play environments: A fuzzy physiological approach. PhD dissertation, School of Computing Science, Simon Fraser University, Burnaby, BC, Canada, 2005.

Mandryk, R. L. Physiological measures for game evaluation. In *Game Usability: Advice from the Experts for Advancing the Player Experience,* Isbister, K. and N. Schaffer, (Eds.). Burlington, MA: CRC Press, pp. 207–235, 2008.

Mandryk, R. L. and M. S. Atkins. A fuzzy physiological approach for continuously modeling emotion during interaction with play technologies. *International Journal of Human–Computer Studies* 65(4), 2007: 329–347.

Mandryk, R. L., M. S. Atkins, and K. M. Inkpen. A continuous and objective evaluation of emotional experience with interactive play environments. In *Proceedings of the SIGCHI Conference on Human Factors in Computing Systems,* Montreal, Canada. ACM, pp. 1027–1036, 2006b.

Mandryk, R. L., S. Dielschneider, M. R. Kalyn, C. P. Bertram, M. Gaetz, A. Doucette, B. A. Taylor, A. Pritchard Orr, and K. Keiver. Games as neurofeedback training for children with FASD. In *Proceedings of the 12th International Conference on Interaction Design and Children,* New York. ACM, pp. 165–172, 2013.

Mandryk, R. L. and K. M. Inkpen. Physiological indicators for the evaluation of co-located collaborative play. In *Proceedings of the 2004 ACM Conference on Computer Supported Cooperative Work,* Chicago, Illinois. ACM, pp. 102–111, 2004.

Mandryk, R. L., K. M. Inkpen, and T. W. Calvert. Using psychophysiological techniques to measure user experience with entertainment technologies. *Behaviour & Information Technology* 25(2), 2006a: 141–158.

Martinez, P., H. Bakardjian, and A. Cichocki. Fully online multicommand brain–computer interface with visual neurofeedback using SSVEP paradigm. *Computational Intelligence and Neuroscience* 2007, 2007: 13–13.

McFarland, D. J., L. A. Miner, T. M. Vaughan, and J. R. Wolpaw. Mu and beta rhythm topographies during motor imagery and actual movements. *Brain Topography* 12(3), 2000: 177–186.

Mirza-Babaei, P., L. E. Nacke, J. Gregory, N. Collins, and G. Fitzpatrick. 2013. How does it play better? exploring user testing and biometric storyboards in games user research. In *Proceedings of the SIGCHI Conference on Human Factors in Computing Systems* (CHI '13). ACM, New York, NY, pp. 1499–1508. DOI: http://dx.doi.org/10.1145/2470654.2466200

Monastra, V. J., J. F. Lubar, M. Linden, P. VanDeusen, G. G. William Wing, A. Phillips, and T. N. Fenger. Assessing attention deficit hyperactivity disorder via quantitative electroencephalography: An initial validation study. *Neuropsychology* 13(3), 1999: 424.

Monastra, V. J., S. Lynn, M. Linden, J. F. Lubar, J. Gruzelier, and T. J. La Vaque. Electroencephalographic biofeedback in the treatment of attention-deficit/hyperactivity disorder. *Journal of Neurotherapy* 9(4), 2006: 5–34.

Monastra, V. J., D. M. Monastra, and S. George. The effects of stimulant therapy, EEG biofeedback, and parenting style on the primary symptoms of attention-deficit/hyperactivity disorder. *Applied Psychophysiology and Biofeedback* 27(4), 2002: 231–249.

Moriyama, T. S., G. Polanczyk, A. Caye, T. Banaschewski, D. Brandeis, and L. A. Rohde. Evidence-based information on the clinical use of neurofeedback for ADHD. *Neurotherapeutics* 9(3), 2012: 588–598.

Mühl, C., H. Gürkök, D. Plass-Oude Bos, M. E. Thurlings, L. Scherffig, M. Duvinage, A. A. Elbakyan, S. W. Kang, M. Poel, and D. Heylen. Bacteria hunt. *Journal on Multimodal User Interfaces* 4(1), 2010: 11–25.

Müller-Putz, G., R. Scherer, and G. Pfurtscheller. Game-like training to learn single switch operated neuroprosthetic control. In *BRAINPLAY 07 Brain–Computer Interfaces and Games Workshop at ACE (Advances in Computer Entertainment) 2007*, Vancouver, BC, Canada. p. 41, 2007.

Nacke, L. E. Wiimote vs. controller: Electroencephalographic measurement of affective gameplay interaction. In *Proceedings of the International Academic Conference on the Future of Game Design and Technology*. ACM, pp. 159–166, 2010.

Nacke, L. E. Directions in physiological game evaluation and interaction. In *Conference on Human Factors in Computing Systems (CHI)*, Vancouver, BC, Canada. 2011.

Nacke, L. E. An introduction to physiological player metrics for evaluating games. In *Game Analytics: Maximizing the Value of Player Data,* M. Seif El-Nasr, A. Drachen, and A. Canossa (Eds.). London: Springer, pp. 585–619, 2013.

Nacke, L. E. Games user research and physiological game evaluation. In *Game User Experience Evaluation,* R. Bernhaupt (Ed.). Cham, Switzerland: Springer International Publishing, pp. 63–86, 2015.

Nacke, L. E., A. Drachen, and S. Göbel. Methods for evaluating gameplay experience in a serious gaming context. *International Journal of Computer Science in Sport* 9(2), 2010a: 1–12.

Nacke, L. E., M. Kalyn, C. Lough, and R. L. Mandryk. Biofeedback game design: Using direct and indirect physiological control to enhance game interaction. In *Proceedings of the SIGCHI Conference on Human Factors in Computing Systems*, Vancouver, BC, Canada. ACM, pp. 103–112, 2011a.

Nacke, L. and C. A. Lindley. Flow and immersion in first-person shooters: Measuring the player's gameplay experience. In *Proceedings of the 2008 Conference on Future Play: Research, Play, Share*, Toronto, Canada. ACM, pp. 81–88, 2008.

Nacke, L., C. Lindley, and S. Stellmach. Log who's playing: Psychophysiological game analysis made easy through event logging. In *Fun and Games*. Heidelberg: Springer Berlin, pp. 150–157, 2008.

Nacke, L. E., S. Stellmach, and C. A. Lindley. Electroencephalographic assessment of player experience: A pilot study in affective ludology. *Simulation & Gaming* 2010b: 1–24.

Nacke, L. E., S. Stellmach, D. Sasse, J. Niesenhaus, and R. Dachselt. LAIF: A logging and interaction framework for gaze-based interfaces in virtual entertainment environments. *Entertainment Computing* 2(4), 2011b: 265–273.

Nan, W., J. P. Rodrigues, J. Ma, X. Qu, F. Wan, P.-I. Mak, P. Un Mak, M. I. Vai, and A. Rosa. Individual alpha neurofeedback training effect on short term memory. *International Journal of Psychophysiology* 86(1), 2012: 83–87.

Negini, F., R. L. Mandryk, and K. G. Stanley. Using affective state to adapt characters, NPCs, and the environment in a first-person shooter game. In *2014 IEEE Games Media Entertainment (GEM)*. Toronto, Canada: IEEE, pp. 1–8, 2014.

NeuroSky. 2015. EEG Hardware Platforms. September 21. http://neurosky.com/biosensors/eeg- sensor/biosensors/

Newzoo. 2015. Global Games Market Will Reach $102.9 Billion in 2017. Retrieved from: http://www.newzoo.com/insights/global-games-market-will-reach-102-9-billion-2017-2/

Nijholt, A., D. P.-O. Bos, and B. Reuderink. Turning shortcomings into challenges: Brain–computer interfaces for games. *Entertainment Computing* 1(2), 2009: 85–94.

Nijholt, A., J. B. F. van Erp, and D. K. J. Heylen. BrainGain: BCI for HCI and games. In *Symposium on Brain Computer Interfaces and Human Computer Interaction: A Convergence of Ideas*, Aberdeen, UK. pp. 32–35, 2008.

Papillo, J. and D. Shapiro. The cardiovascular system. In *Principles of Psychophysiology: Physical, Social and Inferential Elements*, J. T. Cacioppo and L. G. Tassinary (Eds.). Cambridge: Cambridge University Press, pp. 456–512, 1990.

Partala, T., V. Surakka, and T. Vanhala. Person-independent estimation of emotional experiences from facial expressions. In *Proceedings of the 10th International Conference on Intelligent User Interfaces*, San Diego, California. ACM, pp. 246–248, 2005.

Picard, R. W. *Affective Computing*. Vol. 252, Cambridge: MIT Press, 1997.

Pope, A. T. and O. S. Palsson. Helping video games "rewire our minds," NASA TR, 2001.

Ravaja, N., M. Turpeinen, T. Saari, S. Puttonen, and L. Keltikangas-Järvinen. The psychophysiology of James Bond: Phasic emotional responses to violent video game events. *Emotion* 8(1), 2008: 114.

Raymond, J., I. Sajid, L. A. Parkinson, and J. H. Gruzelier. Biofeedback and dance performance: A preliminary investigation. *Applied Psychophysiology and Biofeedback* 30(1), 2005: 65–73.

Rigby, S. and R. M. Ryan. *Glued to Games: How Video Games Draw Us in and Hold Us Spellbound*. Santa Barbara, California: ABC-CLIO, 2011.

Ryan, R. M., M. F. Lynch, M. Vansteenkiste, and E. L. Deci. Motivation and autonomy in counseling, psychotherapy, and behavior change: A look at theory and practice. *The Counseling Psychologist* 39(2), 2010: 193–260.

Ryan, R. M., C. S. Rigby, and A. Przybylski. The motivational pull of video games: A self-determination theory approach. *Motivation and Emotion* 30(4), 2006: 344–360.

Sakurazawa, S., N. Yoshida, N. Munekata et al. A computer game using galvanic skin response. In *Proceedings of the Second International Conference on Entertainment Computing*, Pittsburgh, Pennsylvania. Carnegie Mellon University, pp. 1–3, 2003.

Salen, K. and E. Zimmerman. *Rules of Play: Game Design Fundamentals*. Cambridge, MA: MIT Press, 2004.

Salminen, M., J. M. Kivikangas, N. Ravaja, and K. Kallinen. Frontal EEG asymmetry in the study of player experiences during competitive and cooperative play. In *Proceedings of IADIS International Conference Game and Entertainment Technologies*, Algarve, Portugal, pp. 44–45, 2009.

Salminen, M. and N. Ravaja. Increased oscillatory theta activation evoked by violent digital game events. *Neuroscience Letters* 435(1), 2008: 69–72.

Schild, J., J. LaViola, and M. Masuch. Understanding user experience in stereoscopic 3D games. In *Proceedings of the SIGCHI Conference on Human Factors in Computing Systems*, Austin, Texas. ACM, pp. 89–98, 2012.

Steiner, N. J., E. C. Frenette, K. M. Rene, R. T. Brennan, and E. C. Perrin. Neurofeedback and cognitive attention training for children with attention-deficit hyperactivity disorder in schools. *Journal of Developmental & Behavioral Pediatrics* 35(1), 2014: 18–27.

Sterman, M. B. Basic concepts and clinical findings in the treatment of seizure disorders with EEG operant conditioning. *Clinical EEG and Neuroscience* 31(1), 2000: 45–55.

Stern, R. M., W. J. Ray, and K. S. Quigley. *Psychophysiological Recording*. New York: Oxford University Press, 2001.

Tangermann, M., M. Krauledat, K. Grzeska et al. Playing pinball with non-invasive BCI. In *Advances in Neural Information Processing Systems 21, Proceedings of the Twenty-Second Annual Conference on Neural Information Processing Systems*. Vancouver, Canada, pp. 1641–1648, December 8–11, 2008.

Thompson, L., M. Thompson, and A. Reid. Neurofeedback outcomes in clients with Asperger's syndrome. *Applied Psychophysiology and Biofeedback* 35(1), 2010: 63–81.

Thompson, M. and L. Thompson. *The Neurofeedback Book: An Introduction to Basic Concepts in Applied Psychophysiology.* Wheat Ridge, Colorado: Association for Applied Psychophysiology and Biofeedback, 2003.

van de Laar, B., H. Gurkok, D. Plass-Oude Bos, M. Poel, and A. Nijholt. Experiencing BCI control in a popular computer game. *IEEE Transactions on Computational Intelligence and AI in Games* 5(2), 2013: 176–184.

Vernon, D. J. Can neurofeedback training enhance performance? An evaluation of the evidence with implications for future research. *Applied Psychophysiology and Biofeedback* 30(4), 2005: 347–364.

Vicente, K. J., D. C. Thornton, and N. Moray. Spectral analysis of sinus arrhythmia: A measure of mental effort. *Human Factors: The Journal of the Human Factors and Ergonomics Society* 29(2), 1987: 171–182.

Wehbe, R. R. and L. E. Nacke. An introduction to EEG analysis techniques and brain–computer interfaces for games user researchers. In *Proceedings of DiGRA 2013.* Atlanta, Georgia: DiGRA, pp. 1–16, 2013.

Wehbe, R. R. and L. E. Nacke. Towards understanding the importance of co-located gameplay. In *Proceedings of the 2015 Annual Symposium on Computer–Human Interaction in Play,* London, England. ACM, pp. 733–738, 2015.

Wehbe, R. R., D. L. Kappen, D. Rojas, M. Klauser, B. Kapralos, and L. E. Nacke. 2013. EEG-based assessment of video and in-game learning. In *CHI '13 Extended Abstracts on Human Factors in Computing Systems* (CHI EA '13). ACM, New York, NY, pp. 667–672. DOI: http://dx.doi.org/10.1145/2468356.2468474

Wilkinson, N., R. P. Ang, and D. H. Goh. Online video game therapy for mental health concerns: A review. *International Journal of Social Psychiatry* 54(4), 2008: 370–382.

CHAPTER 7

Biometric Applications in Homeland Security

Mikhail Gofman, Sinjini Mitra,
Maria Villa, and Christina Dudaklian

CONTENTS

7.1 INTRODUCTION

Homeland security is a blanket term used by the U.S. government to refer to national efforts to protect the country against terrorist attacks and other threats. In response to the attacks on New York and Washington DC on September 11, 2001, the U.S. government established the Department of Homeland Security (DHS) as a federal agency. According to the DHS Fiscal Year 2014–2018 Strategic Plan, its key missions are to:

- Prevent terrorism and enhance security

- Secure and manage U.S. borders

- Enforce and administer immigration laws

- Safeguard and secure cyberspace

- Strengthen national preparedness and resilience [1]

The government considers biometric technology to be integral to achieving the above missions. Congress, along with the National Commission on Terrorist Attacks on the United States (thereafter referred to as the 9/11 Commission), urged an increase in the use of biometric technology. A cabinet-level subcommittee created by the White House is responsible for organizing policies to implement biometric technology in various federal agencies. In addition, the United States Visitor and Immigrant Status Indicator Technology (US-VISIT) program was established, to prevent individuals deemed threating from entering the country. [2]. In March 2013, it was replaced by the Office of Biometric Identity Management (OBIM) after the approval of the 2013 Continuing Resolution by U.S. President Barack Obama (although it is still often referred to by many as US-VISIT) [3].

The OBIM falls under the National Protection and Programs Directorate of the DHS, and according to the DHS website, the OBIM's mission is to "supply the technology for collecting and storing biometric data, provide analysis, update its watch list, and ensure the integrity of the data." The US-VISIT program used to perform all the functions that the OBIM performs today, except overstay analysis, which was transferred to the U.S. Immigration and Customs Enforcement (ICE) agency [3]. Many government agencies rely on the OBIM's biometrics technologies, including the Department of Defense, Department of Justice, Department of State, and the Department of Commerce.

The rest of this chapter is organized as follows: Section 7.2 describes the US-VISIT program and Section 7.3 discusses U.S. biometric passports. In

Section 7.4, we present a brief overview of the homeland security applications of biometrics in other countries. In Section 7.5, we introduce new trends in homeland security. Section 7.6 presents a condensed timeline of biometrics in homeland security around the world. Concluding remarks appear in Section 7.7.

7.2 THE US-VISIT PROGRAM OVERVIEW

The 9/11 attacks exposed vulnerabilities in the security infrastructure of the U.S. homeland, particularly in the area of immigration and border control. To address such concerns and protect the nation, the federal government established the DHS. In 2003, the DHS launched the US-VISIT program, which required the collection, analysis, and cross-checking of biometric data (such as fingerprints) from all foreign individuals entering the United States against databases of known terrorists and illegal immigrants.

The use of biometrics was motivated by the fact that this data is harder to steal or forge than visas, passports, and other travel documents. At the same time, biometric systems are convenient for users and have proven to be quite robust in identifying persons considered to be a threat by homeland security. The official brochure in Reference 4 released by the DHS cites the following cases where biometrics helped stop impostors from gaining entry into the country:

Case 1

A man arrived at New York's John F. Kennedy International Airport and presented a valid passport and visa. The name on his travel documents did not raise any concern. However, when his fingerprints were checked through US-VISIT, they revealed that he was trying to use his twin brother's visa, who had no history of criminal or immigration violations. By matching his biometrics, Customs and Border Protection (CBP) officers learned that this man had been apprehended for taking photos of a U.S. military base and had overstayed the term of his admission on a previous visit to the United States. CBP officers refused the man admission to the United States.

Case 2

When a man applied for asylum at a U.S. asylum office, his fingerprints were checked against US-VISIT's data. Although he had used three aliases and a different date of birth to try to evade detection, his biometrics revealed an extensive criminal record, including charges for rape, assault, and an outstanding warrant for kidnapping. As a result of US-VISIT's positive identification of this person, the asylum office contacted Immigration and Customs Enforcement (ICE), who later arrested the man.

Case 3

When a man applied for asylum in the United Kingdom, U.K. immigration officials requested that the United States check the man's fingerprints against the Department of Homeland Security's US-VISIT data. The results revealed that the man had previously traveled to the United States using a different name. This new information confirmed that the asylum applicant was lying about his identity. Upon further investigation, the United Kingdom learned that the man was wanted on rape charges in Australia, and he was later returned there to face court proceedings [4].

7.2.1 US-VISIT Biometrics

The majority of non-U.S. citizens aged between 14 and 49 years who are entering the country or applying for a visa are required to use the US-VISIT program (Canadian citizens are excluded as the United States and Canada have signed agreements allowing visa-free travel of their citizens between each other's countries). Figure 7.1 illustrates a person using the US-VISIT program to provide fingerprints [39].

FIGURE 7.1 (**See color insert.**) A person using a US-VISIT program to provide fingerprints at Washington Dulles Airport. (Photo by Department of Homeland Security, Public Domain.)

When a non-U.S. citizen enters the United States at a major point of arrival (e.g., an airport), U.S. Department of State consular officers and CBP use US-VISIT technology to collect facial photographs and fingerprint scans [6].

The initial fingerprinting system used by US-VISIT in 2003 collected two fingerprints. In 2009, the system was upgraded to collect 10 fingerprints in order to make the verification process more accurate. Much of this optimization of the US-VISIT program has been handled by Accenture Consulting. Currently, Accenture is working to incorporate other biometric modalities into the US-VISIT program, including irises, palm prints, scars/marks/tattoos, and DNA [7].

7.2.2 US-VISIT Performance

According to Accenture, US-VISIT technology has the capability to search through more than 140 million people in a matter of seconds. It also returns ID matches in less than 10 s. Every day, the US-VISIT program identifies an average of 5000 illegal visitors, 2500 immigration violators, and 50 wanted criminals [8].

7.3 BIOMETRIC PASSPORTS

In 2006, the Department of State started issuing biometric passports, or e-passports. A biometric passport is equipped with an electronic chip that stores the passport holder's name, date of birth, other biographic information, and a biometric identifier, which, according to U.S. law, must be a digital photograph of the passport holder [9]. Figure 7.2 shows the

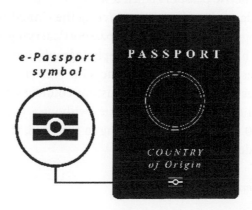

FIGURE 7.2   Symbol used for labeling biometric passports (e-passports). (Digital image from the Department of Homeland Security.)

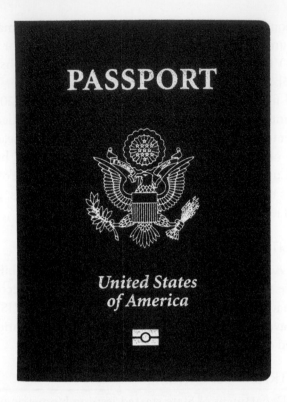

FIGURE 7.3   United States' biometric passport labeled with the international biometric symbol. (From Shutterstock with permission.)

international symbol used for identifying biometric passports. Figure 7.3 shows a U.S. biometric passport labeled with the symbol.

U.S. law mandates that all visitors entering the United States under the Visa Waiver Program must have an e-passport carrying their biometric information (such as the required facial photograph) if their passport was issued on or after October 26, 2006. The Visa Waiver Program includes the United States and 38 mutually trusting countries who allow their citizens to travel to each other's countries without a visa if their stay in the country is 90 days or less. According to the DHS, the benefits of the e-passport include [10]

1. *Securely identify the traveler*

2. *Provide protection against identity theft*

3. *Protect privacy*

4. *Make it difficult to alter a document for use in gaining admission to the United States*

Figure 7.4 illustrates the process for verifying an e-passport [11]. The steps in verifying a biometric passport are as follows:

1. The data page of the person's passport is scanned, and the security features of the data page are verified by the border control system. The data page includes the passport holder's name, date of birth, and other biographic information.

2. The contactless chip on the passport is read by the optical data recognition system, the inspection system then authenticates the information on the chip (which, again, stores the same information as found on the data page in addition to the biometric features). All

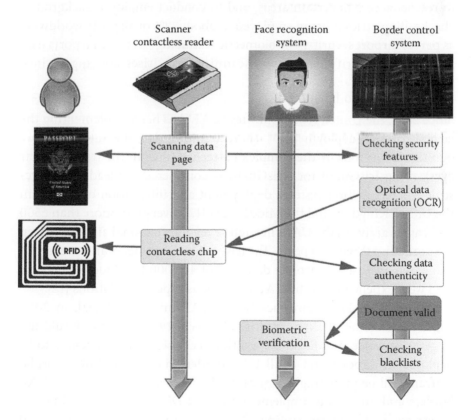

FIGURE 7.4 Process of verifying a biometric passport. (Based on the diagram from Funke, H. Automatic Border Control Systems [eGate]; blog.protocolbench.org.)

U.S. passports and passports issued by the Visa Waiver Program have security features for preventing unauthorized readings of the chip data (also known as skimming) [9].

3. Finally, the person's biometrics (e.g., face and fingerprints) are verified and checked against the databases of known criminals, terrorists, and other individuals who are considered to be a threat. As previously mentioned, some of these databases are shared internationally.

7.4 INTERNATIONAL APPLICATIONS

Although the term *homeland security* is primarily used in the context of immigration and border control in the United States, many countries around the world are also deploying biometrics to secure their homeland. The most extensive use of such technology is at airports in order to simplify and improve efficiency, improve the passenger travel process, to restrict access to certain areas, and to conduct employee background checks. Biometrics is being employed in about 28% of airports worldwide as part of airport security. The biometric technology in these airports uses mechanisms to verify identities via scanning faces, irises, and fingerprints.

7.4.1 United Arab Emirates

Since 2001, the United Arab Emirates (UAE) has been implementing the largest national deployment of iris recognition (i.e., the automatic recognition of persons by the complex patterns visible in the irises of their eyes), using IrisGuard Inc. IrisGuard is considered the leader in large-scale iris recognition systems deployment and integration operating in the United Kingdom and the Middle East [12]. Every day, more than 6500 passengers arrive in the UAE through seven international airports, seven sea ports, and three land ports. The irises of the passengers are extensively compared against an enrolled database of 420,000 IrisCodes of persons who were expelled from the UAE for various types of violations [12].

According to FindBiometrics [13], a UAE ministry official, in 2016, urged the creation of a new multimodal security system that would use fingerprint, voice, and facial recognition technology. The system is to be deployed in airports and at all UAE borders starting in 2016. Morpho (Safran) will be providing the mutlimodal biometric technology to UAE borders and airports to implement *Iris-at-a-Distance* eye scanning and *Finger-on-the-Fly* fingerprinting. The International Airport in Dubai projects service to over 80 million passengers in 2016 when the new multi-modal security biometric system will be implemented [14,15].

7.4.2 Brazil

Brazil has enforced the use of ID cards on its citizens since the early part of the twentieth century. The government led by Dr. Pacheco used the Vucetich system, named after Dr. Juan Vucetich who invented a ten-fingerprint identification system called comparative dactyloscopy. The effectiveness of the system was first illustrated in an Argentina criminal case in 1892. Later, in 1999, Brazil established what became the oldest ID institute, which was integrated into the civil and criminal automatic fingerprint identification system [16]. The Vucetich system was also adopted by Argentina in 1903 and its use later spread to other Spanish-speaking countries [15]. Since 2000, Rio de Janeiro has used fully digitized ID cards that have a signature, a color photo, two fingerprints, and more data about the individual encoded in a two-dimensional barcode. In 2005, Brazil developed its new passport, which was launched in 2007 in Brasilia. The features of this new Brazilian passport include ultraviolet hidden symbols, laser perforation, and a security layer over variable data [16].

7.4.3 Canada

In 2008, the Canadian government started using biometric-based identification in the country's airports. Increased fraud in Canada drove the employment of facial recognition, which includes the scanning of about 34 million images held in the Canadian database. Every year, about 65 genuine passports are identified as having been issued to impostors [17]. Canada has collected the biometric data of about 30 countries, including Afghanistan, Syria, and Egypt. A fee of $85 is charged to visitors to have their biometric data taken; this includes fingerprints and a digital photo. The exception to the biometric data rule applies to citizens who are under 14 or over 80 years old and diplomats. The regulations for biometric scanning are still in development but have an anticipated start date of 2018–2019; the goal is to screen visitors from more than 150 countries, including those with visas for work or school.

7.4.4 Europe

According to the *Wall Street Journal*, airports in Europe have incorporated biometric technology faster than their American counterparts [18]. Visitors to France, Spain, and the United Kingdom are now required to provide their biometric data (facial and fingerprint scans) when applying for visas to travel to these countries. Norway and Sweden introduced biometric passports in 2005, and Sweden even had electronic ID cards that had two microchips: one for traveling and another for identification to log onto various systems [19].

7.4.4.1 Germany

In November 2005, Germany introduced the e-passport with the ePass program. The first generation of passports, from 2005 to 2007, included information about the passport owner, such as the name, date of birth, sex, nationality, and a digital photo. According to the Homeland Security News Wire, smiles and teeth exposure posed a problem for the biometric readers. As a result, people were advised to use a "neutral face expression with closed mouth avoiding a smile" and look straight at the camera [20]. From November 2007 onwards, German passports introduced a machine-readable chip that holds the biometric information of a digital photograph, two fingerprints (index fingers, one from each hand), and a digital signature. The chip, located in the back of the cover page of the passport, is contactless and equipped with a 13.56 MHz loop antenna [21–23]. Iris scans are expected to eventually be incorporated. Figure 7.5 shows a German passport.

7.4.4.2 Naples, Italy

In 2016, Naples International Airport in Italy started employing programmed border control *e-gates*, according to Future Travel Experience [25]. The new e-gates program uses facial recognition to confirm that the

FIGURE 7.5 German passport. (From Application for a German Passport, Welcome to Germany.info.)

FIGURE 7.6   Italian passport. (The Passport Photo Blog by ePassportPhoto.com.)

passenger is the passport holder. Fingerprint verification technology is an additional built-in security feature in the e-gate to be used only when required [25]. The Italian passport is shown in Figure 7.6.

7.4.4.3 The Netherlands

Dutch passports introduced an electronic chip with personal information and the citizen's digitized photo in 2006. It was not until September 21, 2009 that Dutch passports and ID cards began containing the holder's fingerprints in an effort to combat terrorism [16]. However, biometric passports with chips containing digital information regarding facial images and fingerprints have created controversy. The fact that the Netherlands keeps the biometric data in a centralized computer system adds to the opposition groups' concerns [20]. The Vrijbit civil rights group launched legal action at the European Court of Human Rights with these main claims against the new passports:

1. *It's against our human rights that the government takes our bodily data as a kind of property.*

2. *It is very dangerous ... If your fingerprints or your data from the databases are stolen and used by people you don't know, it's irreparable damage.*

3. *All the people who refuse to give their fingerprints can't even function normally in society anymore because there are other laws that order you to show your current identification. It's impossible to get one without fingerprints* [20].

Nonetheless, the intelligence services and the police claim that their access to the biometric database is "vital to catch criminals" and prevent the escalation of terrorism [20].

7.4.5 Australia and New Zealand

Australia and New Zealand have also incorporated the use of biometric technology for their homeland security since 2009. They are two of the countries that use SmartGate or eGate to "self-process through passport control." Anyone with the e-passport symbol (as shown in Figure 7.2), older than 12 years, and traveling from New Zealand, Australia, the United Kingdom, the United States, or Canada, can use SmartGate, but this is still subject to filling out a Passenger Arrival or Departure Card [22]. The SmartGate system is performed in two steps. For instance, at the Auckland Airport in New Zealand, first the traveler uses the kiosk where the passport is inserted and a ticket is issued. If the traveler is eligible, he or she then proceeds to step 2 at the gate. At the gate, the ticket from the kiosk is used and the facial recognition process takes place. The facial recognition system matches the digital image in the e-passport chip with the person's face [26]. If the facial recognition is successful, the traveler proceeds through the gate.

7.4.6 Japan

Japan started using mobile biometric terminals, called *Biocarts,* in its airports in April 2016. A Biocart is a mobile device with a fingerprint reader and a camera attached that gathers a person's face and fingerprint biometrics and transmits the biometric data to the customs booths. As a result, when it is a person's turn to go through customs, the customs agent already has their biometric data [27,28]. Biocarts were introduced to allow passengers to clear the entry routines by themselves and thus reduce the wait time from a maximum of 36 min (i.e., at Kansai International Airport) to 20 min (i.e., at Narita International Airport) [27]. About 80 Biocarts have been installed in the most crowded terminals in Takatsu, Naha, and Kansai International Airports. Since more than 19 million travelers visited Japan in 2015 and more than 30 million are expected in the upcoming years, the government is bringing in more Biocarts to hasten the processing of visitors [29].

7.4.7 India

India's national ID program, operated by the Unique Identification Authority of India, is called *Aadhaar* (meaning *foundation* in Hindi) [30]. Aadhaar is a biometrics-based digital identity platform that verifies identity online, instantly, and at any location [31,32]. It has been called the "biggest biometric database in the world" [33] containing twice as much data as that which is held by the FBI. It has the capacity to authenticate about "one million identities per hour, each one taking about thirty seconds." The Indian government employed Aadhaar to collect fingerprint and iris scans from its 1.2 billion citizens and to provide them with 12-digit-long ID numbers [30].

7.5 NEWER TRENDS

The implementation of biometric technology using facial recognition or fingerprint scanners in the travel industry has transformed the travel experience, making this "the next golden age of air travel" [32].

The Aruba Airport started implementing Aruba Happy Flow [34], a biometric facial recognition system that reduces the boarding process to seconds and into a "single passenger token." With the implementation of Aruba Happy Flow, passengers no longer need to show their passports and boarding passes at numerous points throughout the airport (check-in, border control, bag drop, immigration, and aircraft boarding) [34,35]. The passengers are subject to identification at the first checkpoint, but thereafter, passengers are verified by the new biometric scanners. The Prime Minister of Aruba, Mike Eman, referred to the Happy Flow project as "an extremely innovative and important step in the transportation industry for passengers, not only for Aruba, but worldwide" [36].

Since mid-April 2015, Alaska Airlines has implemented a fingerprint-based passenger token program at San Jose International Airport [23]. Alaska is associated with CLEAR, a biometric secure identity company that implements its "Fast Touch" technology platform [23]. The new biometric technology enables passengers to use fingerprints as a form of identification, instead of a boarding pass, to check bags and at the security point. The new biometric system has been used by hundreds of travelers who have reported that they were "delighted" with the experience [23].

Singapore is implementing a biometric control system made by Morpho (Safran) [40]. This new scheme is to be installed at Terminal 4 at Changi Airport starting in April 2017. The system is used in self-service bag drops, self-service boarding gates, and integrated border clearance by means of the MorphoPass Biometric Applicant Management System and MorphoWay automated gates [37]. MorphoPass uses a passenger's biometrics for identification, speeds up the checkpoints, and makes the bag drops less intrusive [37].

In 2013, London's Gatwick Airport started using biometric technology to scan the irises of passengers when they checked in. Thereafter, the travelers were automatically identified at security checkpoints and gates [18]. Gatwick's website states that iris recognition "is not an optional system" and a "no-fly" policy applies to passengers who do not complete the iris recognition procedure. The iris capture contains the following data:

- *Boarding pass details (which includes the passenger's name)*

- *Passenger photo (taken as identification backup)*

- *Iris algorithm results (taken as the primary identification)* [38]

Some people believe that the automation of traveler identification and verification will allow security personnel to focus on monitoring travelers for suspicious behaviors, such as nervousness and sweating, among others. Others believe that screeners will become too dependent on the technology and it will only serve to cloud their senses. Arnold Barnett is an aviation security expert and a professor at Massachusetts Institute of Technology. He states: "If you're sweating profusely, for example, the person checking your ID would notice, but that computer taking an iris scan wouldn't." Arnold goes on to argue that: "In some situations, like this one at airports, a combined system of biometrics and human personnel may be more efficient in identifying wrongdoers [18]."

Table 7.1 shows a 2001–2017 timeline summarizing some of the uses of biometrics in homeland security applications around the world.

TABLE 7.1   Timeline of Biometrics in Homeland Security

Year	Biometric Implementation
2001, September 11	Attacks on New York, NY and Washington, DC.
2001	The United Arab Emirates (UAE) began to implement the largest national deployment of iris recognition, IrisGuard
2002, November	The federal government established the U.S. Department of Homeland Security (DHS)
2003	DHS launched the United States Visitor and Immigrant Status Indicator Technology (US-VISIT). The system initially collected 2 fingerprints; by 2009, it collected 10 fingerprints.
2005, May	The German government launched the ePass program, whereby all passports issued to German citizens began to contain biometric technology.
2005–2007	Norway introduced biometric passports in 2005. In 2007, the government launched a multimodal biometric enrollment system supplied by Motorola.
	Brazil developed biometric passports in 2005 and released them in 2007 using the biometric Vucetich system, which was subsequently adopted by several other South American countries, such as Argentina.
2006	Department of State in the United States started issuing biometric passports, or e-passports.
2008–2009	The Canadian government launched biometric-based identification in their airports in 2008. Passport Canada began to employ facial recognition technology.
2009, September 21	All new Dutch passports and ID cards began to include the holder's fingerprints.
2009	Australia and New Zealand introduced SmartGate in 2009 in certain airports where electronic passport (e-passport) holders could clear immigration without needing to have their identity checked by a person.
2013, March	The Office of Biometric Identity Management (OBIM) was founded and replaced the US-VISIT.
2015, August	Japan tested an automated facial recognition software at both of Tokyo's airports for Japanese passport holders.
2015	Japan introduced Biocarts. International travelers to Japan have to pass through high-tech Biocarts that capture their fingerprints and photos.
2016, April	Japan announced that it will employ biometric technology in all of its airports beginning in April 2016.
2017	Changi Airport in Singapore plans to implement a biometric control system in 2017 that will include a self-service bag drop.

7.6 CONCLUSION

Biometrics plays critical roles in homeland security and border protection in the United States and beyond. From electronic passports to automatic check-in, the opportunities for biometric applications are endless. Biometrics offers enhanced security in many homeland security applications, and makes processes like airport security more convenient for people and less costly for governments to implement and maintain.

Among the biometric applications that are considered for future implementation are the extension of the capacity of biometric systems and capturing biometric data in a faster and more reliable manner. Canada, for example, is planning to expand the capacity of its biometric system to include visitors from 150 countries, starting in 2018 [17].

Even though the advancements in biometrics for homeland security purposes have reached the point of being automated, as in the case of Japan and the use of *Biocarts*, or *Iris-at-a-Distance* eye scanning and *Finger-on-the-Fly* fingerprinting in the UAE, or self-service bag drops and self-service boarding gates in Singapore, human personnel is still considered necessary to complement biometric systems and identify issues that biometric systems are unable to find at this time, such as the suspicious behaviors of passengers.

REFERENCES

1. Department of Homeland Security. n.d. *Fiscal Years 2014–2018 Strategic Plan.* https://www.dhs.gov/sites/default/files/publications/FY14-18%20Strategic%20Plan.PDF (retrieved October 26, 2016).
2. Seghetti, L. M. and Viña, S. R. 2005. Congressional Research Service Reports on Homeland Security. Congressional Research Service. The Library of Congress CRS Report for Congress Received through the CRS Web Order Code RL32234 US Visitor and Immigrant Status Indicator Technology (US-VISIT) Program, February 23. https://www.fas.org/sgp/crs/homesec/RL32234.pdf (retrieved May 11, 2016).
3. Homeland Security. n.d. *Office of Biometric Identity Management.* https://www.dhs.gov/obim (retrieved May 11, 2016).
4. Homeland Security. 2008. US-VISIT: Enhancing Security through Biometric Identification. Brochure 12/08, December. https://www.dhs.gov/xlibrary/assets/usvisit/usvisit_edu_biometrics_brochure_english.pdf (retrieved May 12, 2016).
5. The Seattle Globalist. 2014. An Easy Fix for Obama to Ease Immigration Backlog. http://www.seattleglobalist.com/2014/11/17/immigration-backlog-obama-visa-rollover/30646 (retrieved May 18, 2016).

6. Nadel, L. 2007. Approaches to Face Image Capture at US-VISIT Ports of Entry. *NIST Biometric Quality Workshop II*, November. http://biometrics. nist.gov/cs_links/quality/workshopII/proc/nadel_Approaches_to_Face_ Image_Capture_at_US-VISIT_POEs.pdf (retrieved May 10, 2016).

7. Homeland Security. 2009. US-VISIT: Fact Sheet Upgrade to 10-Fingerprint Collection, March 1. https://www.dhs.gov/xlibrary/assets/usvisit/usvisit_ edu_10-fingerprint_collection_fact_sheet.pdf (retrieved May 14, 2016).

8. US Department of Homeland Security—Biometrics—Accenture. n.d. https://www.accenture.com/us-en/success-improved-homeland-security- management-biometrics.aspx (retrieved May 14, 2016).

9. Homeland Security. 2016. E-Passports, February 10. https://www.dhs. gov/e-passports (retrieved May 14, 2016).

10. US Department of State. n.d. Visa Waiver Program. https://travel.state. gov/content/visas/en/visit/visa-waiver-program.html (retrieved May 14, 2016).

11. Automatic Border Control (eGate)—Protocolbench. 2013. http://blog.proto- colbench.org/2013/08/automatic-border-control-systems-egate/ (retrieved May 11, 2016).

12. Daugman, J., Malhas, I. 2004. Iris Recognition Border-Crossing System in the UAE. https://www.cl.cam.ac.uk/~jgd1000/UAEdeployment.pdf (retrieved April 13, 2016).

13. UAE Airports Get Multimodal Security—FindBiometrics. 2015. http:// findbiometrics.com/uae-airports-get-multimodal-security-23132/ (retrieved May 18, 2016).

14. Multiple Biometric Modalities to Protect UAE Borders Thanks to New Morpho Contract—FindBiometrics. 2015. http://findbiometrics.com/mul tiple-biometric-modalities-to-protect-uae-borders-thanks-to-new-mor- pho-contract-21292/ (retrieved May 18, 2016).

15. Visible Proofs: Forensic Views of the Body: Galleries: Cases: Juan Vucetich and the origins of forensic fingerprinting. n.d. https://www.nlm.nih.gov/ visibleproofs/galleries/cases/vucetich.html (retrieved May 18, 2016).

16. Countries Applying Biometrics. n.d. http://america.pink/countries-apply- ing-biometrics_1095482.html (retrieved May 19, 2016).

17. CBC News. 2015. Biometric Data Collection Evolved and Expands in Canada. June 5. http://www.cbc.ca/news/politics/biometric-data-collec- tion-evolves-and-expands-in-canada-1.3100872 (retrieved April 13, 2016).

18. Coren, C. 2013. Use of Biometric Security Technology at Airports Raises Concerns. *Newsmax*. December 31. http://www.newsmax.com/Newsfront/ airports-biometrics-technology-automated/2013/12/31/id/544603/ (retrieved May 9, 2016).

19. Setec Provides Biometric Passports to Sweden and Norway—SecureIDNews. 2005, November 3. http://www.secureidnews.com/news-item/setec-provides- biometric-passports-to-sweden-and-norway/ (retrieved May 19, 2016).

20. Dutch Biometric Passports Cause Controversy. n.d. https://www.rnw. org/archive/dutch-biometric-passports-cause-controversy (retrieved May 19, 2016).

21. The Passport Photo Blog by ePassportPhoto.com. n.d. https://www.epass-portphoto.com/blog/2008/07/german-passport-photo-requirements (retrieved May 19, 2016).
22. How to Use SmartGate. n.d. http://www.customs.govt.nz/features/smart-gate/usingsmartgate/Pages/default.aspx (retrieved May 19, 2016).
23. Alaska Testing Biometric Ids, Boarding Passes. 2015. https://blog.alaskaair.com/alaska-airlines/news/biometric-boarding-passes/ (retrieved May 19, 2016).
24. ApplicationforaGermanPassport.n.d.http://www.germany.info/Vertretung/usa/en/03__Consulates/Houston/03/__PassbeantragungHous__e.html (retrieved May 19, 2016).
25. Future Travel Experiences. 2016. Automated Border Control E-Gates Go Live at Naples Airport. January 21. http://www.futuretravelexperi-ence.com/2016/01/automated-border-control-e-gates-go-live-at-naples-airport/# (retrieved April 13, 2016).
26. New Zealand SmartGate. 2014. Using Quantitative Performance Information to Improve Convenience and Security. http://biometrics.nist.gov/ http://biometrics.nist.gov/cs_links/ibpc2014/presentations/05_wednesday_camp-bell_SmartGate_IBPC_2014.pdf (retrieved May 19, 2016).
27. Japan Airports to Install Mobile Biometric Terminals to Screen Foreign Passengers. n.d. http://www.airport-technology.com/news/newsjapan-airports-to-install-mobile-biometric-terminals-to-screen-foreign-passengers-4665642 (retrieved May 19, 2016).
28. Farrell, K. 2015. Japan Transitioning to Biometric Airport Security at All International Airports. *USA Today Travel*, September 8. https://usattravel.wordpress.com/2015/09/08/japan-transitioning-to-biometric-airport-secu-rity-at-all-international-airports/ (retrieved April 13, 2016).
29. Infopass. n.d. https://infopass.uscis.gov/ (retrieved May 19, 2016).
30. India Embarks on Ambitious Biometric Project: 1.2 Billion IDs | Homeland Security News Wire. n.d. http://www.homelandsecuritynewswire.com/india-embarks-ambitious-biometric-project-12-billion-ids (retrieved May 20, 2016).
31. KPMG in India | KPMG | IN. n.d. https://www.kpmg.com/IN/en/IssuesAndInsights/ThoughtLeadership/HomelandSecurityinIndia_ASSOCHAM.pdf (retrieved May 19, 2016).
32. Future Travel Experience. 2015. Report Predicts Biometric Technology Will Enable the "Next Golden Age of Air Travel." http://www.futuretravelex-perience.com/2015/11/report-predicts-biometric-technology-will-enable-next-golden-age-air-travel/ (retrieved April 13, 2016).
33. Biometrics | Homeland Security News Wire. n.d. http://www.homelandse-curitynewswire.com/dr20140505-using-biometrics-to-protect-india-s-one-billion-people-raises-security-privacy-concerns (retrieved May 19, 2016).
34. Future Travel Experience. 2015. Aruba Happy Flow Lays Foundations for European Preclearance. http://www.futuretravelexperience.com/2015/06/aruba-happy-flow-lays-foundations-for-european-preclearance/ (retrieved August 8, 2016).

35. KLM Royal Dutch Airlines. 2015. SkyTeam, Vision-Box. Aruba Happy Flow Secure, Quick, Easy. news.klm.com/download/85456/happyflow-en-29-5-15.pdf (retrieved August 8, 2016).
36. Aruba Travel 2016: Paradise Simplified!—ARUBA TRIP TIPS. 2016. http://www.arubatriptips.com/aruba-travel-2016-paradise-simplified/ (retrieved May 19, 2016).
37. Good News for Tourists to Japan at Airports. 2016. http://www.zaikeinews.com/articles/1536/20160223/good-news-tourists-japan-airports.htm (retrieved May 19, 2016).
38. Flying within the UK & Ireland. n.d. http://www.gatwickairport.com/at-the-airport/flying-out/security/flying-within-the-uk-and-ireland/ (retrieved May 19, 2016).
39. Collins, C. US-VISIT: Biometrics Are Here to Stay | Defense Media Network. 2012. http://www.defensemedianetwork.com/stories/us-visit-biometrics-are-here-to-stay/ (retrieved May 18, 2016).
40. Mayhew, S. Morpho Deploying Facial Recognition Technology at Changi Airport. 2016. http://www.biometricupdate.com/201603/morpho-deploying-facial-recognition-technology-at-changi-airport (retrieved August 8, 2016).

CHAPTER 8

Biometrics in Cloud Computing and Big Data

Yun Tian, Mikhail Gofman, and Maria Villa

CONTENTS

8.1 INTRODUCTION

Sometimes biometric data can be very large in scale and require a substantial amount of resources for its storage and processing. Modern cloud computing systems are capable of providing such resources.

Examples of biometric databases that are growing exponentially are those managed by the Federal Bureau of Investigation (FBI), the Department of Defense, and the Department of Homeland Security (DHS) [1]. By 2010, the DHS IDENT database had hosted 110 million biometric identities, including digital facial photographs, fingerprints, iris scans, palm prints, and latent fingerprints [1,2].

A remarkable example of a large-scale biometric system is "Aadhaar," managed by the *Unique IDentification Authority of India*, which has been referred to as "the most ambitious biometric deployment in history" [3]. The goal of this program is to register/document the iris patterns and fingerprints of all 1.2 billion Indian citizens. It processes an average of 1 million persons per day. As of 2014, more than 600 million citizens had been enrolled with biometric ID [4–6].

With the emergence of big data and cloud computing systems that transfer, store, and process massive amounts of biometric data, proper protection of biometric data in the cloud is critical.

This chapter focuses on the challenges that biometric big data faces in cloud systems. We begin by providing a background on big data and cloud computing in Section 8.2; this will enable us to understand the context within which biometrics are used. Section 8.3 introduces some applications: BioAaaS, BioID, and IriSecureID. Section 8.4 focuses on two broad areas pertaining to the challenges facing biometrics in the big data world: (1) computation challenges and (2) privacy challenges. Section 8.5 concludes with predictions and suggestions for improvement.

8.2 BACKGROUND ON BIG DATA AND CLOUD COMPUTING

8.2.1 Cloud Computing

8.2.1.1 Cloud Computing

Cloud computing has been defined by the National Institute of Standards and Technology (NIST) as "a model for enabling ubiquitous, convenient, on-demand network access to a shared pool of configurable computing resources (e.g., networks, servers, storage applications, and services) that can be rapidly provisioned and released with minimal management effort or service provider interaction" [7].

Businesses, from small to large, implement their own IT infrastructure in-house. This method has some disadvantages, such as the cost of software and hardware, essential upgrades, and the employment of staff to monitor the IT infrastructure 24/7 [7].

Cloud computing offers an innovative solution to those issues and has numerous advantages. The most notable benefits of cloud computing are improvements to cash flow since it offers fixed and predictable costs, and increases in efficiency for IT resources [7].

The basic cloud model is composed of five essential characteristics, three service models, and four deployment models.

8.2.1.2 Cloud Computing: Essential Characteristics

The exponential adoption of cloud computing is mainly due to the following essential characteristics:

- *Elasticity.* Cloud services facilities can be automatically given and taken away, thereby adjusting to demand. In the eyes of the consumer, these capabilities seem to be unlimited and adequate in quantity and time [7].

- *Self-service on demand.* Cloud services can be immediately accessed from any location in the world, at any time. Human interactions with the cloud service provided are not required to provide computer capabilities, such as network storage and computing capabilities.

- *Broad-base network access.* Cloud services can be accessed through any device via any type of network and platform, for example, mobile phones, desktops, laptops, tablets, and more.

- *Resource pooling.* Resources, such as storage, bandwidth, network, processing, and memory, are pooled and serve multiple consumers. Physical and virtual resources are assigned dynamically according to demand.

- *Measured service.* The measured service is usually charged by cloud providers as pay-per-use. A report on the measured services, such as user accounts, processing, and bandwidth is delivered to the consumer and the cloud provider charges the consumer accordingly.

8.2.1.3 Cloud Computing Service Models

There are three common cloud computing service models known as the SPI model (1) software as a service (SaaS), (2) platform as a service (PaaS), and (3) infrastructure as a service (IaaS) [7].

- *SaaS*. SaaS is a software distribution model in which software services and applications are hosted and run by a vendor or service provider and made available to customers over a network. Users are charged for the use of bandwidth according to the amount of time and number of users. The benefits of using SaaS are easier software administration, automatic updates and patch management, software compatibility across the business, easier collaboration, and global accessibility [8].

- *PaaS*. PaaS delivers operating systems and related services over the Internet without the use of downloads or installation, including programming languages and development tools [7]. PaaS provides numerous tools for design, development, application testing, hosting, state management, integration, deployment, an easy-to-use execution environment [9], and related development tools. PaaS offers the advantage of testing on pretested technologies which helps reduce risk upon the deployment of new systems. It provides a development platform for companies that require large data volumes at low cost, risk, and in a secured environment [8].

- *IaaS*. IaaS is a pay-per-use service. In IaaS, client businesses outsource the equipment to support operations to include servers, storage, hardware, and networking components (the "virtual server") [7]. Some advantages of IaaS include business agility, cost-effective scalability, increased financial flexibility, choice of services, and increased security [8]. IaaS is the cloud computing service model with the most attention from the market [8]. Other services offered over the IaaS model are disaster recovery, compute as a service, storage as a service, data center as a service, virtual desktop infrastructure, and cloud bursting [8].

8.2.1.4 Cloud Computing Deployment Models

The setup of a cloud computing paradigm is composed of four deployment models: (1) private cloud, (2) community cloud, (3) public cloud, and (4) hybrid cloud [10].

- *Private cloud.* A private cloud configuration is managed internally by a single organization, such as a bank or retailer. The resources and services are shared within the organization through intranet [8]. The data are not available to the general public [4,11]. Since the cloud resides within the company's firewall, it is considered more secure; however, it is more expensive to monitor and maintain.

- *Community cloud.* NIST defines a community cloud as an infrastructure shared by several organizations supporting a specific community, such as health care, that has shared concerns around mission, policy, and compliance considerations [12].

- *Public cloud.* A public cloud configuration is run by an outsource service provider (i.e., Amazon, Google, or Microsoft). The public cloud provider delivers services to many end-user organizations using pay-as-you-go services. The public cloud is considered to be an external cloud. The businesses do not own the core technology, resources, or services [8]. The cloud infrastructure is provisioned for open use by the general public.

- *Hybrid cloud.* A hybrid cloud is a combination of two or more distinct cloud infrastructures (public, private, or community) [8,11]. A public cloud is generally used to expedite certain tasks that are not available, or limited, in the company's private cloud or data center. The main purpose of using a hybrid cloud is that critical and confidential data are maintained within the company's firewall, while the nonconfidential data can be leveraged in the public cloud infrastructure [8]. The private cloud is maintained internally by company technicians. Employees are able to access the private cloud resources internally and outside the company [8].

8.2.2 Big Data

From a technological perspective, big data is defined as the "data sets whose size is beyond the ability of typical database software tools to capture, store, manage and analyze" [13]. At the same time, big data is a very broad term which is interpreted in many different ways. At the time of this writing, professionals consider the benchmark for big data as multiple terabytes or petabytes. However, as technology moves forward over time, the size of datasets considered to measure up to big data is also expected to increase [9,10]. What is considered big data today may not be in the future [13].

Big data has been generated through an explosion of data collected through social media, smart phones, sensors installed inside machines, and sensors worn by people [13]. According to *Science Daily*, 90% of all the data in the world has been generated over the last five years [14]. Big data market was worth 3.2 billion dollars in 2010 and that value is predicted to grow to 92.2 billion by 2026 [13,15].

Systems that handle big data are very attractive because they help reduce production costs, increase performance, and help companies gain competitive advantages over rival industries. In addition, the effectiveness of knowledge discovery, defined as "the science of finding patterns within sets of data" [16], is very useful to biometric applications since biometric systems can use data mining techniques in order to discover important patterns within biometric data. The biometric big data generated through data mining helps improve processes and performance, thus reducing costs and increasing revenue [13].

An example of the effective use of big data is the "you may also like" engine used by Amazon [17]. A simple visit to amazon.com illustrates how this engine works. Recommendations from discovery to checkout, such as "frequently bought together," or "customers also bought" are a big part of the shopping experience [18]. According to *Fortune* magazine [18], "Amazon's recommendation secret" relies on an algorithm that customizes the browsing experience for returning customers. "Item-to-item collaborative filtering" is generated through the data collected from previously purchased items, products in a virtual shopping cart, rated items, liked items, and viewed items [18]. The "29% sales increase to $12.83 billion during its second fiscal quarter [in 2012], up from $9.9 billion during the same the [previous] year," proves that this big data system's exploitation is successful for Amazon [18].

8.2.2.1 MapReduce

Big data is frequently processed through a programming model known as MapReduce, which was introduced by Google in 2004. MapReduce is a system for processing large volumes of data in parallel by dividing the work into a set of independent tasks. Mike Cafarella and Doug Cutting of Yahoo! created an open source implementation of MapReduce called

Hadoop, which was released in 2005 [19]. MapReduce is used by many companies, such as America Online (AOL), Facebook, *The New York Times*, Joost, Last.fm, and more.

8.3 APPLICATIONS OF BIOMETRICS IN BIG DATA

The most common method used by cloud providers to authenticate their clients is password based. Authentication using a password depends on something the "user knows" (i.e., a PIN, password, and passphrase). However, the use of passwords has serious disadvantages. A password can be guessed or stolen. It is vulnerable to attacks, including the use of brute force, a dictionary, sniffing, shoulder surfing, phishing, and keylogger attacks. Once the attacker has access to the sources, he can manipulate the data and even disable services [20].

A technique to make passwords secure has three safety measures: (1) it must be complex, (2) long, and (3) not easy to remember [21]. However, this method introduces another problem. Even if the password is intricate, for example, a complex combination of case-sensitive numbers, letters, and special symbols, users have a hard time remembering the numerous complex passwords that will need to be used in different systems. Thus, cloud users prefer a simple password and use the same password to access various systems [21].

Biometric authentication provides a stronger verification and offers a solution to the password-related issues. The use of biometrics as a form of authentication depends on something the "user is." The biometrics-based authentication identifies users based on their biological or behavioral characteristics. Biometric traits cannot be stolen, forgotten, or guessed. Moreover, the user does not have to remember a complex and long password.

In cloud computing, biometric authentication is being used more and more as a method of verification for cloud users. This method creates a template of each user's biometric data, which must be protected to preserve the user's privacy. Next, we discuss some concrete examples of biometrics being used in the context of cloud computing and big data.

8.3.1 BioAaaS

A proposed solution to password hacking in the cloud is a Biometric Authentication System as a Cloud Service (BioAaaS). In a method proposed by Vallabhu and Satyanarayana [20], a hybrid biometric technique is used that combines two biometric methods. This scheme fuses fingerprints and voice biometrics that can be encrypted and then used to sign into the cloud service.

The cloud service provider maintains a database of the biometrics of enrolled users authorized to use the cloud service. To help protect the biometric data, the database is encrypted. Then, the user from an organization wishing to sign into the cloud supplies their biometrics which are then matched against the database.

8.3.2 BioID

A current application for BioAaaS is the cloud-based BioID Web Service developed by GmgH. BioID is "built in the cloud to secure the cloud" [22]. BioID provides multimodal (two or more modalities) biometric authentication using face and voice biometrics. BioID services are created for application developers to add multimodal biometric technology to their existing application development frameworks. To add more protection to the privacy of the users, BioID creates an anonymous biometric identifier that is managed by the service provider. The biometric data is stored and transmitted anonymously with no personal identifying information, so BioID only receives the biometrics and "never knows who is being recognized" [22]. BioID services include a Simple Object Access Protocol (SOAP) application program interface (API) protected with an X.509 certificate. The enrollment and verification procedures use a RESTful API with a JSON web token.

8.3.3 IriSecureID

The iris is considered the most promising, reliable, and accurate biometric trait due to two of its characteristics: (1) the iris is stable and does not change with age, and (2) the sophisticated surface of the iris allows high distinction among individuals [23]. Iris recognition has been used in several applications, including personal computers, smart phones, and recently in cloud computing. Services dedicated solely to iris recognition are available to individuals, companies, and government agencies. Iris recognition providers maintain the servers and databases of the iris templates of the enrolled users and provide the clients with an application to capture the iris image and verify the image against the template in the remote database.

Due to the increase in the use of the iris as a source of biometric information, the possibility of an attack on the systems that store and process iris data has become a concern. These attacks are known as "iris spoofing," and are commonly performed with cosmetic contact lenses [23]. Consequently, several solutions to prevent these attacks have been introduced [24–26].

A notable iris recognition service provider is IriTech. IriTech's Cloud-Based Iris Recognition Service launched the IriSecureID system, which is deployed in a cloud infrastructure [11]. IriTech provides its customers with a client application that they can use to connect to IriTech's cloud services. The application can acquire iris images, enroll templates, verify the individual as the person he claims to be, and includes a certificate with cryptography keys. The transfer of data that IriSecureID uses is secured by public key infrastructure (PKI). RSA key pairs are used as well. The customers use standard X509 certificates for public key and PFX/PKCS #12 for the certificate and private key [11].

IriTech has become a strong iris recognition service provider whose clients include the Indian Government, the US Government, the Columbia Police Department, and the United Nations High Commissioner for Refugees [11].

8.4 ISSUES IN BIOMETRICS IN THE BIG DATA WORLD

Security is the main critical challenge of biometrics in the big data world. Other issues related to security are data privacy, confidentiality, authorization (access control), data integrity, and more. Traditional or nonbiometric methods of identification (ID cards, passwords, PINs, and keys) can be lost, forgotten, or stolen. However, an ID card can be replaced, a new password can be created, a new key can be made, and access can be revoked. Once a biometric dataset is compromised, however, it is compromised forever [27].

In this section, we present some of the challenges faced by biometrics in the big data realm. We divide those challenges into computational and privacy issues.

8.4.1 Computation Issues

Biometric big data in cloud computing is subject to computation-intensive procedures to perform biometric functions, including identification and verification, and is subject to local regulations.

8.4.1.1 Local Regulations

Regulations in some countries prohibit biometric information from being sent beyond their borders. An example is the European Data Protection Directive which states that personal information must not travel outside EU borders [28]. Forbidden data transfer includes routing data through a router outside the EU or the backing up of personal data to a foreign data center. Such regulations present a challenge for organizations seeking cloud service providers. Not only would the cloud provider need to offer competitive services at a reasonable price, but it would also have to maintain its data centers locally. A good example of a cloud provider that follows this protocol is the S3 service by Amazon. The Amazon S3 service guarantees that the data will not leave the region where it is stored without the data owner's consent [4].

8.4.1.2 Identification and Verification

Performing biometric identification involves searching one by one through a database of biometric templates to find the best match for a particular biometric trait. Furthermore, when a match is found, another analysis (verification or authentication) is performed to determine if the provided trait and the trait in the database belong to the same individual [27]. In the verification procedure, the live biometric is compared to a stored biometric record typically associated with a user ID [27]. The purpose of the verification process is to make sure that the given biometric matches the stored biometric record. In order to protect sensitive information from users, a biometric identification scheme should only reveal the matching biometric result which is usually associated with an identity ID number or token [1].

The one-to-one search to identify a presented biometric may cause enormous load on the biometric system if we take into consideration that the database and the number of simultaneous requests could be huge. This causes a serious scalability problem and is not practical [27]. In addition, the large-scale storage of biometric data is subject to misuse for purposes other than those to which the individual has agreed, and the information can be stolen [26].

8.4.2 Privacy (Data Confidentiality)

Privacy remains one of the biggest challenges preventing organizations from taking advantage of the biometric cloud's computational resources.

The privacy of biometric data must be preserved while it is being transferred, stored, or processed in the cloud. Stolen biometric data may cause not only fiscal, but also emotional, damage to the affected victims that might take years to recover from [29].

8.4.2.1 Transfer of Biometric Data

Biometric data are sometimes collected at one location and then transferred to another location for storage or processing. One challenge in biometric cloud systems is the sharing of biometric data between nations for the purposes of, for example, fighting terrorism. The Five Country Conference in 2009 concluded with a protocol initiative that established the sharing of biometric data between five countries—the United Kingdom, the United States, Canada, Australia, and New Zealand. The goal of this program was to exchange relevant legal and immigration cases to help track terrorists and help with criminal prosecutions, and foreign national offenders [30]. The program establishes explicit rules governing the sharing and processing of biometric data by member countries. The process of fingerprint matching is anonymous and no information is provided until a definite match is found. The fingerprints must be used "only for the requested purpose" and then destroyed [30]. Although security experts believe that it is imperative to create a formal data sharing program between nations to increase safety, reduce cost, and increase efficiency, the associated transfer of biometric data between nations continues to raise privacy concerns in the civilian community.

8.4.2.2 Storage of Biometric Data

Biometric samples need to be stored for matching purposes. As the number of templates grows, the biometric system must also expand its capacity to match multiple templates in the collected data. Moreover, the storage of biometric samples has been subject to numerous breaches and controversies.

It was once customary to store the big data of biometric samples in one location, until this practice was no longer considered safe. A very significant case highlighting this is the data breach of the United States Office of Personnel Management (OPM) in June 2015. More than 21.5 million records were stolen, including 1.1 million of records of the fingerprints of secret field agents [31]. The affected agents have had their biometric information compromised for life. Even if they change their identities, they can still be recognized by their fingerprint information. The biometric data of the OPM was centralized and accessed with a password, but not encrypted. After the breach, the DHS implemented a three-factor authentication, including a password, smartcard, and a biometric trait.

Authorities around the world have passed legislation to prevent the gathering and centralization of private biometric data to help safeguard civillians [31]. In Canada, the Ontario Privacy Commissioner issued principles on the use of biometrics to mitigate the privacy challenges associated with stored biometric data [24].

Numerous nations and enterprises have adopted the principle of keeping biometric information in local devices rather than storing it in centrally located databases.

Apple's TouchID authentication process to unlock its devices (cellphones and tablets) reads a fingerprint. The fingerprint not only provides access to use the devices, but is also used to make purchases through Apple's applications (iTunes, App Store, iBooks, and Apple Pay) [25]. The biometric security of Apple's products is implemented in the device itself locally as a mathematical representation which is (1) encrypted, (2) isolated from the chip, (3) isolated from the operating system, (4) never sent to Apple's servers, (5) certainly not backed up to the iCloud or anywhere else, and (6) not shared with any other fingerprint databases [25]. Therefore, Apple tries to tackle the issue of storing biometric data in the cloud by avoiding doing so altogether.

8.4.2.3 Processing of Biometric Data

The processing of big biometric data is a very broad problem. It includes all the operations performed on each biometric trait. Some operations include [26]

✓ Collection	✓ Block
✓ Withdrawal	✓ Recording
✓ Consultation	✓ Adjustment
✓ Use	✓ Reveal
✓ Organization	✓ Transmission
✓ Storing	✓ Deletion
✓ Alteration	

The challenges in large-scale biometric systems are related to the purpose, misuse, and threats to the biometric data stored [24]. Data might be stored and used later for purposes to which the users did not agree, or used to discriminate against certain demographics of the population. The Office of the Privacy Commissioner of Canada is implementing the following guidelines to process biometrics [26]:

- People should be informed if their personal information is being collected.

- Personal information should only be used for the purpose for which it was collected.

- Personal information should only be collected for a clearly identified purpose.

These guidelines are a common practice for other nations and organizations.

8.4.2.4 Biometric Data Integrity

Data integrity is defined as "the accuracy and consistency of stored data, in absence of any alteration to the data between two updates of a file or record" [32]. Another definition of data integrity is the guarantee that the received data from the approved entity is intact. Cloud computing providers store their clients' data and users can access these data at any time from any location. Users outsource their information remotely, hence they do not have control over their data. Lack of assurance of data integrity may be an obstacle to a broader adoption of cloud computing to manage biometric big data for both enterprises and individuals [32]. Clients require their data to be safe and protected from any tampering or unauthorized access.

Protection of integrity involves two areas of concern: (1) tampering, and (2) access control [32].

1. Defense from tampering encompasses the design of tools to protect the integrity of the stored data. The tampering might come from intruders or from the cloud service provider which can accidentally

or deliberately alter or delete some of the information from the cloud.

2. Strong authentication is a requirement for protection from access to unauthorized entities [32]. The cloud provider must implement strong authentication mechanisms to ensure that only authorized entities have access to the data in the cloud.

8.4.2.4.1 Authentication of Biometric Data

Authentication is one of the most important applications of biometrics. Although biometric-based authentication is believed to be more secure than the traditional approaches based on passwords or identification cards, it is still susceptible to attacks.

According to the technical author J.R. Vacca [33], there are eight main vulnerabilities in biometric-based authentication systems. These vulnerabilities are listed as follows:

---

1. Presenting a possible reproduction of the template as input into the system.

2. Resubmitting a previously stored digitized template.

3. The matcher is attacked and corrupted so that it produces preselected match scores.

4. The database of stored templates can be attacked with one or more templates modified to authorize a fraudulent individual or deny service to a legitimate person.

5. The feature extractor is attacked by a Trojan horse so that it produces feature sets preselected by the intruder.

6. The stored templates are sent to the matcher through a communication channel. The data traveling through the channel can be intercepted and modified.

7. The features extracted from the input signal are replaced with a different, fraudulent feature set.

8. The final match can be overridden, rendering the authentication system disabled.

8.5 CONCLUSION

There are many challenges facing the use of biometrics in cloud-based systems. The main concerns are how to securely store, manage, and transport biometric data.

As cloud computing technologies evolve, new techniques for handling biometric data in the cloud will likely be developed. The effectiveness of these techniques in addressing the efficiency of cloud computing and its security challenges remain to be seen.

REFERENCES

1. Kohlwey, E., Sussman, A., Trost, J., and Maurer, A. 2011. Leveraging the cloud for big data biometrics: Meeting the performance requirements of the next generation biometric systems. In *2011 IEEE World Congress on Services (SERVICES)*, Washington, DC. IEEE, pp. 597–601, July.
2. Privacy Impact Assessment for the Automated Biometric Identification System (IDENT) DHS/NPPD/USVISIT/PIA-002. US Department of Homeland Security. December 7, 2012. https://www.dhs.gov/sites/default/files/publications/privacy/PIAs/privacy_pia_usvisit_ident_appendixj_jan2013.pdf
3. Defense & Security. n.d. http://spie.org/newsroom/technical-articles/5449-600-million-citizens-of-india-are-now-enrolled-with-biometric-id (retrieved February 28, 2016).
4. Amazon Simple Storage Service (S3)—Object Storage. n.d. http://aws.amazon.com/s3/ (retrieved January 28, 2016).
5. Daugman, J. 600 million citizens of India are now enrolled with biometric ID. Defense & Security, n.d. http://spie.org/newsroom/5449-600-million-citizens-of-india-are-now-enrolled-with-biometric-id (retrieved August 24, 2016).
6. Chen, G. 2014. India's Unique ID Could Generate Big Boost in Financial Access. Consultative Group to Assist the Poor (CGAP). http://www.cgap.org/blog/indias-unique-id-could-be-about-generate-big-boost-access (retrieved August 24, 2016).
7. Das, R. 2013. Biometrics in the cloud. *Keesing Journal of Documents and Identity*, 42, 21–23.
8. Purcell, B. M. 2014. Big data using cloud computing. *Holy Family University Journal of Technology Research*, 8 pages.
9. Microsoft Enterprise Agreement Customer Care (EACC). n.d. http://www.microsoft.com/malaysia/ea/whitepapers.aspx (retrieved February 28, 2016).
10. Bharadi, V. A. and D'Silva, G. M. 2015. Online signature recognition using software as a service (SaaS) model on public cloud. In *2015 International Conference on Computing Communication Control and Automation (ICCUBEA)*, Pune, India. IEEE, pp. 65–72, February.
11. Iris Scanner | Iris Biometrics Technology | Iris Recognition. n.d. http://www.iritech.com/ (retrieved January 14, 2016).
12. Community cloud computing benefits and drawbacks. n.d. http://www.computerweekly.com/news/1510117/Community-cloud-computing-benefits-and-drawbacks (retrieved February 28, 2016).
13. Caldarola, E. G. and Rinaldi, A. M. 2015. Big data: A survey—The new paradigms, methodologies and tools. Conference Paper, July.
14. James, M., Michael, C., Brad, B., and Jacques, B. 2011. *Big Data: The Next Frontier for Innovation, Competition, and Productivity*. The McKinsey Global Institute. http://www.mckinsey.com/global-locations
15. Statista.com/Forecast of Big Data Market Size, Based on Revenue, from 2011 to 2026 (in Billion U.S. Dollars). Rep. Statista Inc., https://www.statista.com/aboutus/ (retrieved October 21, 2016).

16. Knowledge Discovery. n.d. http://www.semagix.com/knowledge-discovery.htm (retrieved February 28, 2016).
17. Manyika, J., Chui, M., Brown, B., Bughin, J., Dobbs, R., Roxburgh, C., and Byers, A. H. 2011. *Big Data: The Next Frontier for Innovation, Competition, and Productivity.* McKinsey Global Institute.
18. Amazon's Recommendation Secret. 2012. http://fortune.com/2012/07/30/amazons-recommendation-secret/ (retrieved February 28, 2016).
19. Apache Hadoop. n.d. https://developer.yahoo.com/hadoop/tutorial/module1.html (retrieved February 10, 2016).
20. Sathyanarayana, R. V. and Vallabhu, H. 2012. Biometric authentication as a service on cloud: A novel solution. *International Journal of Soft Computing and Engineering,* 2, 163–165.
21. Albahdal, A. and Boult, T. E. 2014. Problems and promises of using the cloud and biometrics. In *2014 11th International Conference on Information Technology: New Generations (ITNG),* Las Vegas, Nevada. IEEE, pp. 293–300, April.
22. Face Recognition & Voice Authentication—Multimodal Biometrics. n.d. https://www.bioid.com/ (retrieved February 14, 2016).
23. Silva, P., Luz, E., Baeta, R., Menotti, D., Pedrini, H., and Falcao, A. X. 2015. An approach to iris contact lens detection based on deep image representations. In *2015 28th Conference on Graphics, Patterns and Images (SIBGRAPI),* Salvador, Brazil. IEEE, pp. 157–164, August.
24. At Your Fingertips–Biometrics and the Challenges to Privacy. n.d. https://www.priv.gc.ca/information/pub/gd_bio_201102_e.pdf (retrieved February 28, 2016).
25. Apple. n.d. https://support.apple.com/en-us/HT204587 (retrieved February 26, 2016).
26. Guidelines Regarding the Introduction of Biometric Data. n.d. http://dzlp.mk/sites/default/files/Dokumenti/IPA/Annex%206%20Final%20documents/doc_id_2.1.4-2.pdf (retrieved February 26).
27. Yuan, J. and Yu, S. 2013. Efficient privacy-preserving biometric identification in cloud computing. In *IEEE International Conference on Computer Communications, INFOCOM, 2013 Proceedings IEEE,* Turin, Italy. IEEE, pp. 2652–2660, April.
28. European Data Protection Directive. 1995. [Online], http://eur-lex.europa.eu/legal-content/EN/TXT/?uri=URISERV%3Al14012
29. Soyjaudah, K. M., Ramsawock, G., and Khodabacchus, M. Y. 2013. Cloud computing authentication using cancellable biometrics. In *African Conference: Sustainable Engineering for a Better Future, AFRICON, 2013,* Mauritius, Country in East Africa. IEEE, pp. 1–4, September.
30. What is Biometric Data Sharing? An Introduction & Overview. 2014. http://www.biometricupdate.com/201409/what-is-biometric-data-sharing-an-introduction-overview (retrieved February 28, 2016).
31. The Risk of Centralized Storage for Biometric Data. 2015. White Paper, August 25. http://appliedrec.com/wp-content/uploads/2015/10/White-Paper-Centralized-Storage.pdf

32. Kumar, V. V. and Poornima, G. 2012. Ensuring data integrity in cloud computing, *Journal of Computer Applications.* 5 (EICA2012-4), 2012. ISSN: 0974–1925.

33. Vacca, J. R. 2007. *Biometric Technologies and Verification Systems.* Butterworth-Heinemann, Oxford, United Kingdom, pp. 293.

III

Case Studies of Real-World Mobile Biometric Systems

III

CHAPTER 9

Fingerprint Recognition

Maria Villa and Abhishek Verma

CONTENTS

9.1 FINGERPRINT RECOGNITION IN MOBILE DEVICES

This chapter highlights the most important mechanisms for fingerprint liveness recognition in mobile phones. The structure of this chapter is as follows: Section 9.2 introduces a general definition and an overview of fingerprint recognition methods. Public databases for fingerprint recognition are presented in Section 9.3. Section 9.4 details liveness detection on fingerprints and discusses the following techniques: pore detection, perspiration, skin deformation, image quality, temperature, and skin resistance. Finally, the conclusions are drawn in Section 9.5.

9.2 INTRODUCTION

Fingerprint recognition has been considered the most efficient, popular, and widely acceptable identification method [1]. Currently, it is indisputably the most reliable evidence in the court of law [2]. Fingerprints are unique, not even identical twins have the same set of ridges and lines. Fingerprints stay the same from time one is born until death. This distinctiveness makes fingerprints one of the best ways to identify an individual [3].

Per the *Encyclopedia Britannica* fingerprints are "impressions made by the papillary ridges on the ends of the fingers and thumbs" [4]. The practice of fingerprinting as a means of identification is also known as dactyloscopy and is widely used in current law enforcement [4]. Sweat pores are located on each ridge of the epidermis which is anchored to the dermis by papillae [4]. The fingerprints have patterns that look like loops, arches, or whorls. These forms and outlines evolved onto eight basic patterns, which are still used by the FBI today [5]. The eight patterns can be observed on Figure 9.1. The distribution in the population of the fingerprint patterns is described as follows: 65% have loops, 30% have whorls, and 5% have arches. The most frequent pattern is the ulnar loop [5].

Fingerprinting methods have some challenges, however, they are still very popular and widely used. Numerous fingerprinting methods and

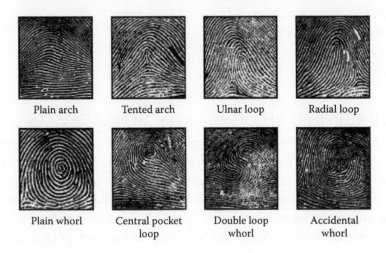

| Plain arch | Tented arch | Ulnar loop | Radial loop |
| Plain whorl | Central pocket loop | Double loop whorl | Accidental whorl |

FIGURE 9.1   Fingerprint patterns. (From viewzone.com.)

enhancements are under development. Some advantages and disadvantages prepared are listed as follows [6]:

Advantages	Disadvantages
• Very high accuracy • Is the most economical biometric PC user authentication technique • It is one of the most developed biometrics • Easy to use • Small storage space required for the biometric template, reducing the size of the database memory required • It is standardized	• It is considered an intrusive method for some people as it seems related to criminal investigations • It can make mistakes with the dryness or dirty of the finger's skin, as well as with the age (is not appropriate with children, because the size of their fingerprint changes quickly) • Image captured at 500 dots per inch (dpi). Resolution: 8 bits per pixel demands a large memory space

Biometric fingerprint recognition is used in several important areas such as forensics, government, immigration border control, identification cards, commercial applications, credit cards, computer login access, and more [1]. Identifying fingerprints can be performed with hardware or software. Hardware methods capture characteristics of life such as temperature, electrical conductivity, and pulse oximetry. Furthermore, hardware systems require additional hardware to be connected and integrated to the biometric sensors. Conversely, software base fingerprint liveness detection uses a "static" approach. This means that a single fingerprint is used and features of multiple frames of the same fingerprint are analyzed [7].

Biometric fingerprint systems can be misled. An attacker may gain entry into a fingerprint system using a false fingerprint sample, this is known as a "spoof attack" [8]. There are numerous methods of fingerprint forgery. For the most part, the moisture-based approach has been able to deceive many fingerprint-based identification systems [1].

Synthetic fingerprints can be produced by two methods: (1) the cooperative process and the (2) noncooperative process.

1. *Cooperative process.* In the cooperative method, the individual presses his finger into a molding material, then the mold is filled with a gelatin-like substance [9]. Creating a fake finger with Play-Doh is economical, simple, and easily available. First, the finger is wrapped around with Play-Doh to create a cast. The cast will then be filled with liquid silicon, gelatin, silicon rubber, wax, or clay and

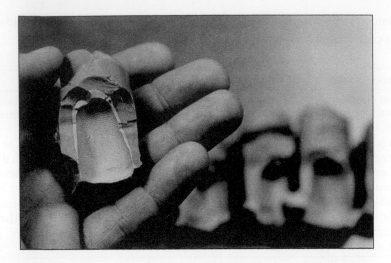

FIGURE 9.2   Play-Doh method. (Photo by biometricbits.com.)

is let dry for a couple of hours [1,9]. The spoofed fingerprint is now a replica of the original one [10]. See an example in Figure 9.2.

2. *The noncooperative process.* The inherent fingerprint is left on a surface in the noncooperative method [9]. In order to obtain a sample of the fingerprint, the surface is enhanced, digitized with a photograph, then the negative is printed on a transparency sheet. The resulted printed image can be used as a mold to duplicate the fingerprint [9]. In the non-cooperative approach, it has been reported that dissected fingers have been used to gain access to systems. BBC News in Malaysia informed that members of a violent gang chopped off a car owner's finger with a machete to steal a Mercedes S-class car, worth about $75,000 [11].

Fingerprint recognition is growing, and along with this growth the use of false fingerprints continues to threaten the security of fingerprint authentication systems. The remarkable popularity fingerprint authentication has gained with mobile phones makes cellphones' users a significant target of spoofing attacks. Ongoing solutions rely upon liveness detection as the main "anti-spoofing mechanism" [7].

9.3 PUBLIC DATABASES FOR FINGERPRINT RECOGNITION

9.3.1 LivDet

An important database used for the creation of liveness detection biometric mechanisms is LivDet Databases. Liveness Detection Competition (livDet.org) organizes a competition every year. The organizers provide biometric fingerprint and iris databases for the competitors. The database contains a total of 17,000 images with "live" and "spoof" fingerprints. The samples are acquired with four different sensors listed below [7]:

- *Biometrika FX2000.* Optical sensor with 569 dpi resolution and 312 × 372 pixels image size.

- *Italdata ET10.* Optical sensor with 500 dpi resolution and 640 × 480 pixels image size.

- *Crossmatch L Scan Guardian.* Optical scanner with 500 dpi resolution and 800 × 750 pixels image size.

- Swipe sensor with 96.

The purpose of the competition is to increase the probability to develop high biometric security mechanisms [7].

9.3.2 CASIA-FingerprintV5

CASIA-FingerprintV5 is a public fingerprint database sponsored by Biometrics Ideal Test (BIT) in China. The database is used for research and educational purposes. This database has the fingerprints of about 500 volunteers (students, workers, waiters, graduate students, and more) adding up to about 20,000 fingerprint images. These images were obtained using a URU4000 fingerprint sensor [12]. BIT focuses on facilitating biometrics research and development to researchers and organizes competitions on fingerprint recognition among other biometrics.

9.3.3 Repository for Individuals of Special Concern

The FBI implemented the Repository for Individuals of Special Concern (RISC), a mobile system to check for fingerprints of suspects. This system is part of the Next Generation Identification system. RISC is free, but agencies provide their own mobile devices to obtain the fingerprints [13]. Law enforcement officers use the RISC system to match the fingerprints against a national registry of about 2.5 million sets of fingerprints [14]. RISC's registry includes

- Wanted Persons including the Immigration Violator File

- National Sexual Offender Registry Subjects

- Known or Suspected Terrorists

- Other Persons of Special Interest

RISC is distinguished for quick identification. It only takes 10 s for the system to send a response to the officer [14]. The responses are red = highly probable, yellow = possible, and green = no candidate in RISC. RISC's official flyer for the FBI [13] reports a success story of the mobile fingerprint identification system. An individual was wanted by the Gwinnett county sheriff's office in Georgia for murder and aggravated assault. He had an outstanding warrant for 8 years and was finally arrested when stopped by an officer for driving with headlights off.

9.4 LIVENESS DETECTION ON FINGERPRINTS

One method to detect spoofed fingerprints is by reading the physiological signs of life (liveness or vitality detection) on templates for enrollment, verification, and identification into biometric systems [1]. A system designed to protect against attacks with spoofed fingerprints must also check if the presented biometric sample matches with the sample originally enrolled in the system. Most biometric systems today have a decision process which first checks liveness [16]:

if data = live

perform acquisition and extraction

else if data = not live

do not perform acquisition and extraction

Some physiological features that can be monitored to detect the physiological signs of life are perspiration, pulsation detection, pulse oximetry, temperature sensing, electrical conductivity, EGC, active sweat pores, and among other attributes [1,10].

- *Perspiration.* Detects the change of moisture level in areas around the sweat pores which spread across the ridges over some time [1,13]. Perspiration is also known as sweat. Sweat is a dilute sodium chloride solution secreted by the sweat glands of the skin on to the surface of the skin through small pores. In live fingers, the perspiration starts from the pores then diffuses along the ridges during time. This makes the semidry areas among the pores moister or darker in an image. The human skin has about 600 sweat glands per square inch. The perspiration process does not occur in cadavers or artificial fingerprints [17].

- *Pulsation detection.* The pulsation detection focuses in the fine movements of the skin. Pulsation differs from person to person, the emotional state, and previous activity. A normal pulse rate ranges between 200 and 220 heart beats per minute [13]. Changes in the pulse generate problems [17].

- *Pulse oximetry.* Measures the saturation of oxygen in hemoglobin and the heart pulse of the tip of the finger. The blood oxygenation involves hardware with two light sources: infrared (940 nm) and red (550 nm) [13]. Recognition of pulse oximetry can be tricked by means of a translucent false fingerprint, for example, one made with gelatin, on top of an impostor's live finger. The pulse oximetry will measure the saturation of oxygen of hemoglobin in the blood of the trespasser's finger [17].

- *Temperature sensing.* The average temperature of the human epidermis in fingertips ranges between 26°C and 30°C [13]. This is a simple method, however, some physiological variation in persons may make this method difficult to detect liveness. For example, a person with poor blood circulation can change the body's temperature and the finger sensor may read a wrong vitality signal [18].

- *Electrical conductivity.* Measures the dielectric constant property of human living skin [13]. The conductivity or resistance in human skin depends on the humidity. Humidity is also dependent on the person's biological characteristics and the environment. For example, some persons have dry fingers and others have sweaty ones. The seasons also affect the moisture [18]. Live fingers have a 16% moisture level whereas a gelatin fingerprint has a 23% [17]. The difference in moisture level between gelatin fingerprints and living fingers is insignificant enough to be able to fool sensors with gelatin prints [17].

- *Active sweat pores.* The pores discharge sweat fluid drops as part of a thermoregulation process. The openings and closing of the sweat pores can be used for liveness detection in fingerprint images [1]. A fingerprint sensor with a very high resolution camera can capture the sweat pores in a fingerprint [17]. Those details might be very difficult to reproduce in an artificial fingerprint. Intraridge pores can be made with gelatin, but not good enough to reproduce the exact size and position of the pores on the mold and the print [17].

Fingerprint liveness detection can be grouped in five categories: (1) pore detection-based, (2) skin deformation-based, (3) image quality-based, (4) perspiration-based, and (5) combined approaches [10]. In this section, we describe some emerging approaches of fingerprint liveness detection that include one or more of the previously listed categories.

9.4.1 Pore Detection-Based

Pore detection-based procedures sense pores as a sign of fingerprint liveliness. Usually, the detection of pores encompasses locating the pores' position and the extraction of active sweat pores [10]. Other methods use pore quantity to distinguish between a query image and a reference image (real or false) [10]. The pore detection process is usually combined with the perspiration-based approach.

9.4.2 Perspiration-Based

Perspiration-based fingerprint detection schemes study perspiration shapes existing in the fingerprint. Pores are defined as the "openings of subcutaneous eccrine sweat glands located in the epidermis" [1]. A pore detection-based approach aims to distinguish active pores from inactive ones. Active pores tend to be bigger than inactive finger pores by a factor of 5–10. Moreover, active pores discharge sweat fluid drops [1] as can be seen in Figure 9.3 (sweat fluid).

Liveness detection for pores in fingerprints can be performed by various methods. Some methods are as follows:

- *Fingerprint pore extraction* aims to locate the sweat pores in fingerprint images and uses the location as a unique identification [20].

- *Pores and ridge contours extraction* in which wavelength transform and Gabor filters are used to extract the pores with ridge counters [21].

- *Analysis of pore's location* analyzes the distribution of pores [22].

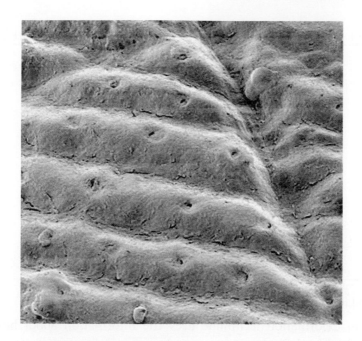

FIGURE 9.3   Sweat pores with fluid in ridges. (From Wordpress, image of pore.)

A method proposed by Memon, Manivannan, and Balachandran implements an advanced image processing algorithm named high-pass and correlation filtering (HCFA) [1]. HCFA uses high-pass filtering from the image of a fingerprint and then performs a correlation filtering and then binarization [1].

The HCFA first takes an original color image of high resolution of at least 800 dpi. Then, the image is converted into gray scale, inverted, and normalized. This enhanced image is passed through a high-pass filter stage which uses a high-pass filter transfer function [1]. Once the image is passed through the filter, the low frequency ridge-valley structures are removed, leaving the small active pore-like shapes that will provide a number of correlation peaks in the output. In the final stage, a binarized black image with white spots is generated in which the white spots indicate the presence of active pores [1].

The tests were performed with 20 images. The results compared manual identification of active pores against the HCFA method. The statistics of the results were very positive. The correlation coefficient of the four measured thresholds was very close to one as displayed in Table 9.1. In this case, one means there is a perfect match between the two sets—manual and HCFA.

TABLE 9.1   Statistical Measures for Four Threshold Values: 0.05, 0.1, 0.15, and 0.2

		Type of Statistical Measure	Threshold			
			0.05	0.10	0.15	0.20
1		Coefficient	0.90	0.83	0.81	0.79
2		Mean	62.4	53.2	42.0	38.0
3		Median	63.6	50.0	40.0	35.0
4		LQ	48.9	42.4	28.3	19.4
5		UQ	74.2	66.8	51.7	51.7
6	DE	IQR	25.3	24.4	23.4	32.3
7		Mean	59.8	70.9	73.5	72.7
8		Median	60.0	75.0	80.0	75.0
9		LQ	41.3	52.8	54.9	54.2
10		UQ	74.2	85.4	97.2	97.2
11	DA	IQR	32.9	32.6	42.3	42.5

9.4.3 Skin Deformation-Based

The skin deformation technique uses the information about how the fingertip's skin deforms when pressed against a scanner surface. This approach exploits the elasticity properties of the skin [10]. A method to capture finger distortion is the use of a thin plate spline model with different angles of rotation [23]. Another approach to detect skin deformation in fingerprint is via the correlation coefficient and standard deviation based on the elasticity of the skin [24].

Nonetheless, a thin fake fingerprint attached on a live finger is able to produce comparable nonlinear deformation as a live finger would. Another disadvantage is that the skin deformation-based systems need special training and well-calibrated scanners to deliver frames at a proper rate to identify spoofs [10].

9.4.4 Image Quality-Based

Image-based techniques to identify liveness of fingerprints concentrate on finding the difference between the image of a live and a fabricated fingerprint.

9.4.4.1 Profiling and Wavelet: Joint Time Frequency Analysis

An image processing technique for detecting liveness on fingerprint images is joint time frequency analysis using profiling and wavelet [10]. In a proposal by Bhanarkar and Doshi [25], a single-image-based method was used for liveness detection. This procedure assumes that the fingerprint images of a live person are different from spoofed ones. The individual characteristics of live and spoofed fingerprints are analyzed using profiling method and wavelet-based analysis techniques.

This method is performed in the following sequence: (1) the subject trying to access the system scans the finger, (2) an image of the fingerprint is obtained, and (3) the fingerprint image is processed in two stages: profiling and wavelet-based profiling [10]. This technique tested 50 samples of live and 50 samples of silicon fake fingerprint images. The result of the tests indicated that the live fingerprint samples are identified as live by indicating 1, but the spoof fingerprint images indicated 0 as fake [10].

This approach is a software-based application thus allows for a high level of customization and reduces the cost of the fingerprint biometric system. Furthermore, there is no need for additional hardware [10].

The joint time frequency analysis based on liveness fingerprint detection has numerous advantages: (1) only a single image of a fingerprint is used, (2) it only takes 1 s for liveness detection, and (3) it can be used in real time applications [10]. These advantages make this method very promising for mobile phone biometric applications.

9.4.4.2 3D Image Quality: FPCLiveTouch™

There are numerous innovative commercial solutions for fingerprint liveness detection. A commercial option for fingerprint liveness detection Fingerprint Cards (FPC) created FPCLiveTouch as a solution to enhance the security for fingerprint sensors to recognize spoofs. The new fingerprint recognition system including liveness detection was released in February 2016. This technology was created in response to the increased demand for secure mobile payments. The accuracy rate ranges from 96.5% to 99.5% to catch and reject "fake fingers" using different sensors including touch, swipe, optical, and capacitance [26]. This biometric equipment offers "unique image quality, extreme robustness, and low power consumption" [26]. FPC technology is implemented in smartphones, tablets, and biometric cards. A distinctive advantage of FPC fingerprint liveness identification is that does not need additional hardware for a fast and secure verification. The latest release mobile with FPCLiveTouch technology is a flagship mobile model Mi5 with an FPC1245 sensor. It includes ceramic coating, 360° finger rotation capability, fast response, and a three-dimensional (3D) image. This innovative mobile phone was released on February 26, 2016 and it has already reached its expected revenues for 2016. Figure 9.4 shows the touch sensor verification.

FIGURE 9.4   Touch sensor verification. (From Fingerprints.com.)

9.4.5 Temperature-Based

Temperature is considered an involuntary generated body signal [18]. The temperature on a fingertip is easy to measure, though, it is also easy to be deceived. The average temperature on fingertips ranges between 26°C and 30°C [18]. A thin silicone artificial fingerprint can be used on top of the finger. The temperature on the silicone is only 2°C below the live finger. Since 2°C is within the range of acceptance by the sensor, it will not be difficult to have the temperature of an artificial fingertip within the margins of the sensor [17].

Trials measuring human skin's temperature were performed with a FLIR ThermoCAM PM545G. Ten healthy users contributed and all 10 fingers were measured four times. All the trials were made at room temperature of 26°C and humidity of about 64% within the same day. The results of the trials provided a skin temperature range from 21.5°C to 35.7°C. In addition, the difference between the right and left fingers was roughly 0.6°C. The wide-ranging temperatures in this approach are not effective to detect liveness [18]. Thus, this methodology is not suitable for liveness detection implementation on mobile devices.

9.4.6 Skin Resistance-Based

The resistance or conductivity of the human skin is based on humidity. The electrical properties of the human body can be used as a possible solution to detect liveness. Moisture, in turn, depends on an individual's biological features and environmental conditions. With respect to biological features, some persons have very dry skin which results in high resistance (low conductivity), and other persons have sweaty skin which leads to low resistance (high conductivity) [18]. Environmental conditions are related to the seasons which influence humidity variations as well. Consequently, the extent of acceptable resistance levels has to be large enough to be used by fingerprint liveness detection systems [18].

In a trial on Reference 17, the electric resistance in a live finger measured 16 Mohms/cm. A fabricated fingerprint made out of gelatin measured 20 Mohms/cm. Figure 9.5 displays a recently made gelatin fingerprint. The difference between the live and artificial electrical resistance was very minor. Moisture levels of live fingers and gelatin made ones were taken as well. The results indicated that live fingers have a moisture level of 16%, while gelatin ones have a moisture level of 23% [17]. Furthermore, it is easy to add a salty solution of similar concentration of sweat or saliva on a fake finger to add moisture and imitate the humidity of a real finger.

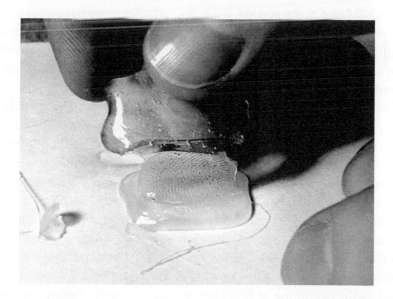

FIGURE 9.5   Making a gelatin fingerprint. (From Kaseva, A., and Stén, A. 2003. Creating an artificial finger using the actual finger, March 18.)

The slight difference between the moisture levels of the real and gelatin made fingerprints and the capacity to add moisture to a fake fingerprint, make this method not feasible to use as liveness detection option on mobile devices.

9.5 CONCLUSION

Spoofing is a real concern with regard to the security of biometric system in the mobile industry. In this chapter, we explained various approaches to prevent the attacker from fooling the biometric system with fake fingerprints and we also discussed some of the challenges of each method.

Software methods, image-based, have more popularity due to the diversity of algorithms that can be used to analyze the obtained fingerprints. A promising liveness detection approach, from among the many possible techniques, is the profiling and wavelet procedure presented in this chapter. This scheme has an advantage over other methods for liveness detection on fingerprints since only one image is used to detect spoof attacks [10]. Profiling and wavelet process only requires 1 s for liveness detection thus making this approach suitable for real time applications such as mobile phone biometric user authentication.

Another optimistic answer to liveness detection on fingerprints is FPCLiveTouch(TM)'s commercially available solution introduced before. Although is new in the market, the sales and popularity have already surpassed the expectations within months of its release. The sophisticated design includes swipe, touch, and optical properties with a 95%–99% accuracy of fingerprint spoof detection. The liveness detection can be applied in tablets, cellphones, and biometric cards.

Conversely, approaches that did not meet the criteria to be suitable for fingerprint liveness detection are, among several others, the pore detection and temperature-based methods. The pore detection method achieved good results, but it works best in the presence of more active pores. This method seems a good fit for mobile devices although it needs further development to become more practical. The temperature-based liveness detection is not a feasible method to detect fingerprint liveness since the scanner can be easily deceived using a thin silicone fingerprint over a live finger. In addition, some fake fingers moisturized or warmed up were recognized by the system as live fingers. The pulse oximetry approach presented in the beginning of this chapter was also easily fooled. The same applied for the skin resistance-based approach.

The amount of spoofing attempts is continuously increasing and new methods are emerging. Both industry and academic circles are working on creating more robust biometric devices. Still every counterstep can sooner or later be bypassed. Thus, research and development efforts must be continuous. The solutions should be precise, fast, and easy to use. The technology for mobile fingerprint authentication is evolving rapidly and it is just a matter of including liveness detection for better authentication.

Single modal biometric techniques for liveness fingerprint recognition are under continuous research and have achieved very good results. However, the integration of multimodal biometric systems for fingerprint authentication is under initial development. Further research is needed to integrate the liveness detection method into multimodal biometric systems. The challenge would be to choose a property or multiple properties in the fingerprints that are very difficult or impossible to imitate.

REFERENCES

1. Memon, S., Manivannan, N., and Balachandran, W. 2011. Active pore detection for liveness in fingerprint identification system. In *2011 19th Telecommunications Forum (TELFOR)*, Belgrade, Serbia. IEEE, pp. 619–622, November.
2. Shinde, M. K. and Annadate, S. A. 2015. Analysis of fingerprint image for gender classification or identification: Using wavelet transform and singular value decomposition. In *2015 International Conference on Computing Communication Control and Automation (ICCUBEA)*, Pune, India. IEEE, pp. 650–654, February.
3. What's So Special about Your Fingerprints? n.d. http://wonderopolis.org/wonder/what-s-so-special-about-your-fingerprints (retrieved March 8, 2016).
4. Hoover, J. E. n.d. Fingerprint. http://www.britannica.com/topic/fingerprint (retrieved March 2, 2016).
5. Understanding Fingerprints. n.d. http://www.viewzone.com/fingerprintsx.html (retrieved February 25, 2016).
6. Advantages and Disadvantages of Technology. PB Works. http://biometrics.pbworks.com/ (retrieved March 1, 2016).
7. Gottschlich, C., Marasco, E., Yang, A. Y., and Cukic, B. 2014. Fingerprint liveness detection based on histograms of invariant gradients. In *2014 IEEE International Joint Conference on Biometrics (IJCB)*, Clearwater, Florida. IEEE, pp. 1–7, September.
8. Abhyankar, A. and Schuckers, S. 2006. Fingerprint liveness detection using local ridge frequencies and multiresolution analysis techniques. In *International Conference on Image Processing*, Atlanta, Georgia, pp. 321–324.

9. LivDet—Liveness Detection Competitions. n.d. http://livdet.org/ (retrieved February 25, 2016).

10. Akhtar, Z., Michelon, C., and Foresti, G. L. 2014. Liveness detection for biometric authentication in mobile applications. In *2014 International Carnahan Conference on Security Technology (ICCST)*, Rome, Italy. IEEE, pp. 1–6, October.

11. Kent, J. Malaysia car thieves steal finger. *BBC News*, Kuala Lumpur, http://news.bbc.co.uk/2/hi/asia-pacific/4396831.stm

12. Institute of Automation, Chinese Academy of Sciences (CASIA). Biometrics Ideal Test. http://biometrics.idealtest.org/ (retrieved March 1, 2016).

13. Reddy, P., Kumar, A., Rahman, S., and Mundra, T. 2007. A new method for fingerprint antispoofing using pulse oxiometry. In *IEEE Biometrics: Theory, Applications and Systems (BTAS)*, Washington, DC, pp. 1–6.

14. FCW: The Business of Federal Technology. https://fcw.com/articles/2011/08/25/fbi-fingerprint-check-system-national-database-mobile.aspx

15. The FBI's big, bad identification system. By Michael Cooney, Network World |Sep 25, 2014 8:31 AM PT. http://www.networkworld.com/article/2687913/security/164703-The-FBI-s-big-bad-identification-system.html#slide9

16. Aggarwal, T. 2014. *CS Journals*, May 1. http://www.csjournals.com/ (retrieved March 1, 2016).

17. Sandström, M. 2004. Liveness detection in fingerprint recognition systems, Master thesis, http://www.ep.liu.se/exjobb/isy/2004/3557/exjobb.pdf

18. Drahansky, M. 2008. Experiments with skin resistance and temperature for liveness detection. In *International Conference on Intelligent Information Hiding and Multimedia Signal Processing*, Harbin, China. IEEE, pp. 1075–1079, August.

19. Image of Pore. https://handfacts.files.wordpress.com/2011/04/sweat-pores-skin-ridges.jpg

20. Ray, M., Meenen, P., and Adhami, R. 2005. A novel approach to fingerprint pore extraction. In *Proceedings of the Thirty-Seventh Southeastern Symposium on System Theory, SSST '05*. IEEE, pp. 282–286.

21. Watson, C. and Wilson, C. L. 2008. *NIST Special Database 4, Fingerprint Database*. National Institute of Standards and Technology. http://www.nist.gov/srd/nistsd4.cfm

22. Parthasaradhi, S.T.V., Derakhshani, R., Hornak, L.A., and Schuckers, S.A.C. 2005. Time-series detection of perspiration as a liveness test in fingerprint devices. *IEEE Transactions on Systems, Man, and Cybernetics, Part C: Applications and Reviews*, 35, 335–343.

23. Zhang, Y., Tian, X., Chen, X., Yang, X., and Shi, P. 2007. Fake finger detection based on thin-plate spline distortion model. *Advances in Biometrics Lecture Notes in Computer Science*, 4642, 742–749.

24. Jia, J., Cai, L., Zhang, K., and Chen, D. 2007. A new approach to fake finger detection based on skin elasticity analysis. In *Proceedings of the 2007 International Conference on Advances in Biometrics (ICB'07)*, S.-W. Lee and S. Z. Li (Eds.). Springer-Verlag, Berlin, Heidelberg, pp. 309–318.

25. Bhanarkar, A., Doshi, P., Abhyankar, A., and Bang, A. 2013. Joint time frequency analysis based liveness fingerprint detection. In *2013 IEEE Second International Conference on Image Information Processing (ICIIP)*, Shimla, India. IEEE, pp. 166–169, December.
26. Fingerprint cards extends security for fingerprint sensors. 2016, February 17. http://www.fingerprints.com/corporate/en/fingerprint-cards-extends-security-for-fingerprint-sensors/ (retrieved February 28, 2016).
27. Kaseva, A. and Stén, A. 2003. Creating an artificial finger using the actual finger, March 18. http://biometrics.mainguet.org/ (retrieved March 9, 2016).

CHAPTER 10

Face Recognition

Andrey Gubenko and Abhishek Verma

CONTENTS

10.1 PUBLIC DATASETS

Since the face recognition problem has been here for a while, there are several public datasets available. In most cases, there is no need to adjust the general purposes datasets for mobile biometrics. Of course, some observation could be made regarding features more important for biometrics, such as environment, noise, different illumination, and rotation. Below we describe a few datasets.

10.1.1 PubFig: Public Figures Face Database

The PubFig dataset consists of 58,797 real-world images of 200 people collected from the Internet. Most of these images were taken in uncontrolled situations which makes a huge difference from other popular datasets.

10.1.2 Labeled Faces in the Wild

Labeled faces in the wild is a dataset of face images developed to test an algorithm in solving the unconstrained face recognition problem. The dataset consists of more than 13,000 images collected from the Internet. Each image was classified according to the name of person. A total of 1680 of these people have two or more distinct pictures in this dataset. Faces in these dataset were detected using the Viola–Jones face detector.

10.1.3 Columbia Gaze Dataset

Columbia gaze dataset contains 5880 images of 56 people taken with varying gaze directions and head poses. For each person, there are 5 head poses and 21 gaze directions per head pose. The dataset's subjects are ethnically diverse and 21 of the people wore glasses. This dataset was created to train a detector to sense eye contact, but it can be used for any other gaze estimation or tracking problems.

10.1.4 3D Mask Attack Database

The 3D mask attack database (3DMAD) is a biometric (face) spoofing database. It currently comprises 76,500 frames covering 17 people. These were recorded using Kinect for both real access and spoofing attacks. Each frame consists of a depth image, the corresponding RGB image and manually annotated eye positions (with respect to the RGB image). The data were collected in three different sessions from the subjects. Five videos of 300 frames were captured for each session. The recordings were done under controlled conditions and depict frontal view and neutral expression.

10.1.5 10k US Adult Faces Database

US adult faces dataset contains 10,168 natural face photographs and several measures for 2222 of the faces, including memorability scores, computer vision and psychology attributes, and landmark point annotations. The face pictures are stored in as a JPEGs format 72 pixels/in resolution and 256-pixel height.

10.2 RELEVANT WORK ON MOBILE FACE RECOGNITION

One of the most important requirements for mobile biometrics in comparison with classical approaches is that they have to work in real time. Due to the use cases, images should be captured and processed immediately when authentication is required.

CASE STUDY 1

Choi et al. [1] introduce the extraction method of local features using a random basis alongside with sequential neural network. An algorithm uses these extracted features to train the neural network incrementally, adjusting weights on each step. This paper also introduces a real-time training process which is essential for mobile biometrics. Secondary, the introduced model solves the problem of large variation pictures of the same faces, taken with different illumination and with occlusions.

There are two main distinctive features of this algorithm:

1. *Local random basis.* The algorithm generates a nonorthogonal local random basis which is robust to local deformation. Compared with a common basis which extracts orthogonal and global features, a nonorthogonal basis is more efficient in terms of computational requirements.
2. *Real-time incremental training.* The model is trained incrementally using a nontraining-based feature extractor with a sequential classifier. This method avoids retraining which significantly decreases computational time.

While most of the well-known training-based features extraction methods require a lot of training samples and hyper parameters tuning, random projection (RP) [2] was created as a dimensional reduction technique which can operate without a lot of training samples. Because there is no need in training samples, the basis generation approach doesn't require a lot of computational power which makes it perfect to use for mobile platforms. Besides this, applying of the local random basis allows the convolution of high-dimensional features to low-dimensional features and we decrease amount of memory required.

RP projects multidimensional data to low-dimensional subspaces using a set of randomly generated basis, in such a way that the projection matrix consists of entries with zero mean and a constant variance. This approach is based on the sparse RP method proposed by Achlioptas [3], when the matrix is projected onto low-dimensional spaces without normalization.

Another part of the proposed method is the multilayer feedforward neural network (MLP). This machine learning technique is widely used for solving different classification problems. If we think about MLP as a single hidden layer an output layer will be formed by neurons with linear activation functions. Such a model is called a single layer feedforward network (SLFN) [4]. SLFN can be used as a universal approximator with adjustable weights. Normally, a hidden neuron parameter can be randomly generated according to any continuous sampling distribution. In this case, hidden node parameters can be independent of the training data and by new incoming data the learning machine can be retained only by using additional samples via a recursive least-squares formulation. In one of the previous works, the authors propose to call that online sequential extreme learning machine (OS-ELM) [5]. OS-ELM provides great accuracy along with robustness, but is highly computational intensive for high-dimensional face images.

The authors introduce an architecture which uses both techniques together. First, local implementation of RP applies to image, which performs projection from high- to low-dimensional space. Local RP is more robust to local deformations and illumination conditions. The effect is achieved by using local techniques such as independent component analysis [6], local features analysis [7], and local nonnegative matrix factorization [8]. After this the online sequential ELM is applied to the projection. Because we have already decreased the number of dimensions, OS-ELM does not require a lot computational resources which makes it applicable for mobile platforms.

Experiments reveal that such an approach works fast on most of the datasets with acceptable good accuracy. Although experiments showed different training time on different datasets, it showed low constant time in most cases.

CASE STUDY 2

There is much implementation of face detection using dedicated hardware and coprocessors built in digital cameras. However, most of these approaches cannot be applied to mobile biometrics due to high computational or memory costs.

As it was mentioned before, it is critical for mobile biometrics to perform image recognition in real time. Observing existing face recognition algorithms shows that the key algorithm for face detection is the algorithm introduced by Viola and Jones [9]. This algorithm uses a cascaded Adaboost classifier, trained on a number of sub images. One of the requirements of the Adaboost is that the classifier has to be previously trained offline, due to the amount of time and computational resources. While algorithms based on the Viola approach give good accuracy, it has a limitation when there is rotation or occlusion. This can be solved by using different assembling models with pretraining. However, pretraining requires additional computational and storage resources and it is not possible to do it in real time.

Viola and Jones [10] present a hybrid solution for robust face detection which does not require any pretraining and image preprocessing. The authors introduce a hybrid solution which consists of the Viola algorithm alongside a color-based approach.

In the color-based part of the algorithm, skin color in Cr–Cb color space is represented by the Gaussian mixture model (GMM). Experimentally it was shown [11] that the optimal number of Gaussians is two, which gives the best accuracy–speed ratio.

The procedure for face detecting consists of two stages. In the first stage of the algorithm, the images convert into a binary image by applying skin color extraction using the GMM with 1's representing pixels of the image corresponding to skin color pixels and 0's representing nonskin color pixels. Then, by applying a subblock shape processing scheme to the binary image algorithm detects the face based on face size, aspect ratio, and probability.

Such a skin color detection approach increases robustness to the rotational variance as well as decreases computational requirements. The favorable difference of this algorithm to other similar algorithms is that it still works well when the surroundings have the same color as the skin.

Adding the Viola and Jones algorithm to this hybrid solution helps to avoid the limitations of illumination conditions and computation requirements which are incredibly important for real-time mobile face detection.

Since the Viola and Jones algorithm has already shown its robustness to lighting and brightness variations, the authors use it to detect frontal view faces. Then, the detected area is used to calibrate a previously introduced color-based model for illumination conditions. After calibration, the color-based algorithm can detect faces regardless of any brightness issues. Also, this hybrid approach does not require any additional data collection for classifier training.

The real-time implementation of the algorithm was tested using Texas Instruments OMAP3430 mobile platform. Platform consists of ARM Cortex-A8 processor, GPU, and C6400 DSP. For testing, the authors used combination of tests with different lighting such as florescent (average accuracy 94.4%), incandescent (91.8%), mixed (93%), and sunlight (92.3%). Experiments were performed under different image conditions, for example, rotation, covered eyes, and frontal faces. Also, experiments showed that average processing time was around 800 ms of the OMAP3430 mobile device.

CASE STUDY 3

As we know, most face recognition techniques rely on sophisticated machine learning algorithms which can be computationally intensive. Due to the limited resources of mobile devices, client–server architecture becomes more and more popular, because all data processing can be completed on the more powerful server side.

Kremic et al. [12] proposed a new authentication model, which reduces risks with cell phone authentication. At the very beginning of wireless technology, most mobile authentication systems were an adaptation of the classic client–server model. However, due to the specifics of mobile biometrics this was not perfect (Figure 10.1).

System proposed by authors aimed to decrease all potential vulnerabilities by having multiple authentication frameworks.

A system's architecture consists of server and client side. When the client side is a personal cell phone, the server side is more sophisticated. The key part of the server part is a machine learning MATLAB algorithm, which operates with the client through the Tomcat server.

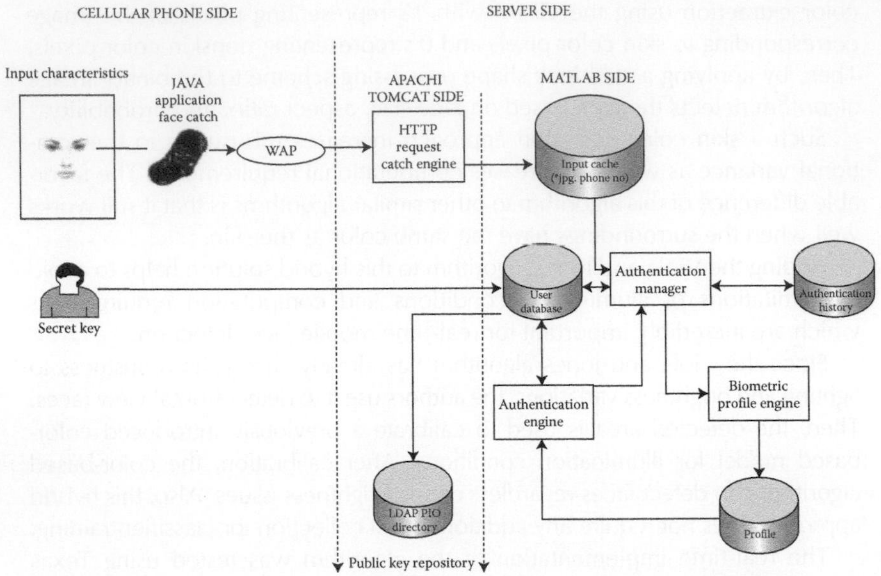

FIGURE 10.1   Client–server based mobile authentication system.

Machine learning algorithm in MATLAB works with the user database, authentication engine, biometric profile, and authentication manager. The authentication manager is the key of the systems as it redirects queries depending on input.

The database stores information about users and mobile devices, which are configured to work with this system, as well as supported biometric systems. The proposed system has great flexibility, any biometrics system can be used. Also in the presented system public key repository using public key infrastructure (PKI) was implemented, which aims to guarantee image authenticity after the image was sent to the server over the network.

CASE STUDY 4

Park and Yoo [13] propose a mobile face recognition algorithm which operates at low computational and memory cost. The algorithm is based on extracting features using Gabor– linear binary pattern (LBP) histogram alongside the scale invariant feature transform (SIFT)-based local feature descriptor.

Gabor–LBP is well known for detection texture features of objects, that is why this extractor is responsible for representing the local texture and shape of the face.

On the other hand, the SIFT-based part works better on the detection of local feature points in regions of interest (regions most likely to contain distinct information for each face). Such regions are eyes, mouth, nose, ears, etc.

The algorithm divided into two stages: train and test. In the training stage 40 Gabor filters are applied to one image which produces 40 different Gabor images. We need many different filters to decompose the images. Next, these images are transformed into Gabor–LBP images by applying the LBP operator. For each image, we extract the LBP histogram on the regular regions. During the test stage, the algorithm extracts the LBP histogram using the same technique. Besides, local feature points are extracted using the SIFT descriptor. SIFT-based features points are used in order to select local feature blocks. At the last stage, both LBP histograms are compared between training local features and test local features.

The proposed algorithm showed great accuracy performance: 96.1% for Electronics and Telecommunications Research Institute (ETRI) dataset and 98.4% for XM2VTS dataset with a small processing time which is critical for mobile devices.

10.3 CONCLUSION

Face recognition algorithms have been known for a while. New challenges in mobile biometrics created a new set of problems to be solved by researchers. Most of these solutions aim to decrease the differences between face recognition approaches on desktop computers and mobile devices. Observing the latest research, there are a few different ways to do this.

Using distributed architecture, with the client on a mobile device and a sophisticated face classification algorithm on servers is a straightforward naive solution. Such an approach allows the adoption of classic face classification algorithms and uses them for mobile biometrics. The downside of this method is that it requires a connection between the mobile device and server, which makes the method unreliable and vulnerable to hackers' attacks.

Another way of implementing mobile biometrics is to change the algorithms in the way they will be using the advantages of mobile platforms, such as graphics processing units (GPUs). Since GPUs were designed for matrix multiplication which makes them perfect fit for computer vision.

Due to the limited amount of memory resources and the necessity of getting results without long pretraining, online machine learning is another helpful approach. Instead of using computationally heavy offline training, in this case the prediction model which is stored on the mobile device itself gets updated with every new input.

Besides the techniques presented, there are several different assemblies of these methods, which are used depending on current tasks and resources.

REFERENCES

1. K Choi, KA Toh, H Byun. Realtime training on mobile devices for face recognition applications. *Pattern Recognition*, 44(2), 386–400, 2011.
2. N Goel, G Bebis, A Nefian. Face recognition experiments with random projection. In *Defense and Security*, Orlando, Florida, 2005.
3. D Achlioptas. Database-friendly random projections. *Proceedings of the Twentieth ACM*, Santa Barbara, California, 2001. pp. 274–281.
4. KA Toh. Deterministic neural classification. *Neural Computation*, 20(6), 1565–1595, 2008, MIT Press.
5. NY Liang, GB Huang, P Saratchandran. A fast and accurate online sequential learning algorithm for feedforward networks. *Neural Networks*, 17, 1411–1423, 2006.
6. MS Bartlett, JR Movellan, TJ Sejnowski. Face recognition by independent component analysis. *IEEE Transactions on Neural Networks*, 13(6), 1450–1464, 2002.
7. PS Penev, JJ Atick. Local feature analysis: A general statistical theory for object representation. *Network: Computation in Neural Systems*, 7(3), 477–500, 1996.
8. DD Lee, HS Seung. Algorithms for non-negative matrix factorization. In *Advances in Neural Information Processing*, Vancouver, BC, Canada, 2001.
9. M Rahman, N Kehtarnavaz. A hybrid face detection approach for real-time depolyment on mobile devices. In *Image Processing (ICIP)*, Cairo, Egypt, 2009.
10. P Viola, M Jones. Rapid object detection using a boosted cascade of simple features. In *IEEE Computer Society Conference on Computer Vision and Pattern Recognition*, Kauai, Hawaii. Vol. 1, 511–518, December 2001.
11. T Caetanoa, S Olabarriagab, D Baronea. Do mixture models in chromaticity space improve skin detection? *Pattern Recognition*, 36(12), 3019–3021, 2003.
12. E Kremic, A Subasi, K Hajdarevic. Face recognition implementation for client server mobile application using PCA. In *Technology Interfaces (ITI)*, Dubrovnik, Croatia, 2012.
13. S Park, JH Yoo. Real-time face recognition with SIFT-based local feature points for mobile devices. In *Modelling and Simulation (AIMS)*, Kota Kinabalu, Malaysia, 2013.

CHAPTER 11

Voice Recognition

Rodrigo Martinez and Abhishek Verma

CONTENTS

11.1 PUBLIC DATASETS

11.1.1 CHAINS Corpus

CHAracterizing Individual Speakers (CHAINS) was used to determine the accuracy of identifying an individual by an assortment of methods. The CHAINS project is used to identify key features in voices unique to individuals, which are possibly shared between speakers who adopt each other's style of speaking. The datasets included 36 speakers (18 males and 18 females) from East Ireland, from those who speak Eastern Hiberno-English, from the United Kingdom, and the United States. All subjects are recorded under several speaking conditions. This allows speaker comparison across a variety of well-defined speech styles (http://chains.ucd.ie/ftpaccess.php).

11.1.2 MIT Mobile Device Speaker Verification Corpus

This dataset is comprised of 48 speakers; 26 males and 22 females. The process consisted of having speakers recite short phrases, names, and ice-cream flavors within 20-min sessions. There were two separate sessions, one had the 48 speakers while the other contained imposters allowing each individual speaker to have their own dedicated imposter. In doing this, it allowed all imposter files for a speaker to be provided by the same imposter.

CASE STUDY 1

By having a microphone conveniently installed into any mobile device, the user is capable of verifying their identity in a manner more secure than having a four-digit passcode. In the article "Mobile biometrics: Joint face and voice verification for a mobile platform," by P.A. Tresadern [1], both facial recognition and voice verification are combined to investigate the possibility of having a reliable method of security. To ensure the ability to verify one's identity with one's voice, the system must be able to actively detect the vocal activities of the speaker and then verify that the speaker is in fact the owner of the mobile device, or is authorized to use the said device.

The first step in being able to validate one's identity through voice on a mobile device, comes from the ability to detect voice activity. In order to use a sample collected from the microphone, the system needs to separate the speaker's voice from the background noise (or anything that isn't the speaker). This provides the system with a clear sample without any factor that might interfere in successfully authenticating the owner. Because there are many variations in speech, be it physiological traits (lisps or accents) or other forms of vocal habits that might alter the clarity of the voice, the ability to detect the speaker's voice for the initial sample and overall verification differs between speakers. For example, someone with a cold, flu, or varied form of allergies, will have an altered voice producing varied results that could affect the outcome of the authentication process. When capturing voice, its shape can be represented as a feature vector and must be condensed into a fragment at any desired location. The summarized vector can be displayed using a technique known as *cepstral analysis* which helps calculate the spectrum using Fourier transform to breakdown the logarithm of the vector with a second Fourier transform or discrete cosine transform [1], eventually charting the results onto the *mel* scale; this scale helps to perceive the variances due to distance in pitch. The second breakdown produces *mel-frequency cepstral coefficients* (MFCCs).

To determine what classifies feature vectors as actual *speech* or *nonspeech*, the Gaussian mixture model is used to categorize these, while disregarding the ordering of the feature vectors. Using the GMM is efficient for samples with a high signal-to-noise ratio (SNR), but falls short when provided with environments with significant amounts of background noise. In these occasions, artificial neural networks (ANNs) assist in classifying the vectors as either a phoneme, the smallest unit of speech that determines the difference between words and nonspeech. According to Tresadern et al. [1], the output of the ANN produces a vector of probabilities that correspond to phonemes and nonspeech which are leveled over time using a hidden Markov model;

this accounts for the phoneme frequency studied from training data and allows the phoneme to merge into speech samples.

After removing nonspeech, or unnecessary noise, the remaining sample can be used to determine if it is a match with the authorized individual; in doing so, the system can then approve or deny access into the system. To begin with the verification of the speaker, we use the MFCC depiction to define the sound of the voice provided. Once silence is filtered out of the sample's frames created with the MFCC, a cepstral mean and variance normalization is utilized. To categorize feature vectors, joint factor analysis based on parametric Gaussian mixture model [1] is used. In this process of categorizing or classifying, various examples are gone through to generate a more client-specific model to produce a tested connection. According to Tresadern et al. [1], their results concluded with an equal error rate (EER) of 3%–4% when it came to speaker verification.

CASE STUDY 2

When it comes to testing the capability of verifying voice in noise-riddled surroundings, it tends to be in locations with controlled noises. These examples or tests become less effective when faced with arbitrary noises that occur in everyday environments. "Robust speaker recognition in noisy conditions" [2] focuses on being able to distinguish, or recognize, a speaker while immersed in noise that you would find without prior knowledge of the noise.

The approach they took for modeling noise contained two steps. To begin, various copies of an original training set, a set containing clean speech data, were produced. From there, they would be able to introduce several different types of noise to simulate corruption of the cleanliness; done by introducing white noise at varying SNRs. The formula provided in Reference 2 takes frame vectors, corrupted samples, and probability of the occurrence of the noise condition for the speaker, and in doing so should improve the robustness of the noise in the test samples. The second step is to focus solely on test cases where the sub-bands, or noise samples, are matched to identifiable noise; done by ignoring the sub-bands that failed to match. In doing this, they can define the likelihood of producing vocal samples that match and pass verification. White noise wasn't exclusively used, because this type of electronically added noise wasn't natural or arbitrarily found in real-world environments; this was remedied by using acoustic sounds to imitate more realistic noise. To do this, they fed the samples to loudspeakers, that is, one speaker was playing the white noise and the second speaker was playing the clean sample. New acoustic sets of data were recorded by making the corruption occur at varying SNR while simultaneously playing the clean data. Using several corruption sources, like pop songs, street traffic, restaurant noise, and mobile ringtones. Ming et al. [2] were able to create a table providing the results of their testing. This table describes the effectiveness of being able to correctly identify speech when placed in these arbitrary sounds at different SNR. The BSLN-Cln from testing the clean data was able to produce an accuracy of 98.41%. The rest of the data tends to vary, becoming more accurate with higher SNR amounts, and becoming less efficient at lower levels.

To test the actual capability of verifying a speaker, Ming et al. [2] used MIT's Mobile Device Speaker Verification Corpus, a database created for speaker verification. The recordings were gathered from mobile devices and were surrounded by realistic, environmental conditions. The database itself consists of 48 speakers, 26 males and 22 females, and 40 fake speakers, 23 males and 17 females. When conducting the experiment, the subjects (both groups) were to recite a list of ice-cream flavors numerous times to perform the training sessions and actual recording sessions. The testing itself took place in two different environments, the first being an office setting which provided low levels of background noise acting as corruption, and a street intersection which provided high levels of background noise.

During the process of gathering results for the speaker verification, it was determined that the office data was not entirely clean due to abrupt noise when microphones were turned on and off, and arbitrary background noises. By training the models in narrow-band noise, mismatching was able to be reduced providing better performances; training with wide-band noise produced worse results. The results revealed that having knowledge, or familiarity, with the noise bandwidth would help improve the performance of the model by being able to correctly filter white noise that matches the said bandwidth. By performing these types of multicondition tests, adding noises at varying SNR to simulate unknown sound, Ming et al. [2] concluded that multicondition training may or may not provide improved performance, but can help improve robustness.

CASE STUDY 3

It is rather difficult to bypass mobile devices that are protected by vocal biometrics, but it isn't impossible. Johnson et al. [3] proposed using a protocol called vaulted verification, improving on it to produce vaulted voice verification to ensure a more protected experience when using vocal biometrics for mobile devices. The vaulted voice verification process starts off by gathering information from the user, enough to better identify the real user in the future, through questions and responses. These samples allow feature vectors to be formed and divided into blocks. Chaff blocks, or dummy blocks, are formed for each of the feature blocks previously made; their appearance being identical to the original feature vector (allowing only the user to distinguish between them). Once this process is completed, the system is now secured.

The process for verifying the user begins immediately once the user attempts to access the protected system. To begin, the unidentified user must declare who they are by speaking their name/identification or by manually typing it in. Following the initially requested information, the system will ask the user for their password. Failing to provide the password will cause the system to end the process, providing no follow-up questions. If the user is able to successfully input the correct password, the series of challenge questions will begin.

The challenge questions would be sent from the software to the device in a random order, making the order different whenever a new verification attempt is made. The response request would vary depending on the type of question asked; with multiple choice questions, the user would have to recite the correct answer, for passages required to be read, the user would have to read what is asked correctly. The responses given are then processed into a model; the system then makes a decision by comparing the responses made by the unidentified user and the saved responses from the original user. The responses will be converted into a bit string, having the questions end once the stopping condition is met; this would generally be when the required amount of bits is achieved. Once the server evaluates the bit string, it will decide whether to allow access or deny it.

Johnson et al. [3] utilized the same dataset as Ming et al. [2], that being the MIT mobile device speaker verification corpus. In doing so, they were able to produce models from the data they can use to determine the effectiveness of their security. The effectiveness of the results is measured in terms of the false reject rate (FRR) and false accept rate (FAR). The FRR depicted the percentage of users who are falsely denied access to the mobile device. FAR depicts the percentage of people allowed into the system while pretending to be someone else. Where both of these rates meet is considered the EER and is only applicable once the attacker has already cracked or entered the software; before entering the initial name and password, the attacker wouldn't be able to gather any information.

In their experiments, they assumed that the system was compromised to determine the level of security vaulted voice verification provides. In small scale tests where the initial password was not compromised, the EER generated was 0%; the baseline or average EER being 11%. Due to the need to know how protected the software is without the initial password check, another model and test were done. The EER of the new tests was 8%, still lower than the general baseline of 11%. With more tests on a larger scale, they were able to produce a baseline of approximately 6% for EER. Johnson et al. [3] state that vaulted voice verification is determined on a case-by-case bases allowing it to identify between the imposters in the tests conducted.

In terms of security, the vaulted voice verification has many layers to it. The communication between the user and system occurs over a secured encryption protocol, preventing someone from eavesdropping. If the encryption on the communication is broken somehow, and the culprit attempts a "man in the middle" attack, they wouldn't receive any additional information due to the data and keys still being encrypted. Even if the attacker were to obtain the name/id and password of the user, they would still need to make

2^n correct guesses (2^{58} due to having the 58 blocks) in which case the user can always issue new answers and keys.

CASE STUDY 4

The ability to identify a person based on their voice, specifically their characteristics and mannerisms, opens up a wide variety of applications. Novakovic [4] wants to illustrate the dependability of person identification using vocal characteristics in smarts, all while using multilayer perceptron (MLP).

Speaker identification can be classified as being able to verify a speaker simply by their voice. Speaker verification is being able to decide if the speaker, or client, is who they state they are. Speaker identification can be described as 1:N where the voice is being compared against N templates. A speaker identification system would not only be able to authenticate or verify a speaker when asked, but it should also be able to do so covertly while users are speaking normally. The speaker identification system must begin with an enrollment phase; gathering recorded voices to extract features to form voice prints. In the verification phase, the sample previously recorded is compared against several voice prints to determine the best matches possible.

There are several factors that can affect the ability of the system to identify a user, be it mispronounced words or phrases, heightened emotional states, room acoustics, or even aging and illness. Because of these reasons, identifying someone can be difficult throughout the day due to the fact that at any given moment they can be affected by an arbitrary variable that will alter the speaker's voice. Background noise also affects the efficacy of identification because environmental noise could cause speakers to raise their voices to match or surpass the noise around them, also known as the Lombard effect. When collecting voice samples, it is important to have silence before and after each spoken phrase. In doing this, it allows the system to more easily determine where speech is occurring, and it allows that silence to be effortlessly cut out. In some occasions, a speaker might vary the speed at which they talk, causing some vowels to be pronounced longer or shorter than normal; a problem that can be remedied by time aligning the samples.

To compare and identify speakers, a supervised learning technique is implemented. Novakovic [4] utilizes the MLP ANN for their supervised learning technique as it can be utilized for real-world applications. MLP contains a set of inputs which represent the input layer of the network, a layer of computational nodes, and an output layer of computational nodes. A perk of MLP is that the nodes (neurons) of any layer are connected to all of the nodes of the previous layer, meaning it is fully connected. MLP's network also contains layers of neurons allowing it to learn complex nonlinear tasks by mining significant features from the input gathered. An algorithm that is used frequently with MLP is the error back-propagation algorithm, which consists of a forward pass and a backward pass. The forward pass contains synaptic weights that are fixed, while they are adjusted according to the error-correction rule during the backward pass. During the backward pass, the synaptic weights are adjusted to make the final output relatively close to what was desired.

CHAINS utilizes speaking conditions to determine vocal properties. There are six speaking conditions: solo speech, retelling, synchronous speech, repetitive synchronous imitation, fast speech, and whispered speech. Solo speech has the speaker read the entirety of a text sample at a natural rate after they read it silently to themselves. Retelling allowed speakers to freely read the text in their own words with no time limit. Synchronous speech had speakers, in pairs, read the text together while attempting to remain in synch. Repetitive synchronous imitation required speakers to listen to a recording of the speech, attempting to match the recorded model as best they could. Fast speech had speakers read the entire text at an accelerated rate, and in whispered speech, speakers read the text aloud in a whispered tone.

To run the experiment, Novakovic [4] used CfsSubSet evaluation, chi-squared attribute evaluation, and principal component analysis. Along with MLP, which contained additional feature ranking and feature selection techniques, Novakovic [4] used test datasets for 8 and 16 speakers with 25 features. The feature ranking and feature selection techniques would be used to discard irrelevant features in any feature vector. The results showed that the classification, or identification of a speaker, was dependent on the speaking condition; having a 23% variance in accuracy. Whispered speech had the worst accuracy when it came to speech classification, retelling being the most accurate. With MLP, the results provided showed an average accuracy of 65% when it came to identifying the speaker, concluding that vocal identification can be accurate enough to work in conjunction with other personal characteristics.

11.2 CONCLUSION

With the current need for advanced forms of security, biometric protection can be very appealing. Although most of a person's body is unique to themselves, one's voice can be difficult, nearly impossible, to imitate; allowing voice biometrics to be a more secure form of protection. With the ability to authenticate one's identity through speech (allowing access to their desired content) being currently available, the fear of having one's information taken is slowly diminishing. Although the data show that voice authorization and identification aren't 100% accurate, the chance to improve is high. Because of the possible limitations to software and the tools (microphones, etc.) used currently, it may take time for advancements to occur. The possibility of being able to walk into a smart environment and have the local system identify a speaker to better customize the experience will be plausible. In the future, it will be possible to maintain your work, or information, private and secured behind a layer of protection only your authorized voice will be able to bypass.

REFERENCES

1. Tresadern, P., T. F. Cootes, N. Poh, P. Matejka, A. Hadid, C. Levy, C. McCool, and S. Marcel. Mobile biometrics: Combined face and voice verification for a mobile platform. *IEEE Pervasive Computing*, 12(1), 79–87, 2013.
2. Ming, J., T. J. Hazen, J. R. Glass, and D. A. Reynolds. Robust speaker recognition in noisy conditions. *IEEE Transactions on Audio, Speech, and Language Processing*, 15(5), 1711–1723, 2007.
3. Johnson, R. C., W. J. Scheirer, and T. E. Boult. Secure voice-based authentication for mobile devices: Vaulted voice verification. In *The SPIE Defense, Security + Sensing Symposium*, Baltimore, Maryland, May 2013.
4. Novakovic, J. Speaker identification in smart environments with multilayer perceptron. In *2011 19th Telecommunications Forum (TELFOR)*, Belgrade, Serbia. 2011, pp. 1418–1421.

CHAPTER 12

Iris Recognition in Mobile Devices

Alec Yenter and Abhishek Verma

CONTENTS

W ITH THE POPULARITY OF mobile devices (phones, tablets, and other portable devices), people have begun to trust their contraptions with sensitive information. The requirement for security on mobile devices has become prevalent; many devices are marketed on their ability to protect user data. Many phones, such as the Apple iPhone and Samsung Galaxy phones, are also marketed based on their innovative camera technologies. The imaging advancements beg to be the solution to society's security requirement; hence the attractiveness of iris recognition.

12.1 OVERVIEW

12.1.1 History

Daugman (2014) was the first to explore the use of iris as a biometric identification indicator. His work implemented integro-differentials operators to focus on the iris and 2D Gabor filters to extract features from the iris texture. Among the first, Jeong et al. (2005) and Cho et al. (2005) proposed mobile methods for extracting the iris information and localizing the pupil, respectively. There have been many other contributors to the building of a reliable iris identification method.

12.1.2 Methods

Although there are several approaches to iris recognition and identification, the majority of current and new methods can be split into six generic phases. The first phase is simply the *Capturing* of the iris. This is typically accomplished with a camera that operates in the visual (VIS) spectrum, but could possibly be done with a near infrared (NIR) sensor (Jillela and Ross 2015). The second phase is *Image Correction*. Since images can be taken in multiple different lighting environments, corrections need to be made to transport images onto a common baseline. The third phase, *Iris Segmentation*, is the analytical process of separating iris information from the rest of the image. Once the critical information is isolated, *Normalization* converts information gathered from the iris texture into a standard format. From this format, *Feature Extraction* collects essential information into a quantitative form. The final phase is the *Matching* of features to identify the iris. These phases often overlap during the overall process of identification.

12.1.3 Challenges

The majority of mobile iris recognition struggles are rooted in the imperfect imaging process. While the iris is a semiperfect circle, eyelids and eyelashes interfere to allow only a partial view of the iris. *Iris Segmentation* attempts to capture the visible iris despite the interference (Jillela and Ross 2015). Specular reflections and improper illumination (such as shadows and high-intensity lighting) can also interfere with the multiple phases of recognition; *Image Correction* attempts to minimize the effect of such noise. Imaging also finds a dilemma in the use of front-facing and rear-facing cameras. While front-facing cameras are ideal because of their ease of use, the imaging produces lower resolutions on a weaker sensor. In contrast, rear-facing cameras typically have higher resolutions and premium sensors, but require the mobile device to be turned around and tediously aligned for imaging (Jillela and Ross 2015). While imaging of the iris can still be managed, the use of the more common VIS sensor is less accurate than the NIR sensors for imaging iris texture (Jillela and Ross 2015). A final challenge is the consideration of false positives from the imaging of deceptive iris; therefore, liveness detection must be considered during *Capturing*.

12.2 MOBILE DEVICE EXPERIMENT

Barra et al. (2015) experimented iris recognition with modern mobile device while utilizing homogeneity algorithms for segmentation and spatial histograms for matching.

12.2.1 Data

Since Barra et al. (2015) had a focus on use in mobile devices; they created a new database, MICHE-I, that would serve as a rigorous examination of mobile iris recognition. The database contains a collection of images imitating typical attempts of iris recognition from an Apple iPhone 5, Samsung Galaxy S4, and Samsung Galaxy Tab 2. The VIS images were taken both indoors and outdoors with both the rear-facing and front-facing camera at variable distances. (Due to the low quality of the rear-facing camera, the Samsung Galaxy Tab 2's front-facing camera was the only tablet sensor applied for the database.) With a database focused on mobile environment noise, the experiment can be better tested as a realistic form of mobile iris recognition.

Barra et al. (2015) included two additional databases, UPOL and UBIRIS, to understand the performance of their proposed method. UPOL is a collection of VIS images that are under near-perfect conditions; the images are at a high resolution with only the pupil, iris, and portion of sclera visible. UPOL will determine if their method performs as expected without noise. UBIRIS is a collection of noisy VIS images that simulate less constrained capturing but are of higher resolution and cropped properly to the eye area. UBIRIS serves as a viable comparison to the noisier MICHE-I database.

12.2.2 Methods

Barra et al. (2015) applied a series of image corrections on the collected iris images. First, an image is quantified by a grayscale histogram passed through an enhancement filter to remove interference. A "canny" and a median filter are also applied to distinguish the pupil area. Assuming the pupil area is circular, the algorithm developed by Taubin (1991) is utilized to find circular regions. The circular regions are then scored based on the homogeneity and separability of the corresponding pixels to accurately define the iris and sclera boundary. Once the iris circle is defined, the circle region is normalized with polar coordinates. A median filter is used to discard unnecessary sclera inclusion.

To extract features, Barra et al. (2015) utilized a spatial histogram (or spatiogram) calculated from the iris image. The spatiogram is utilized because it preserves the image's geometric orientation without the need for exact geometric transformations. The spatiograms can be used to efficiently calculate differences between two irises for matching.

12.2.3 Results and Conclusion

To first determine the performance of the method, Barra et al. (2015) utilized the UPOL and UBIRIS databases against the MICHE-I image set. The results of the proposed method on UPOL and UBIRIS were mostly effective according to the receiver operating characteristic (ROC) graph (Figure 12.1). MICHE-I with the method proved less effective (Figure 12.2); the database proved too difficult for the method. While the method may benefit from refinement, the results pointed to the need for more controlled conditions of imaging from the user.

12.3 MOBILE DEVICE EXPERIMENT WITH PERIOCULAR INFORMATION

People typically do not recognize others based on their iris texture alone. We absorb the features around the eye also known as the periocular. Since iris is difficult to detect, Santos et al. (2015) utilized the periocular information for recognition. Detecting both the periocular and iris information separately and fusing them together results in powerful recognition.

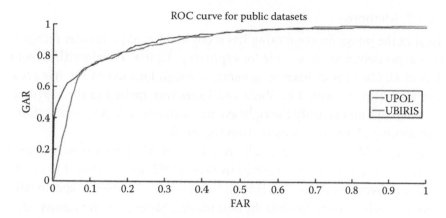

FIGURE 12.1   ROC curve shows effectiveness for UPOL and IBIRIS. (From Barra S. et al. 2015. *Pattern Recognition Letters*, 57, 66–73.)

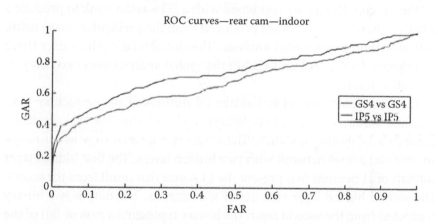

FIGURE 12.2   ROC curve of indoor use of rear-facing cameras prove less effective. (From Barra S. et al. 2015. *Pattern Recognition Letters*, 57, 66–73.)

12.3.1 Data

Santos et al. (2015) created their own iris database for the purpose of incorporating the mobile aspect of the iris recognition. To ensure cross-platform capability, the database consisted of 50 subjects with 4 devices in 10 different setups. These setups included both the rear-facing and forward-facing cameras with both no flash and flash if available. The simulation included multiple lightning situations because mobile use involves iris recognition in a variety of environments. The images also contain significant noise, such as image rotation, deviated gaze, focus issues, and obstructions.

12.3.2 Methods

To split the image for computing iris recognition and periocular recognition separately, a mask is made for capturing the iris. The algorithm from Tan et al. (2010) is utilized to generate a rough location of the iris area. The algorithm presented by Viola and Jones was applied to the captured area to refine and identify the right eye in a binary mask. A reflection filter removes high levels of intensity from the mask.

To normalize the color from different devices, MacBeth ColorChecker® Chart and the algorithm described in Wolf (2003) are combined to create a color correction matrix. The Hough transform is also used to specifically find the iris boundary. Within the boundary, a histogram and Canny edge detector is applied to isolate the pupil boundary. Pixels of the resulting area between the iris and pupil boundaries are mapped to pseudopolar coordinates for normalization.

The iris coordinates are combined with a 2D wavelet bank to produce a binary "iriscode." Features are produced from the periocular image using both distributed and global analysis. The distributed analysis uses three descriptors: HOG, LBP, and ULBP; the global analysis uses two descriptors: SIFT and GIST.

The distributed- and global-extracted features of the periocular were matched through X^2 distance. Binary codes of the iris were matched through a Hamming distance. These scores are fused together through an artificial neural network with two hidden layers. The first hidden layer consists of 11 neurons to represent the 11 scores that result from the scores. The second hidden layer consists of six neurons. The output is a binary computed from the second layer; the binary represents a pass or fail of the inputted image. The training data used to build the neural network were separated from the test data.

12.3.3 Results and Conclusion

Santos et al. (2015) compared the use of the color correction method against no color tampering; color correction proved to enhance detection but decrease clarity of the image's details. Additionally, iris detection was compared with periocular detection and found that the latter performed better than the former. Periocular detection had the ability to work semiconsistently on its own; however, the fusion of periocular and iris detection improves the recognition rate. Certain descriptors, such as GIST, were more successful than others, yet have a lower computational cost.

Santos et al. (2015) compared the performance of recognition between capturing setups. The rear-facing cameras proved to preform best; yet, this was not exclusively the result of higher resolutions. The outcomes also showed that flash-less images had better performance resulting in the best imaging originating from a flash-less, rear-facing camera setup. Images from the same device proved to improve performance, but cross-platform recognition was still effective.

12.4 MOBILE IRIS LIVENESS DETECTION

Since security is the primary focus, the iris recognition must detect false access attacks. Biometric spoofing is addressed by Akhtar et al. (2014) with a liveness detection system to prevent spoof attacks of face, iris, and fingerprint recognition. Iris spoofing can be accomplished by photos, videos, or contact lenses that imitate an accepted iris texture. Many liveness detection focus on involuntary light reactions and reflection analysis; however, these are still risks to spoofing. Akhtar et al. (2014) proposed a level-based security system to eliminate the effectiveness of biometric deceiving including iris spoofing.

12.4.1 Data

Akhtar et al. (2014) utilize the publicly available ATVS-Flr database that includes 8 images of both the eyes of 50 subjects and spoofed versions of each image. The database was split for 40% to be used for training and the other 60% to be used for testing.

12.4.2 Methods

Akhtar et al. (2014) did not use iris detection or segmentation, but instead utilized three-feature analysis algorithms on the entire image. Locally uniform comparison image descriptor (LUCID) calculates order permutations on distributed local information. Census Transform Histogram (CENTRIST) compares pixel intensities to neighboring pixels globally. Pattern of Oriented Edges Magnitude (POEM) uses both global and local information; a gradient image is calculated for all pixels before local histograms are collected on neighboring pixels and encoded together. The security system has three levels: low uses LUCID alone; medium fuses LUCID and CENTRIST; and high incorporates LUCID, CENTRIST, and POEM.

12.4.3 Results and Conclusion

After five deployments of the data through the proposed method, Akhtar et al. (2014) establish success from their system. The system was effective at detecting liveness from spoofing at all three levels. The three analysis processes were isolated for comparison of performance. While LUCID alone proved applicable, CENTRIST had an enhanced performance and POEM resulted in the superlative performance. Together in level high, the effectiveness was drastically increased. The half total error rate percentage was decreased by over 0.7% when using high level over low level.

12.5 LIMITATIONS

While the experimented iris recognition methods proved effective, they have not reached the point of commercial use due to the security priority and rate of false acceptances. Today's mobile security requires virtually flawless recognition systems.

Errors are mainly being produced by the limitations in capturing the environment. The hardware of current mobile devices is not optimized for iris detection because precision cameras are located on the back of devices. While the front-facing cameras are ideal for imaging orientation and ease of use, the resolution and accuracy of these sensors are insufficient in adequately detecting the iris texture. Additionally, users are required to deliver significant effort to image correctly in appropriate lighting. An attempt to circumnavigate imaging constraints would result in too high of computational costs for mobile devices.

12.6 CURRENT TECHNOLOGY

Capabilities are expanding with the improvement of mobile hardware in computational and imaging abilities. Although higher resolutions proved semiirrelevant to iris detection, newer devices are being released with higher resolution sensors. More importantly, the mobile device sensors have reached DSLR-level quality in clarity, color, and low-light sensitivity. The most ideal device will supplement the VIS sensor with a NIR sensor for a better capture of the iris texture.

REFERENCES

Akhtar, Z., Micheloni, C., Piciarelli, C., Foresti, G. 2014. Mobiolivdet: Mobile biometric liveness detection. *2014 11th IEEE International Conference on Advanced Video and Signal Based Surveillance (AVSS)*, August 26–29, 2014, Seoul, Korea, pp. 187–192.

Barra, S., Casanova, A., Narducci, F., Ricciardi, S. 2015. Ubiquitous iris recognition by means of mobile devices, *Pattern Recognition Letters*, 57, 66–73.

Cho, D. H., Park, K. R., Rhee, D. W. 2005. Real-time iris localization for iris recognition in cellular phone. In *Software Engineering, Artificial*

Intelligence, Networking and Parallel/Distributed Computing, 2005 and First ACIS International Workshop on Self-Assembling Wireless Networks. SNPD/SAWN 2005. Sixth International Conference on, pp. 254–259.

Daugman, J. 2004. How iris recognition works, *IEEE Transactions on Circuits and Systems for Video Technology*, 14(1), 21–30.

Jeong, D. S., Park, H.-A., Park, K. R., Kim, J. 2005. Advances in Biometrics: International Conference, ICB 2006, Hong Kong, China, January 5–7, 2006. Proceedings. In D. Zhang, A. K. Jain (ed.), (pp. 457–463). Springer Berlin Heidelberg. (ISBN: 978-3-540-31621-3.) Retrieved from http://dx.doi.org/10.1007/11608288_61.

Jillela, R., Ross, A. 2015. Segmenting iris images in the visible spectrum with applications in mobile biometrics, *Pattern Recognition Letters*, 57, 4–16.

Santos, G., Grancho, E., Bernardo, M., Fiacleiro, P. 2015. Fusing iris and periocular information for cross-sensor recognition, *Pattern Recognition Letters*, 57, 52–59.

Tan, T., He, Z. Sun, Z. 2010. Efficient and robust segmentation of noisy iris images for non-cooperative iris recognition, *Image and Vision Computing*, 28(2), 223–230, doi: http://dx.doi.org/10.1016/j.imavis.2009.05.008. Retrieved from http://www.sciencedirect.com/science/article/pii/S0262885609001115

Taubin, G. 1991. Estimation of planar curves, surfaces, and nonplanar space curves defined by implicit equations with applications to edge and range image segmentation, *IEEE Transactions on Pattern Analysis and Machine Intelligence*, 13(11), 1115–1138.

Wolf, S. 2003. *Color Correction Matrix for Digital Still and Video Imaging Systems*, National Telecommunications and Information Administration, Washington, D.C.

CHAPTER 13

Biometric Signature for Mobile Devices

Maria Villa and Abhishek Verma

CONTENTS

13.1 BIOMETRIC SIGNATURE RECOGNITION

This chapter talks about the most recent mechanisms for biometric signature in mobile devices. The structure of this chapter is as follows: Section 13.2 introduces a general background and definitions of biometric signature on mobile methods. Section 13.3 presents some public databases for biometric signature. Next, Section 13.4 discusses different approaches for liveness detection on biometric signature and presents four case studies. Finally, the conclusions are drawn in Section 13.5.

13.2 INTRODUCTION

The expression signature originates from Latin *signare* (to sign) and is typically a handwritten representation of a person's name [1]. The individual that signs is known as signer. Some signatures require a witness and a notary public for further legal strength such as the event of a marriage, purchase of a property, and more. A signature gives indication of both identity (proves identity) and will (informed consent) [1]. The verification of a signature can be divided into two categories [1]:

1. *Offline signature verification* takes as input the image of a signature and is used in banks and on documents.

2. *Online signature verification* uses signatures, captures by pressure-sensitive surfaces.

In the last 5 years a variety of devices with touch screens have emerged. This headed to the idea of using a touch screen as the capture device, dropping the cost and at the same time reaching the final user in point of service terminals, smartphones, tablets, and more [2].

13.2.1 How Biometric Signature Works

Signature is considered to be a behavioral biometric trait. A behavioral feature studies the motions of an individual [3] and it is based on interactive characteristics. Some approaches use the image of the signature [4]. Figure 13.1 shows the signature of John Hancock which became synonym for "signature" in the United States [1]. John Hancock's signature is the most outstanding on the United States Declaration of Independence [1].

Biometric signature recognition measures and analyzes the physical motion of signing including speed, the stroke order, and applied pressure

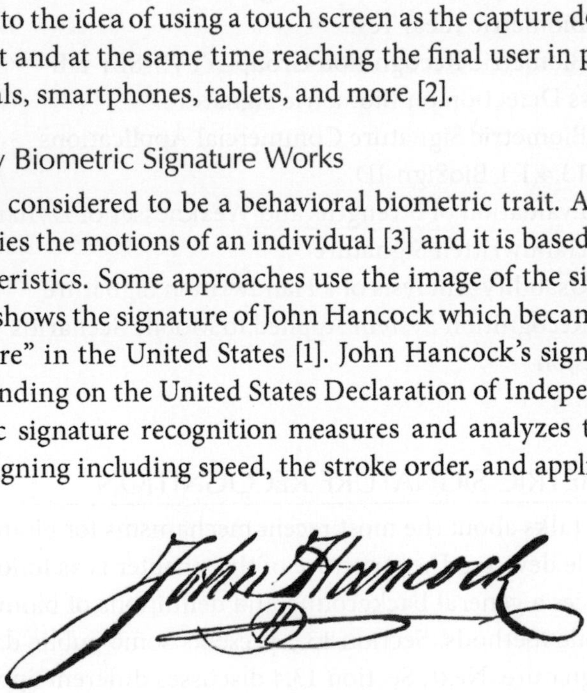

FIGURE 13.1   Signature of John Hancock. (From https://en.wikipedia.org/wiki/Signature#/media/File:JohnHancocksSignature.svg)

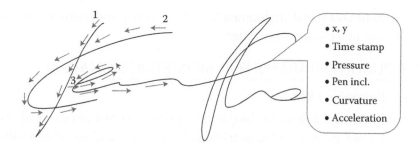

FIGURE 13.2   Biometric signature analysis. (From Biometrics Research Group.)

as illustrated in Figure 13.2 [4]. Some systems could also match graphic images of signatures, but the core of a signature biometric system is interactive or behavioral (how it is signed rather than visual).

Handwritten signature is used worldwide in different situations [2]:

1. As an agreement to the content of the signed document

2. As legal background

3. Used in forensic analysis

4. Links the document with the signer's identity

13.2.2 Benefits of Biometric Signature Biometric Systems

In our culture, handwritten signature is used in everyday life to gain access to documents, contract and agreement execution, acknowledgement of goods or services received, and banking services [6]. After electronic documents emerged, an electronic signature system using cryptographic algorithms was designed and it has been implemented in several countries.

Some biometric signature benefits are as follows [6]:

• The image of a signature is easy to falsify, however, the behavior of signing is exceptionally difficult [6]

• Low false acceptance rates (FAR) [6]

• Signature is perceived as not invasive since people are used to sign documents in daily basis [6]

• Remove the use of handling and storage of paper dl at shops and parcel delivery [2]

A weakness of signature biometric systems is that individuals may not always sign in a consistent manner.

13.3 PUBLIC DATABASES FOR BIOMETRIC SIGNATURE

13.3.1 Biometric Ideal Test

A distinguished database for biometric signature is biometrics ideal test (BIT). BIT is a website for biometric database supply and algorithm valuation. Among the databases available through BIT are iris, face, fingerprint, palm print, multispectral palm, and handwriting databases [7]. Researchers can download the public databases and submit algorithms online to be tested by third parties and also provides certification free of charge [7]. Figure 13.3 shows biometric signature workflow.

With respect to biometric signature, BIT is supported and certified by the following organizations [7]:

- International Association of Pattern Recognition (IAPR)

- Technical Committee on Biometrics (IAPR TC4)

- Asian Biometrics Consortium (ABC)

- Committee on Testing and Standards (ACTS)

- Testing results of algorithms are certified by IAPR TC4 and ACTS

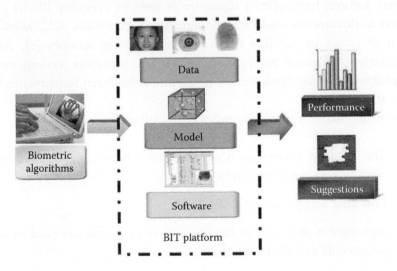

FIGURE 13.3 BIT biometric signature workflow. (From http://www.idealtest.org/images/idea_17.jpg)

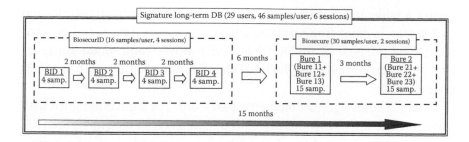

FIGURE 13.4 Time diagram of the different acquisition sessions that confirm the ATVS online signature long-term DB. (From ATVS—Biometric Recognition Group » Databases » ATVS-FFp.)

- BIT diagnoses algorithms are based on performance metrics and suggest improvements

13.3.2 Biometric Recognition Group-ATVS-SLT DB

Biometric Recognition Group—ATVS from the Autonomous University of Madrid has numerous biometric databases, all available for research at no charge [8]. The database available for biometric signature is ATVS-SLT DB. This dataset contains the online signature data of the 29 users to the BiosecurID and the Biosecure databases. The two signature subsets were developed within 15 months and they present some unique features that make them especially appropriate for aging evaluation of online signature recognition systems [PONE2013]. The general time distribution of the different sessions of the database is presented in Figure 13.4.

13.4 LIVENESS DETECTION ON BIOMETRIC SIGNATURE

Biometric signature recognition systems measure and study the physical motion of signing. Dynamic signature recognition has been accomplished using a pen stylus [9]. The applications using smartphones with a small touch screen are questionable since only a small touch display is used and the signature is performed with the finger [9].

The following case studies introduce different approaches for liveness detection of biometric signature systems.

13.4.1 Biometric Signature Commercial Applications
13.4.1.1 BioSign-ID

Among commercial applications for liveness detection for biometric signature is biometric signature ID (BSI). BSI designed BioSig-ID™ to secure a wide array of transactions in banking, health care, education and research, financing services, online purchases, retail, and government. The purpose of BioSig-ID is to diminish fraud, maintain security, and keep compliance. BioSig-ID has been implemented in about 70 countries [10].

BioSig-ID uses a gesture biometric password. The login is designed with a four unique digit password that is drawn by users as seen in Figure 13.5. It does not require tokens, keys, fobs, or passwords and no sensitive biometric data is required [10]. It offers two options to use as a layer or to replace the security method used. BioSig-ID system captures the user's unique movements when drawing four digit password including:

- Direction
- Speed
- Length
- Angle
- Pressure
- Height

Biometric signature is not considered threatening to people since they are used to signing paper documents (i.e., checks, contracts, and

FIGURE 13.5 BioSign technology on mobile. (From Blog—Biometric Signature ID.)

applications) and electronic surfaces (i.e., credit card transactions and mail receipt electronic surfaces). Therefore, the system of BioSign-ID is very user friendly.

Not only BioSig-ID is user friendly but also is effective at keeping imposters out with 99.98% accuracy as reported by independent auditor Tolly Group [11].

13.4.2 Evaluation of Strengths and Weaknesses of Dynamic Handwritten Signature

The evaluation of strength and weaknesses of dynamic handwritten signature study presents a toolbox, Windows-based program with a Wacom STU 500 connected, which stores data from a signing pad connected to a computer and a touch screen device located in a smartphone or a tablet. This study introduces a DTW-based algorithm and uses a database of genuine signatures obtained with a STU-500 pad as input. This approach presents some strengths and weaknesses of biometric signature modality [2].

This study considers the following features for a signature biometric system [2]:

- Altitude
- Positioning of the capture device
- Enrollment process
- Policies for accepting acquired signatures
- Capture device
- Impact of stress in the act of signing

In the acquisition tool box step, when a counterfeit signature is recognized in the system, it is requested to choose a genuine signature identifier from the ones that have not been forged beforehand. Once the genuine signature is designated, the different levels start sequentially, with no possibility of toing to a previous level and with the option to cancel the attempt as soon as the forged signature is recognized.

- The error rates obtained when using the STU-500 are mentioned below:

1.59% (level 1)

6.77%

12.86%

23.35% (level 4)

17.73%

19.51%

33.43% (level 7)

19.27%, 18.27%

16.93%, 18.21%

(level 11)

- Results when using mobile devices are mentioned below:

  APCERs of (in all cases for levels 8, 9, 10, and 11) 19.98%

  20.43%

  18.73% and 19.02%

  Note4-S; 18.4%, 18.45%, 16.73%, and 17.25%

  Note4-F; 15.32%, 14.72%, 15.06%, and 14.7% for iPad

13.4.3 Usability Analysis of a Handwritten Signature Recognition System Applied to Mobile Scenarios

With the growth of the use of smartphones and mobile devices in general, the sensitive data stored in them creates the need to protect it. This defense of delicate data started to be covered by biometrics [13]. The work of this case study is primarily focused on online signature. The method to obtain the biometric signature is by using the fingertip instead of a stylus. In addition, the system in this case uses a DTW-based handwritten signature recognition algorithm in mobile scenarios. The trials use a state evaluation and the users sign in four different devices, in five different positions, and three sessions separated by 1 week each. The results also display satisfaction and efficiency as shown in Figures 13.6 and 13.7.

The satisfaction results of this case study indicate that users scored 3.85 over 5. The preferred factor was the easiness (3.9) and the less favorite the

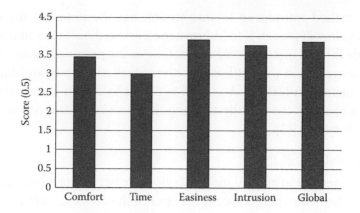

FIGURE 13.6   Satisfaction factors.

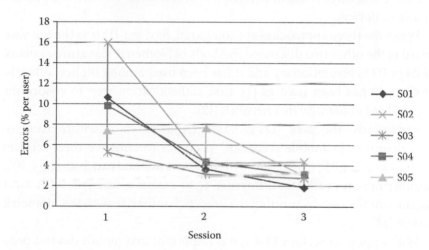

FIGURE 13.7   Efficiency.

time (3). 80% of the operators would use handwritten signature recognition on mobiles again in the future with the exception of one of them that chose stylus. The favorite devices were the STU using the stylus and the iPad using the fingertip. The preferred scenarios were arranged as follows: S01 > S03 > S04 > S02 > S05. Refer to Figure 13.6 [13].

Figure 13.7 indicates the efficiency results. The STU is the scheme that offers the most constant performance in the assessment, as anticipated it is the reference device. However, the iPad in scenario 2 shows the best results. The iPad also obtained an equal error rate (EER) over 7% in the reference scenario. Figure 13.7 demonstrates the high importance or the order of scenarios and the devices in the performance [13].

The method introduced in this section has the potential for future work. The first approach is to improve the liveness detection and usability in handwritten signature recognition. One of the proposals is to conduct a similar evaluation with different methods such as the human-biometric sensor interaction (HBSI). A second option is to design a scenario with more comfort for the user by training the users to familiarize with the biometric system [13].

13.5 CONCLUSION

Smartphones and in general mobile devices are becoming more and more sophisticated. Thus, people's daily life opened the doors for many building blocks for applications. This chapter presented two databases for biometric signature and three liveness detection approaches for biometric signature in mobile devices.

When the three approaches are compared, BioSign-ID is at the top vanguard of the other two discussed methods of biometric signature systems. BioSign-ID is revolutionary and it has been used among highest officials. BioSign-ID has been used as the first authentication step to ensure the highest level of identity in a network [12].

Particularly, the case "DTW-based handwritten signature recognition algorithm in mobile scenarios" proposes to enhance their services to conduct a similar evaluation with different methods such as the HBSI. Another option available to improve is to design a scenario with more comfort for the user by training the users to familiarize with the biometric system [13].

With respect to Section 13.4.2, it is important that mobile devices present the same level of vulnerability with trained forgers when comparing with the biometric reference obtained with the same device, no matter whether the forger uses a stylus or a finger. However, the results obtained in this study can be used as reference for further studies dealing with other algorithm and in particular, for those incorporating PAD mechanisms.

REFERENCES

1. Biometrics Research Group. n.d. http://biometrics.sabanciuniv.edu/signature.html (retrieved February 28, 2016).
2. Sanchez-Reillo, R., Quiros-Sandoval, H. C., Liu-Jimenez, J., Goicoechea-Telleria, I. 2015, September. Evaluation of strengths and weaknesses of dynamic handwritten signature recognition against forgeries. In *Security Technology (ICCST), 2015 International Carnahan Conference on*, Taipei, Taiwan, pp. 373–378. IEEE.

3. Welcome to the Technology Executives Club. n.d. http://www.technology-executivesclub.com/Articles/security/artBiometricsSignatureRecognition.php (retrieved April 17, 2016).
4. Signature Biometrics. n.d. http://www.biometricnewsportal.com/signature_biometrics.asp (retrieved February 28, 2016).
5. Signature. n.d. https://en.wikipedia.org/wiki/Signature (retrieved April 17, 2016).
6. Signature Biometrics. n.d. http://www.biometricnewsportal.com/signature_biometrics.asp (retrieved April 17, 2016).
7. http://biometrics.idealtest.org/dbDetailForUser.do?id=12
8. ATVS—Biometric Recognition Group » Databases » ATVS-FFp. n.d. http://atvs.ii.uam.es/slt_db.html (retrieved April 17, 2016).
9. Vera-Rodriguez, R., Tolosana, R., Ortega-Garcia, J., Fierrez, J. 2015, March. e-BioSign: Stylus-and finger-input multi-device database for dynamic signature recognition. In *Biometrics and Forensics (IWBF), 2015 International Workshop on*, Gjøvik, Norway, pp. 1–6. IEEE.
10. The World's First Biometric Password. n.d. https://www.biosig-id.com/ (retrieved April 17, 2016).
11. Tolly Enterprises, LLC. January 19, 2011. Biometric Signature ID—BioSig-ID 2.0 User Authentication Solution. Test Report Tolly #211104, no. January 2011, pp. 1–7. http://biosig-id.com/images/docs/Tolly_BioSigID_Accuracy.pdf (retrieved April 16, 2016).
12. Blog—Biometric Signature ID. n.d. https://www.biosig-id.com/resources/blog (retrieved April 18, 2016).
13. Blanco-Gonzalo, R., Miguel-Hurtado, O., Sanchez-Reillo, R., Gonzalez-Ramirez, A. 2013, October. Usability analysis of a handwritten signature recognition system applied to mobile scenarios. In *Security Technology (ICCST), 2013 47th International Carnahan Conference on*, Medellin, Colombia, pp. 1–6. IEEE.

CHAPTER 14

Hand Biometric Case Study

Yukhe Lavinia and Abhishek Verma

CONTENTS

T HIS SECTION PRESENTS A summary of four papers on hand mobile biometrics. Among the four, only the first one uses a touch method, while the other three use a touchless method. Overall, method and experimental results are compared and tabulated at the end of this section.

The first paper discusses Tartz and Gooding's study [1] on hand biometric authentication method using raw capacitance data on a mobile phone. The algorithm follows the following sequence: raw capacitance data acquisition, preprocessing, two-step segmentation, feature extraction, matching, and decision-making.

The data are obtained by placing the full four fingers (excluding the thumb) and the top part of the right hand palm for about 3 s on a 7-inch screen mobile phone with a 40×64 resolution display that is connected to a data logger. All noises are normalized and filtered.

Next, the images are segmented. The first segmentation process concerns the finger length features. In this step, the capacitance sensor data are averaged and all the sensor rows are totaled and plotted. With the touch capacitance sensor, any crease in the hand appears as a dip in the curve—the deeper the crease, the sharper the dip. Using this technique, the fingers can be separated from the palm by first looking at the end of the curve and then locating the final sharp drop, which is interpreted as the longest finger. Next is locating an earlier sharp drop in the curve that lies within certain limit from the final sharp drop. This one is interpreted as the deep crease between the palm and the fingers. Anything between this dip and the final dip are extracted as the finger length features.

The second segmentation extracts finger width features. This step takes only the finger data, sums the capacitance touch sensor columns, and plots the sum result. The dips in the curve are interpreted as separation between the four fingers from which the finger width features are extracted. The extraction results from these two segmentation processes (finger length and finger width) are then used to create finger profiles. These profiles are the features used for matching and decision-making.

This raw capacitance study was done twice. The first study consists of 8000 comparisons taken from 40 subjects (20 males and 20 females) aged 18–58. Out of eight data collection trials, the first three trials are used as the template for matching, while the five trials are used for authentication attempts. The study yielded a 2.5% equal error rate (EER). Results are calculated using normalized coefficient correlation (NCC) in matching and then varying the threshold value. The second study is a longitudinal study of 6100 comparisons, taken from 10 subjects (five males and five females). There were also eight data collection trials, but this one is taken over the course of only 1 month. It yielded a 2.3% EER.

While the previous study is using touch for authentication, many studies in hand biometrics opted for a contactless method. Choraś and Kozik [2] proposed a contactless mobile hand biometric that is based not only on palm print but also on knuckles features. The palmprint features are extracted using three-valued mask function, while the knuckle features are extracted using Probabilistic Hough Transform (PHT) and Speeded Up Robust Features (SURF). The images are taken using standard mobile cameras.

In palmprint feature extraction, the palmprint images are acquired using mobile phone cameras. The images are preprocessed by detecting the skin color, determining the corners, separating the palm from the background, and marking the most significant points in the palm to obtain the rectangular shape features.

Skin color detection is done by using a specific set of RGB color space to classify a section of an image as skin: $R > 95$, $G > 40$, $B > 20$, $\max(R, G, B)$ min $(R, G, B) > 15$, $|R - G| > 15$, $R > G$, $R > B$. Corner or edge determination is done by blurring the image. Separating palm from the background is done through binarizing the image with the value of 1 for the palm and 0 for the background. Although the study extracted both polygonal shape palm region and rectangular shape, only the rectangular shape is used in the next extraction step.

This rectangular shape region is obtained by locating seven points and four lines on the palm in order to perform palm rotation. Finding this seven points started from first locating a P.0 point representing the longest finger, which is the tip of the middle finger, then locating four more points: one at the joint between the index and middle fingers (denoted as P.1), one at the joint between the middle and ring fingers (denoted as P.2), one at the joint between the index and the thumb (denoted as P.3), and another at the joint between the ring and little fingers (denoted as P.4). The first line L1 is created by connecting P.1 and P.4. Using P.1 as a pivot, two more lines can be generated from L1: (1) L2, by rotating L1 30° counterclockwise and (2) L3, by rotating L1 60° counterclockwise. Another line, L4, is determined by using P.4 as pivot and rotating L1 60° clockwise. The following three points are generated from the intersection of each of these lines with the palm edge: (1) P.7, being the intersection of L2 and the palm edge; (2) P.5, being the intersection of L3 and the palm edge; and (3) P.6, being the intersection of L4 and the palm edge. Connecting these seven points create the polygonal palm region and combining this polygonal shape with L1 allows palmprint rotation. The rectangular palm region can be extracted from this rotation result by once again locating P.1 and P.4.

The next extraction step concerns the mask function generation and size. The mask is in the form a matrix that contains only three values: −1, 0, and 1. Choraś and Kozik investigated three methods to select the appropriate mask (randomly, manually, and by implementing "eigen-palms"). They also investigated three different mask sizes (15×15, 20×20, and 45×45) that generate three different resolutions. The results are evaluated based on effectiveness, which is measured by computing the percentage of the lowest equal values of false acceptance ratio (FAR) and false rejection ratio (FRR).

Choraś and Kozik's palmprint study used 252 images taken from 84 subjects (three images per subject). Their results showed that the lowest FAR = FRR percent rates are yielded by the eigen-palms mask generation method (FAR = FRR of 2.5%) and the 45×45 mask (FAR = FRR of 1.7%).

To improve performance, Choraś and Kozik proposed to combine the palmprint features with the knuckle features, although they did the palmprint and knuckle experiments separately. Their knuckle feature extraction experiment sample images are preprocessed by (1) obtaining the lines on knuckle skin where the fingers bend and (2) removing the noise using PHT. The classification method had three steps. First, 50 images are selected using basic feature vectors. Second, five images with the lowest distance are selected using PHT feature vectors. Third, one image out of these five is selected using the SURF descriptor. In the case where the SURF descriptor failed to find an image, the first of the five PHT results is used.

For the knuckle identification study, Choraś and Kozik used the IIT Delhi Knuckle Database. The database contains 790 images that are taken from 158 subjects aged between 16 and 55. The images are in bitmap format with the resolution of 80×100 pixels.

The experiment yielded an average EER value of 1.02%. The PHT method by itself yields 95.56% accuracy, while the SURF 85.57%. Combined PHT–SURF method, however, yielded better result than PHT-only or SURF-only methods.

Another contactless mobile hand biometric is proposed by Franzgrote et al. [3]. Their method allows mobile palmprint authentication system using hand orientation normalization method and accelerated Competitive Code. Their preprocessing stage mainly concerns region of interest (ROI) extraction, which is achieved by performing hand orientation normalization, valley points determination, and ROI formation. The image resolution started with 640×480 and was later reduced to 100×100 after ROI extraction. The images are taken using a smartphone camera.

The algorithm used is the accelerated version of Competitive Code, which is first proposed by Kong and Zhang [4]. The original Competitive Code consists of two steps: (1) code computation and (2) matching. Franzgrote et al. [3] modified the code computation step by using a different set of Gabor functions described as the following:

$$\Psi(x, y, \theta) = e^{-\frac{x'^2 + \gamma^2 y'^2}{2\sigma^2}} \cos\left(2\pi \frac{x'}{\lambda} + \varphi\right)$$

$$x' = x \cos\theta + y \sin\theta$$

$$y' = -x \sin\theta + y \cos\theta,$$

where $\gamma = 0.3$, $\lambda = 4$, $\sigma = 2$, and $\varphi = 0$.

The six two-dimensional Gabor filters $\psi(x, y, \theta)$ with orientation θ_p are applied to the ROI $I(x, y)$ to create the following rule for the winner to take all [3]

$$\arg\min_{\theta_p}[I(x, y) * \Psi(x, y, \theta)].$$

In the matching step, Franzgrote et al. computed the angular distance using bitwise operations [3]

$$D(P, Q) = \frac{\sum_{x=1}^{n} \sum_{y=1}^{n} \sum_{i=1}^{3} P_M(x, y) \wedge Q_M(x, y) \wedge \left(P_i^b(x, y) \oplus Q_i^b(x, y)\right)}{3 \sum_{x=1}^{n} \sum_{y=1}^{n} P_M(x, y) \wedge Q_M(x, y)},$$

where P and Q are competitive codes, n is the size, P_M and Q_M are the binary masks representing nonpalmprint pixels, p_i^b and Q_{-i}^b are the i-th bit plane of P and Q, respectively, $\wedge$ is the bitwise operator "and," and $\oplus$ is the bitwise operator "exclusive or." The Competitive Code is then accelerated through comparing only a smaller section, calculating the matching score, and applying it to the whole.

Franzgrote et al. used 600 palmprint images that are taken from 30 subjects; 10 images per hand for each subject. The results show that starting from 0.46 threshold value, the palmprint matching success rate achieved higher percentage and much lower rejection rate. Regarding the computation time of the Competitive Code, the code computation step in the nonaccelerated competitive code is 87 ms, while its accelerated version is 5 ms. Moreover, the code matching step of a regular Competitive Code took 4.258 s to complete, while its accelerated version took only 0.116 s.

Also contributing to contactless mobile hand biometric authentication method is Ota et al. [5]. Their study introduced a variation to the previously discussed method, as they used remote palmprint recognition system. In this method, a mobile phone acts as an end-user system that communicates with a server on which a palmprint authentication algorithm is stored.

The algorithm has two stages as it combines a preprocessing method that includes a technique proposed by Yörük et al. [6] with a palmprint recognition algorithm proposed by Ito et al. [7–12] that is based on phase-only correlation (POC). The new preprocessing stage comprises six steps with the fifth step using the method proposed by Yörük et al.

The first preprocessing step is image extraction. The process extracted only the right half of the image since key point detection only requires the right half of an image. The image is then reduced to half its size in the second step. The third step converts the previous RGB color space to HUE saturation value (HSV) to allow skin color detection using the following:

$$\begin{cases} 0 \leq H \leq 50 \\ 300 \leq H \leq 360 \end{cases}.$$

The resulting image is then converted to binary image using the H channel. The fourth step is the opening process, which consists of the erosion and dilation processes. Each process is executed once using a kernel with a structuring element in a shape of a 3-pixel radius disk. The fifth step is determining significant points. The algorithm determined significant points located at the joining points between the fingers; one between the index and middle fingers and another between the ring and little fingers. In the sixth step, these significant points are used to form a rectangular shape palmprint region. The image is then normalized and converted to grayscale. The resulting palmprint region is a 160×160 pixel grayscale image.

The next stage in the algorithm, which is the matching stage, consists of two steps. The first matching step maps between images using the POC, generating a 32×32 pixel block and 16 "corresponding points" [5]. The second matching step took this block and the corresponding points to compute the matching score.

In addition to combining two existing methods, Ota et al. proposed a remote system consisting of a mobile phone and a server. The mobile phone is used to take the palm images, convert these images using the above preprocessing method, send and receive data to and from the server, and display results. The server is used to store data, query the database, customize authentication service, compute the matching score, make decision regarding matching result, and send the result back to the mobile phone.

In this study, Ota et al. sampled 12 subjects, taking five pictures of each subject's left palm. Among the 1770 possible combinations for those 60 images, 120 combinations are used as genuine users to test the FRR, while the 1650 combinations are used as impostor users to test the FAR value. The results show that the lowest EER is 3.3% at 0.263 threshold value and that best accuracy is achieved when the minimum threshold is set to be greater than 0.182 and the maximum greater than 0.283. In assessing the computation time, Ota et al. found that the algorithm took 0.94 s to complete, while the communication between mobile phone and server took 5.48 s.

Excluding Franzgrote et al. study that presented the results using receiver operating characteristic (ROC) instead of EER, the lowest EER of the three-hand biometric study is 1.02%, which is achieved by Choraś and Kozik's knuckle identification study. Although Choraś and Kozik did the palmprint and knuckle study separately, each study generated the lowest EER. Considering a slightly lower number of subjects, Tartz and Gooding's results of 2.5% and 2.3% fare well with Choraś and Kozik's. The lowest performance is 3.3%, achieved by Ota et al. in their remote palmprint recognition study. Table 14.1 shows how the four studies fare against each other.

TABLE 14.1 Comparison of Studies Done by Tarts and Gooding, Choraś and Kozik, Franzgrote et al., and Ota et al.

Publication	Sensor	Subjects/ Database	Technique	Hand	Results (%)
Tartz and Gooding [1]	Mobile phone capacitance	40 subjects (1st) 10 subjects (2nd)	Capacitance	Right	EER = 2.5 (1st) EER = 2.3 (2nd)
Choraś and Kozik [2]	Mobile camera	84 subjects	Palm print	Right	EER = 2.5 (eigen-palms) EER = 1.7 (45 × 45 size)
		IIT Delhi Knuckle Database: 158 subjects, bitmap format	Knuckle	Not described	EER = 1.02
Franzgrote et al. [3]	Smartphone camera	30 subjects	Palm print	Both	ROC curve
Ota et al. [5]	Smartphone camera	12 subjects	Palm print	Left	EER = 3.3

EER, equal error rate.

REFERENCES

1. Tartz, R., Gooding, T. 2015. Hand biometrics using capacitive touch-screens. In *Adjunct Proceedings on the 28th Annual ACM Symposium on User Interface Software and Technology (UIST'15 Adjunct)*, pp. 67–68, Charlotte, NC, USA.
2. Choraś, M., Kozik, R. 2012. Contactless palmprint and knuckle biometrics for mobile devices, *Pattern Analysis and Applications*, 15(1):73–85.
3. Franzgrote, M., Borg, C., Tobias Ries, B.J., Büssemaker, S., Jiang, X., Fieseler, M., Zhang, L. 2011. Palmprint verification on mobile phones using accelerated competitive code. In *International Conference on Hand-Based Biometrics (ICHB'11)*, pp. 1–6, Hongkong.
4. Kong, A.W.-K., Zhang, D. 2004. Competitive coding scheme for palmprint verification. In *Proceedings of 17th International Conference on Pattern Recognition (ICPR'04)*, Cambridge, UK, pp. 520–523.
5. Ota, H., Watanabe, R., Ito, K., Tanaka, T., Aoki, T. 2010. Implementation of remote system using touchless palmprint recognition algorithm. In *Proceedings of the 8th International Conference on Advances in Mobile Computing and Multimedia (MoMM'10)*, pp. 33–41, Paris, France.
6. Yörük, E., Konukoğlu, E., Sankur, B., Darbon, J. 2006. Shape-based hand recognition, *IEEE Transactions on Image Processing*, 15(7):1803–1815.
7. Iitsuka, S., Ito, K., Aoki, T. 2008. A practical palmprint recognition algorithm using phase information. In *Proceedings of 19th International Conference on Pattern Recognition (ICPR'08)*, Tampa, Florida, pp. 1–4.
8. Iitsuka, S., Miyazawa, K., Aoki, T. 2009. A palmprint recognition algorithm using principal component analysis of phase information. In *Proceedings of 16th IEEE International Conference on Image Processing (ICIP'09)*, Cairo, Egypt, pp. 1973–1976.
9. Ito, K., Aoki, T., Nakajima, H., Kobayashi, K., Higuchi, T. 2006. A palmprint recognition algorithm using phase-based image matching. In *Proceedings of 13th IEEE International Conference on Image Processing (ICIP'06)*, Atlanta, Georgia, pp. 2669–2672.
10. Ito, K., Aoki, T., Nakajima, H., Kobayashi, K., Higuchi, T. 2006. A phase-based palmprint recognition algorithm and its experimental evaluation. In *Proceedings of 2006 International Symposium on Intelligent Signal Processing and Communication Systems (ISPACS'06)*, Tottori, Japan, pp. 215–218.
11. Ito, K., Aoki, T., Nakajima, H., Kobayashi, K., Higuchi, T. 2008. A palmprint recognition algorithm using phase-only correlation, *IEICE Transactions on Fundamentals of Electronics, Communications and Computer Sciences*, E91-A(4):1023–1030.
12. Ito, K., Iitsuka, S., Aoki, T. 2009. A palmprint recognition algorithm using phase-based correspondence matching. In *Proceedings of 16th IEEE International Conference on Image Processing (ICIP'09)*, Cairo, Egypt, pp. 1977–1980.

CHAPTER 15

Keystroke Dynamics

Jason Ligon and Abhishek Verma

CONTENTS

15.1 EXISTING BENCHMARK DATASETS FOR KEYSTROKE DYNAMICS

Unlike other biometric modalities, there are only a few public datasets available for keystroke dynamics, some of which are composed of several subdatasets. Giot et al. [1] compiled a list of current public databases for keystroke dynamics using a keyboard in collecting the data. The data provided by these, though not mobile, can be extended into mobile in the future.

15.1.1 GREYC

GREYC is an important public dataset due to its large number of users. The dataset contains 133 users with 100 of them providing samples of at least five distinct sessions. The majority of these sessions were spaced out for at least 1 week. All of the users typed the password "greyc laboratory"

12 times on two distinct keyboards per session, thus giving 60 samples for the 100 users that participated in each session. Both the extracted features (hold time and latencies) and raw data are available and allow computing of other extracted features. This data are stored in a SQLite dataset file.

15.1.2 WEBGREYC{A,B}

Another important public dataset is WEBGREYC due to its number and length of sessions. A total of 118 users' keystroke samples were acquired once a week for 18 months. The maximum number of sessions per user was 47 sessions. The importance of this dataset is that it contains two kinds of samples:

1. An imposed login and password (typical of the usual keystroke dynamic dataset samples) (WEBGREYCA).

2. Login and password information were chosen by the user (WEBGREYCB). It is worth nothing that several imposters were also asked to type this.

This is the first public dataset where each user designates their own password. It, therefore, provides the most realistic scenario. The dataset is stored in a set of text files containing both raw and extracted features.

15.1.3 DSN2009

A significant dataset in terms of *number of samples per user* is the DSN2009. The dataset contains 51 users, each providing 400 samples captured in eight sessions (50 inputs per session). Each session has a 1 day delay. Though this dataset has a large number of samples per user, the samples have been captured in a relatively short-time period. Each data has been captured typing the password ".tie5Roan." The dataset contains other extracted features such as: hold time, interval between two pressures, interval between the release of a key, and pressure of the next one. The dataset is stored in a raw text, CSV, and Excel files.

15.1.4 PRESSURE{0,1,2}

A public keystroke dynamic dataset called PRESSURE{0,1,2} uses a pressure sensitive keyboard to collect data. The keyboard embeds the following raw data: key code, time when pressed, time when released, and pressure force. There were a total of 104 users on the dataset, but only seven provided a significant amount of data (89–504 samples). The other users have only provided 3–15 samples. Three different keystroke samples were used: "pr7qlz" (PRESSURE2), "jeffrey allen" (PRESSURE1), and "drizzle" (PESSURE3). The dataset is available in a CSV or SQL file.

15.1.5 BIOCHAVES{A,B,C}

Created by the biochaves team, this database consists of three subdatasets (A, B, C) for static-text keystrokes and one dataset (D) for free text. The maximum number of 15 users in a dataset provided 10 samples each. Each dataset contained a unique group of users. The dataset is composed of a couple of ASCII codes of the pressed key and elapsed time since the last key down event. The release of a key, however, is not tracked. Each dataset is stored in raw text files.

15.1.6 Keystroke 100

Keystroke 100 contains keystroke latency and keystroke pressure. The dataset also contains keystroke patterns of users typing the password "try4-mbs." There are a total of 100 users providing 10 samples each.

15.1.7 GREYC-NISLAB{A,B,C,D,E}

This dataset created by GREYC labs revolved around the study of recognizing soft biometric traits for keystroke dynamics. The dataset can also be used for classical keystroke dynamics authentication. There are a total of 110 users, each providing 10 inputs of 5 different passwords in several sessions typed with one hand and another 10 using both hands. The data were obtained using the same software as the GREYC database. The dataset is available in an Excel file.

15.2 RELEVANT WORKS ON MOBILE KEYSTROKE DYNAMICS

In today's market, smartphones usually rely on a four digit PIN that the user must remember and a fingerprint biometric authentication system to protect mobile phones from intruders. As mobile phones become more integrated into consumers' lives, there is an ever increasing need to secure the data in the devices used every day.

CASE STUDY 1

In order to better protect user data, the keyboard on mobile devices can help better secure sensitive information. Luca et al. [2] examined the best method of keystroke behavior as a method for authentication and the resilience of the system against attacks. An application was developed for data gathering in this study. It involved four different unlock methods: horizontal, vertical, diagonal, and two finger vertical. The application kept track of four factors: pressure (how hard the finger presses), size (area of the finger touching the screen), X- and Y-coordinates, and time. The two-finger-unlock method differed from the other methods because it provided two sets of X- and Y-coordinates, pressure, and size. There were 48 participants in this study and each was tasked to unlock the device 160 times over a period of 2 days. The method of unlocking the screen was counterbalanced in order to minimize learning effects.

In this study, it was assumed that the attacker had the device at hand, presumably stolen, and knowledge of the user's password pattern (shape for unlocking the phone). This meant that the first security barrier was already compromised. As with other available commercial systems, the attacker then has three tries until the device is blocked.

The methods presented in this work were designed to provide security against such attacks. Furthermore, even after a user loses the mobile device and authentication system, the mobile device should still be protected.

On the first day, the participants were asked to unlock the screens 80 times with each method. They were also instructed to unlock the mobile device using the same finger. After 20 tries, the users were asked to perform a different task, such as typing a text message, then resumed unlocking the device again using the same finger they used before. After 2 days, they were asked to perform the same task again, which was done in order to reflect more realistic data by observing how performance would change over time. In addition, each unlock that was provided was used as an attack against other users.

The algorithm used to analyze the data was the dynamic time warping (DTW) algorithm. This allowed for the comparison of two sets of data. The algorithm looks for similarities between the given sets and calculates the costs match of one set to the other. The result is a value called *warp distance*. The smaller the warp distance value is, the more similar the two sets are (i.e., if warp distance is 0, the two sets are identical). The larger the values are, the sets differ from each other. A set was composed of the time series of a touch screen (combinations of X- and Y-coordinates, pressure, size, and time).

A reference set was also implemented to represent the baseline for comparison and act as an ID for users. This was captured by taking the first 20 unlocks for each user. Each unlock was compared to the 19 other unlocks using DTW. The average warp distance for each respective unlock was then calculated. The unlock method with the lowest average warp distance was then chosen to be the reference set for the user.

The unlock attempts that were not used in creating the reference sets were compared to the reference set using DTW. In order to check the resistance of the system to attacks, the unlock attempts of other participants were also compared to the reference set. Furthermore, the parameters used to determine the success of the system were true positive (TP): correctly accepted users, true negative (TN): correctly rejected attackers, false positive (FP): wrongly accepted attackers, and false negative (FN): wrongly rejected users. Each value was calculated per method (i.e., vertical unlock have TP, TN, FP, and FN values) which was then used to determine which unlock method was the most efficient.

The results of the study were based on 30,720 unlocks (640 per user). The ideal result would show that the method(s) would have very high TP and TN values and low FP and FN values. The results of the study have shown that the diagonal unlock method provided the highest accuracy in determining keystroke biometrics compared to other methods. It produced the highest accuracy values in FP and FN and also contained the lowest FP and FN values. The two-finger vertical unlock method performed the poorest with the lowest TN value, meaning to say that the majority of the attacks were successful.

Overall, the result of this study has shown that the developed system could identify users well (high TP values), regardless of the method used. Despite these results, however, there is a drawback to using this approach for keystroke biometrics. In the best case (diagonal unlock method), the TN value was relatively high. Meaning to say, attacks are still possible (~4 out of 10 attacks would be successful). In terms of security, the result of this statistic does not provide a satisfying result. Despite the room for improvement for the unlock method, the more promising way to go is using a method that allows collecting more significant data per dataset.

CASE STUDY 2

Jeanjaitrong and Bhattarakosol [3] determined the feasibility of applying keystroke dynamics on mobile phones in their case study. They developed a web-application where the participants were granted passwords based on symbols. The symbols used for this study were heart, spade, club, and diamond with each symbol having different color: black, red, blue, and green. The web-application had three pages; registration, data collecting, and forgot password page. The registration page asks each user personal information and remembers the granted password. The data collection page is where the user performs the unlocking task. The page shows 16 symbols arranged as a 4×4 matrix. The password forgot page shows the users of their granted password.

There were a total of 10 random iPhone users that were selected for this study. The web-application provides the users a password that they would have to enter. A password consists of 4 out of the 16 symbols. The length of the password is based off an ATM machine and iPhone passcode length. Each user was asked to perform the unlock procedure 10 times per round and there was a total of 10 rounds. The data collected in this experiment were button-pressed time, button-released time, and an ordered pair of screen position (X-, Y-coordinate). Using this data, the authors were able to calculate dwell time, interval time, and distance.

The dwell time refers to the amount of time the participant took while pressing down a button. This was calculated using the difference between the time a button was pressed and the release time. Interval time ratio refers to the ratio of the interval time between button presses and the overall time used to press the whole password. The distance value is the distance between two different points on the screen that was pressed by the user.

The values used as performance metrics in this study were the false acceptance rate (FAR) and the false rejection rate (FRR). The authors determined the FAR, FRR, and accuracy for a single factor authentication and multifactor authentication. Their study has shown that the triple-factor used to authenticate a user yielded a higher accuracy rate compared to dual and single factor authentication. Using the dwell time, interval time, and distance factors to authenticate a user yielded the best values FAR, FRR, and accuracy.

In order to show that keystroke dynamics in mobile touch screen devices have similarities to their keyboard counterpart, the authors generated FAR, FRR, and accuracy percentages for a keyboard. Their results have shown a close relationship in terms of FAR, FRR, and accuracy values using dwell time and interval as factors.

Based on the results of this study, the keystroke dynamic mechanism has shown that it can be just as effective as the keyboard. Furthermore, this proves to be a cost efficient method in securing data in mobile phones.

CASE STUDY 3

In Reference 4, a software prototype was implemented on a Microsoft Windows phone. Each user was instructed to create two passwords, a simple four-digit PIN and an alphanumeric password. The password textbox implemented in the software captures key events and interkeystroke latencies. These values were evaluated based on three classifiers: Euclidean distance, Mahalanobis distance, and feed-forward multilayered perceptron (FF MLP) neural network. Both the Euclidean and Mahalanobis distance are statistical-based methods that have low processing requirements which is an important factor to consider on mobile platforms. FF MLP, on the other hand requires high processing requirements in exchange for better performance rate.

There were 20 people who participated in this study. And in a single session, each participant was asked enroll by entering a password they had chosen 20 times and authenticate it by entering it 10 more times.

The results have shown the importance of limited process capacity of mobile devices. While neural network-based approaches have outperformed the statistical-based methods, it has exceeded the process capability of the device. Due to the poor performance of the neural network algorithm, it was not possible to calculate the performance rates of the system (both FAR and FRR).

The two statistical analysis methods have little difference in performance in obtaining either the PIN or alphanumeric password. However, the results do show that the performance of the classifiers on the alphanumeric password is stronger than the PIN. This suggests that a short PIN is an ineffective tool for keystroke analysis. The alphanumeric password yielded much lower FRR and FAR values than the PIN password.

After the study, the authors also took a survey asking the participants which authentication method they would use on a mobile device. The vast majority of the participants preferred fingerprint-based solutions, with speech recognition solutions coming in second, and keystroke analysis third.

Half of the participants thought that entering 20 samples to be time consuming. However, 18 out of the 20 participants said that they would use the keystroke solution if it were available and thought that it would provide more security.

15.3 CONCLUSION

Due to the fast evolution of smartphones over the last few years, keystroke dynamics authentication used in computers could also be implemented in the near future. There are significant advantages in using this method, making it a viable method in securing phones. One of the advantages of this method is the lack of need for hardware. All the hardware required to implement this system is inherently built into the system. Another benefit to keystroke dynamics is the small amount of data that is needed to train a recognition system. Compared to other biometric techniques such as facial recognition the amount of data needed in sufficiently implementing keystroke dynamics requires a much smaller sample size. This leads to a shorter processing time. External environmental conditions also do not affect the verification process making the authentication process easier for the user [5]. Based on these advantages, keystroke dynamics provides a reliable method in securing sensitive data in mobile devices.

Despite the advantages this method has over other biometric techniques, there are still some drawbacks using keystroke dynamics. In Reference 4, the case study using neural networks, which can produce optimal results, exceeded the processing capability of the mobile device used. Another disadvantage is despite having a small sample size requirement, users in his study found providing multiple samples troublesome. Depending on the position of the user (sitting down, walking, or standing), the performance of the verification process can also be affected. This could possibly lead to false rejection by the system if the user tries to login in a different position and the system was trained when the user was standing up.

Considering the advantages and disadvantages of applying keystroke dynamics on mobile phones, it is within reason to think that this can be applied to mobile devices in the near future [5]. As mobile phone technology rapidly advances, obtaining performance that rivals desktop computers is within reach.

REFERENCES

1. Giot, R., B. Dorizzi, and C. Rosenberger. A review on the public benchmark databases for static keystroke dynamics. *Computers and Security*, Elsevier, 2015, Vol. 55, pp. 46–61.
2. Luca, A. D., A. Hang, F. Brudy, C. Lindner, and H. Hussmann. Touch me once and i know it's you! In *Proceedings of the 2012 ACM Annual Conference on Human Factors in Computing Systems—CHI '12*, Austin, Texas, 2012. n. pag. Web.
3. Jeanjaitrong, N. and P. Bhattarakosol. Feasibility study on authentication based keystroke dynamic over touch-screen devices. In *2013 13th International Symposium on Communications and Information Technologies (ISCIT)*, Surat Thani, Thailand, 2013. n. pag. Web.
4. Buchoux, A. and N. L. Clarke. Deployment of keystroke analysis on a smartphone. *Research Online*. Edith Cowan University, 2008, p. 48. Web. February 22, 2016, http://ro.ecu.edu.au/ism/48
5. Avila, C. S., J. G. Casanova, F. Ballesteros, L. J. M. Garcia, M. F. A. Gomez, D. De Santos Sierra, and G. B. Del Pozo. PCAS—Personalised Centralized Authentication System. *European Union's Seventh Framework Programme*, January 31, 2014. Web. February 22, 2016, https://www.pcas-project.eu/

CHAPTER 16

Gait Recognition

Yu Liu and Abhishek Verma

CONTENTS

16.1 DATASETS

Gait analysis databases are used in a myriad of fields that include human motion study, kinesiology, and surveillance, which are typically based on vision. These gait data are mostly collected by camera in a laboratory that has a specially designed walking belt. However, the available data acquired from mobile devices are still very limited. Gait authentication from a wearable sensor is still a rather new research area and thus not many datasets are available yet. In recent years, as more researchers show interest exploring gait on mobile devices and conduct experiments, we are fortunately able to find the following public databases for gait research:

1. University of California—Irvine released their gait database on their website. Twenty-two participants walk in the wild over a predefined path with their Android smartphone positioned in their chest pockets. Accelerometer data are collected for motion patterns research and authentication.

2. Another database was collected by Dr. Jordan Frank at McGill University. In this case, HTC Nexus One and HumanSense open-source Android Data Collection Platform were used for gait data acquisition. Twenty participants performed two separate 15-min walks on two different days with the mobile phone in their pockets.

3. The OU-ISIR (Osaka University—I Research) Gait Database was collected by using one smartphone (Motorola ME860) with accelerometer and three inertial sensors with each embedded with a triaxial accelerometer and triaxial gyroscope. In all, 744 volunteers participated in this experiment. Three sensors are positioned in the back, center and left, and right of the subject's waist. Each subject walked in and out on the level path and upslope and downslope.

4. Pattern Recognition Lab in University Erlangen—Nuremberg used two sensors for gait data acquisition. Each sensor node was equipped with a triaxial accelerometer and a triaxial gyroscope. Data were sampled with 200 Hz and stored on an SD card. Fifteen participants performed seven daily life activities: sitting, lying, standing, walking outside, jogging outside, ascending stairs, and descending stairs.

Study Cases

Gait authentication using a cell phone-based accelerometer sensor offers an unobtrusive, user-friendly, and periodic way of authenticating individuals on their cell phones. Here, we present three study cases for gait authentication on a mobile platform.

5. Case 1: Unobtrusive User-Authentication on Mobile Phones Using Biometric Gait—In 2010, researchers from the Norwegian Information Security Lab in Gjovik University in Norway did an experiment on 51 participants carrying Google G1 mobile phones equipped with accelerometers to record their gait data. The mobile phone was placed on the belt on the right-hand side of the subject's hip. The phone's screen pointed to the subject's body and the top pointed to the walking direction, which means the phone was in the same direction as the person who was walking.

The G1 has an integrated sensor (AK8976A) for measuring accelerations in three axes. The sensor is a piezoresistive micro electro mechanical system (MEMS) accelerometer. Accelerations in all directions can be collected with three sensors perpendicular to each other that represents x, y, and z directions, respectively. The accelerometer can obtain 40–50 samples per second.

A total of 51 subjects performed two sets of walking, each of two walks, that is a round trip of 37 m of flat carpeted hall. The author defines a cycle as two steps because every a person repeats the same walking every two steps. Notice from all four walks, the first one is used as a template and only the other three are used as test data.

The x-axis data have the best performance among all three (x, y, z), from the gait data obtained and thus x-axis is used as the measurement in this case. To extract features, the author preprocessed the data by interpolating time and filtering data, and then performed cycle estimation and detection.

Since the accelerometer only detects when there is motion change, the data interval is not always equal. Time interpolation is necessary in order to fix this problem. For filtering, apply a weighted moving average [1] filter to remove noise of the data.

From the data, we observed a cycle length is about 40–60 samples per second. The average cycle length is computed based on the distance scores from the small subset to the center of the data.

Cycle detection is conducted after computing the cycle estimate. A cycle starts with the minimum point, which is set as the starting point and goes to both directions by the length of the average cycle length that is computed from the last step. Instead of specifying a particular point, a 10% positive and negative estimation around that point is applied for accuracy and robustness.

As to the average cycle, the authors first drop out the irregular cycles and then use the dynamic time warping (DTW) [2] algorithm to calculate the distances between all cycles and deleting the ones which have an unusually large distance to the other cycles. The cycle with the lowest average DTW distance to the remaining cycles will be used as the average cycle. Average cycle is a feature vector (of real values) of an average length of around 45 samples.

This experiment and algorithm resulted in 20.5% equal error rate [3]. It is not 50% higher than the one using a more advanced sensor that is capable of obtaining twice the data samples.

6. Case 2: Orientation Independent Cell Phone-Based Gait Authentication—The previous research experiment was conducted under a nearly perfect situation where the mobile phone was stably positioned. However, this is not close to a real-life situation at all. People usually put their phone in their pocket and the orientation of the phone-based accelerator continuously changes. This author conducted a research experiment under a more realistic scenario, contributed in compensating the orientation error, and showed the

authentication results by using the modified cycle length estimation and detection algorithm he proposed.

In this research, 35 participants' gait data are collected using the Google Nexus Android phone. An Android application is developed to record three-dimensional accelerometer data at a sampling rate of 100 Hz, and a text file with timestamps is written out. Participants were asked to put their phone in the pant's right-hand side front pocket and walk two round trips in a 68 m long straight corridor at their normal pace.

From the subject's gait data, a total of four walks are observed and each walk roughly lasts 50 s. The walking activity data vary person to person. To separate each walk, the author monitored the variances of data along one axis and examined the variances for every second and compared the data variances with the predefined threshold. If the data variances are above the threshold, it is set as the start of a walk. If the data variances are below the threshold, then it is set as the end of the walk. After all the walk cycles are marked, the walk that is longer than 10 s was selected and the Euclidean resultant vector computed.

A few preprocessing procedures are applied including reshaping of the data for equal time interval, and rescaling the feature with zero normalization and the wavelet-based noise removal modules. It was the same with the last study case, since the data are collected only when the sensors detect the motion change, the time interval between every two input data is not equal. Therefore, the author applied interpolation to reshape the data in equal time intervals.

Data normalization is necessary before any furthering gait analysis. In this case, the author simply obtained the new acceleration data by subtracting the mean acceleration for each axis. The multilevel Daubechiess orthogonal wavelet (db6) [4] with level 3 and soft thresholding is used to eliminate the noise from the walking signal.

In this example, the cycle length estimation is based upon the assumption that the center of the walk is the most stable data. So, it starts with extracting 80 small sets of walk data as samples around the center of the walk, and stores them in a reference window. Compare the reference window with the rest of the data subset to get the difference vector. Then, store the minimum indices found from it which results in a new vector. Compute every two adjacent values in the new vector and the mode, which is the most frequent data of the resultant set of numbers, is used to estimate the cycle length. However, if the mode does not exist, it means that every step of the subject varies and the cycle length can be computed by averaging the values of the difference vector.

To reduce the risk of picking the wrong minimum, the author takes a segment of the size twice of the estimated cycle length in the center of the walk, therefore obtaining two minima. The smaller minima is picked and used as the start of a cycle. Similarly with the last study case, the cycle's ending is obtained by adding and subtracting a cycle length time. Since not all the minimas in the walk occur in the equal interval, applying an offset (0.2*estimated cycle length) helps to increase the accuracy. Finally, all the gait cycles are normalized and unusual cycles are removed by computing the pairwise distance using DTW.

Once the references and the probe cycles are generated, they are compared against each other to compute the intraclass (genuine) and interclass (imposter) distances. If 50% cycles of a walk have distances below the threshold value, it is considered as genuine, and vice versa.

The author compares the gait analysis on the same day and crossdays and found big differences. Since people's gait changes over time, he points to an online learning method to cope with the aging factor as future work.

7. Case 3: Secure and Privacy Enhanced Gait Authentication on Smartphone—In this paper, the author proposes a gait biometric cryptosystem (BCS) using a fuzzy commitment scheme on mobile platform. The gait features are used to biometrically encrypt a cryptographic key which acts as the authentication factor. Gait signals are acquired by the mobile phone-based triaxial accelerometer. Error correcting codes are adopted to deal with the natural variation of gait measurements. The gait sample is merely used to retrieve the cryptographic key and then discarded.

The author collected 34 participants' gait data. Each subject walked with the Google Nexus One smartphone inside the front pant pocket. The experiment achieved the lowest false acceptance rate and the false rejection rate of 3.92% and 11.76%, in terms of key length of 50 bits.

There are two phases in this gait BCS, namely enrollment and authentication. In the enrollment phase, a user's gait features are collected. Similarly with the previous two examples, the acquired gait data are preprocessed in a few steps: data interpolation to achieve equal time interval and noise filter using Daubechie orthogonal wavelet (db6) [4] with level 2. Feature vectors are extracted in both time and frequency domains. Euclidean distance in 3D space is calculated for measurement. Then, the vectors are binarized. A reliable binary feature vector w is extracted based on the user's gait. Meanwhile, a randomly generated cryptographic key m is encoded to a codeword c by using error correcting codes. The fuzzy commitment scheme F computes the hash value of m and a secured δ using a cryptographic hash function h and a binding function. The helper data which are used to extract reliable binary feature vectors and values of h(m), δ are stored for later use in the authentication phase.

In the authentication phase, the user provides a different gait sample. It is also preprocessed to extract a feature vector and a reliable w′ is extracted by using helper data which is stored in the enrollment phase. The decoding function f computes the corrupted codeword c′ via binding w′ with δ and then retrieves a cryptographic key m′ from c′ using the corresponding error correcting code decoding algorithm. Finally, the hash value of m′ will be matched with h(m) for authentication decision.

There is good potential to construct an effective gait-based authentication system. Design and construct better discriminant feature vectors (using global feature transformations), finding optimal quantization scheme for binarization can help to achieve better performance.

16.2 CONCLUSION

Humans walk in their own unique style with a natural repetitive mode. A mobile-based accelerator is able to collect the gait data. A gait cycle which is the time interval between two successive occurrences of one of the repetitive events when walking is used to study and analyze the characteristics of the gait. The key of the gait analysis lies on a good algorithm for cycle length estimation and cycle detection—points where a cycle starts and ends.

Under the realistic situation where the phone's positions change all the time, the orientation of the sensor changes frequently and much noise is created by random motions of the mobile phone. The human gait can be affected by clothes, weight lifting, carrying burdens, etc., besides the fact that the human gait may change with aging. All these factors affect accuracy recognition and pose challenges. More work may be needed in improving the cycle extraction algorithms and exploring various walking environment settings.

Regardless of a number of challenges, gait authentication on mobile devices is a feasible and promising field. The three case studies detailed here achieved good results and meanwhile indicate that there is more that can be done. In order to improve gait authentication performance, we need a continuous research effort in developing a more robust cycle estimation and detection algorithm and a sophisticated adaptive learning system to compensate the constant position changes with mobile devices.

REFERENCES

1. https://en.wikipedia.org/wiki/Moving_average
2. https://en.wikipedia.org/wiki/Dynamic_time_warping
3. https://en.wikipedia.org/wiki/Biometrics
4. http://wavelets.pybytes.com/wavelet/db6/

IV

The Future

CHAPTER 17

Current and Future Trends in Biometrics

Sinjini Mitra and Bo Wen

CONTENTS

17.1 INTRODUCTION

According to the *M2SYS blog on Biometric Technology*, a recent report projects a bright future for the global market for emerging biometric technologies, predicting a market currently valued at $555 million to quickly double in the next 4 years to $1.04 billion [1]. Biometrics is a field that is undergoing a rapid evolution with a host of new modalities emerging that offer higher levels of accuracy than traditional traits, such as face and fingerprints. Fueling the growth for these emerging biometric technologies is the growth of the industry in government, gaming, and health care, thus moving beyond the initial applications in law enforcement and in immigration and border control for identification of criminals. Although the preceding chapters presented comprehensive descriptions of all these different modern applications of biometrics-based authentication, there are several even more novel directions that are emerging on a daily basis.

Another report by Future Market Insights [2] predicts that the market will undergo a double-digit growth rate by 2019 from its previous global market value of $6357.7 million in 2012. The report states that the global biometrics market is driven by a handful of factors, including security concerns due to increasing crimes and terror attacks, and the unique and simple features of biometric systems. But conversely, the unreliability and high cost involved in the implementation of biometrics technologies will decelerate the growth of the global biometrics system market in the near future, the report said. However, it is still believed that the biometrics system market will be greatly improved in the future. Tractica, a company that focuses on biometrics market research, projects that the global biometrics market will increase from $2.0 billion in 2015 to $14.9 billion by 2024, with a compound annual growth rate (CAGR) of 25.3% and cumulative revenue for the 10-year period totaling $67.8 billion [3]. Figure 17.1 shows the trend of annual biometrics revenue by region in the world market, from 2015 to 2024.

The rest of this chapter is organized as follows. Section 17.2 presents brief summaries of some recent trends in biometric applications.

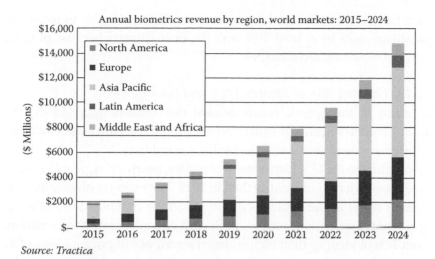

Annual biometrics revenue by region, world markets: 2015–2024

Legend:
- North America
- Europe
- Asia Pacific
- Latin America
- Middle East and Africa

($ Millions)

Source: Tractica

FIGURE 17.1 **(See color insert.)** Biometrics market overview over the next 10 years. (From Tractica. 2015. Biometrics market revenue to total $67 billion worldwide over the next 10 years. With permission from Tractica.)

Section 17.3 describes some newer biometric modalities that are coming into the market, and we finally conclude with a discussion in Section 17.4.

17.2 NEWER TRENDS IN BIOMETRIC APPLICATIONS

Some recent applications of biometrics-based authentication have been enumerated in this book that includes mobile security, health care, gaming and entertainment, and big data. All of these fields are still growing, while newer domains for biometrics applications are emerging on a regular basis. In this section, we briefly outline some of these recent trends, along with potential opportunities.

17.2.1 Biometrics in Banking

Since security is a major risk in the banking industry, many financial institutions are willing to implement biometrics systems as a means of client authentication. The report [4], published by the Biometrics Research Group Inc., states that revenue streams for biometrics utilized in the global banking sector will rise from $900 million in 2012 to $1.8 billion by the end of the year. As seen in the report, developed countries will still take the lead in biometric technology research; however, implementation in emerging economics will be the primary revenue source. Also, the group forecasts that the banking industry is likely to be able to reduce its operational risks by at least 20% over the next 10 years because of more advanced biometric technologies.

17.2.1.1 Growing Risk of Identity Theft and Banking Fraud

According to the generic organizational risk context figure in [5], the banking industry normally experiences the highest security risks followed by the government sector and the healthcare industry.

According to the U.S. Department of Justice, nearly 7% of people aged 16 or older were victims of identity theft in 2012. The majority of identity theft incidents (85%) in the United States involved the fraudulent use of existing account information, such as credit card or bank account information. About 14% of identity theft victims experienced out-of-pocket losses of $1 or more, whereas about half suffered losses of less than $100. Victims who experienced the misuse of their personal information reported a mean loss of $9650 and a median loss of $1900. Victims of new account fraud incurred an average loss per incident of $7135, victims of multiple types of fraud suffered an average loss of $2140, while victims of existing account misuse incurred an average loss of $1003 per incident. In addition to any direct financial loss, 6% of all identity theft victims reported indirect losses associated with the most recent incident of identity theft. Victims who suffered an indirect loss reported an average indirect loss of $4168 [6].

Identity theft victims reported a total of $24.7 billion in direct and indirect losses attributed to all incidents of identity theft experienced in 2012. These losses exceeded the $14 billion victims lost from all other property crimes (burglary, motor vehicle theft, and theft) as measured by the National Crime Victimization Survey in 2012. Identity theft losses were over our times greater than losses due to stolen money and property in burglaries ($5.2 billion) and theft ($5.7 billion), and eight times the total losses associated with motor vehicle theft ($3.1 billion) [6]. Surprisingly, a recent report even shows there is a new victim of identity theft every 3 s [7].

Due to such increasing concerns over security of personal information, banks and other financial institutions around the world are becoming more and more inclined toward deploying biometric-based authentication for their clients.

17.2.1.2 Biometrics in Automatic Teller Machines

Biometric Automatic Teller Machines (ATMs) are machines that utilize biometric measures to verify the identity of customers and allow them

FIGURE 17.2   An ATM using biometrics. Biometric ATM gives cash via fingerprint scan through a mobile device. (With permission from Shutterstock.)

to use the cash machine for carrying out banking transactions, such as withdrawing cash, depositing checks, and so on. Some ATMS solely use biometric authentication for identification, whereas others may use this in conjunction with another format, such as a payment card, a mobile device, or an additional security credential like a Personal Identification Number (PIN). The biometric measures used in biometric ATMs typically include palm or finger vein print biometrics; however, more advanced technologies, such as iris recognition are now gradually becoming available as well. Countries such as Brazil, India, Poland, and Japan already support ATM cash withdrawals by means of biometrics, while we believe that many other countries will follow the trend in the near future as well, especially in Asia and Africa [4]. Figure 17.2 shows an ATM from where cash is being withdrawn using a fingerprint scan.

17.2.2 Government-Driven Identification Initiatives

The other major application space for biometrics is government-related initiatives for secure identification and banking. Indeed, governments in emerging economies have rapidly been embracing biometric technologies for payment verification in the retail industry. Several countries have started using biometric technologies to verify recipients of government payments. For instance, the Philippines government uses biometric technology to authenticate cash grant beneficiaries for poor households. In Pakistan, the government has begun to issue biometric smart cards to pensioners, which can be used to withdraw pensions from banks and post offices [8]. But the most demonstrative example of government-driven biometric application in the recent years is the Indian government's proposed use of *Aadhaar* that provides identity cards to citizens as well as issues bank accounts for all Indian households [9]. Figure 17.3 shows a prototype of an Aadhaar card issued by the Indian government to Indian citizens.

Aadhaar is the world's largest biometric database. Recently, the Indian government allocated $340 million to accelerate resident registration. Currently governed by the Unique Identification Authority of India (UIDAI), Aadhaar is used to authenticate delivery of social services, including school attendance, natural gas subsidies to India's poor population in rural areas, and direct wage payments to bank accounts. With already about 700 million enrolled Indians in the Aadhaar program, the government's objective is now to enroll 100 million more residents [10]. This expansion of the Aadhaar system is primarily targeted toward the delivery of more welfare initiatives and programs, including Prime Minister Narendra Modi's new "Pradhan Mantri Jan Dhan Yojana" scheme. The new program, which means "Prime Minister Scheme for People's Wealth" aims to provide a bank account for each household in India, a scheme that is an important step toward converting the Indian economy into a cashless and digital economy [11].

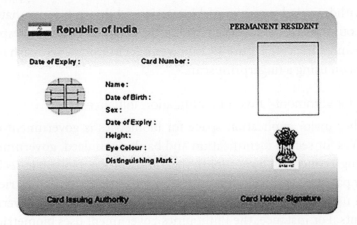

FIGURE 17.3 A prototype of an "Aadhaar" card issued by the Government of India. (With permission from The Alternative.)

17.2.3 Biometrics in Health Care

Health care is one of the most important expenditure categories within the U.S. economy. According to the World Health Organization (WHO), total health care spending in the United States was 17.9% of its gross domestic product (GDP) in 2011, the highest in the world. Further, this is expected to continue its historical upward trend, reaching 19.5% of GDP by 2017. Despite these trends, most analysts rank the United States last in the quality of care provided, on the basis of economic investment versus actual health outcomes [12]. The use of biometrics in several areas of health care today is expected to help mitigate some of these shortcomings, and some more recent applications and potential application areas for the future are described below.

17.2.3.1 Reduced Healthcare Fraud

Health care fraud is a pervasive and a costly drain on the U.S. healthcare system. In 2008, of the $2.26 trillion spent on health care, between $68 and $226 billion (3%–10%) was lost to healthcare fraud [13]. This susceptibility to fraud is attributed to the complexity of a fragmented health insurance regime in the United States. Of the many times of fraudulent healthcare schemes in the United States, the most common kind report edly involves a false statement, misrepresentation, or deliberate omission made by a healthcare recipient that is critical to the determination of benefits payable. Such fraudulent activities are usually criminal, although the specific nature or degree of criminal acts varies from state to state [12]. To reduce some of these frauds, biometric-based identification can be used. For example, biometrics instead of paper insurance cards can be deployed to prevent a common type of fraud that occurs when one patient poses as another to obtain insurance benefits. It can also deter unscrupulous providers from filing phantom claims, because a biometric scan proves a patient's physical presence at a healthcare facility. Therefore, the use of biometrics to secure patient and provider identities can prevent certain healthcare fraud, thus increasing the efficiency and effectiveness of healthcare programs [14].

17.2.3.2 Provide Access Control to Critical Medical Sources

Many hospitals and healthcare organizations are currently deploying biometric security architecture. Secure identification is critical in the healthcare system to control logical access to centralized archives of digitized patients' data, to limit physical access to buildings and hospital wards, and to authenticate medical and social support personnel. As electronic health records (EHRs) and personal health records (PHRs) become more commonly used, biometrics are being utilized as an authentication mechanism by both medical facilities and insurers. Under U.S. federal legislation, specifically the Health Insurance Portability and Accountability (HIPAA) Act, records must be kept every time a patient's EHR is accessed. Biometrics permit medical professionals to do this easily since their use of a biometric identifier can be automatically and digitally recorded each time a medical record is opened. A number of biometric equipment manufacturers and service providers therefore offer turnkey applications that maintain and track access to EHRs [12].

17.2.3.3 Workflow Improvement

The use of biometric authentication tools provides the option for healthcare facilities to extend physical control over access to medicine cabinets and laboratories. The use of such systems also streamlines workflow by adding sign-off capacity for diagnostic results, patient medication and treatments, and for data capture for pharmaceutical trials. It can potentially replace patient wristbands and barcodes as identifiers when nurses are administering medication at the bedside. Therefore, it greatly reduces medication errors [12].

Nurses may also be soon required to use biometrics to access digitized patient information in place of passwords that are more vulnerable to fraud. Many systems that are currently in use automatically time out, forcing nurses to log on repeatedly throughout the shift. On the other hand, if a nurse could log in and out simply by touching his or her fingertip to a sensor or laying his or her hand down on a scanner, it would save a lot of valuable time and make the overall process highly efficient. Facial recognition technologies can be even more efficient—a facial scanner on top of a computer monitor can log a person in as soon as he or she sits down at the workstation and log him or her out as soon as he or she moves away. The smart badges used by nurses to gain access to secure areas or supply cabinets are also moving toward replacement by biometric security measures. Such measures can help guarantee the physical safety of patients, newborn babies in the maternity wards, and prevent the loss and theft of inventory (such as pharmaceuticals and narcotics) by making a positive identification of people rather than badges that can be stolen and misused [14].

17.2.3.4 Secure Mobile Healthcare Applications

Mobile health or *mHealth* is an increasingly popular consideration because of its capacity to increase access to health care and health-related information, particularly in hard-to-reach populations and in developing countries. mHealth applications can improve the ability to diagnose and track diseases and can provide timelier, more actionable public health information. Further, mHealth applications can provide expanded access to ongoing medical education and training for health workers [15].

Due to the sensitivity of the data being collected and relayed via mHealth applications, we expect that biometric technology will be highly leveraged to protect mHealth devices, applications, and resources in the future. We anticipate that fingerprint recognition technology will be utilized the most since it is the primary biometric technology utilized in smartphones and other consumer mobile devices, such as iPhones, iPads, and Samsung Galaxy phones and tablets. Fingerprint recognition is therefore becoming a globally accepted method for positive identification and we expect it to be increasingly used in mHealth applications moving forward [12].

17.2.3.5 Other Healthcare Areas

Some other areas in the domain of health care that can potentially benefit from biometrics applications include the following:

- Assisting providers to obtain faster payments for services rendered by verifying at the provider's location that a patient is eligible at the time of service.

- Reducing the costs and risks associated with programs that attempt to recoup inaccurate and fraudulent payments.

- Increasing patient safety by reducing medical errors due to mismatched or incomplete records. The unique biometric identifier ensures an accurate match to their electronic healthcare record under most care conditions.

- Providing a unique and more accurate means for ensuring that patient records in multiple provider locations can be linked accurately. This increases the usefulness of EHRs, their safety, and privacy.

- Protecting patients' identity and healthcare information by providing an efficient and convenient means of authenticating both patients and providers before allowing access to records.

- Verifying that an individual requesting a particular treatment is eligible or not under his or her specific benefits plan.

17.2.4 Biometrics in Education

According to a report published by Technavio, "Biometrics Market in the United States in Education Sector 2015–2019," the biometrics market in the U.S. education sector is predicted to grow at a rate of 23.65% over the period 2014–2019 [16].

Biometrics can be employed in schools widely to save time and money, and make operations more efficient. Many areas in a school require identification, the most common ones used today include picture ID cards, PINs, and, of course, visual identification. Each of these methods suffer from drawbacks and are a drain on the time and resources of schools and cities. Cards are regularly forgotten, lost, and shared; PINs are easily forgotten, swapped, or stolen. Also, visual identification can be deceptive due to makeup and other external variations that affect a face. By using biometrics for identification, the problems and costs associated with the current methods can be avoided and new standards of accountability can be put into place in today's educational institutions [17].

Biometric technology can also provide benefits to educational institutions in terms of convenience, safety, and security. A typical first installation in a school is in the cafeteria, where accurate records are critical for reimbursement from the federal government's $9 billion free and reduced lunch program. According to a report, many cafeterias around the world are being fitted with biometric payment systems for students to purchase lunch, and these systems offer great benefits: kids do not need to carry cash, kids who lose money do not need to go without food, and lunch lines will move quickly, thus making the system more efficient [18]. The biometric payment systems for cafeterias work this way: student biometrics are registered in the system and converted to a numerical sequence for verification, parents or students can load money into an account, and then students are verified by their biometrics when buying food and money is taken out of their preloaded account [18]. Schools can then use the same biometric database to identify students in other applications, such as those used for attendance, in the nurse's office, in the library or media center, gym, at athletic events, social functions, and on the bus. The latter is particularly important because school bus drivers change frequently—new drivers are hired or routes are changed frequently, thus making it difficult for them to get to know the students well enough to visually identify them and where they belong. School districts have implemented finger scanning on buses in order to help the driver know if the student is on the correct bus, goes to the correct school, and gets off at the correct stop [19]. Once biometrics is being used successfully in one part of a school, the idea has a higher chance of being accepted and embraced in other areas as well [19].

A controlled and secure environment is critical to a school's success. Access to the school must be permitted only to authorized persons. Students, teachers, staff, and recurring visitors can be accurately time stamped and identified using biometric finger scanning technology, thus providing administrators with an irrefutable record of the date and time of each person's entry into the building. Such systems can thus assure administrators that those entering their schools actually belong there [17].

17.2.4.1 Examples of Biometric Applications in Schools

Some current example applications of biometric technologies in schools around the world are described below:

- A high school in North Wales has started fingerprinting its pupils in order to manage access on the school premises [20]. This has significantly helped in ensuring security for the large school campuses where certain buildings and areas should only be accessible to certain staff.

- According to a recent article [21], facial biometrics is going to be launched soon at a California school district for children in the elementary school (K-6) for logging into their iPads, thus replacing manual online passwords. Figure 17.4 shows some students using iPads for their schoolwork.

- Planet Biometrics [22] discusses how U.K. aid is supporting the "Adolescent Girls Initiative—Kenya" (AGI-Kenya) which registered 3000 adolescent girls in 60 schools in the Wajir County, Kenya using easy-to-use and inexpensive equipment to read students' fingerprints to record daily attendance. Those students who met the conditional threshold of 80% attendance had their households qualify for an

FIGURE 17.4 Students using iPads at school. (With permission from Shutterstock.)

electronic cash transfer, which was set up via biometric technology as well. This has helped boost attendance in these schools.

- Schools in Westerville, Ohio, are piloting a biometric payment system for their cafeterias. At a cost of $3731, three schools in Westerville City School District—which itself comprises 21 schools—are currently testing out fingerprint scanning devices at their cafeteria point of sale (POS) terminals [23].

- In September 2015, Antelope Valley Schools Transportation Agency conducted a pilot program to test an iris reader recognition solution on its special needs buses. The system, called *IRITRANS*, will alert the bus driver visibly and audibly if the child passenger is about to get on or off at the wrong stop. When the bus reaches the end of its daily route, the driver ends the route on the IRITRANS mobile device application. If all students have not exited the bus, the device will notify the driver to recheck the bus for any passengers. The system is in constant communication with the district office to provide officials with real-time specific information about the bus passengers and location [24].

17.2.4.2 Online Learning
When it comes to education, academic integrity has always been of the utmost concern. It is extremely important to know for certain that tests

are taken by the correct students and not by impostors. Student identity verification is more challenging in the online learning environment than in a face-to-face environment. Many programs still rely on the typical username/password protection. Others have implemented live remote proctoring via webcam, despite a number of logistical, financial, and in some cases legal challenges related to doing so.

Biometrics going mainstream via the iPhone 5S holds a lot of promise, not only for the owners of high-tech gadgets but also for academia as well. *Propero* is a self-paced online learning program from Pearson that allows students to master rigorous material at their own pace. Students in select courses under Propero will soon be asked to verify their identity by drawing a password using their mouse, stylus, or touchscreen. This gesture biometrics technology works on any device and analyzes not only what is drawn but also how it is drawn, including speed, angle, height, width, and direction. The popping up of this identity verification during an exam sends a strong message to students that academic integrity is taken seriously, and provides a great preventive measure against cheating. Behind the scenes, IP detection tracks each student's location during the exam, which provides useful evidence in the event that a suspicious case ever arises. According to Pearson [25], "biometrics can help us verify student identity in the online environment, and give our partner institutions peace of mind that their courses are secure."

17.2.4.3 Online Proctoring

Just as the need to introduce self-paced curriculum is gaining momentum, so is the need for efficient remote proctoring to ensure academic integrity. As institutions migrate more of their academic programs online with various learning management systems, the need for online proctoring and identity authentication solutions has become ever more apparent in order to ensure and protect academic integrity. Some institutions have elected to use online live proctors, but this solution has a major shortcoming, scheduling. Students are burdened by the time and costs associated with scheduling a live online proctor. Often it is the instructors who are overwhelmed with coordinating student schedule changes. Hence institutions are now seeking a proctoring solution that can scale and be flexible to students' growing need to take exams any time of the day and at the place of their choosing [26].

As a solution, *Proctortrack*, a proctoring service offered by Verificient, Inc., focuses on identity verification through the use of machine learning, facial recognition, and biometrics, thus providing time and cost advantages over live human proctors. Unlike other online exam proctoring system that verifies students' identity at the beginning of the exam, Proctortrack provides a continuous online identity verification solution [27]. The system uses a variety of biometric techniques, including vision-based cues, audio cues, test data, key-stroke patterns, and knuckle and mouse movements in order to continuously verify the identity of online test takers. It detects if the test taker is replaced, leaves the test, receives assistance from another people in the room, or opens up another browser. So far, the technology has been implemented by major institutions, such as Rutgers University, University of Southern California, and St. George's Medical University (SGU) [28]. In a 2015 online course at SGU, after the introduction of ProctorTrack, online exam cheating progressively declined from 11 incidents during the first exam to one during the last [29].

Since Proctortrack actively partners with learning management systems on solutions for earning online degrees, it is already seamlessly integrated with major learning management systems, such as Blackboard, Canvas, Moodle, eCollege, and Desire2Learn [28].

17.2.4.3.1 Security and Privacy Concerns with Proctortrack

As more and more universities choose to implement Proctortrack in their online classes, students seem to be outraged at the lack of concern over privacy. Many students were unaware of the program until it was too late to drop the course. Rutgers' student Betsy Chao, who began the change. org petition "Stop Use of Proctortrack in Online Courses," complained that the University gave no prior notice about the software [31]. After a few months, the Daily Targum, a Rutgers University Newspaper, wrote an article to express the major concerns in using the Proctortrack system, such as those related to secured data storage, security of the remote connection through which the biometrics monitoring takes place and whether the stored biometric data is used appropriately. For example, If a student accidentally leaves a personal or embarrassing website in their browser during an online course, a Proctortrack instructor might stumble upon their activity. Monitoring student's browser history is extremely invasive and might not be common knowledge to many students utilizing the Proctortrack software [32].

According to a blog post [33], since at least one person has already come up with ways to try to fool the Proctortrack system, it is not hard to understand why Proctortrack poses a major security risk. The author discusses several approaches to bypassing the system, including "intercepting the video feed," "the non-standard hardware approach" using an extra monitor or LAN, "the non-standard software approach" using virtual machine (VM), and so on.

On the other hand, Verificient seems to take privacy more serious. According to an article in New York Times [34], "In hopes of alleviating students' concerns, Verificient recently posted a pledge on its blog saying that Proctortrack did not share students' data with third parties; that it typically deleted students' data after 30 to 60 days; and that students could remove the software from their computers once they had uploaded their test data." This, however, also was proved to be controversial [35,36].

17.2.4.3.2 Other Online Exam Proctoring System Vendors

Although there are many online proctoring providers in the market, their products can be divided into three main categories [37]:

- *Fully automated solutions:* The computer monitors students and determines whether they are cheating.

- *Record and review:* Sessions are recorded as the computer monitors students. A human can then review the video at any time afterward.

- *Fully live:* Students are on video and watched remotely by a live proctor.

Some vendors for such online proctoring, with or without biometrics, include

- *Kryterion:* Kryterion sets a variety of biometrics standards in test taker identification verification. A digital photo match of the test taker is completed utilizing facial recognition software and a visual match at test launch which is stored with the test taker's test record. The solution also uses patented software that differentiates individuals based on their keystroke patterns [38].

- *ProctorCam:* ProctorCam offers online proctoring via seamless integration into the existing workflows of learning management systems and is currently part of Pearson VUE [39].

- *Proctorio:* Proctorio utilizes machine learning and facial recognition to monitor students during online exams [40].

- *Respondus Monitor:* Respondus Monitor is a companion application for Respondus LockDown Browser [41]. It uses webcam and video technology to prevent cheating during online exams that are administered remotely. Further, it allows seamless integration with learning management systems.

- *eProktor:* Swiss-based facial recognition company KeyLemon and U.S. e-learning firm eProktor have announced a partnership that aims to use facial biometrics to make student authentication more secure [42].

- *ProctorU:* ProctorU is an online proctoring service that uses a layered verification process (along with a live proctor), which resembles multifactor authentication, to verify a student's identity online [43]. The process works by the proctor viewing the student via a webcam, checking their ID, and capturing their photo to store on file. The student is then asked to answer a set of challenges or knowledge-based questions to further validate their identity. Finally, the system's keystroke analysis software adds a behavioral biometrics element to add to the student's profile for any subsequent logins.

- *SoftwareSecure:* SoftwareSecure provides both live and on-demand secure online proctoring solutions via identity verification (called *Remote Proctor NOW* or RPNow), which are scalable, affordable, and can be easily integrated with any Learning Management System (LMS).

17.2.4.4 Easy-to-Use versus Privacy Concerns

As more students participated in use of biometrics, security and student identification became more complicated issues. In United Kingdom, more than a million pupils have been fingerprinted at their secondary school and four out of ten secondary schools now use biometric technology as a means of identifying pupils—with nearly a third failing to seek parental consent before introducing the system [44].

In fact, Florida has moved to prohibit facial recognition or voice pattern technology from being used as solutions. Citing privacy concerns, Florida lawmakers banned collection of biometric data from students and their families [45]. While Florida is the first state to enact a total ban on the collection of this information, it is not the first to consider doing so. In March 2013, the Maryland Senate proposed legislation that banned the collection of students' biometric information throughout the state. After an amendment limited the ban to a single school district, the bill unanimously passed the Maryland Senate before the district voluntarily stopped the collection of biometric information [46]. Additionally, legislation currently working through the New Hampshire House would bar the state from collecting biometric information—as well as 16 other categories of information—from students for any reason [47].

However, some people believe that use of biometrics in education will not pose a threat to student privacy but enhances it [48].

- The data that need the most protection is one's biographic data, such as name, address, date of birth, sex, and social security number, but not biometrics. In all of the highly publicized thefts of identity, the data that were used were biographic and NOT biometric.

- Biometric data are already protected. In the difficult and unlikely case that a person hacks a biometric database, all the hacker receives is the digital representation of the biometric (a string of ones and zeros). This digital representation does not provide access either to the biometric image or the biographic data, contrary to hacking into a database of personal biographic data.

- As a best practice to protect student privacy, it is recommended to store only the biometric templates, which should be deleted when a student leaves the school. Student privacy is further enhanced because templates cannot be used to search law enforcement biometric databases.

17.3 EMERGENCE OF NEW BIOMETRIC TECHNOLOGIES

Although fingerprints, face, and iris are still popularly used biometric technologies, several newer biometrics are also emerging for different applications. In this section, we briefly review some of these more recent biometrics and their applications.

17.3.1 Vein/Vascular Pattern Recognition

Vascular pattern recognition, also commonly referred to as vein pattern authentication, uses near-infrared (IR) light to reflect or transmit images of blood vessels. Researchers have determined that the vascular pattern of the human body is unique to a specific individual and does not change as people age. The potential for the use of the technology can be traced to a research paper in 1992 [49], which discussed optical trans-body imaging and potential optical CT scanning applications. The first paper about the use of vascular patterns for biometric recognition was published in 2000 that described technology to use subcutaneous blood vessels in the back of the hand, and that was the first to become a commercially available vascular pattern recognition system [50]. Additional research improved that technology and inspired additional research and commercialization of finger- and palm-based systems [51,52].

Typically, the technology for vein/vascular recognition either identifies vascular patterns in the back of hands or fingers. To do this, near-IR rays generated from a bank of light-emitting diodes (LEDs) penetrate the skin of the back of the hand. Due to the difference in absorbance of blood vessels and other tissues, the reflected near-IR rays produce an extracted vascular pattern via image processing techniques. From the extracted vascular pattern, various feature-rich data, such as vessel branching points, vessel thickness, and branching angels are extracted and stored as a template [53].

This technology is difficult to forge, and is contact-less. Vascular patterns are difficult to recreate because they are inside the hand and, for some approaches, blood needs to flow to register an image. Users do not touch the sensing surface, which address hygiene concerns and improves user acceptance. This technology has been deployed in ATMs, hospitals, and universities in Japan. Applications include ID verification, high-security physical access control, high-security data access, and point-of-sale access control. The technology is also highly respected due to its dual matching capacity, as users' vascular patterns can be matched against personalized ID cards and smart cards or against a database of many scanned vascular patterns [54]. Some disadvantages associated with vein/vascular biometric technology are as [54] (i) there are numerous factors that can affect the quality of the captured image, such as body temperature, ambient temperature, humidity, unevenly distribution of heat, heat radiation, nearness of vein to surface, camera calibration, and focus and (ii) the technology is invasive because it creates apprehension among users that it can be a painful process.

17.3.2 Ear Shape Recognition

Using ear in person identification has been interesting for at least 100 years. The most famous work in the area of ear identification is by Alfred

Iannarelli in 1989, when he gathered over 10,000 ears and found that they all were different [55–58]. In 1906, Imhofer found that in a set of 500 ears, only four characteristics of the ear were needed to prove the uniqueness of the organ across individuals [58].

There are three primary methods for obtaining ear images for the purpose of identification: (i) taking a photo of a ear, (ii) taking "earmarks" by pushing the ear against a flat glass surface, and (iii) taking thermogram pictures of the ear. The most interesting parts of the ear are the outer ear and ear lobe, but the structure and shape of the whole ear are often used as well. The most commonly used methods in research for ear recognition are based on photos taken of a ear. The photo taken is combined with previously obtained photos stored in a database for identifying a person. The earmarks are used mainly in solving crimes by law enforcement officials, although currently they are not accepted in courts. The thermogram pictures, on the other hand, could be one potential solution to the problem of hair or hat which sometimes tend to obscure the ear when taking a photo [59].

According to a recent study by Mark Nixon, a computer scientist at the University of Southampton's School of Electronics and Computer Science, the ear, however, may prove to be an even more effective identification tool than any of the existing techniques, such as face and fingerprints, due to a new technology known as the "image ray transform." This technique takes advantage of the tubular features of the outer ear. Rays of light are shined on the ear, and the manner in which the light reflects off its curved features is analyzed by software in order to create an image. By repeating this process several times (say, thousands), a clear image of the ear is formed. Subsequently, these curves are translated into a series of numbers that can be used for matching during the identification process. According to the scientists that developed and implemented this program for ear recognition, this method offers a 99.6% success rate in test experiments involving over 250 ear images. Because ears are not affected by facial expressions or by differences in the background, Nixon alleges that the image ray transform technology for ears can be used as a reliable biometric indicator [60,61].

Some advantages of ear recognition are as follows:

- Ears are remarkably consistent—unlike faces, they do not change shape with different expressions or age, and remain fixed in the middle of the side of the head against a predictable background.

- Can be performed from long distance.

- The method for capturing ear images in noninvasive.

There are some disadvantages of ear recognition as well, which are summarized below [60]:

- The possibility of ear transformation with age—although the ear is fully formed at birth, whether it significantly changes due to aging over time remains a controversial point.

- The possibility of ear transformation with jewelry that can alter the shape of the ear.

- Hair and glass frames covering the ears, insufficient lighting conditions, and varying angles of ear images may prove to be hindrances to capturing good-quality images.

Currently, there are no commercially available ear recognition systems. However, the future holds tremendous potential for incorporating ear images with face images in a multimodal biometric configuration, even as researchers continue to refine the technology. For example, assigning a ear image to one of several predefined categories based on shape and structure, for example, could allow for rapid retrieval of candidate identities from a large database. In addition, the use of ear thermograms could help mitigate the problem of occlusion due to hair and accessories. As the technology matures, both forensic and biometric domains will benefit from this new biometric [62]. According to Westlake [63], Amazon has patented a ear recognition technology for smartphones that may feature in their new Fire mobile phones.

17.3.3 Facial Thermography

In the mid-1990s, it was demonstrated by scientist Prokoski that *facial thermograms* are unique to individuals, and that these could be potentially used to devise methods and systems for biometric identification [64]. Thermograms, generally, are "visual displays of the amount of IR energy emitted, transmitted, and reflected by an object, which are then converted into a temperature, and displayed as an image of temperature distribution."

IR energy, and IR light itself, is an electromagnetic radiation with longer wavelengths than those of visible light, extending from the nominal red edge of the visible spectrum at 700 mm to 1 mm [65]. This range of wavelengths corresponds to a frequency range of approximately 430 THz down to 300 GHz and includes most of the thermal radiation emitted by objects near room temperature [65]. IR light is emitted or absorbed by molecules when they change their rotational–vibrational movements that can be observed through *spectroscopy*—the study of the interaction between matter and radiated energy [66]. Historically, spectroscopy originated through the study of visible light dispersed according to its wavelength, by way of a prism. Later the concept was expanded greatly to comprise any interaction with radiative energy as a function of its wavelength or frequency. Spectroscopic data are often represented as a plot of the response of interest as a function of wavelength or frequency, known as *spectrum*.

Thermography works very much like facial recognition, except that an IR camera is used to capture the images in place of a regular digital camera. Prokoski however found that facial thermogram technology capability is inherently more accurate and more robust over varying lighting and environment conditions than video images. The technology involves the use of biosensor data for uniquely and automatically identifying individuals. The connectedness of the physiological systems of the human body enables elemental shapes to be derived from any biological sensor data and presented as an image. The elemental shapes and their locations provide an identification capability. Biosensors, which produce very detailed localized data, such as high-resolution IR images, can result in unique identification of an individual from the determination of elemental shapes and their distribution. The market for such devices and services includes all facilities which seek to restrict access to physical areas, distribution systems, or information files [67].

Thermograms as a mechanism of biometric identification are advantageous since the technology is nonintrusive. While not used prolifically, electronic thermography is increasingly used as a noninvasive alternative method for medical diagnostics. Unlike using the visible spectrum, recognition of faces using multispectral imaging modalities like IR imaging sensors [68–73] has become an area of growing interest. So, thermal images can be used to mitigate some of the challenges underlying regular face recognition based on video images [74]. Some of these are enumerated below:

- Face (and skin) detection, location, and segmentation are easier when using thermal images.

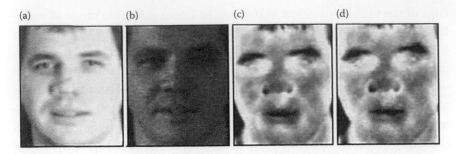

FIGURE 17.5 Thermal images have no effect of illumination: (c) and (d) are the corresponding thermal images of the visual images shown in (a) and (b), respectively. (From Bhowmik MK et al. 2011. Thermal infrared face recognition—A biometric identification technique for robust security system. In *Reviews, Refinements and New Ideas in Face Recognition*, Corcoran, P. (Ed). © 2011. InTech Open. Available from: http://dx.doi.org/10.5772/18986. With permission.)

- Within-class variance is much smaller for thermal images as they are not affected as much by external distortions.

- Nearly invariant to illumination changes and facial expressions.

- Works even in total darkness.

- Useful for detecting disguises (including artificial makeup) that is probably the biggest obstacle to effective facial recognition.

Figure 17.5 shows that thermal face images of a human being have no effect of illumination.

17.3.4 Odor Sensing

People's body odor identification is not a new idea considering since it has been conducted for over a century by the police force with the help of bloodhound dogs which are trained for such tasks. The ability of these dogs to follow the trail of a person from a sample of his or her personal odor is well known and proves that using body odor is an effective biometric identifier. Although the sensors used today have not yet achieved the accuracy of a dog's sense of smell, the research has used a system developed by the Ilí Sistemas Company that has a high sensitivity to detect volatile elements present in body odor [76].

Body odor can vary considerably due to instances of diseases, diet changes, or even mood swings. However, the research carried out by the "Group of Biometrics, Biosignals, and Security" (GB2S) of the Universidad Politécnica de Madrid (UPM) showed that the analysis of a group of 13 people during 28 sessions proved that recognizable patterns on each person's body odor have an identification error rate of 15%. This successful experiment and result confirm that the odor biometric system is a novel technique with an enormous potential [76].

Swiss researchers have discovered a way to identify humans through their unique *breathprints*. In a research paper titled, *Human Breath Analysis May Support the Existence of Individual Metabolic Phenotypes*, researchers conclude that individual signatures of breath composition exist, suitable enough to identify humans [77]. Eleven subjects were included in this study, and during the course of the study, they did not change their routine life style. For 9 days, the participants' breaths were measured, averaging 18 measurements each for the duration of the study as they breathed through a heated Teflon tube connected to the curtain gas port of a quadrupole time-of-flight mass spectrometer. Each time, a subject provided a full exhalation, while keeping pressure. Though the researchers noticed slight changes between samples, a core signature remained, which the researchers believe could facilitate human identification [77].

Some advantages of body odor identification are

- Nonintrusive: A scanner can simply "sniff" a person's odor as they walk through a booth, for instance, at a border checkpoint [78].

- Fool-proof: Even deodorants and perfumes cannot mask the basic human odor. These artificial scents do not eliminate the organic compounds present in the odor. As of now, it is impossible to replicate human odor [79].

The main disadvantage of this type of biometric identification relates to privacy concern—the body odor carries a significant amount of sensitive personal information since it is possible to diagnose some disease or activities in the last hours by analyzing body odor [80].

17.3.5 Gait Recognition

Gait recognition is a behavioral biometric modality that identifies people based on their unique walking pattern. Human movement consists of synchronized movements of hundreds of muscles and joints. Although basic movement patterns are similar, gait does vary from one person to another in terms of timing and magnitude [81]. Therefore, minor variations in gait style can be used as a biometric identifier to identify individuals.

Gait recognition groups spatial–temporal parameters, such as step length, step width, walking speed, and cycle time with kinematic parameters, such as joint rotation of the hip, knee, and ankle; mean joint angles of the hip, knee, and ankle; and thigh, trunk, and foot angles. Also considered is the correlation between step length and the height of an individual. Because human ambulation is one form of human movement, gait recognition is closely related to vision methods that detect, track, and analyze human behaviors in human motion analysis [82].

Gait recognition technologies are currently in their infancy. Currently, there are two main types of gait recognition techniques in development. The first is gait recognition based on the automatic analysis of video imagery. This approach is the most popular one and involves analysis of video samples of a subject's walk and the trajectories of joints and angles. A mathematical model of the motion is created, and is subsequently compared against other samples in order to determine identity. The second method uses a radar system, which records the gait cycle that the various body parts of the subject creates. These data are then compared to other samples in order to perform identification [83]. In both models, human body analysis is employed in an unobtrusive way using technical instrumentation that measures body movements, body mechanics, and the activity of specific muscle groups [84]. Such technologies are projected for use in criminal justice and national security applications. Figure 17.6 shows how the gait recognition system enrolls biometrics data.

Some advantages of gait recognition are [85]

- Does not require subject cooperation or body contact.

- The sensor may be located remotely, so it is good for criminal identification (e.g., bank robbers often wear masks, glasses, and gloves, which invalidate the possibility of using other biometric techniques, such as face or fingerprint).

- Effective where only low-quality image is available, as with closed-circuit television (CCTV) cameras.

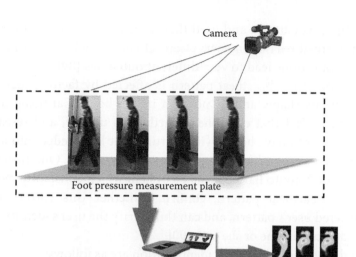

FIGURE 17.6   Diagram showing the enrollment process of a gait recognition system [87]. (With permission from author.)

Some disadvantages of gait recognition, on the other hand, are

- It might not work if a person wears an attire, such as a trench coat, or a footwear, such as flip-flops, that affects a person's walking style.

- The walking surface, downhill, uphill, and so on, could also cause a problem.

17.3.6 Heartbeat Authentication

In September 2013, the U.S. Department of Homeland Security's Science and Technology Directorate demonstrated a prototype of the *FINDER* radar technology device, which uses microwave radar to detect the unique signature of a human's breathing pattern and heartbeat, through 20 feet of solid concrete, 30 feet of a crushed mixture of concrete and rebar, and 100 feet of open space [87].

Heartbeat not only can detect human beings but also can be used to identify people. According to a recent research reported by New Scientist [88], our heartbeats follow an irregular pattern that never quite repeats and is unique to everyone. Researchers at Taiwan used an electrocardiograph (ECG) to extract the unique mathematical features underlying this pattern, and used that information to generate a secret key that formed part of an encryption scheme, by which small changes in initial conditions lead to very different outcomes [89].

The shape of the heartbeat pattern is affected by factors, such as the heart's size, its shape, and its position in the body. Cardiologists have known since 1964 that everyone's heartbeat is unique, and researchers around the world have been trying to turn that knowledge into a viable biometric system. Until now, they have had little success. One group at the University of Toronto have patented a system which constantly measures a person's heartbeat pattern, confirms whether this corresponds to the registered user's pattern, and can thus verify the user's identity for the various devices that he or she uses [90].

The advantages of heartbeat identification are as follows:

- Heartbeats are difficult to clone—cloning a biometric marker obtained via ECG is hard, making them more secure than fingerprints, which can be recovered from nearly anything that has been touched. Moreover, spoofing an ECG-based system is much harder that a face recognition system for instance (can be done with disguises and makeup). The wristband heartbeat sensor can sense whether it is in contact with a person, so a con man would have to use electrical components to imitate both the ECG and the body [90].

- The security feature derives from the fact that a user's ECG cannot be lifted or captured without a person's consent. For fingerprints, on the other hand, it is easy to leave behind "latent samples" (i.e., smudges) that can be replicated or forged [91].

- Noninvasive/user friendly.

The primary disadvantages of heartbeat identification include (i) difficulty in obtaining samples compared to other biometrics like face and fingerprints—capturing heartbeat patterns via ECG requires sophisticated medical equipment that may not be always available everywhere, and (ii) transformation with age—one obvious worry is that a person's ECG pattern might change beyond recognition in response to exercise or—over a longer period—as he ages [90]. Figure 17.7 shows a currently deployed payment method that is based on heartbeat authentication.

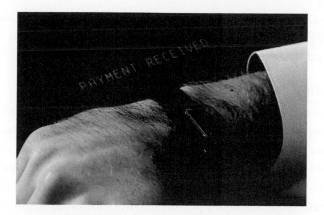

FIGURE 17.7   An illustration of a heartbeat-authenticated payment system [93].
(With permission from Nymi.)

Some recent applications of heartbeat identification are enumerated
below:

- *Nymi Band* is the first heartbeat-authenticated payment system with
  a wearable device that can be used at cash registers by connecting
  with a companion device, such as a smartphone or a computer [89],
  developed by Toronto-based biometrics firm Nymi. Additionally,
  MasterCard has partnered with the Royal Bank of Canada and Nymi
  to pilot a payment wristband that uses the electric wave pattern of
  the individual's heartbeat (electrocardiogram or ECG) for verification [93].

- *Heartbeat ID:* Apple has the first-mover advantage for creating a
  heartbeat ID since everyone knows about Touch ID, its fingerprint-
  based authentication scheme that is available on iPhones. And Apple
  also has an advantage because of its huge iPhone and iPad customer
  base. As a result, fingerprints—not heartbeats—are the *de facto*
  industry standard for authenticating digital devices, digital services,
  and mobile payment transactions [94]. But there are signs that the
  heartbeat could replace the fingerprint in the future. Last year, a
  company called *Bionym* raised a $14 million round of venture capi-
  tal investment and reached out to hospitality providers in order to
  convince them to use heartbeat identification as a way to recognize
  users. They hope to license the heartbeat recognition technology to

others, so that it can become a new standard for all wearable devices. Finally, they are opening up to developers, asking them to design around the technology.

17.3.7 Brain Waves/Activity

Brain wave as a biometric identifier is a relatively new concept. The research, which first comes from UC Berkeley, essentially turns brain activity into a biometric identifier. In much the same way that one's DNA or the blood vessels in one's retina are unique, one's brainwaves also are unique and can be used to identify a person. This can be useful for logging on a computer and establish a person's identity for other applications [95]. According to this research, a commercial electroencephalogram (EEG) is used (costing about $100), which resembles a Bluetooth headset with a single electrode that rests on a person's forehead, over the brain's left frontal lobe [96]. This electrode measures the person's brainwaves, which is then transmitted via a Bluetooth link to a nearby computer. The Berkeley researchers claim that their system has an error rate of below 1%, which is quite impressive.

To develop brain biometrics, participants were asked to complete seven different tasks with the EEG after being equipped with the machine. Three of the tasks were generic, such as focus on breathing in and out, to imagine moving their finger up and down, and listening for an audio tone; the other four tasks required participants to focus on an individual/ personalized secret, such as singing a song of their choice or performing a repetitive action. While performing these tasks, some software on a nearby computer watched the participant's brainwaves to discern a pattern that could be used to identify his/her brain. The experimental results had shown that all seven tasks—even just sitting there and focusing on your own breathing—provide enough information to authenticate one's identity [95].

In order to further study the feasibility of brainwaves as a biometric, a research team led by Blair Armstrong of Basque Center on Cognition, Brain, and Language in Spain observed the brain signals of 45 subjects while they read a list of 75 acronyms, then used computational algorithms to identify any discrepancies between individuals [97]. The responses varied sufficiently enough across individuals for the computer programs to identify them with an accuracy rate of about 94% when the test was repeated. The research clearly suggests that brainwave activity could serve as a method for security systems to verify an individuals' identity.

Though other methods of identifying people based on the electrical signals in their brain have been developed in the past, the noise related to the measurements of all the brain's signals has made the data particularly difficult to analyze. Armstrong's method solves this issue by solely focusing on brainwaves from the area of the brain that relates to the function of reading and recognizing words, producing a clearer signal that can be measured faster, as reported by Lee [98].

Moreover, another new way to identify humans using brain activity has been found in late 2015. A team of researchers at Yale University discovered that images of brain activity scanned by using functional magnetic resonance imaging (fMRI) can act as a signature pattern to accurately identify certain individuals, according to The Conversation [99]. Published in the journal "Nature Neuroscience," the study details a technique that measures neural activity via blood flow in the brain while people are awake and mentally active. The research team analyzed hundreds of fMRI image scans taken of 126 participants supplied by the *Human Connectome Project*, where they were able to successfully identify individuals based on their "connectivity profile." The team looked at activity across 268 different regions in the brain by scanning each participant six times. During certain sessions, the researchers asked participants to perform a cognitive task during the fMRI scan, while in other sessions participants remained at rest during the scan. Based on these tests, the researchers were able to identify individual participants with up to 99% accuracy when comparing scans of the same individual performing a similar cognitive task. However, their accuracy rate dropped to approximately 80% if the scan showed the same individual performing a disparate task or being at rest [100].

The main advantages of brainwave identification are that it is fool-proof in the sense that it is almost impossible to clone or spoof, while the disadvantages include the fact that the technology is intrusive and not user friendly, and the need for highly specialized equipment. Nonetheless, this relatively newer biometric demonstrates the potential to mature and be deployed in serious security applications in the future.

17.4 CONCLUSION

Biometrics as a field is burgeoning at a very rapid pace as is clearly shown by newer technologies and applications that are emerging on a regular basis. Reference 101 summarizes the current and future trends in biometric applications that we presented in this chapter—from law enforcement and immigration to access control, health care, and education. It aptly describes the breadth of possibilities in this domain, along with the associated benefits such as cost reduction, mobility, usability, and ease of integration with already existing infrastructure.

We can thus clearly see the huge potential and reach of this technology that has its roots in prehistoric times. Nonetheless, there are widespread concerns about privacy of the general people who are constantly being subject to surveillance and scrutiny in different walks of life, for the sake of ensuring security. The latter is of foremost concern in today's world, and biometrics has proved time and again to be valuable toward that. As technology advances, opportunities for research and development in the area of biometrics are vast, and if properly utilized, can go a long way toward making the world a safer place to live in for our future generation.

REFERENCES

1. Trader, J. 2015. M2SYS named a "key player" in Emerging Biometrics Tech, September. http://blog.m2sys.com/biometric-resources/m2sys-named-a-key-player-in-emerging-biometrics-tech/ (retrieved October 15, 2015).
2. Future Market Insights. Biometrics services market: Global industry analysis and opportunity assessment 2015–2020. http://www.futuremarketinsights.com/reports/global-biometrics-services-market (retrieved October 15, 2015).
3. Tractica. 2015. Biometrics market revenue to total $67 billion worldwide over the next 10 years, May. https://www.tractica.com/newsroom/press-releases/biometrics-market-revenue-to-total-67-billion-worldwide-over-the-next-10-years/ (retrieved October 15, 2015).
4. King, R.O., Biometrics Research Group, Inc. 2014. Banking and biometrics white paper, November. http://www.scribd.com/doc/249699706/Biometrics-and-Banking-Special-Report (retrieved October 15, 2015).
5. Stallings, W., Brown, L. 2012. *Computer Security: Principles and Practice*, 2nd Edition, Prentice Hall, Inc., 479, 2012.
6. Harrell, E., Langton, L. 2013. Victims of identity theft, 2012, December. http://www.bjs.gov/content/pub/pdf/vit12.pdf (retrieved October 16, 2015).
7. Rogers, K. 2013. One new identity theft victim every 3 seconds in 2012, February. http://www.foxbusiness.com/personal-finance/2013/02/20/one-new-identity-theft-victim-every-3-seconds-in-2012/ (retrieved October 16, 2015).
8. King, R.O. 2012. Biometric research note: Emerging economies embracing biometric banking technologies, December. http://www.biometricupdate.com/201212/emerging-economies-embracing-biometric-banking-technologies (retrieved October 18, 2015).

9. King, R.O. 2014. Aadhaar to be used to issue bank accounts to all Indian households, September. http://www.biometricupdate.com/201409/aadhaar-to-be-used-to-issue-bank-accounts-to-all-indian-households (retrieved October 18, 2015).
10. King, R.O. 2014. $340 Million allocated for aadhaar expansion in Indian budget, July. http://www.biometricupdate.com/201407/340-million-allocated-for-aadhaar-expansion-in-indian-budget (retrieved October 18, 2015).
11. King, R.O. 2014. India pursuing multi-fold expansion of citizen biometric registration scheme, October. http://www.biometricupdate.com/201410/india-pursuing-multi-fold-expansion-of-citizen-biometric-registration-scheme (retrieved October 18, 2015).
12. King, R.O., Biometrics Research Group, Inc. 2015. Biometrics and health-care, January. http://www.scribd.com/doc/255979360/Biometrics-in-Healthcare (retrieved October 19, 2015).
13. Federal Bureau of Investigation. 2007. Financial crimes report to the public 2007. https://www.fbi.gov/stats-services/publications/fcs_report2007 (retrieved October 20, 2015).
14. American Sentinel University. 2014. Biometrics as a security measure in health care, January. http://www.americansentinel.edu/blog/2014/01/08/biometrics-as-a-security-measure-in-health-care-2/ (retrieved October 20, 2015).
15. Vital Wave Consulting. 2009. *mHealth for Development: The Opportunity of Mobile Technology for Healthcare in the Developing World*. Washington, D.C. and Berkshire, UK: UN Foundation-Vodafone Foundation Partnership. http://unpan1.un.org/intradoc/groups/public/documents/unpan/unpan037268.pdf (retrieved October 20, 2015).
16. Technavio. 2015. Biometrics market in the United States in education sector 2015–2019, September. http://www.technavio.com/report/biometrics-market-in-the-united-states-in-education-sector-2015–2019 (retrieved October 21, 2015).
17. Ugwoke, F.N., Anyakorah, O.V. 2015. Biometric system for class attendance, *International Journal of Current Research and Academic Review*, 3(2), 261–281.
18. Vrankuli, A. 2013. Biometric payments in school cafeterias: Privacy nightmare or lunchroom revolution? April. http://www.biometricupdate.com/201304/biometric-payments-in-school-cafeterias-privacy-nightmare-or-lunchroom-revolution (retrieved October 21, 2015).
19. identiMetrics. 2009. Biometric student identification: Practical solutions for accountability & security in schools, June. http://www.identimetrics.net/images/Biometric-Student-ID-Schools-White-Paper-2016.pdf (retrieved October 21, 2015).
20. Mayhew, S. 2012. Fingerprint Scanner used for Welsh high school access, June. http://www.biometricupdate.com/201206/fingerprint-scanner-used-for-welsh-high-school-access (retrieved October 21, 2015).
21. Hope, M. 2015. Facial recognition "Biometrics" coming to California school district, May. http://www.breitbart.com/texas/2015/03/21/facial-recognition-biometrics-coming-to-california-school-district/ (retrieved October 21, 2015).

22. Planet Biometrics. 2015. British biometric project boosting school attendance in Kenya, October. http://www.planetbiometrics.com/article-details/i/3624/desc/british-biometric-project-boosting-school-attendance-in-kenya/ (retrieved October 22, 2015).
23. Gillum, D. 2015. Paying for meals just got a touch faster, August. http://www.thisweeknews.com/content/stories/westerville/news/2015/08/18/paying-for-meals-just-got-a-touch-faster.html (retrieved October 22, 2015).
24. Mayhew, S. 2015. California school districts testing iris recognition system for school bus safety. http://www.biometricupdate.com/201509/california-school-districts-testing-iris-recognition-system-for-school-bus-safety (retrieved October 23, 2015).
25. Pearson. 2013. Biometrics in education: Preserving *integrity in online learning*, September. http://www.pearsoned.com/education-blog/biometrics-in-education-preserving-integrity-in-online-learning/ (retrieved October 23, 2015).
26. Verificient Technologies. Proctortrack. http://olc.onlinelearningconsortium.org/sites/default/files/Full%20Compliance%20TM.pdf (retrieved October 24, 2015).
27. Mayhew, S. 2015. Verificient technologies receives patent for continuous online identity verification solution, January. http://www.biometricupdate.com/201501/verificient-technologies-receives-patent-for-continuous-online-identity-verification-solution (retrieved October 24, 2015).
28. Planet Biometrics. 2015. Verificient patents "world's first" automated remote proctoring solution, January. http://www.planetbiometrics.com/article-details/i/2657/ (retrieved October 25, 2015).
29. Verificient Technologies, Inc. 2015. Case study ensuring medical school excellence.
30. Kale, N. 2014. Using automated proctoring to safeguard against cheating in online test taking. DEN//gapp.usc.edu/files/u32/Fall%202014%20DEN%20Faculty%20Forum_Kale.pdf (retrieved October 25, 2015).
31. Chao, B. 2015. Stop use of proctortrack in online courses. https://www.change.org/p/rutgers-university-stop-use-of-proctortrack-in-online-courses#petition-letter (retrieved October 25, 2015).
32. Wythe, P. 2015. U. online facial recognition system presents major privacy risk—Nothing, if not critical. *The Daily Targum*, February. http://www.dailytargum.com/article/2015/02/u-online-facial-recognition-system-presents-major-privacy-risk (retrieved October 25, 2015).
33. Jake. 2015. On knuckle scanners and cheating—how to bypass proctortrack, January. http://madebyknight.com/knuckle-scanners-cheating-how-to-bypass-proctortrack/ (retrieved October 28, 2015).
34. Singer, N. 2015. Online test-takers feel anti-cheating software's uneasy glare. *The New York Times*, April. http://www.nytimes.com/2015/04/06/technology/online-test-takers-feel-anti-cheating-softwares-uneasy-glare.html?_r=0 (retrieved October 28, 2015).

35. Munoz, D. 2015. Proctor track company not complying with Rutgers contract. *New Brunswick Today*, September. http://newbrunswicktoday.com/article/proctortrack-company-not-complying-rutgers-contract (retrieved October 28, 2015).

36. Verificient Technologies. 2015. Privacy policy, August. http://www.verificient.com/privacy-policy (retrieved October 28, 2015).

37. Alderson, J. 2015. The developing market for online proctoring, August. http://www.eduventures.com/2015/08/the-developing-market-for-online-proctoring/ (retrieved October 29, 2015).

38. Kryterion. Online proctoring. https://www.kryteriononline.com/Delivery-Options/Online-Proctoring (retrieved October 29, 2015).

39. Proctor Cam, Inc. How it works. http://www.proctorcam.com/#!how-it-works/c1vdt (retrieved October 29, 2015).

40. Proctorio. Student guide. https://foothillcollege.instructure.com/courses/197/pages/getting-started-with-proctorio-student-guide (retrieved October 29, 2015).

41. Respondus website. http://www.respondus.com/products/monitor/index.shtml (retrieved August 10, 2016).

42. Planet Biometrics. 2014. Biometrics firms face up to online classroom cheating, September. http://www.planetbiometrics.com/article-details/i/2152/ (retrieved October 29, 2015).

43. Lee, J. 2015. Monitoring behavioral biometrics helps proctor U curb academic fraud, April. http://www.biometricupdate.com/201504/monitoring-behavioral-biometrics-helps-proctoru-curb-academic-fraud (retrieved October 29, 2015).

44. Garner, R. 2014. Privacy concerns raised as more than one million pupils are fingerprinted in schools, January. http://www.independent.co.uk/news/education/education-news/privacy-concerns-raised-as-more-than-one-million-pupils-are-fingerprinted-in-schools-9034897.html (retrieved October 30, 2015).

45. Jordan, G. 2014. Lawmakers ban biometric data collection in Florida schools, April. http://wlrn.org/post/lawmakers-ban-biometric-data-collection-florida-schools (retrieved October 30, 2015).

46. Vrankuli, A. 2013. Senate bill could ban biometric data collection from school children in Maryland, March. http://www.biometricupdate.com/201303/senate-bill-could-ban-biometric-data-collection-from-school-children-in-maryland (retrieved October 30, 2015).

47. Womble Carlyle Sandridge & Rice, LLP. 2014. Florida bans use of biometric data in schools, June. http://www.wcsr.com/Insights/Alerts/2014/June/Florida-Bans-Use-of-Biometric-Data-in-Schools (retrieved October 30, 2015).

48. International Biometrics & Identification Association. Biometric identity assurance for school children: Enhancing child security, safety and privacy. https://www.ibia.org/download/document/38/IBIABriefingDocument-Biometric-Identity-Assurance-for-School-Children-on-LH.pdfm (retrieved October 30, 2015).

49. Shimizu, K. 1992. Optical trans-body imaging—Feasibility of optical CT and functional imaging of living body, *Medicina Philosophica*, 11, 620–629.

50. Im, S.K., Park, H.M., Kim, Y.W., Han, S.C., Kim, S.W., Kang, C.H. 2011. Biometric identification system by extracting hand vein patterns, *Journal of the Korean Physical Society*, 38(3), 268–272.

51. Taka, Y., Kato, Y., Shimizu, K. 2000. Transillumination imaging of physiological functions by NIR light. World Congress on Medical Physics and Biomedical Engineering 2000, CD-ROM, 4982–14105.

52. Card Technology. 2005. New biometric technologies get beneath the surface, *ID Newswire*, 4(18), October. http://www.fujitsu.com/downloads/COMP/fcpa/reviews/idnewswire.pdf (retrieved November 1, 2015).

53. NSTC Subcommittee on Biometrics. 2005. Biometrics "Foundation Documents", October http://www.biometrics.gov/documents/biofoundationdocs.pdf (retrieved November 1, 2015).

54. Ademuyiwa, S.I. 2010. *Vein Pattern Recognition Biometric Systems*. University of East London. http://www.scribd.com/doc/16288152/Vein-Pattern-Recognition-in-Biometric-Systems (retrieved November 1, 2015).

55. Burge, M., Burger, W. Ear biometrics in computer vision. 2000. In *the 15th International Conference of Pattern Recognition, ICPR 2000*, Barcelona, Spain, pp. 826–830.

56. Victor, B., Bowyer, K., Sarkar, S. 2002. An evaluation of face and ear biometrics. In *Proceedings of International Conference on Pattern Recognition*, Quebec, Canada, pp. 429–432.

57. Chang, K., Bowyer, K.W., Sarkar, S., Victor, B. 2003. Comparison and combination of ear and face images in appearance-based biometrics, *IEEE Transactions on Pattern Analysis and Machine Intelligence*, 25(9), 1160–1165.

58. Hoogstrate, A.J., Van den Heuvel, H., Huyben, E. 2001. Ear identification based on surveillance Camera's images, *Science & Justice: Journal of the Forensic Science Society*, 41(3), 167–172.

59. Lammi, H.K. 2004. *Ear Biometrics*. Lappeenranta University of Technology. http://citeseerx.ist.psu.edu/viewdoc/download?doi=10.1.1.96.6204&rep=repl&type=pdf (retrieved November 2, 2015).

60. Yale Scientific. 2011. Ears: The new fingerprints?, May. http://www.yalescientific.org/2011/05/ears-the-new-fingerprints/ (retrieved November 2, 2015).

61. Mainguet, J.F. Ear geometry. http://biometrics.mainguet.org/types/ear.htm (retrieved November 2, 2015).

62. Ross, A., Abaza, A. 2011. Human ear recognition, *IEEE Computer Society*, 44(11), 79–81.

63. Westlake, A. 2015. Amazon patents ear-scanning technology for unlocking smartphones, June. http://www.slashgear.com/amazon-patents-ear-scanning-technology-for-unlocking-smartphones-15388431/ (retrieved November 3, 2015).

64. Prokoski, F.J., Riedel, R.B. 1996. Infrared identification of faces and body parts, In: *Biometrics: Personal Identification in Networked Society*, Springer, USA, pp. 191–212.

65. Liew, S.C. Electromagnetic waves. Centre for Remote Imaging, Sensing and Processing. http://www.crisp.nus.edu.sg/~research/tutorial/em.htm (retrieved November 5, 2015).

66. William, R. 1999. *Infrared Spectroscopy*. Michigan State University, East Lansing, Michigan.

67. Prokoski, F.J., Riedel, R.B., Coffin, J.S. 1992. Identification of individuals by means of facial thermography. In *Security Technology, 1992. Crime Countermeasures, Proceedings*, pp. 120–125.

68. Yoshitomi, Y., Miyaura, T., Tomita, S., Kimura, S. 1997. Face identification using thermal image processing. In *Proceedings of IEEE Int. Workshop on Robot and Human Communication*, Sendai, Japan, pp. 374–379.

69. Prokoski F. 2000. History, current status, and future of infrared identification. In *Proceedings of IEEE Workshop on Computer Vision Beyond the Visible Spectrum: Methods and Applications*, Hilton Head, SC, pp. 514.

70. Selinger, A., Socolinsky, D.A. 2001. Appearance-based facial recognition using visible and thermal imagery: A comparative study, Technical Report, Equinox Corporation.

71. Wolff, L.B., Socolinsky, D.A., Eveland, C.K. 2006. Face recognition in the thermal infrared. *Computer Vision beyond the Visible Spectrum Book*, Springer, London, pp. 167–191.

72. Wolff, L.B., Socolinsky, D.A., Eveland, C.K. 2001. Quantitative measurement of illumination invariance for face recognition using thermal infrared imagery. In *Proceedings of CVPR Workshop on Computer Vision beyond the Visible Spectrum*, Kauai, Hawaii.

73. Heo, J., Kong, S., Abidi, B., Abidi, M. 2004. Fusion of visual and thermal signatures with eyeglass removal for Robust face recognition. *IEEE Workshop on Object Tracking and Classification beyond the Visible Spectrum in conjunction with CVPR 2004*, pp. 94–99. Washington, DC.

74. Kong, S.G., Heo, J., Abidi, B.R., Paik, J., Abidi, M.A. 2005. Recent advances in visual and infrared face recognition—A review, *Computer Vision and Image Understanding*, 97(1), 103–135.

75. Bhowmik, M.K., Saha, K., Majumder, S., Majumder, G., Saha, A., Sarma, A.N., Bhattacharjee, D., Basu, D.K., Nasipuri, M. 2011. Thermal infrared face recognition—A biometric identification technique for robust security system. In *Reviews, Refinements and New Ideas in Face Recognition*, Corcoran, P. (Ed). InTech Open. Available from: http://dx.doi.org/10.5772/18986.

76. Science Daily. 2015. Identity Verification: Body odor as a biometric identifier, February. http://www.sciencedaily.com/releases/2014/02/140204073823.htm (retrieved November 5, 2015).

77. Martinez-Lozano Sinues, P., Kohler, M., Zenobi, R. 2013. Human breath analysis may support the existence of individual metabolic phenotypes, *PLoS One*, 8(4): e59909. doi: 10.1371/journal.pone.0059909.

78. Thompson, A. 2008. Your odor: Unique as fingerprint, November. http://www.livescience.com/5188-odor-unique-fingerprint.html (retrieved November 6, 2015).

79. Inbavalli, P., Nandhini, G. 2014. Body odor as a biometric authentication, *International Journal of Computer Science and Information Technologies*, 5(5), 6270–6274.
80. Pagani, M. 2005. *Encyclopedia of Multimedia Technology and Networking*, IGI Global, USA, pp. 59.
81. BenAbdelkader, C., Cutler, R., Davis, L. 2002. Stride and cadence as a biometric in automatic person identification and verification. In *Proceedings of Fifth IEEE International Conference on Automatic Face and Gesture Recognition*, Washington, DC, pp. 372–377.
82. BenAbdelkader, C., Cutler, R., Davis, L. 2002. Motion-based recognition of people in eigen gait space. In *Proceedings of International Conference on Automatic Face and Gesture Recognition*, Washington, DC, pp. 267–274.
83. Swarna Lakshmi, V.S. 2014. Application of biometrics in commercial security, *International Journal of Computer Science and Information Technology Research*, 2(2), 381–389.
84. Levine, D., Richards, J., Whittle, M.W. 2012. *Whittle's Gait Analysis*, 5th Edition. Churchill Livingstone, London.
85. Han, X. 2010. *Gait Recognition Considering Walking Direction*. University of Rochester, USA. ftp://ftp.cs.rochester.edu/pub/papers/robotics/10.tr961. Gait_Recognition_Considering_Walking%20Direction.pdf (retrieved November 6, 2015).
86. Zheng, S., Zhang, J., Huang, K., He, R., Tan, T. 2011. Robust view transformation model for gait recognition. In *Proceedings of ICIP*, Brussels, Belgium.
87. Department of Homeland Security. 2015. Detecting heartbeats in Rubble: DHS and NASA Team up to save victims of disasters. http://www.dhs.gov/detecting-heartbeats-rubble-dhs-and-nasa-team-save-victims-disasters (retrieved November 8, 2015).
88. Aron, J. 2012. Your heartbeat could keep your data safe, February. https://www.newscientist.com/article/mg21328516.500-your-heartbeat-could-keep-your-data-safe/ (retrieved November 8, 2015).
89. Chena, C.-K., Lina, C.-L., Chiangb, C.-T., Linc, S.-L. 2012. Personalized information encryption using ECG signals with chaotic functions, *Information Sciences*, 193, 125–140.
90. The Economist. 2013. A heart to my key, May. http://www.economist.com/blogs/babbage/2013/05/biometrics (retrieved November 9, 2015).
91. Nymi Inc. 2015. Nymi white paper, August. https://nymi.com/sites/default/files/Nymi%20Whitepaper.pdf (retrieved November 10, 2015).
92. Hamilton, D. 2015. Nymi band completes first heartbeat-authenticated payment with a wearable device, August. http://www.biometricupdate.com/201508/nymi-band-completes-first-heartbeat-authenticated-payment-with-a-wearable-device (retrieved November 11, 2015).
93. Broverman, A. 2015. Face value: Biometric verification gains speed, July. http://canada.creditcards.com/credit-card-news/biometric-verification-gains-speed-1273.php (retrieved November 11, 2015).

94. Basulto, D. 2014. The heartbeat vs. the fingerprint in the battle for biometric authentication. *The Washington Post*, November. https://www.washingtonpost.com/news/innovations/wp/2014/11/21/the-heartbeat-vs-the-fingerprint-in-the-battle-for-biometric-authentication/ (retrieved November 12, 2015).

95. Anthony, S. 2013. Berkeley researchers replace passwords with pass thoughts by reading your mind, April. http://www.extremetech.com/computing/152827-berkeley-researchers-authenticate-your-identity-with-just-your-brainwaves-replace-passwords-with-passthoughts (retrieved November 15, 2015).

96. UC Berkeley School of Information. 2015. New research: Computers that can identify you by your thoughts, April. http://www.ischool.berkeley.edu/newsandevents/news/20130403brainwaveauthentication (retrieved November 15, 2015).

97. Hond, B. 2015. Your brain's unique response to words can reveal your identity. *New Scientist*, May. https://www.newscientist.com/article/dn27555-your-brains-unique-response-to-words-can-reveal-your-identity/ (retrieved November 18, 2015).

98. Lee, J. 2015. Researcher says brainwaves could be a way for security systems to verify identity, May. http://www.biometricupdate.com/201505/researcher-says-brainwaves-could-be-a-way-for-security-systems-to-verify-identity (retrieved November 20, 2015).

99. The Conversation. 2015. Brain activity is as unique—and identifying—as a fingerprint, October. https://theconversation.com/brain-activity-is-as-unique-and-identifying-as-a-fingerprint-48723 (retrieved November 22, 2015).

100. Finn, E.S., Shen, X., Scheinost, D., Rosenberg, M.D., Huang, J., Chun, M.M., Papademetris, X., Constable, R.T. 2015. Functional connectome fingerprinting: Identifying individuals using patterns of brain connectivity, *Nature Neuroscience*, 18, 1664–1671.

101. Cannon, G., Cambier, J. 2011. A Future in Biometrics. http://www.biometrics.org/bc2011/presentations/FutureTech/0929_1130_Rm13_Cannon.pdf (retrieved November 25, 2015).

Index

Printed and bound by CPI Group (UK) Ltd, Croydon, CR0 4YY

24/10/2024

01778301-0014